Theoretical Perspectives on
Native American Languages

SUNY Series in Linguistics
Mark R. Aronoff, Editor

THEORETICAL PERSPECTIVES ON NATIVE AMERICAN LANGUAGES

Edited by
Donna B. Gerdts
and
Karin Michelson

State University of New York Press

Published by
State University of New York Press, Albany

Printed in the United States of America

For information, address State University of New York Press, State University Plaza, Albany, N. Y., 12246

Library of Congress Cataloging-in-Publication Data

Theoretical perspectives on native American languages.

(SUNY series in linguistics)
Papers stemming from a symposium sponsored by and held at the State University of New York at Buffalo, Mar. 14–16, 1985.
Includes index.
1. Indians of North America—Canada—Languages—Phonology. 2. Indians of North America—Canada—Languages—Syntax. 3. Indians of North America—Canada—Languages—Morphology. I. Gerdts, Donna B. II. Michelson, Karin. III. State University of New York at Buffalo. IV. Series.
PM232.T48 1988 497 87-13226
ISBN 0-88706-642-9

ISBN 0-88706-643-7 (pbk.)

CONTENTS

PART TWO: THE MORPHO-SYNTAX OF COMPLEX VERBAL MORPHOLOGY

CONTRIBUTORS

Eung-Do Cook, Department of Linguistics, University of Calgary, Calgary, Alberta, Canada.

J. Peter Denny, Department of Psychology, University of Western Ontario, London, Ontario, Canada.

Donna B. Gerdts, Department of Linguistics, State University of New York at Buffalo, Buffalo, New York.

Ann Grafstein, Linguistics Program, University of Western Ontario, London, Ontario, Canada.

Sharon Hargus, Department of Linguistics, University of Washington, Seattle, Washington.

John T. Jensen, Department of Linguistics, University of Ottawa, Ottawa, Ontario, Canada.

Alana Johns, Department of Linguistics, Memorial University of Newfoundland, St. John's, Newfoundland, Canada.

Karin Michelson, Department of Linguistics, Harvard University, Cambridge, Massachusetts.

Glyne L. Piggott, Department of Linguistics, McGill University, Montreal, Quebec, Canada.

Keren D. Rice, Department of Linguistics, University of Toronto, Toronto, Ontario, Canada.

Leslie Saxon, Department of Linguistics, Memorial University of Newfoundland, St. John's, Newfoundland, Canada.

Patricia A. Shaw, Department of Linguistics, University of British Columbia, Vancouver, British Columbia, Canada.

PREFACE

Native American languages have played a unique role in the development of theoretical linguistics in America. Investigation of these languages has uncovered many phenomena that are rarer in the more commonly studied languages. The analyses of these phenomena often contribute to the development of theoretical principles. At the same time, theoretical insights frequently have suggested solutions to recalcitrant data that have challenged researchers on these languages. Continuing in the tradition of the interaction of field research and theory, the studies in this volume present analyses that bear on a variety of phonological and syntactic issues.

The five papers in Part One address the phonological representation of segments and the interaction of such representations with rules and rule levels. First, Shaw provides evidence for the complex segment analysis of ejective and aspirate consonants in Dakota (Siouan). Michelson provides a solution within *CV Phonology* to the interaction of stress and epenthesis in Mohawk (Iroquoian). The next two papers deal with Athabaskan languages within *Lexical Phonology*. Hargus examines the effects of several rules in Sekani and their implications for underspecification theory. Rice provides an analysis for several problematic vowel-initial prefixes in Slave, supporting the distinction between lexical and postlexical rules. Finally, Cook investigates the articulatory and acoustic correlates of the feature Advanced Tongue Root, in two British Columbia Athabaskan languages, Babine and Carrier.

Part Two addresses issues concerning the syntactic or semantic status of complex verbal morphology, a characteristic feature of native American languages. The six papers represent research within four current frameworks. Arguing within *Government/Binding*, Saxon discusses the status of "empty"

NP positions associated with agreement morphology in Dogrib (Athapaskan), concluding that they are arguments and thus have theta roles. Three papers develop a lexical view of morphosyntax referencing *Argument Structure*. Grafstein discusses Disjoint Reference in Ojibwa, formulating a principle based upon the concept of obligatory argument. Piggott treats Ojibwa personal affixes, finals, and theme signs, showing how such verbal morphology modifies argument structure. Jensen and Johns use percolation conventions to provide a lexical analysis of Eskimo Causatives, Passives, and Antipassives. Using concepts of *Logical Semantics*, Denny develops a nonsyntactic view of noun classifiers and noun incorporation in Algonquian and Eskimo. Finally, Gerdts gives a *Relational Grammar* analysis of the two morphological reflexives in Halkomelem (Salish) based on the notion of ''multiattachment''.

The eleven papers in this volume discuss languages from six of the major families of Canada: Athapaskan, Algonquian, Eskimo, Iroquoian, Salishan, and Siouan. The studies in this volume represent a research strategy that combines extended fieldwork and linguistic theory. By presenting data that for the most part have not been previously published or treated from the viewpoint of contemporary theory, these papers make both a descriptive and theoretical contribution.

This volume stems from a symposium held at State University of New York at Buffalo, March 14–16, 1985. We wish to thank all the participants for their enthusiastic questions and comments. Many colleagues and students from the Department of Linguistics, SUNY at Buffalo, helped with the organization and execution of the conference and we thank them for their assistance, especially Daniel Devitt, who served as administrator. We gratefully acknowledge the financial assistance we received for the symposium from the Canadian American Studies Center (SUNY at Buffalo), the Department of Linguistics (SUNY at Buffalo), the Graduate Linguistics Club (SUNY at Buffalo), Canadian Pacific Airlines, and the United States Division, International Relations Ministry, the Government of Quebec.

Part One

PROBLEMS IN PHONOLOGICAL REPRESENTATION

THE COMPLEX STATUS OF COMPLEX SEGMENTS IN DAKOTA

Patricia A. Shaw

INTRODUCTION

One of the major and well-documented inadequacies of the conception of phonological representations within the standard theory of *SPE* is its failure to account for a variety of sub- and supra-segmental phenomena. Thus, when examined against the hypothesis that each individual segment comprises an unordered set of atomic features, all synchronized in time, the phonological behavior of certain classes of sounds that are articulatorily complex (e.g., affricates, prenasalized stops, diphthongs, ejectives, etc.) presents a number of serious problems (cf. Campbell 1974, Anderson 1976, Ewen 1982, Kaye 1983, Walli-Sagey 1986, etc.).

Of particular interest in the present paper are cases where there is not only some internal articulatory change of state, but also what appears to be an internal phonologically functional change of unit status. For example, the phonological status of affricates in the German dialect of Zurich reportedly varies as follows (Riemsdijk & Smith 1973, cited in Hulst & Smith 1982): at the underlying level, affricates function as unitary segments but, at later levels, it is necessary to refer to the constituent parts, i.e., the internal structure of the sounds. Clearly, this kind of access to internal substructure is impossible in any framework that treats features as atomic and fully coextensive with the scope of underlying segments. Furthermore, such cases raise questions of to what extent and under what conditions a complex segment may change its phonemic status from one segment to two, or vice versa.

The major focus of this paper is on an analysis of aspirate and ejective stops in Dakota, a Siouan language, spoken on the Canadian prairies and the mid-northwest plains in the United States, for it will be shown that Dakota appears to offer a case that is an exact opposite type from Zurich German. That is, at the underlying level, aspirates and ejectives seem in certain respects to function as clusters [Ch, Cʔ], whereas later phonological processes clearly treat them as unitary segments. In the analysis I propose, this apparent duality or change in phonemic status will be shown to be essentially illusory, for the relevant facts can be derived from a single conception of the representation of these segments that will hold throughout the course of the derivation. Integral to the analysis of ejectives and aspirates as complex segments is the issue of the phonemic status and representation of [h] and [ʔ] as simplex segments. It is concluded that [h] may have full and independent phonemic status, but glottal stop does not. Rather, the behavior of all lexical instances of glottal stop is claimed to be more appropriately characterized by the concept of a "floating" segment as defined within autosegmental theory.

The paper is organized as follows. Section 1 details a variety of distributional restrictions on aspirates and ejectives, as well as on [h] and [ʔ]. In Section 2, the behavior of these segments with respect to two processes of morphophonemic alternation is presented. The analysis developed in Section 3 offers a unified and systematic treatment of these several facts, drawing on certain insights of syllable structure and of autosegmental melodic representation. Finally, the conclusions are summarized in Section 4.

1. DISTRIBUTIONAL PROPERTIES OF ASPIRATES AND EJECTIVES

To introduce the discussion of Dakota, it is illuminating to look at previous treatments of these issues in the available Siouan literature. Given that earlier frameworks, both structuralist and generative, adhered fairly rigorously to a notion of atomic and coterminous features, Siouan scholars took it upon themselves to defend a consistent position either on one side of the fence or on the other. Consequently, there is an extended debate in the literature: on the one hand, Boas & Deloria (1941), Matthews in his later work (1958, 1970), and Carter (1974) argue cogently that aspirates and ejectives must be treated as clusters; but, on the other hand, Hollow (1970) and Shaw (1980) counter these arguments with the apparently opposite claim that they function as unitary segments.

Therefore, let us consider the evidence for each position. A major set of arguments relates to certain anomalies regarding their distribution.

1.1. Root-Final Position and Syllable-Final Position

As initially observed by Boas and Deloria (1932, 98; 1941, 12, 25), there are severe restrictions on the class of consonants that may occur in final position. Traditionally (Boas & Deloria, 1932, 98; 1941, 12, 25; Carter 1974, 102; Shaw 1980, 117; etc.), these constraints have been characterized in terms of Morpheme Structure Conditions (MSCs) of various sorts. Given the productive amount of recent study within theoretical frameworks recognizing syllable structure as subject to well-defined constraints, it will prove insightful in the following discussion to compare the more traditional claims regarding root-final position to generalizations applicable to the independent domain of syllable-final position.

Let us consider first constraints on the canonical form of consonant-final (henceforth C-final) lexical roots. Characteristically, roots are maximally bisyllabic and may be characterized by the general morpheme structure template $(C_0^2V)C_0^2VC_0^1$. Of present interest is the fact that the class of consonants which may occur in the root-final slot is strictly limited. Specifically, only /p t č k s š x l n y/ may occur here, i.e., plain stops, voiceless fricatives, and the central liquid, nasal, and glide.[1] This class may be compared with the following full phonemic inventory[2] of Dakota, with a temporary caveat of course on the phonemic status of C′, C^h, and ʔ.

[1] Phonemic Inventory of Dakota:

p	t	č	k		i	į	a	ą	u	ų
p^h	t^h	$č^h$	k^h							
p′	t′	č′	k′	(ʔ)	i	į			u	ų
b	(d)				e				o	
	s	š	x	h			a	ą		
	s′	š′	x′							
	z	ž	γ							
	l									
m	n	y	w							

What is absolutely uncontroversial in all analyses of MSCs on C-final roots is that aspirates and ejectives, as well as consonant clusters, are prohibited in root-final position. A major argument for treating the aspirates and ejectives as clusters has been this distributional parallelism (cf. Boas & Deloria 1941, 25–26; Carter 1974, 41 ff.).

Despite the prima facie appeal of this conclusion, one must question (as pointed out in Shaw 1980, 66) what independent principle would justify classifying the ejectives and aspirates with clusters rather than with the other sets of segments also prohibited in final position; namely, the voiced stops (*b* in all dialects, and *d* in the Santee dialects), the voiced fricatives, the sonorants /m w/, as well as the laryngeals /h/ and [ʔ] (setting aside for the moment the issue of the latter's phonemic status). Since all these segments are uncontroversially single phonemic units and not clusters, there is no a priori reason why aspirates and ejectives could not be treated as single phonemes, with their absence in root-final position deemed parallel to the voiced obstruents and other unitary elements that also have to be excluded from root-final position. Indeed, it surely would be circular to arbitrarily identify the distribution of aspirates and ejectives with clusters and then to claim that they are clusters because of this distributional parallelism.

A reasonable evaluation measure would be the relative naturalness of the resultant classes of segments. The Standard Theory simplicity metric assumes a direct correlation between relative complexity and the number of distinctive features which must be specified. Consequently, we may ask which analysis of the ejectives and aspirates leads to a ''simpler'' feature specification of the set of possible root-final segments. By this criterion, the cluster analysis arguably is simpler, as is evident from a comparison of [2a] and [2b] below. Under the unitary analysis of aspirates and ejectives, the formalization of the class of permissible root-final obstruents must expressly exclude them, this requiring the use of two additional features.

[2] Possible Root-Final Obstruents:

a. Unitary Analysis

$$\begin{bmatrix} -\text{sonorant} \\ -\text{voice} \\ -\text{spr. gl} \\ -\text{constr. gl.} \end{bmatrix}$$

b. Cluster Analysis

$$\begin{bmatrix} -\text{sonorant} \\ -\text{voice} \end{bmatrix}$$

In anticipation of the argumentation to be developed later in the paper, it may be noted at this point that there is a significant distributional parallelism that analysis in [2] fails to capture; namely, that the voiced obstruents class with the aspirates and ejectives in being prohibited in final position. In both the feature matrix specifications, [−voice] must simply be stipulated.

Before proceeding, it is worth reconsidering briefly the particular facts just discussed in the context of syllable structure constraints in Dakota. First, a rather unusual restriction on the distribution of closed syllables may be noted: *all* syllables preceding root-final position, not only in lexical roots but also in derivational and inflectional prefixes, are open. Although this observation essentially is of orthogonal relevance to the present discussion, I suspect it is partially responsible for the lack of focussed attention in the previous literature on differentiating between syllable structure constraints and MSCs.

Moreover, there is considerable overlap between the set of consonants permitted in syllable coda position and the set occurring in root-final position, although the two sets are not entirely coextensive. The set of allowable syllable-final consonants consists of [p k s š x l m n].[3] Notably, no ejectives or aspirates can ever occur in coda position—nor can any clusters. Consequently, the observed parallelism between the complex segments and clusters also can be viewed as a pervasive generalization characterizing syllable structure in Dakota.

1.2. Onsets

A second distributional anomaly is that ejectives and aspirates never appear in clusters, even though Dakota manifests some rather unusual combinatory possibilities in onset position, as illustrated by the chart in [3a][4] and the data in [3b].

[3] Syllable-Initial Clusters (L-dialect):

a.

1\2	p	t	č	k	s	š	x	l	n	m	w
p	−	+	+	−	+	+	−	+[5]	+[6]	−	−
t	−	−	−	+	−	−	−	−	−	−	−
č	−	−	−	−	−	−	−	−	−	−	−
k	+	+	+	−	+	+	−	+[5]	+[5]	+[5]	+[5]
s	+	+	+	+	−	−	−	+	+	+	+
š	+	+	−	+	−	−	−	+	+	+	+
x	+	+	+	−	−	−	−	+	+	+	+

b.

pte	'buffalo'	psiča	'jump'
kpa	'to swell'	ksapa	'be wise'
kča	'loose'	kte	'kill'
xča	'intensifier'	tke	'be heavy'

Onsets are limited to a maximum of two consonants in Dakota; therefore, if one were to treat the ejectives and aspirates as sequences, then their failure to cluster would be accounted for automatically. This parallelism is illustrated informally in [4a] and [4b]:

[4] Unitary Hypothesis:

a.

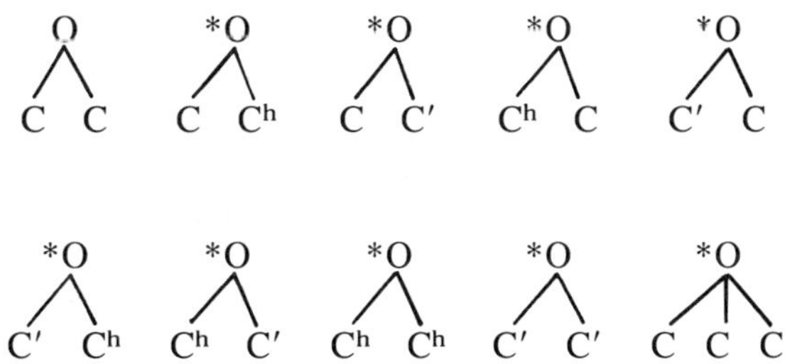

b. Cluster Hypothesis:

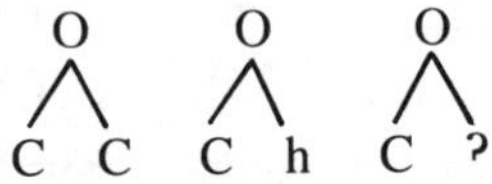

These observations constituted one of Boas and Deloria's principal reasons for adopting a cluster hypothesis: "The morphological treatment of verbs suggests that the aspirate and glottalized consonants must be considered as double consonants . . . [T]hese consonants rarely appear in consonantic clusters. Since no triconsonantic clusters are admitted, this may be conceived as a corroboration of our assumption" (Boas & Deloria 1941, 5).

Before considering some relevant morphophonemic behavior, two further aspects regarding distribution merit consideration.

1.3. Phonemic Status of [ʔ] and [h]

First, since a cluster analysis assumes the independent phonemic status of /ʔ/ and /h/, one must ask whether this assumption is justified.[7] Boas and Deloria (1941, 4) and Carter (1974), for example, list both in their inventories, whereas Hollow (1970) lists /h/ but not /ʔ/. However, none of these authors provides explicit motivation for their position; moreover none comments on what is really a striking difference in their freedom of occurrence.

As illustrated by the examples in [5], [h] may freely occur in medial (i.e., intervocalic) position in polysyllabic roots [5a], as well as in root-initial position [5b]. Moreover, a root-initial [h] remains stable when preceded by an affix or lexical stem [5c].

[5] a.	paha	'hill, mound'	**b.**	hi	'tooth'
	okihi	'be able'		heya	'louse'
	sloh̨a	'to crawl'		ha	'skin, bark'
	yuho	'to move'		hokšila	'boy'
	siha	'foot'		hu	'leg'

c.	/wič^{h}a-hi/	[wič^{h}ahi]	'human teeth' (human-tooth)
	/wič^{h}a-hu-hu/	[wič^{h}ahuhu]	'human skeleton' (human-bone-Redup)
	/o-ha-mna/	[ʔohamna]	'smelling of skin' (Loc-skin-smell)
	/i-ha/	[ʔiha]	'the lower lip' (mouth-skin)

One may conclude, therefore, that [h] should indeed be accorded full phonemic status.

In contrast, [ˀ] is extremely limited in distribution. Significantly, /ˀ/ is never found in medial position in polysyllabic roots [6a]. An optimal analysis should account for this distributional anomaly: /h/ can fill an intervocalic C-slot in lexical representation, but /ˀ/ cannot.

[6] a. $*C_0^2V{}^{ʔ}VC_0^1$

b.

[ˀi]	'mouth'
[ˀia]	'to talk'
[ˀeya]	'to say'
[ˀapʰa]	'to strike'
[ˀopʰetų]	'to buy'
[ˀu]	'to come'

c.

/ia/	[ˀia]	'to talk'
/a-ia/	[ˀaia]	'to gossip' (about-talk)
/ųk-ia/	[ˀųkia]	'we (2) talk' (Dual-talk)
/o-ia-i/	[ˀoie]	'word' (Loc-talk-Nom)
/wičʰa-o-ia-i/	[wičʰoie]	'speech' (human-word) [a → Ø/_o][8]
/i/	[ˀi]	'mouth'
/o-i/	[ˀoi]	'to put into the mouth' (Loc-mouth)
/wičʰa-i/	[wičʰai]	'human mouth' (human-mouth)
/wičʰa-i-ha/	[wičʰaiha]	'human lips' (human-mouth-skin)

Now consider the data of [6b], where it is seen that a phonetic [ˀ] does occur in word-initial (or what may be termed "stem-initial"[9]) position. However, it is evident from inflectionally and derivationally related forms as in [6c], that such instances of [ˀ] are not part of the lexical representation, but result instead from a general process of ˀ-Epenthesis. The principles governing the insertion of [ˀ] are given in [7].

[7] *Empty Onset Principle (EOP):*[10]

An onset is obligatory in stem-initial position. Elsewhere, an onset position will be filled if possible.[11]

ˀ-Epenthesis: [+constr. gl.] will function as the default value to fill an otherwise empty onset slot.

Thus, in addition to the contrast between [5a] and [6a], a comparison of the forms in [5c] and [6c] further emphasizes the nonparallel status of [h] and [ˀ] in the phonological system. Whereas [hi] 'tooth' [5b] and [ˀi] 'mouth' [6b] look at first like minimal pairs, their different behavior following /wičʰa/

reveals the essential difference: /h/ is present in the underlying phonemic representation, but [ʔ] is not.

Interestingly, Matthews' (1955) brief but insightful phonemic analysis of a Yankton/Teton dialect entails the recognition of a fundamental distributional asymmetry similar in part to that just noted. Matthews postulates only phonemic /h/. Phonetic [ʔ] has two sources: one is epenthetic, under conditions comparable to those formalized here in [7]; the second is introduced as an allophone of /h/ in final position. This latter set of cases is intended, if I am interpreting Matthews correctly, to account for the so-called declarative [ʔ] (cf. discussion of data in [8]). Although the particulars both of the analysis and of the theoretical assumptions in this work differ significantly from Matthews', a major thrust of the argumentation here is to further substantiate Matthews' essential insight as to the nonphonemic status of [ʔ].

Only two sets of facts lend some credence to the possibility of [ʔ] having independent phonemic status. First, in the so-called L-dialect or Teton Lakhota (but not in the Santee or Stoney dialects), the declarative mode is indicated by an utterance final glottal closure.[12] Boas and Deloria (1941, 109) characterize the distinctive function of this glottal closure as follows: ''The end of a declarative statement of a commonly known fact, or the mere statement of a fact not previously known to the hearer and without expression of an opinion regarding it is expressed by the terminal glottal stop, both by men and women.'' This is illustrated by the Teton data in [8a], in contrast to the imperative and interrogative statements in [8b]:

[8] a.	kiyąʔ	'he is flying'	(fly-Decl)
	kiyąpiʔ	they are flying'	(fly-Pl-Decl)
	kiyąpišniʔ	'they are not flying'	(fly-Pl-Neg-Decl)
b.	kiyą yo	'fly'	(fly Male-Imp)
	kiyą hą	'is he flying?'	(fly Q)

A further phonetic fact about the articulation of this declarative is that the closure tends to be followed by an echo vowel, or what is described as an extremely short voiceless copy of the preceding vowel, although it is clear that it does not constitute an independent syllable, e.g., [kiyąˀą̥] 'he is flying', [kiyąpiʔi̥] 'they are flying'. The morphemic function of this glottalic closure is, it would seem, a major reason why some previous scholars have included the /ʔ/ in the phonemic inventory.[13]

A second set of forms further suggests an underlyingly distinctive role for /ʔ/. Some relevant data are given in [9] (cf. also Boas and Deloria 1941, 77):

[9] a.	[ʔi]	'to go (perf)'	[ʔųki]	'we (incl) go'	/i/
	[ʔu]	'to come (dur)'	[ʔųku]	'we come'	/u/
	[ʔųspe]	'to know'	[ʔųkųspe]	'we know'	/ųspe/

b.	[ʔį]	'to wear'	[ʔųk'į]	'we wear'	/ʔį/
	[ʔų]	'to be, use'	[ʔųk'ų]	'we are, use'	/ʔų/
	[ʔo]	'to shoot'	[ʔųk'o]	'we shoot'	/ʔo/

The verb forms in [9a] exemplify the expected behavior of underlying vowel-initial roots. Thus, the word-initial [ʔ] is attributable to the epenthesis rule of [7], this being corroborated by its systematic absence in roots prefixed by the first person inclusive morpheme /ųk/. In contrast, there is a very small set of verb roots (about eight to ten, to my knowledge) represented by the forms in [9b], which retain a glottalic closure in the comparable inflected forms, this being realized phonetically as an ejective [k'].

This suggests an analysis, as postulated in Carter (1974) and Shaw (1980), where the stems of [9b] have an underlying phonemic /ʔ/ root-initially which merges morphophonemically with the previous C to create the ejective output. Carter further proposes that this morphophonemic rule merging [k] plus [ʔ] into an ejective be generalized to derive all ejectives from an underlying sequence of obstruent and [ʔ]. This would provide a third kind of argument, advanced for example by Carter, for a cluster analysis.

It should be emphasized that this glottalic merger would have to be postulated as an extremely early rule in the phonology, applying pervasively to morpheme-internal /Cʔ/ clusters but restricted in its intermorphemic application only to forms involving prefixation of the first dual inclusive morpheme /ųk/, for there is abundant evidence that no other obstruent plus [ʔ] sequences created through morphological concatenation are subject to it: e.g., /šųk-ʔo-pi/ → [šųkʔópi] not *[šųk'ópi] 'they are shooting dogs' (dog-shoot-Pl), etc. In such forms, the two segments [k] and [ʔ] are clearly distinct, with the obstruent closing the first syllable and the glottal functioning as the onset to the second (see also Boas and Deloria's (1941, 4) attestation of the phonetic distinction here).

One last concern mitigating against utilizing a "generalized" rule of glottatic merger (GM) to derive all ejectives from underlying clusters relates to the well established role (e.g., Kiparsky 1985, Shaw 1985, etc.) of the Strict Cycle Condition (SCC) as a constraint on phonological rules. Given that all input to the putative GM rule, other than the morphologically derived data of [9b], would consist of underlyingly tautomorphemic "sequences", one might well question how they could possibly serve as input to the merger rule, since the SCC would automatically block the rule from applying to any non-derived input. Nor could the application of GM be postponed until later in the phonology where the SCC was no longer active, for then there would be no way of preventing other derived forms e.g., [šųkʔópi] (cf. above) from incorrectly undergoing the rule. In essence, an analysis relying on a generalized rule of merger to derive all ejectives from underlying clusters is simply not possible in a framework which accepts the SCC as a substantive constraint on phonological derivation.

1.4. (Non)Parallelism

The final consideration I wish to raise is that previous analyses have assumed that whatever the appropriate analysis might be for ejectives, aspirates should be treated in parallel fashion. Despite the prima facie appeal of such "generalization" within the grammar, I will claim that this conclusion does not necessarily follow. In fact, there is compelling evidence against it. Specifically, as shown in [10a], *h*-initial (similarly *x*-initial, see note 7) stems do not coalesce with a preceding [k] to create an aspirate [k^h]. Rather, the final [k] of the first person inclusive prefix drops before *h*- (and *x*-) initial stems, just as it does before all other C-initial stems (where C includes liquids and glides).

[10] a.	/hi/	'to arrive at'	/ųk-hi/	[^{ʔ}ųhi]	'we arrive'
	/xa/	'to bury'	/ųk-xa/	[^{ʔ}ųxa]	'we bury'
b.	/t^{h}i/	'to live'	/ųk-t^{h}i/	[^{ʔ}ųt^{h}i]	'we live'
	/ši/	'to order'	/ųk-ši/	[^{ʔ}ųši]	'we order'
	/yat^{h}ą/	'to praise'	/ųk-yat^{h}ą/	[^{ʔ}ųyat^{h}ą]	'we praise'

In conjunction with the distributional evidence cited in [5] and [6], the morphophonemic data of [9] and [10] provide strong evidence that [^{ʔ}] and [h] do not have equivalent status within the phonological system of Dakota, and consequently the analysis of ejectives and aspirates will not be entirely parallel.

2. MORPHOPHONEMIC ALTERNATION

Let us turn from what, up until this point, has been a major focus on distribution to consider some other morphophonemic evidence. Here, the behavior of ejectives and aspirates with respect to two very general, broad-based phonological processes of the language strongly argues for their functional status as unitary segments.

2.1. Cluster Simplification

The reduplication data in [11a] illustrate a pervasive process in Dakota, whereby the first consonant of a triconsonantal sequence is deleted. A comparison with the data in [11b] establishes, first, that the final maximal syllable (i.e., $C_0^2VC_0^1$) of the root is copied to the right in the reduplication process. Similar data from compounding, which illustrates the deletion of the first of a triconsonantal sequence, is given in [11c].

[11] a.	/ksap-ksap/	[ksa ksapa]	'be wise'
	/xlok-xlok/	[xlo xloka]	'to have holes'
	/ptus-ptus/	[ptu ptuza][14]	'bent over'

b.	/wikčemna/	[wikčemnamna]	'by tens'
	/yatką/	[yatkątką]	'drink'
	/ček/	[čekčeka]	'stagger'
	/yus/	[yusyuza]	'to hold'
	/kax/	[kaxkaγa]	'make'
	/pus/	[puspuza]	'be dry'
c.	/šųk-blok/	[šųbloka]	'stallion' (horse-male)
	/pʰet-šnis/	[pʰešniza]	'embers' (fire-fade)

Now consider, in contrast, the behavior of aspirate and ejective segments in the reduplicated forms in [12].

[12]	/t'ax-t'ax/	[t'axt'aγa]	'rough'
	/yu-k'ex-k'ex/	[yuk'exk'eγa]	'scratch' (by pulling)
	/čʰep-čʰep/	[čʰepčʰepa]	'fat'
	/tʰąk-tʰąk/	[tʰąktʰąka]	'large'

It is evident that aspirates and ejectives do not function as clusters here since they do not trigger the cluster-simplification process.

2.2. Palatalization

The second set of data that provides clear evidence for ejectives and aspirates functioning as unitary segments is their behavior with respect to Velar Palatalization.

[13]	**a.**	/i-kax-i/	[ičaγe]	'instrument' (Instr-make-Nom)
		/wa-iči-k'a/	[wéčič'a]	'I dig it for him' (I-Dat$_2$-dig)
		/kiči-kʰute-pi/	[kičičʰutepi]	'they shoot each other' (Recip-shoot-Pl)
	b.	/kiči-kte-pi/	[kičiktepi]	'they are killing each other' (Recip-kill-Pl)
		/wa-iči-ksu/	[wéčiksu]	'I bead it for him' (I Dat$_2$ bead)

As shown in [13a], a velar stop palatalizes after the high front oral vowel [i]. Crucially, note that aspirate and ejective velars pattern with the plain velars in this regard. The data of [13b], however, show that palatalization never occurs if a [k] is followed by any other nonvocalic segment. Referring back to the cluster possibilities summarized in [3a], it will be noted that [č] never occurs as the initial member of a cluster. On the one hand, therefore, it is not surprising that Velar Palatalization is blocked here, for one would assume that the independent principle of Structure Preservation (e.g., Kiparsky 1985) would automatically prevent the creation of č-initial clusters. By this same line of argument, however, to postulate that the ejective [č′] and aspirate [čʰ] derive from underlying clusters, i.e., /čʔ/ and /čh/, would entail treating these clusters as the only exceptions to the otherwise valid generalization that [č] never occurs as the initial member of a cluster.

2.3. Summary of the Cluster/Sequence Paradoxes

To summarize thus far, three arguments have been presented in favor of a cluster analysis. First, as shown in [2a], no ejectives or aspirates occur in root-final or syllable-final position; nor do clusters. Second, as shown in [3], a maximum of two segments can occur within an onset position but ejectives and aspirates do not cluster in onsets. Third, as in [9], there is independent evidence of a morphophonemic merger of [k] and [ʔ] to [k′] in first-person-inclusive prefixation onto ʔ-initial roots. This coalescence could then be generalized (albeit only if one abandons the Strict Cycle Condition as a constraint on phonological rules) to subsume at least all other ejectives as deriving from an underlying sequence.

On the other hand, however, two arguments against a cluster analysis also have been advanced. First, as in [11] and [12], the ejectives and aspirates do not behave as clusters with respect to the general rule of triconsonantal cluster simplification. Second, as illustrated in [13], they do not behave as clusters would to block palatalization.

At least superficially, therefore, this looks like the opposite kind of case to that exemplified by the Zurich German analysis referred to earlier. Whereas, in the Zurich dialect, affricates purportedly function as unitary at the phonemic level but as separately accessible elements for later phonological rules, the Dakota segments appear to behave as clusters with respect to the underlying morpheme structure conditions and one early phonological rule (coalescence of [k] plus [ʔ]) but as unitary segments for the proper application of later phonological rules.

3. AN ALTERNATIVE ANALYSIS

Rather than postulating a formal 'change' of phonemic status in the course of a derivation, I would like to suggest that, if viewed within the framework of 3-dimensional phonology as developed in recent literature, all the relevant facts of Dakota can be derived from a single consistent conception of the phonological representation of affricates and ejectives.

The proposed analysis assumes a number of independent but interacting subtheories of phonological organization. First, a particular advantage of the autosegmental framework is the postulation of the autonomy of a skeletal tier, representative of a sequence of timing units, as distinct from the melodic tier, representative of the distinctive feature content of phonological segments. Crucially, the theory characterizes various situations where the relationship between units on the timing tier and units on the melodic tier is not one-to-one. One such possibility is where a melodic element has no corresponding skeletal slot in lexical representation. It is argued here that this conception of a "floating" segment provides a systematic explanation for the behavior of underlying [ʔ] compared with [h].

A further assumption in the present treatment is that the distinctive features on the melodic tier are internally organized in terms of subsets which function together as natural classes. Various proposals have been advanced to motivate particular hierarchical groupings (e.g., Clements 1985, Sagey 1986, Archangeli and Pulleyblank 1986). All these models are consistent in separating the laryngeal features from the supralaryngeal features. This provides a formal representation of the frequently attested autonomy of each of these two sets of features. Schematically, this subdivision of melodic structure may be represented as follows, where the features [voice], [constricted glottis], and [spread glottis] occur under the laryngeal node, and the manner and place features are dominated by the supralaryngeal node (these latter features are hierarchically organized amongst themselves, but the details of this representation are simplified here as they are not directly relevant to the present analysis):

[14]

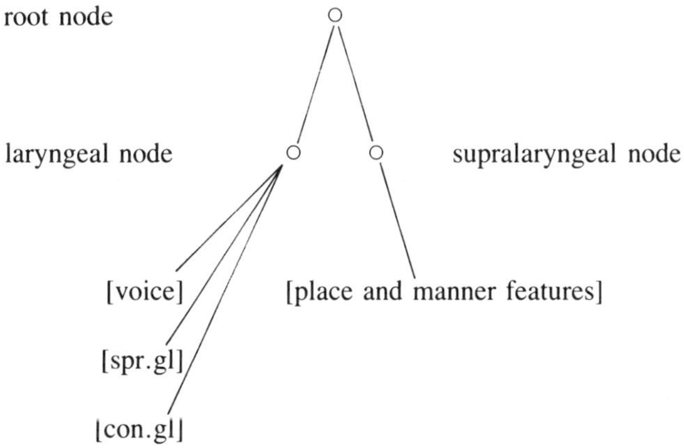

A third body of hypotheses regarding melodic representation derives from underspecification and markedness theory (e.g., Trubetzkoy 1949, Chomsky and Halle 1968, Kean 1975, Kiparsky 1985, Archangeli and Pulleyblank 1986, and so forth). The present analysis is constrained by the strong hypothesis that only the marked and non-redundant values of phonologically distinctive features are specified in lexical representation and may be accessed by lexical phonological rules. Thus, for example, in Dakota the only segments marked for [voice] are the [+voice] obstruents: voiceless obstruents and voiced sonorants are both unmarked for this feature. The redundant feature values will be filled in later in the phonological derivation by default rules, e.g., [Øvoice] → [−voice]/[−sonor] and [Øvoice] → [+voice] elsewhere.

The final subtheory assumed here is one regarding the internal structure of the syllable, a prosodic unit which defines an organization of the skeletal tier in terms of a head N (the nucleus), a rime constituent N′ (the nucleus plus any following elements in the coda), and the maximal projection N″ (which incorporates the onset). It is further assumed that certain dependency relations may exist between adjacent, but not necessarily tautosyllabic, skeletal elements. This relation of prosodic "licensing" is defined with reference to prosodic constituency within an X-bar theory of the syllable, and functions as a constraint on the prosodic and melodic well-formedness of underlying and lexically derived phonological structure.[15]

Once the properties of Dakota aspirates and ejectives are viewed within a theoretical framework embodying the above assumptions, it can be seen that many of their attributes follow from their structural representation and from general constraints relating to the integrated interaction of the various levels of phonological organization.

3.1. Distributional Properties

Let us establish, first, the appropriate underlying representation for aspirates and ejectives. Following Kaye and Lowenstamm (1982) and others, it is assumed here that a series of empty x-slots on the skeletal tier determines the phonological timing. If aspirates and ejectives are truly a sequence of two phonological units, they would be represented with an independent skeletal slot for each melodic element, e.g.:

[15] Cluster analysis:

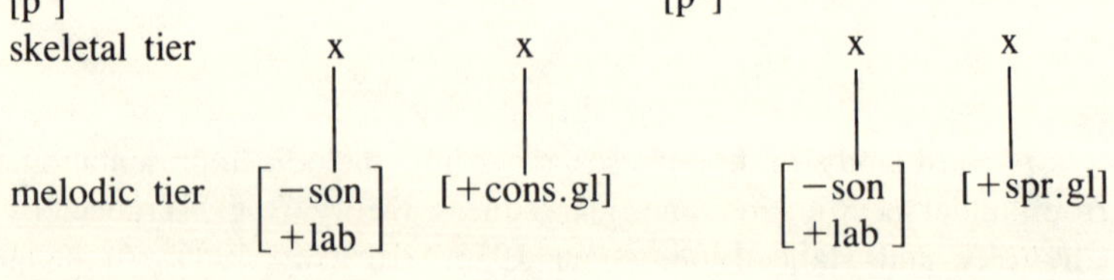

One would consequently expect them to function as two independent units for syllabification, cluster-reduction, or any other phonological process related to timing or sequencing constraints.

The alternative hypothesis is that aspirates and ejectives function as complex segments (Campbell 1974, Clements and Keyser 1983, Walli-Sagey 1986, among others), i.e., segments with configurational complexity in their melodic representation, which are mapped onto a single skeletal node. More specifically, given the frequently attested functional independence of glottal vs. supraglottal articulation (Thráinsson 1978, Clements 1985), it is hypothesized that the laryngeal (L) and supralaryngeal (SL) features are represented on independent branches of a hierarchically structured melodic model. These separate branches are jointly dominated by a single root node, which is in turn linked (by the association conventions) to a single skeletal slot. This model thus predicts a segmental unity with respect to skeletally-sensitive phonological processes, but a potential independence of the laryngeal features at the melodic level. Further, one might expect certain restrictions relating to the internal configurational complexity. This internal branching structure of ejectives and aspirates is illustrated in [16a].

[16a] Complex segment analysis:

[p'] [pʰ]

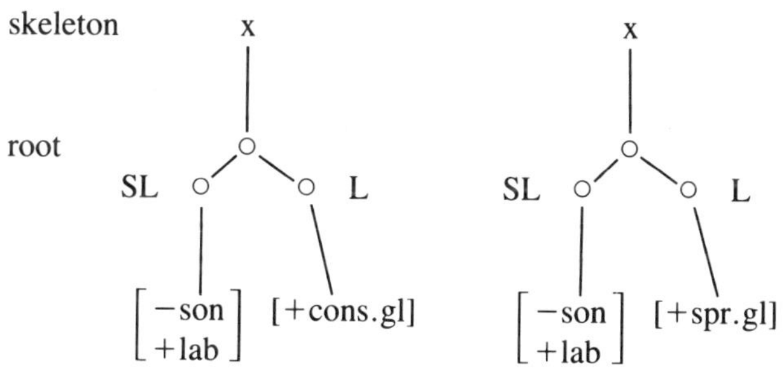

It is argued here that this complex segment representation offers a systematic explanation of several distributional properties.

3.1.1. Root-Final Consonants

First, reconsider the discussion (Section 1.1) related to the proposed feature matrix specifications given in [2] of the class of permissible root-final consonants. It will be recalled that a complication inherent in both statements of the feature class involved was that voiced obstruents had to be expressly excluded by stipulating the feature [−voice]. That is, there was no way of formally capturing the generalization that voiced obstruents in final position were behaving like the aspirates and ejectives. Now, however, let us compare a formalization of voiced and voiceless obstruents in the autosegmental framework adopted here. Given standard assumptions regarding markedness in consonants (e.g., Chomsky & Halle 1968; Kiparsky 1985; and so forth), voiced obstruents will be overtly marked with respect to the laryngeal feature [+voice], whereas the voiceless obstruents will be unmarked, as in [16b]:

[16b]

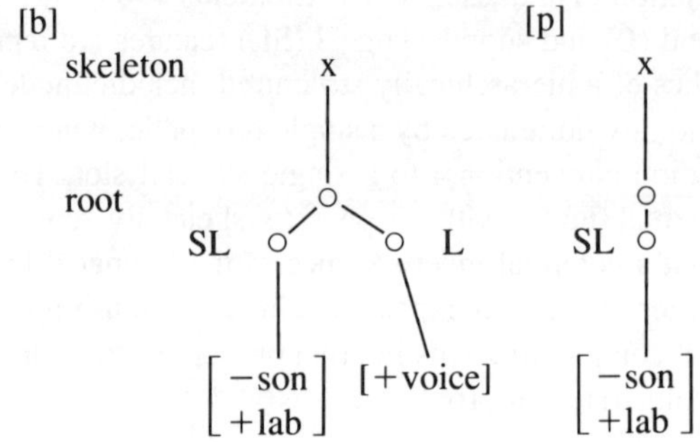

It will be immediately evident that the characterizations in [16a] and [16b] provide a straightforward grouping of the voiced obstruents with the ejectives and aspirates as a natural class: each is a complex segment, expressed by internal branching structure with overtly marked laryngeal articulation, in contrast to the nonbranching representation of the voiceless obstruents.

As pointed out by Kaye and Lowenstamm (1984, 5) in observing a parallel distributional restriction in Sanskrit, ''if one assumes that the syllable coda position is recessive, the constraint against complex segments occupying this position reduces to something akin to the constraint against branching structures in recessive metrical positions.'' In other words, this distributional property is neither particular to Dakota nor to aspirates and ejectives. There is a general constraint against complex segments in a weak prosodic position.

From this discussion it is evident that the initial argument purportedly in support of the cluster analysis—viz. the 'simpler' feature specification in [2b] compared with [2a]—disappears. Rather, under the complex segment hypothesis, the unitary analysis allows for a significantly more general and principled treatment. In sum, the class of permissible root-final obstruents is restricted to precisely those which, on the basis of universal markedness theory, have *no* specified laryngeal features.

3.1.2. Licensing

Before proceeding, the notion of codas constituting a recessive or weak metrical position in Dakota must be made more precise. To do so, I will characterize certain dependency relations between adjacent skeletal elements in terms of a notion of prosodic licensing. With respect to syllable codas, we have noted the severely restricted distribution of closed syllables in Dakota: they occur only in absolute final position of a root, stem, or word, i.e., at the extreme right margin of an independently defined prosodically relevant morphological domain.[16] Although this class of contexts conforms to a possible characterization of extrametricality (Hayes 1982), there is independent evidence (from Stress (Shaw 1985) and Reduplication (Shaw 1984)) that the consonants under consideration do function as syllabic coda constituents. Consequently, I propose to characterize the observed prosodic dependency on the occurrence of codas in the following way: a post-nuclear consonant (coda) is "licensed" if it occurs in stem- or word-final position.

The question arises as to what happens to root-final codas when they are no longer in stem-final position. When a derivational process such as Reduplication, which suffixes a copy of the root-final syllable, applies to create a stem-internal closed syllable, various phonological modifications apply to the non-final coda consonant. These processes may be functionally interpreted as attempts to rectify or at least ameliorate this violation of the otherwise pervasive constraint against stem-internal codas. For example, the root /nič/ 'to lack' would be expected to reduplicate as *[ničnič]. However, a process of Coronal Dissimilation (see Shaw 1980) applies to change the first of any two coronal segments thus juxtaposed into a [k], yielding in this case [niknič]. A straightforward explanation would be to interpret this dissimilation as an effect of resyllabification of the coda /č/ into the initial onset slot of the following syllable: the constraints on onset clusters already seen in [3] do allow two segments, but absolutely prohibit coronal consonants in the initial slot (except for [tk]). The deletion of a marked [+cor] feature on [č], and the subsequent realization of the default [-cor] value (giving [k]) would therefore be an automatic consequence of the syllable structure constraints of the language. The problem with this proposal, however, is that if the /č/ were fully resyllabified into the following onset, the resultant [kn] sequence would be expected to surface phonetically as [gn] (see note 7). This does not happen however.

Rather, it is clear from the non-application of such syllable-sensitive postlexical rules that the [k] is syllabically still a coda within the preceding syllable, but is nonetheless being subject to the lexical constraints determined by the following onset (for several other examples of such apparent paradoxes, see Shaw 1984).

This second kind of prosodic dependency of the realization of codas here is characterized as a second kind of licensing. Specifically, it is contended that the severe restrictions on the distribution and phonological content of codas in Dakota may be expressed by the following constraint:

[17] A post-nuclear (N′-dominated) skeletal slot in Dakota must be licensed. It is licensed only if it meets one of the two following conditions:
(a) it occurs in stem- or word-final position; or
(b) it conforms to the lexically-defined structural constraints on pre-nuclear (N″-dominated) constituents of the following syllable.
If through morphological concatenation, a post-nuclear skeletal slot in a derived context cannot meet either of these conditions, then it will delete.

Schematically, licensing will be represented by a dotted line.

In essence, the licensing constraint of [17] provides an immediate explanation of why the phonological changes which apply to the output of Reduplication are so broadly structure-preserving, in the sense that the output must be readjusted to conform with the lexical constraints of [3].

To exemplify this, consider the representations in [18]. Given a derived internal sequence [čn] as in the Reduplicated form *[ničnič], the skeletal slot will be licensed by the following syllable, because the N″ node can accommodate a maximum of two skeletal positions [18a]. However, although this slot is structurally licensed, its melodic content is not, for the initial [č] violates the *[+cor][+cor] constraint. This triggers Coronal Dissimilation, whereby [č] → [k], which then constitutes a fully licensed coda [18b].

[18]

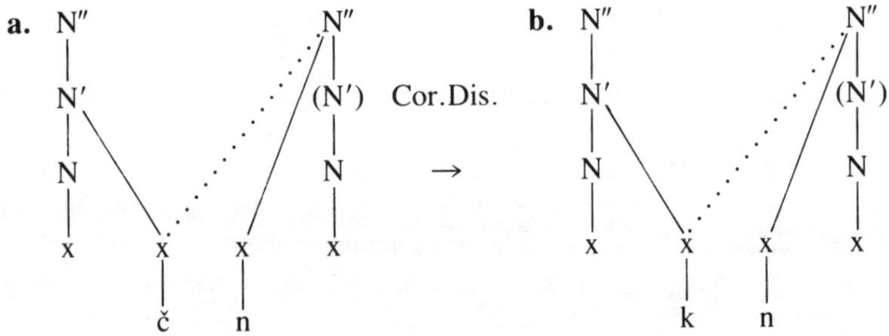

3.1.3. Distributional Restrictions in Onsets

Let us return to reconsider the second distributional argument in favor of a cluster analysis: that is, that the maximal number of positions in the onset is two, and that ejectives and aspirates do not generally cluster.

An analysis which could relate the onset restrictions to the postulated constraint against complex segments in coda position would provide a more unified and principled treatment. From the perspective of the complex segment hypothesis, the observation that complex obstruents never cluster translates configurationally into a constraint against melodic branching within a branching onset:

[19] a.

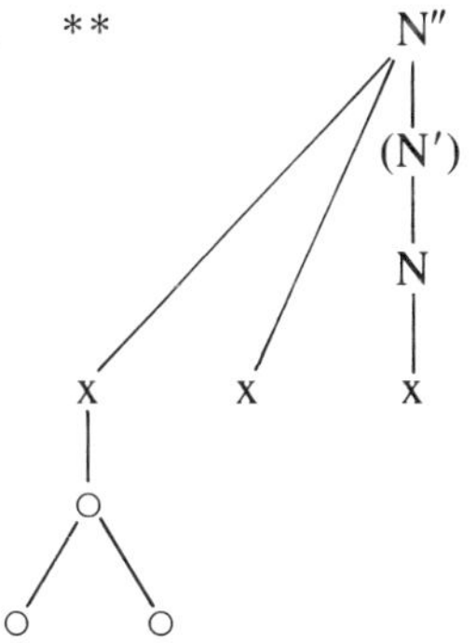

b.

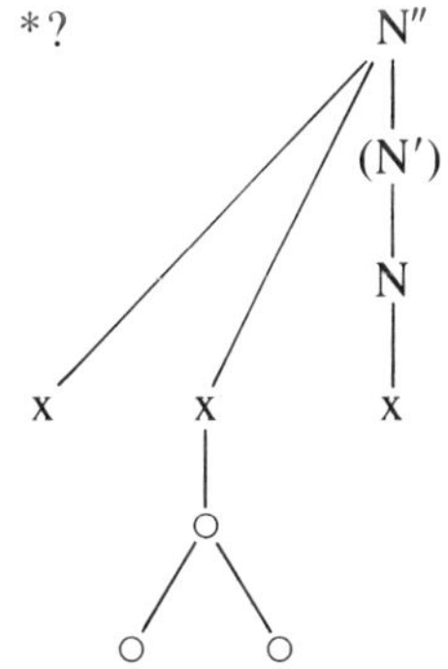

There is some evidence of an asymmetry in the status of [19a] vs. [19b]. [19a] appears to be absolutely inviolable, and is undoubtedly reducible to the universal constraint cited above against branching in a recessive metrical position. However, some very limited data suggest that [19b] is more tolerable.[17] Given that the second onset slot is adjacent to the Nucleus, i.e., to the head of the syllable, one might hypothesize that this skeletal position is therefore prosodically stronger. This would also accord with the fact, documented in [3], that there is a greater inventory of possible segments in the second onset slot than in the first. However, as this observed asymmetry is essentially marginal, a formalization of metrical government in prenuclear position will not be pursued here. The principal claim is that the structural representation of complex segments as branching constituents is directly related to the constraints on their occurrence in complex onsets, as represented configurationally in [19].[18]

3.2. Morphophonemic Alternation

Let us now examine the various morphophonemic facts from the perspective of the complex segment analysis proposed here.

3.2.1. Cluster Simplification

First, reconsider the Cluster Simplification process, illustrated previously by the data in [11] versus [12], in the light of the proposed constraints in [17] on the licensing of codas. The basic question here is: given a segment which is in principle (and in fact, on the preceding cycle) a permissible coda, why is it forced to delete when followed by an onset cluster but not when followed by a single onset segment? Again, if one could claim that the coda segment were necessarily resyllabified into the following onset, these facts would be automatically explained, but as argued above, there is clear evidence against resyllabification on the basis of the observed inapplicability of several syllable-sensitive postlexical rules.

Rather, it was hypothesized in [17] that a coda which is no longer licensed by being in final position, must be licensed by the following onset. More specifically, it must conform to the constraints on N″ constituency of the following syllable. As the maximal number of pre-nuclear skeletal slots which can be incorporated into an N″ in Dakota is two, and in a case such as [20a] the two slots are already filled, the result is that this stem-internal coda cannot be licensed. It consequently must delete.

[20] a.

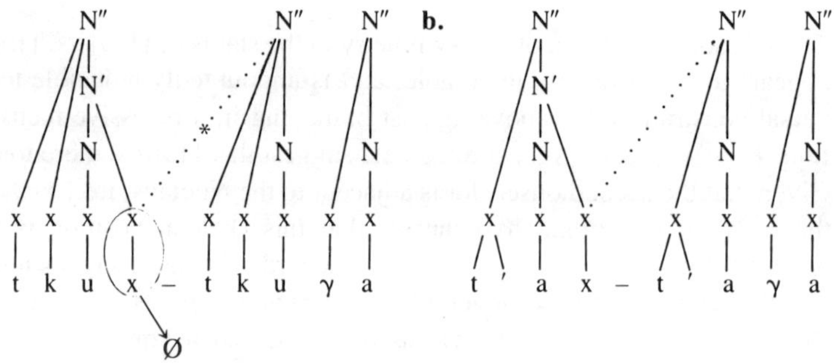

‘break off’ (REDUP) ‘rough’ (REDUP)

In contrast, since ejectives and aspirates are represented by only a single skeletal slot, when they are preceded by a syllable with a filled coda position, as in [20b] [t'ax-t'aγa], the Reduplicated form of ‘rough’, the constraint on licensing the preceding coda can be met, since the N″ can accommodate a second skeletal slot. These facts would receive no systematic explanation under the cluster analysis of aspirates and ejectives.

3.2.2. Palatalization

Secondly, reconsider the Palatalization facts of [13]. Assuming this to be the result of an autosegmental spreading of the [-back] feature of /i/ over to the melodic representation of a following /k/, we note in [21a] that this is blocked.

[21] a.

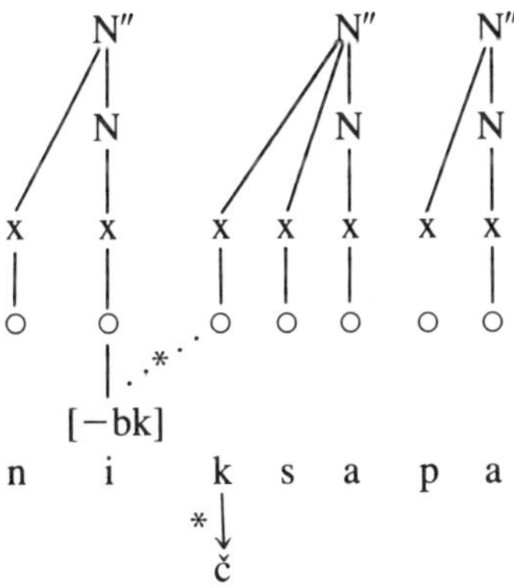

'you are wise'
(2sg-wise)

b.

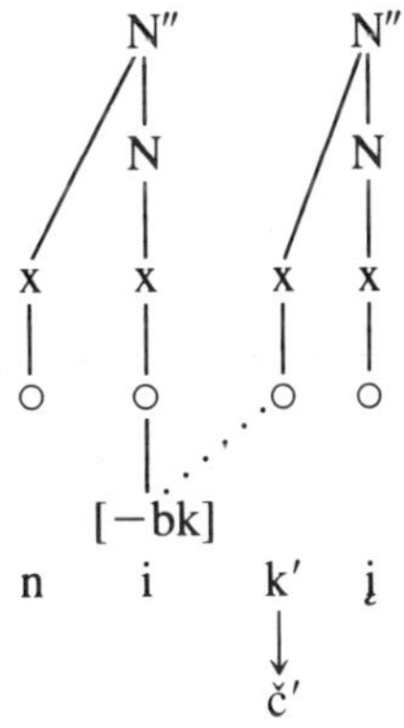

's/he carries you'
(2sg-carry)

c.

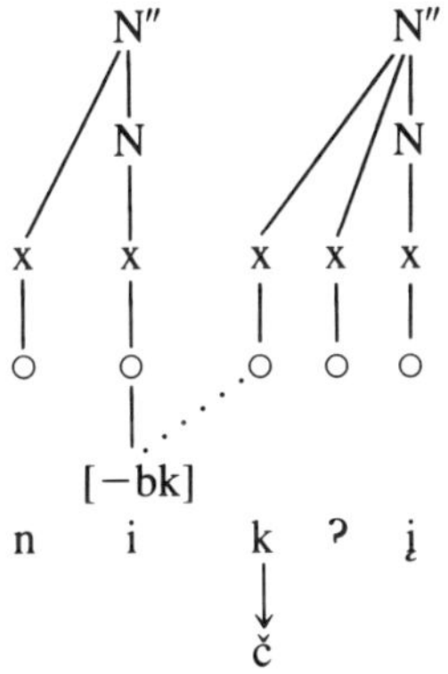

The explanation follows directly from the facts of [3] and the principle of Structure Preservation. That is, the spreading of [-back] would change /k/ to [č]. However, since a *[čC] onset sequence is prohibited by the cluster constraints of [3], Structure Preservation would prevent any *[čC] cluster from being derived in the course of the phonological derivation.[19]

In contrast, note that in [21b], [nič′į], the [-back] palatalizing feature can propagate over to a following ejective (or similarly to an aspirate) since, although the melodic representation itself branches, there is nonetheless only one skeletal slot in the onset, and consequently no cluster restrictions to block the derivation of [č].

Finally, consider as in [21c] the implications of the cluster analysis where /k/ and /ʔ/ are each dominated by their own skeletal slot. In order to derive the correct output, [-back] would have to be permitted to propagate to the /k/, which would in turn require some kind of ad hoc stipulation that [č] can occur as the initial member of a cluster only if /h/ or /ʔ/ were the second member. Once again, the unitary segment analysis entails a much more principled account.

3.3. The Behavior of [ʔ]

Let us now reconsider the facts reflected in the Teton data of [8a], where the declarative mode morpheme is represented by a final glottal closure. It will be remembered that the morphemic status of [ʔ] here has been advanced as a major justification for according it full phonemic status in previous treatments. Here it is argued that a more explanatory analysis derives from another feature of the autosegmental framework: the postulation of floating elements. That is, given the claim that there need not be a one-to-one relationship between the melodic elements of a language and the skeletal tier, it follows that a lexical representation may consist of (or may include within its melodic specification) an element that does not have a corresponding slot on the skeletal tier. Indeed, in tone languages, the phenomenon of a "floating tone" is frequently attested.

If [ʔ], or more specifically the feature [+cons.gl.], is treated as a "floating" element in the lexical representations where it consistently appears in Dakota, then several aspects of its distribution and behavior are accounted for.[20]

3.3.1. The Declarative

First, it is here hypothesized that the declarative morpheme exemplified in [8a] consists solely of the floating feature [+cons.gl.] on the melodic tier. When it is concatenated with a preceding verb stem, it spreads leftward to anchor under the skeletal point of the vowel element which precedes it,[21] as illustrated schematically in [22a], and formally in [22b].

[22] a. [kiyąʔą̥]

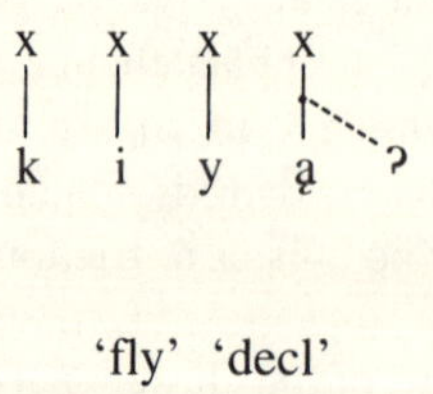

b.

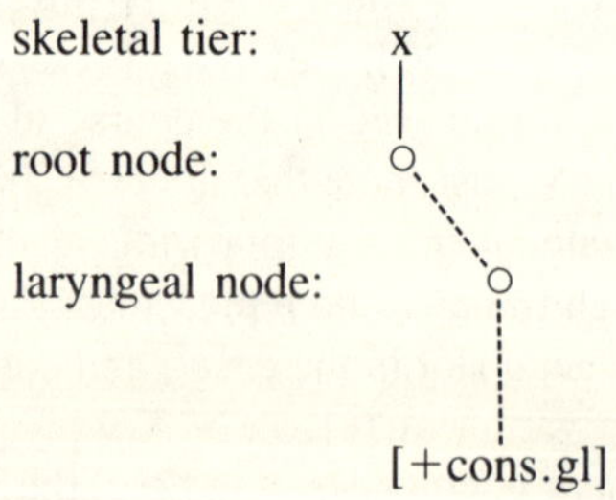

Before discussing the explanatory implications of this analysis, one might ask whether this leftward spread must be stipulated as a particular rule of the grammar, or if it follows from some more general principle. First, we note that this "declarative mode marker" is always utterance-final. Consequently, even within the maximal domain of the "sentence", there is never a possible skeletal node to its right for it to anchor onto. Thus, if this [ʔ] morpheme is to be phonetically realized at all, there are only two other conceivable alternatives: (i) it could function as a coda of the preceding syllable, or (ii) it could spread into the nucleus of the preceding syllable. The first alternative is automatically blocked by several independent factors already seen to be functional within the Dakota phonological system. Most significantly, this would require a skeletal slot to be generated in coda position, but as we have already noted, codas are highly marked in Dakota. Although there is strong motivation to justify the generation of a skeletal slot into an otherwise empty onset position under appropriate circumstances (e.g., the Empty Onset Principle of [7] above), there is no independent evidence for the generation of a skeletal slot into a coda position in Dakota. Therefore, this would be a unique and highly marked rule, inconsistent with several other phonological factors. The second alternative, i.e., for the floating [+cons.gl.] to anchor leftward under the nucleus, is then the only viable path for it to follow. One might hypothesize, therefore, that rather than this leftward spread being stipulated as a "rule", it follows as an automatic consequence of a more general principle that morphemic content will be phonetically realized if possible, i.e., unless blocked by some active rule or constraint of the language.

One significant advantage of analyzing the 'declarative' glottal closure phenomenon as in [22] is that it provides an immediate explanation of the phonetic realization of the final echo vowel associated with these declarative forms. The echo vowel has no independent syllabic status; rather, it is like a "broken" vowel, where the glottal closure is superimposed on the vowel articulation, creating a transitory interruption. This kind of simultaneity or overlay of articulation is exactly what would be expected from the proposed analysis, which links the vowel and the feature of [+cons.gl.] together as a complex segment under a single skeletal point.

A second advantage of this analysis is that it offers a reasonable explanation of the seemingly marginal phonemic status of [ʔ] in Teton. Consider the analysis where the fact that this utterance-final glottal closure is the only phonological manifestation of the 'declarative' morpheme constitutes evidence of the phonemic status of [ʔ]. The rationale behind this conclusion presumably derives from the assumption that the capability of differentiating meaning is held to be a criterial property of distinctive *phonemes*. What this conclusion does not account for, however, is why [ʔ] is so very limited and so largely predictable in its distribution elsewhere. The present analysis relies first on the recognition that the capability of differentiating meaning reduces to the level of distinctive *features* that comprise the phonemes of a language. The feature [+cons.gl.] is clearly distinctive in Dakota, but this distinctive role does not automatically accord it independent status as a phoneme, any more so than one would want to postulate the distinctive features [+voice] or [+labial] as phonemes. What has influenced traditional analyses at this point is the classical problem of how to represent a morpheme (the declarative) which surfaces only with something analogous to suprasegmental or prosodic content being superimposed on another segment. The only assumption which is necessary here is that a morpheme can be lexically specified with phonological content on the melodic tier (here the laryngeal specification [+cons.gl.]), without any specified content on the skeletal tier. Thus, the lexical status of [+cons.gl.] does not, in and of itself, justify according it phonemic status.

The present claim that [+cons.gl.] is not an independent phoneme in Dakota, i.e., is never linked to its own skeletal slot in lexical representation, makes very different predictions regarding its distribution. Because [+cons.gl.] is not a phoneme, it follows automatically that [ʔ] does not have the observed freedom of distribution of other phonemes in the language. Moreover, because [+cons.gl.] is postulated to be lexically floating, one might ask whether the theory predicts any further restrictions on its distribution. Indeed, if we hypothesize that floating segments are universally constrained to occur only at the extreme margin of a lexical domain,[22] this would prohibit any morpheme-internal occurrences of [ʔ]. This is exactly the distributional "anomaly" noted in [6a]. The fact that it is a necessary consequence of the present analysis is, again, strongly supportive of this autosegmental treatment.

A third advantage is that the analysis presented here offers a much more uniform treatment of the several Dakota dialects. That is, unlike the Teton dialect, many of the other dialects (e.g., Santee, Sioux Valley, Stoney) do not utilize the "declarative" glottal closure described for Teton above. Consequently the status of "phonemic" [ʔ] is even more marginal in these other dialects. The only role potentially justifying /ʔ/ in Santee and Sioux Valley is the "glottalizing" behavior of some vowel-initial roots, as shown in the Teton data of [9] above and discussed in 3.3.4.

3.3.2. The Nonparallelism of [h] versus [ʔ]

A further advantage of treating all lexical instances of [+cons.gl.] as floating is that this accounts very nicely for the observed differences in distribution between [h] and [ʔ]. Thus, as noted in [5], [h] has a much greater freedom of occurrence and truly exhibits full phonemic stature when it occurs morpheme initially and intervocalically. Therefore, such instances of [h], or more specifically the feature [+spread glottis], all have a corresponding skeletal slot in their lexical representation. In contrast, the fact that [ʔ] never occurs medially follows necessarily, as previously discussed, from its not having a corresponding skeletal slot. Further, with the exception of the very limited set of forms represented in [9b], its occurrence in initial position is due to ʔ-

epenthesis. Thus, the extremely marginal lexical status of [ʔ] is explained by including it in the feature inventory as an available articulatory gesture but never with its own skeletal slot in lexical representation.

3.3.3. The First-Person Dual-Inclusive Morpheme

In order to motivate a principled account of the data of [9b], viz. verbs with an apparent underlying root-initial [ʔ], it is necessary first to understand the behavior and lexical form of the first-person dual-inclusive morpheme [ų̧k]. This pronominal prefix is unusual in two respects: first, it is the only prefix in the language that is consonant final, and second, its final [k] will not cluster with any following single consonant, even when the resultant cluster would produce an acceptable onset, e.g., /ų̧k-ši/ → [ų̧ši] 'we order', but compare [kšiža] 'bent, doubled up', [ų̧kšiža] 'we are doubled up', [kšu] 'to bead', etc. The failure of the dual-inclusive [k] to surface in preconsonantal contexts clearly is not a function of the cluster simplification process we saw to be broadly operative in the data of [11]. Indeed, the fact that [k] of [ų̧k] will only surface before true V-initial stems and stems with an initial floating [ʔ] suggests that it also is "floating" and will be realized only when required to fill an otherwise empty onset. Compare, therefore, the derivations given in [23a] and [23b].

[23] a.

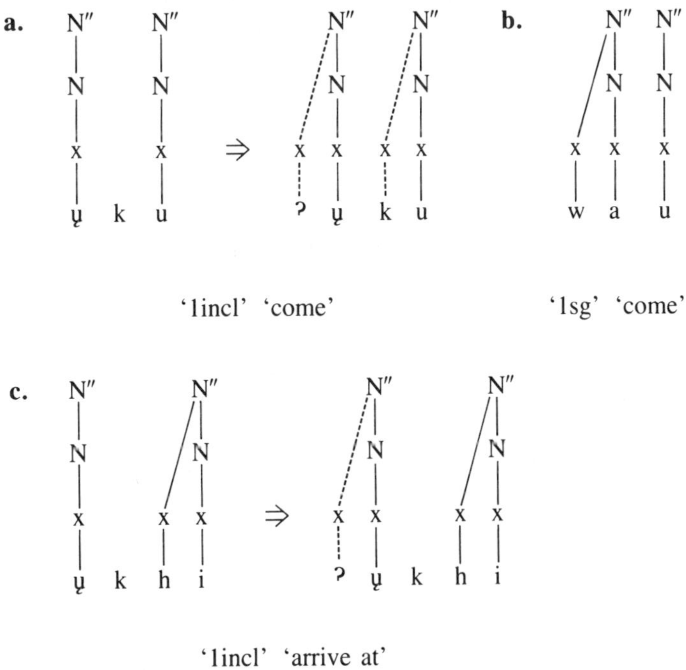

In the underlying representation of [23a], there is no segment with an anchored skeletal point that can serve as the onset to the second syllable. Rather than leaving this as an onsetless syllable, the conditions on syllable structure, i.e., the Empty Onset Principle in [7], stipulate that an onset position must be filled, if possible. In this situation, the presence of the [k] on the melodic tier will trigger the creation of a skeletal slot for it to associate to, thus satisfying the EOP condition. The stem-initial syllable must always have an onset, so here a truly epenthetic glottal stop is inserted.

Consider, in contrast, this same verb with a vowel-final prefix such as the first singular /wa-/. As shown in [23b], there is no possible segment, anchored or floating, to serve as the onset to the second syllable. In regular speech, therefore, this form surfaces with the vowel sequence, i.e., [waú]. In slow or careful speech (see note 11), it is possible to have a weak epenthetic glottal transition here, i.e., [waʔú], but this is indisputably a low-level, optional phenomenon, unlike the obligatory realization of both the [k] and the stem-initial [ʔ] in [23a].

Compare now [23a] with [23c], where [ųk] is prefixed onto a skeletally anchored consonant-initial stem. Here the underlying /h/ with its associated skeletal slot already fills the onset position. Consequently, the floating [k] is preempted from having its own x slot created. Further, we note although [k^h] is indeed a possible complex segment, the [k] cannot associate under an x slot that is already linked. Following Pulleyblank (1983) and others, I will assume this failure to link to the x slot in [23c] follows from the general principle that multiple linking is the marked case, and will only result from the application of a specific rule. In the absence of such a 'rule' and given that the EOP is not called into play here (since the onset in question is already filled), the floating [k] will fail to be realized in the phonetic output.

3.3.4. ʔ-initial Verb Roots

Having discussed the underlying form of the first dual inclusive and illustrated the principles governing its realization with both vowel-initial and consonant-initial roots, let us investigate its interaction with the ʔ-initial verb roots of [9b]. Consistent with the earlier claim that all lexical instances of [ʔ] in Dakota are floating, it is hypothesized that the appropriate representation of these roots is as in [24a], where the symbol [ʔ] is used to represent the floating feature [+cons.gl.]:

[24] a. **b.**

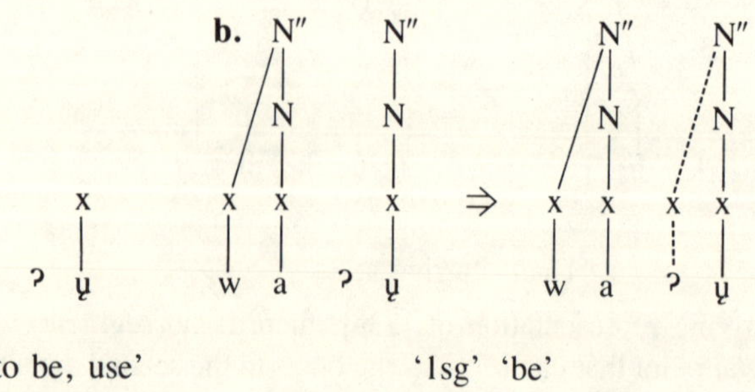

'to be, use' '1sg' 'be'

Their realization with vowel-final prefixes is straightforward, for the derivation in [24b] exactly parallels that of [23a]. That is, in accordance with the mandate to fill an empty onset slot if possible, a skeletal point will be generated for the lexically present floating [ʔ] to dock onto, yielding [waʔų] 'I am'.

The most revealing cases, however, arise when a ʔ-initial root is prefixed with the first person inclusive morpheme /ųk/, for this inflection places two postulated floating elements side by side. The fact that both these segments get realized follows automatically from two assumptions: (i) all skeletally linked segments must be syllabified, and (ii) the creation of skeletal slots for floating segments to anchor onto is strictly constrained by the EOP of [7]. Consider the underlying representation of [25]:

[25]

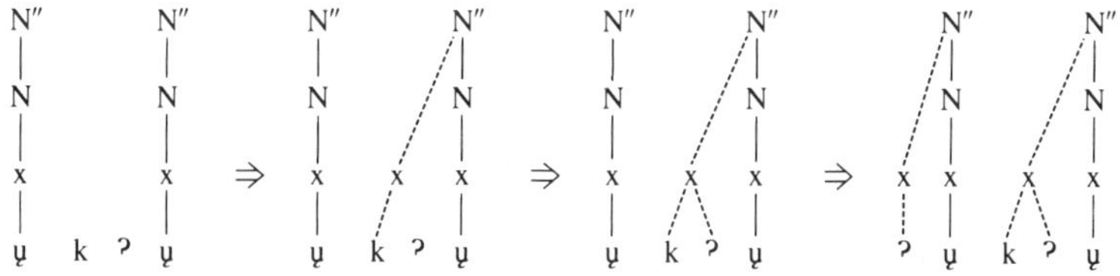

'1incl' 'be'

First, it has been noted that, except where the EOP creates a required onset slot, the feature [+cons.gl.] cannot have its own skeletal point. It can only join a skeletal point that already is linked to another segment. Thus, it will link either to a preceding vowel, as in [22], or to a preceding consonant, resulting in an ejective as in [16a]. In both types of cases, the link is to the immediate left and to a previously anchored point. Consequently, since the [ʔ] in [25] does not have an already linked segment on its left, it cannot be the first element to link. Rather, as we already saw in [23a], the EOP will create a skeletal slot to fill the medial onset position which the floating [k] will dock onto. Once the [k] is associated, then the [ʔ] can link to this anchored point on its left. Finally, the general rule of ʔ-epenthesis [7] will generate a word-initial onset slot with the default [ʔ], thus giving the correct phonetic output [ʔuk′ų].

4. CONCLUSION

To summarize, this paper has attempted to show that what initially seemed to be a kind of paradoxical duality in the behavior of aspirates and ejectives reduces to a principled and unified explanation if a complex segment analysis within the autosegmental framework is adopted. The fundamental claim defended here is that aspirates and ejectives indeed are unitary phonemes, represented by a single point on the skeletal tier. The apparent cluster properties they manifest derive from their subskeletal branching configuration.

Furthermore, the proposals advanced here offer a much more systematic and coherent treatment of several previously unrelated facts regarding the behavior and distribution of [ʔ] and [h] as simple segments. It is concluded that the glottal stop /ʔ/ does not function as an independent segmental phoneme in Teton, nor by extension in any of the Dakota dialects. Rather, it is postulated that the articulatory feature of [+cons.gl.] is lexically available but never with its own skeletal slot at the level of underlying representation.

Thus, it is hoped on the one hand that the present analysis, by drawing on the resources of the autosegmental framework, has contributed some insights into questions of long-standing debate within the Siouan literature.

On the other hand, the data investigated here have raised several questions of theoretical interest, motivating the postulation of constraints on the distribution and realization of floating features, and constraints on the prosodic organization of skeletal elements. In this latter regard, it is hypothesized that a notion of prosodic licensing interacts with canonical syllable structure constraints to explain the severely limited distribution of closed syllables in Dakota, and the particular phonological changes which are manifest in coda position.

NOTES

Earlier versions of this paper were presented at the Western Conference on Linguistics (WECOL) in Vancouver, British Columbia in October 1984, at the University of Ottawa in November 1984, and at the Symposium on Canadian Native Languages in Theoretical Perspective at SUNY, Buffalo, New York in March 1985. I am particularly grateful to Elan Dresher, Karin Michelson, Glyne Piggott, and David Rood for their helpful comments and to Cathy Howett and Don Johnson for computer programming. Partial funding for this research was generously provided by NSF (BNS–8406236) and NEH (RD–20477–84) grants.

1. In the statements of permissible root-final consonants, two issues have been the subject of some controversy in the Dakotan Literature. The first concerns the underlying value for [voice] of the fricative series. Arguments for a [+voice] value are found in Boas and Deloria (1941, 12), Carter (1974, 73 ff.), and Shaw (1980, 55–63), whereas motivation for adopting the [−voice] value is found in Matthews (1970, 98–99) and Shaw (1985). Two major advantages of the latter position are (1) the unmarked status of the voiceless set, and (2) the clear parallelism with the voiceless stops, as /p t č k s š x/ constitutes a much more natural set than does /p t č k z ž γ/. The reader is referred to the cited references for fuller discussion.

The second issue of debate has been the extent of the set of consonants that occur in root-final position. For example, Boas and Deloria (1932, 98) identify /p t k z ž γ w y/, but in their later work (1941, 25) list /p t č k z ž γ/. Abstracting away from the previously mentioned issue of the [voice] value of the fricative series, at variance here is whether any nonobstruent segments should be included. Although not numerous, there are some roots that behave both phonologically and morphologically as consonant-final, but that terminate in /l n y/. Representative examples of such roots are given below. However, I have not found any convincing examples of a /w/-final root. Given space limitations, it is not possible to motivate fully the criteria differentiating C-final from V-final roots (see Shaw 1980, 116ff.). For the present purposes, note the different stress and reduplication patterns below. Roots that are strictly V-final show regular second syllable stress, and reduplicate the final syllable. Those that are underlyingly C-final surface with a terminal epenthetic (also called a stem formative) vowel, which never participates in stress or reduplication. What therefore appears as irregular initial stress results from what in fact is the regular application of stress to the underlyingly monosyllabic root, with subsequent epenthesis of the final -a vowel. Similarly, reduplication applies regularly to these roots to copy the last (C-final) syllable prior to epenthesis (ancillary and exceptionless processes of Coronal Dissimilation and Coronal Lenition are detailed in Shaw 1980; Triconsonantal simplification is discussed in Section 2.1 of this paper).

V-final

/kala/	kalá	kaláła	'to spill'
/zuya/	zuyá	zuyáya	'to go on a war party'

C-final

/lil/	líla	/lil-lil/	→	liglíla	'very'
/k^huy/	k^húya	/k^huy-k^huy/	→	k^hulk^húya	'below'
/spay/	spáya	/spay-spay/	→	spaspáya	'be wet'
/čon/	čóna	/čon-čon/	→	čokčóna	'be few'

On the basis of the dozen or so forms that behave like those in the C-final set, I have included /l y n/ in the class of possible root-final consonants. Viewed statistically, however, it is certainly true that the vast majority of root-final consonants are the obstruents.

2. Phonemic /l/ in the Teton dialect, from which the data for the present paper are drawn, is realized as /d/ in the Santee dialects. Consequently, either one or the other may occur but not both.

3. This identification of possible segments in syllable-final position abstracts away from various low-level phonetic processes which may apply to voice final obstruents. Such voicing is transparently phonetic in nature, as well as subject to a considerable degree of dialect variability, and consequently is not directly relevant to the present discussion (see Shaw (1984) for extensive discussion). For example, there is (non-contrastive) regressive voicing assimilation in Sioux Valley: /top/ [toptopa] 'by fours', but /ɣop/ [ɣobɣopa] 'to snore' showing [b] in syllable-final position.

4. The reader is referred to Boas & Deloria (1941, 5), Carter (1974, 52) and Hollow (1970, 297) for similar observations regarding intramorphemic clustering restrictions.

5. Within the domain of the onset, voicing of a sonorant spreads leftward to a noncontinuant giving /pl/ → [bl], /kl/ → [gl], /kn/ → [gn], etc. Thus, tautosyllabic [pl], [kl], [kn], etc., clusters do not surface phonetically though such clusters do arise

heterosyllabically through morphological concatenation, e.g., [šųk-mánitu] 'coyote' (dog-wilderness), [šųk-lúza-hą] 'race horse' (dog-swift-Adv).

6. Nasality spreads leftward giving [mn] from /pn/, e.g., [mni] 'water'. Note however that this does not affect a back noncontinuant, where simply voicing spreads, i.e. /kn/ → [gn].

7. An alternative cluster approach, advanced by Matthews (1955, 58) and subsequently N. Levin (1964), treats ejectives as deriving from geminates. As there appears to be little support for such a position (see Hollow 1970, 296; and Shaw 1980, 64–65, for explicit counterarguments) and as Matthews himself switches to a consonant plus [ʔ] representation in his later works (1958, 1970), I will not specifically address the geminate hypothesis here.

Carter (1974, 49 ff), following Matthews (1955), pursues an alternative representation for the aspirates; namely, that the second member of an aspirate cluster is /x/ rather than /h/. In the absense of morphophonemic evidence, Carter's argumentation is based primarily on formal issues of rule notation, questions of rule interaction, and putative economy of Morpheme Structure Conditions. As much of Carter's argumentation is dependent on the correctness of the initial hypothesis that aspirates are underlyingly clusters and as the basic claim being defended here is that they are not, in the interest of brevity, I cannot pursue a detailed defense of the /h/ versus /x/ debate. Suffice it to say that markedness conditions, in conjunction with the fact that /h/ and /ʔ/ class together as laryngeals, more plausibly justify the choice of /h/ in the present analysis.

8. For further details governing the conditions under which the vowel [a] deletes before another vowel, see Shaw 1980, 1985, although it should be noted that not all aspects of vowel deletion are well understood. The nominalizing suffix (Nom) is here hypothesized to be a floating /−i/ which coalesces with a preceding ablauting /a/ to surface as [e].

9. Stem is here used to refer to the maximal morphological structure that comprises a lexical root plus prefixes. Evidence that "stem-initial" position (rather than word-initial position) is the most appropriate domain for the process of ʔ-epenthesis is the fact that the epenthetic glottal most often remains on the second member of a lexical compound, even if the first member is C-final, e.g., [[čʰap][i-gmųka]] → [čʰapʔígmųke] 'beaver-trap' [[beaver][instrumental-trap]]. There is both lexical and dialectal variability in this regard, however, for even the same V-initial stem may not have the epenthetic [ʔ] in another compound, e.g., [[šųk][i-gmųka]] → [šųkígmųke] 'poison; anything to use in trapping wolves' (Beuchel 1970, 469).

Consistent with several other observations in the literature (Aronoff 1976, and so forth), I would hypothesize that the presence of an internal epenthetic [ʔ] correlates directly with the degree of morphological transparency of the internal compound structure. A formal account of this would therefore follow from the morphological bracketing structure of the compounds. If a compound is morphologically transparent, then one may assume the internal bracketing to be available to trigger the application of ʔ-epenthesis on the internal stem. If, however, there is a greater degree of lexicalization (reflected, for e.g., in less transparent semantic compositionality, e.g., "poison" above), one may assume the internal bracketing to have been erased and therefore inaccessible to ʔ-epenthesis.

10. The Empty Onset Principle of [7] may be related to a more general principle of grammar, viz. the Obligatory Contour Principle (OCP), if this latter is held to apply at the level of syllabic representation to optimize a non-nucleus/nucleus contour sequence (i.e., CVCV. . .) with the unmarked initiator being non-nuclear.

11. As argued in Section 3 below, a lexically present floating [k] or [ʔ] will obligatorily fill an empty onset. Of less relevance to the present argumentation are various optional epenthetic transitions whose occurrence is variable and dependent on rate of speech. Thus, a VV sequence may be broken by [y] if the initial vowel is front, by [w] if it is round, and otherwise by [ʔ], e.g., /ia/ [ʔiʸá] 'speak', /oa-a/ [ʔoʷáʔa] 'be moldy' (Redup).

12. Although Teton is the only documented Dakota dialect to have "glottal closure" bearing the morphemic function of the declarative mode marker, a comparable case is reported for the related Siouan language Hidatsa, where a final glottal prosody is realized as a glottal interruption of a preceding vowel to mark the interrogative mode (Matthews 1965, 101).

13. I would like to thank David Rood for initially bringing this tacit assumption to my attention.

14. The voicing alternation in the fricative series is attributable to a cyclic intervocalic voicing rule (see Shaw 1985).

15. This characterization of licensing draws heavily on Kaye, Lowenstamm, and Vergnaud's (1985) notion of prosodic government. I shall assume, however, that government may only hold between two constituents which are configurationally related within independently defined prosodic dominance relations; e.g., a coda may be governed by the nucleus. Licensing, on the other hand, is defined here with reference to prosodic constituency, but strictly on the basis of adjacency: thus, for example, a coda may be licensed by a following onset, or vice versa.

The use of the terms 'coda' and 'onset' is not intended to imply the existence of intermediate constituent nodes with these labels. Rather, the terms are here used solely as mnemonics to reference a post-nuclear skeletal position dominated by N′ and a pre-nuclear skeletal position dominated by N″, respectively.

16. Regarding the independently motivated role of "stem" and "word" domains in the determination of Dakota stress, see Shaw 1985.

17. First, the 'counterfactual' [tkʰa] in Teton (diachronically derived by unstressed hi V deletion, cf. cognate [tukʰá] in Santee and [kʰá] in Western Oglala (Boas and Deloria 1941, 112)) sustains an aspirate in second position. Secondly, the Santee dialects systematically have the voiced segments [b] and [d] (cognate to the resonants /w/ and /l/ in Teton) in second position, e.g., Santee [šbu] (T. [šwu]) 'to drip', [xba] (T. [xwa]) 'be sleepy', [sda] (T. [sla]) 'grease'. Thirdly, the affricate [č] can occur (albeit rarely) in second position in onsets, but never in initial position, e.g., [xča] 'intensifier'. Although following Walli-Sagey (1986), I assume /č/ to be a "contour"

rather than a "complex" segment, it nonetheless has internal melodic branching (of [−cont][+cont]) and is subject to essentially identical distributional constraints.

18. Under the assumption (Kiparsky 1985) that Structure Preservation operates lexically, [19] is postulated as a lexical constraint. Consequently, [19] will not block the application various postlexical processes that create branching representational structure. Consider, for example, that certain voiced segments are tolerated as the second member of a cluster, e.g., /pl/, /kn/, etc., as in the chart in [3a]. All these permissible voiced segments are sonorants, and, therefore, voiced redundantly. Assuming that only distinctive features are present in underlying representation and throughout the lexical component, the sonorants will have no laryngeal specification (and consequently no branching structure) until the appropriate redundancy rules apply at the postlexical level to insert the requisite feature values.

Similarly, consider the nasal and voicing assimilation processes that occur within the onsets, e.g., surface [mn] from /pn/, [bl] from /pl/, etc. (see notes 5 and 6). The autosegmental spreading of [voice] or [nasal] might initially appear to violate the constraint in [19]. Thus, in the following example, which makes minimal assumptions as to the internal structure of /n/, the value of [+nasal] must spread over to the unmarked /p/, thereby creating a branching structure under a branching onset:

[mn]

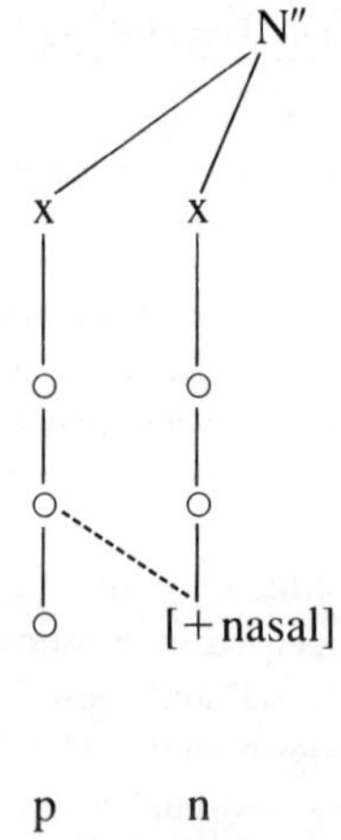

However, as such voice/nasal assimilations are low-level, fully pervasive allophonic phenomena, i.e., clearly postlexical, they are not subject to the lexical constraint [19].

19. This account assumes that Palatalization is a lexical rule, for postlexical rules would not be expected to be subject to Structure Preservation. That Palatalization is indeed lexical is confirmed by such facts as (1) it is constrained by Strict Cyclicity not to apply morpheme-internally, e.g., [sik-sika] 'Blackfoot'; (2) it does not apply across stronger lexical boundaries, e.g., [mni-kį], not *[mni-çį] 'the water' (water-the); and (3) it is sensitive to the categorial subclassification of verbs, applying only to active transitive stems.

20. See Archangeli (1984) for a prosodic treatment of [ʔ] in Yawelmani.

21. Given that all verbal stems and suffixes in Dakota are vowel-final, the declarative [ʔ] simply never occurs postconsonantally. The only possible exception would be the "adversative" suffix /-š/, but its morphological distribution and semantic value are such that it never concatenates with the declarative.

22. The postulated constraint on floating elements occurring only at the margins on a lexical domain would follow from the Mapping Convention which, in effecting a one-to-one directional linking between root nodes and skeletal elements, will not skip over any medial elements. The only possible residue from a mismatch will be at the terminal margin.

REFERENCES

Anderson, S. R. 1976. Nasal Consonants and the Internal Structure of Segments. *Language* 52, 326–44.

Archangeli, D. B. 1984. *Underspecification in Yawelmani Phonology and Morphology*. Ph.D. Diss., Massachusetts Institute of Technology.

Archangeli, D. and D. Pulleyblank. 1986. The Content and Structure of Phonological Representations. Unpublished ms., University of Arizona, Tuscon, and University of Southern California.

Aronoff, M. 1976. *Word Formation in Generative Grammar*. Cambridge: Massachusetts Institute of Technology Press.

Beuchel, Rev. E., S. J. 1970. *Dictionary of the Teton Dakota Sioux Language,* Rev. P. Manhart (ed.) Pine Ridge, S.D.: Red Cloud Indian School, Inc.

Boas, F., and E. Deloria. 1932. Notes on the Dakota, Teton dialect. *International Journal of American Linguistics* 7, 97–121.

Boas, F., and E. Deloria. 1941. *Dakota Grammar,* Memoirs of the National Academy of Sciences 23, Part 2.

Campbell, L. 1974. Phonological Features: Problems and Proposals. *Language* 50, 52–65.

Carter, R. T., Jr. 1974. *Teton Dakota Phonology*. University of Manitoba Anthropology Papers 10.

Chomsky, N. and M. Halle. 1968. *The Sound Pattern of English*. New York: Harper and Row.

Clements, G. N. 1985. The Geometry of Phonological Features. *Phonology Yearbook 2*.

Clements, G. N. and S. J. Keyser. 1983. *CV Phonology: A Generative Theory of the Syllable*. Linguistic Inquiry Monograph 9. Cambridge: Massachusetts Institute of Technology Press.

Ewen, C. J. 1982. The Internal Structure of Complex Segments. In *The Structure of Phonological Representations, Part II,* Harry van der Hulst and Norval Smith, eds., pp. 27–67. Dordrecht, Holland: Foris Publications.

Hayes, B. 1982. Extrametricality and English Stress. *Linguistic Inquiry* 13.2, 227–276.

Hollow, R. C. 1970. A Note on Assiniboine Phonology. *International Journal of American Linguistics* 36, 4, 296–98.

Hulst, H. van der and N. Smith. 1982. Introduction. In *The Structure of Phonological Representations, Part I*. Dordrecht, Holland: Foris Publications.

Kaye, J. 1983. On the Syllable Structure of Certain West African Languages. In Goyvaerts (ed.) *African Linguistics: Essays in Memory of M. W. K. Semikenke*. Studies in the Sciences of Language Series, Vol. 6. Pp. 285–308.

Kaye, J. and J. Lowenstamm. 1982. On the Internal Structure of the Rime. Paper presented at GLOW, Paris.

Kaye, J. and J. Lowenstamm. 1984. A Non-linear Treatment of Grassman's Law. Paper presented at NELS 15, Brown University.

Kaye, J., J. Lowenstamm, and J. R. Vergnaud. 1985. The Internal Structure of Phonological Elements: A Theory of Charm and Government. In *Phonology Yearbook 2*, 305–328.

Kean, M-L. 1975. *The Theory of Markedness in Generative Phonology*. Ph.D. Diss., Massachusetts Institute of Technology.

Kiparsky, P. 1985. Some Consequences of Lexical Phonology. *Phonology Yearbook 2*, 85–138.

Levin, N. B. 1964. *The Assiniboine Language*. Publication No. 32, Research Center in Anthropology, Folklore, and Linguistics. Bloomington: University of Indiana.

Matthews, H. G. 1955. A Phonemic Analysis of a Dakota Dialect. *International Journal of American Linguistics* 21, 56–59.

Matthews, H. G. 1958. *Handbook of Siouan Languages*. Ph.D. Diss., University of Pennsylvania.

Matthews, H. G. 1965. *Hidatsa Syntax*. The Hague: Mouton.

Matthews, H. G. 1970. Some Notes on PSi Continuants. *International Journal of American Linguistics* 36, 98–110.

Pulleyblank, D. 1983. *Tone in Lexical Phonology*. Ph.D. Diss., Massachusetts Institute of Technology.

Riemsdijk, H. C. van and N. S. H. Smith. 1973. Zur Instabilität komplexer phonologischer Segmente. In *Linguistische Perspectiven*, A. P. ten Cate and P. Jordens (eds.) Niemeyer.

Sagey, E. C. 1986. *The Representation of Features and Relations in Nonlinear Phonology*. Ph.D. Diss., Massachusetts Institute of Technology. Technology.

Shaw, P. A. 1980. *Theoretical Issues in Dakota Phonology and Morphology*. New York: Garland.

Shaw, P. A. 1984. Syllable Structure Paradoxcs in Dakota. Unpublished ms., presented at the Canadian Linguistic Association, Guelph.

Shaw, P. A. 1985. Modularization and Substantive Constraints in Dakota Lexical Phonology. *Phonology Yearbook 2,* 173–202.

Thráinsson, H. 1978. On the Phonology of Icelandic Preaspiration. *Nordic Journal of Linguistics* 1, 1, 3–54.

Trubetzkoy, N. S. 1967. [1949] *Principes de Phonologie.* Paris: Klincksieck.

Walli-Sagey, B. 1986. On the Representation of Complex Segments and their Formation in Kinyarwanda. In *Studies in Compensatory Lengthening,* Engin Sezer and Leo Wetzels (eds.) Dordrecht, Holland: Foris Publications. Pp. 251–278.

INVISIBILITY: VOWELS WITHOUT A TIMING SLOT IN MOHAWK

Karin Michelson

INTRODUCTION

Various aspects of epenthesis processes have been studied within nonlinear phonology in recent years: for example, the evidence from epenthesis for universal principles of syllable structure assignment (Lowenstamm 1981); the interaction of stress and epenthesis (e.g. Broselow 1982); and the representation of epenthetic vowels (e.g. Archangeli 1984). Mohawk, a Northern Iroquoian language, exhibits several epenthesis processes involving three different vowels as well as a complex interaction with prosodic phenomena; a study of Mohawk epenthesis thus bears directly on the last two issues mentioned.

A very basic description of epenthesis in Mohawk is that it involves the insertion of an epenthetic vowel *e* into certain consonant clusters, except at the boundary between an incorporated noun root and a following verb root, where an epenthetic *a* (the *joiner*) is inserted instead (e.g. Postal 1968, 253; Bonvillain 1973, 56; Chafe 1977, 171; Mithun 1979a, 179 and 1979b, 345). A third epenthetic vowel, a prothetic *i*, is inserted word-initially into verb forms that have fewer than two vowels.

Both epenthetic *e* and epenthetic *a* show an interesting interaction with stress. Stress regularly occurs on the penult in Mohawk, except that certain syllables containing epenthetic *e* or *a* are ignored in determining the penult.

For example, [1] and [2] below contain an epenthetic *e* while [3] and [4] contain an epenthetic *a* or joiner.[1] In each pair of examples, the epenthetic vowel occurs under identical morphological conditions and nearly identical phonological conditions, yet in [1] and [3] the epenthetic vowel is unstressed while in [2] and [4] it is stressed. (The clusters broken up by an epenthetic vowel are italicized in the segmented versions of the examples.)

[1] tékeriks 'I put them together, next to each other'
te-*k*-*r*ik-s
DUALIC-1SG.AGT-put together, next to each other-HABITUAL

[2] kérhaʔ[2] 'I fill it in'
k-*r*-haʔ
1SG.AGT-fill something in-HABITUAL

[3] tekaʔshá:rariks 'I put the knives side by side'
te-k-aʔsha*r*-*r*ik-s
DUALIC-1SG.AGT-knife-place side by side-HABITUAL

[4] wakiʔtuhkwárhos 'I have a fever'
wak-iʔtuhk*w*-*r*ho-s
1SG.PAT-flame, fever-coat, spread-HABITUAL

One possible solution is to posit two rules of *e*-epenthesis and two rules of *a*-epenthesis, crucially ordered with respect to stress. Those epenthetic vowels that are ignored by the stress rule would be inserted by rules ordered after stress, while those epenthetic vowels that are potentially stressed are inserted by rules ordered before stress. In this paper, it is argued that the most insightful treatment of the complex interaction in Mohawk of the phonological environment of epenthesis, the grammatical categories involved, and the quality of the epenthetic vowel is an analysis that makes use of the distinction in CV phonology of the timing tier and the melody tier. It is further shown that there is an alternative approach to deriving the accent of forms containing epenthetic vowels once the notion is abandoned that epenthesis involves the unitary insertion of a segmental feature matrix together with its associated element on the timing tier (e.g. V-slot).

The organization of the paper is as follows. In section 1, I describe the environments into which epenthetic *e* and epenthetic *a* are inserted and the interaction of the epenthetic vowels with accentual phenomena. I believe the clearest way to present the rather complex data is in terms of a rule-ordering analysis, similar to the one presented in an earlier paper (Michelson 1981). Section 2 presents an alternative analysis to the rule-ordering solution. Section 3 is a discussion of some of the implications of the new analysis. Section 4 is a brief summary of the paper. In addition, I have provided two appendixes. The first outlines the evidence for a particular formulation of *e*-epenthesis, which is not crucial to the analysis but interesting in its own right; the second gives additional examples of epenthesis with the intention of providing a complete range of relevant data.

1. THE DATA

In this part of the paper, I describe the conditions under which epenthetic vowels occur in Mohawk and the interaction of epenthesis with stress, vowel lengthening, and a rule of prothesis (which inserts the third epenthetic vowel, an initial prothetic *i*). A short remark on terminology will make the discussion clearer. I make a distinction, in the case of both epenthetic *e* and the joiner, between those epenthetic vowels that intervene between two morphemes, for which a synchronic rule of epenthesis therefore is motivated; and certain vowels that show the same behavior with respect to prosodic phenomena as the first type but always occur morpheme internally and never alternate with Ø, for which a synchronic rule therefore is not motivated. Since the second type is not properly an epenthetic vowel from a synchronic point of view, I will sometimes use the term *weightless vowel* (taken from Lounsbury 1942) to refer to either or both vowels when they exhibit similar behavior with respect to accent.

All the examples in this paper are from Mike and Catherine Norton of Kahnawà:ke, Québec, with whom I have worked off and on since 1974 and whose kindness and expertise I gratefully acknowledge.

1.1. Epenthetic e

An epenthetic *e,* whose phonetic realization is identical to the phonetic realization of underlying /e/, occurs under the following conditions. First, *e* is inserted into *consonant plus n, r,* or *w* clusters, when the *n, r,* or *w* is the initial segment of certain morphemes which I will simply designate *stem* here (see Michelson 1983, 1988, for the specific morphemes involved). The clusters broken up by epenthetic *e* are italicized in the segmented versions of the examples in [5], and the rule that inserts the epenthetic *e* is stated formally in [6]. Note that *Cr* clusters never occur on the surface in Mohawk. (See Appendix 1 for the CC clusters that occur in Mohawk.)[3]

[5] a. wakeruhyá:kʌ 'I suffer'
wa*k-r*uhyakʌ-Ø
1SG.PAT-suffer-STATIVE

b. kerúnyus 'I put it into something; I sketch'
*k-r*unyu-s
1SG.AGT-fill in-HABITUAL

c. wahakena?kú:ni? 'he made me angry'
wa-ha*k*-*n*a?kuni-?
FACTUAL-MASC.SG.AGT/1SG.PAT-make angry-PUNCTUAL

d. senohkwánerʌk 'Tie it!'
s-*n*ohkwanerʌk-Ø
2SG.AGT-tie-IMPERATIVE

e. ratatewʌniyóstha? 'he takes advantage of everything'
r-ata*t*-*w*ʌniyost-ha?
MASC.SG.AGT-REFLEXIVE-take advantage of-HABITUAL

f. tekera?neká:rus 'I burst it, popped it'
te-*k*-*r*a?nekar-us
DUALIC-1SG.AGT-burst, pop-HABITUAL

g. ʌ́kerʌ? 'I will put it into a container'
ʌ-*k*-*r*-ʌ?
FUT-1SG.AGT-fill into-PUNCTUAL

h. ʌ́kerahkwe? 'I will use it as a container'
ʌ-*k*-*r*ahkw-?
FUT-1SG.AGT-use as a container-PUNCTUAL

i. wà:kerihte? 'I will cook it'
wa?-*k*-*r*iht-?
FACTUAL-1SG.AGT-cook-PUNCTUAL

j. tʌ́kerike? 'I will put together side by side'
t-ʌ-*k*-*r*ik-?
DUALIC-FUT-1SG.AGT-put side by side-HABITUAL

k. wa?tkatátenake? 'I scratched myself'
wa?-t-k-ata*t*-*n*ak-?
FACTUAL-DUALIC-1SG.AGT-REFLEXIVE-scratch-PUNCTUAL

[6] *e*-Epenthesis I:

$$\emptyset \rightarrow \underset{\substack{| \\ e}}{V} \;/\; C \_\_\_\_ \underset{\substack{| \\ [+\text{son}]}}{[C}$$

Condition: [C belongs to *stem*

Second, an epenthetic *e* intervenes between an oral (i.e. [-low]) consonant and a following consonant cluster whose first member is any nonsyllabic segment except *h* or *s*. Examples are given in [7a] through [7g]. Clusters consisting of *ChC* and *CsC* are not broken up by an epenthetic *e,* as shown by the examples in [7h] and [7i]. The second rule of *e*-epenthesis is stated in [8]. The C that conditions epenthesis is characterized as an *extrasyllabic* (i.e. a nonsyllabic segment that cannot be syllabified by the syllabification rules of Mohawk) sonorant or an extrasyllabic noncontinuant obstruent (*k, t,* ʔ).[4] The [-low] condition on the first C prevents the rule from inserting an epenthetic *e* into clusters whose first member is *h* or ʔ (e.g. *hny,* ʔ*kt),* which remain intact as implied by the first sentence of this paragraph. (See also Appendix 1 and note 4 on the formal statement of this rule.)

[7] a. kethè:thaʔ 'I pound, am pounding'
*k-t*heʔt-haʔ
1SG.AGT-pound-HABITUAL

b. ʌkeʔnekʌ̀:naʔ 'I will go and beg'
ʌ-*k*- ʔnekʌ-hna-ʔ
FUT-1SG.AGT-beg-DISLOCATIVE-PUNCTUAL

c. watè:skuteʔ 'a roast'
w-a*t*- ʔskut-ʔ
NEUTER AGT-SEMI-REFLEXIVE-roast-STATIVE

d. wakényaks 'I get married'
wa*k*-*n*yak-s
1SG.PAT-get married-HABITUAL

e. sérhos 'you coat it with something'
s-*r*ho-s
2SG.AGT-coat something-HABITUAL

f. ʌkétheʔteʔ 'I will pound'
ʌ-*k*-*t*heʔt-ʔ
FUT-1SG.AGT-pound-PUNCTUAL

g. akétsheʔ 'my container, jar'
a*k*-*t*she-ʔ
1SG.POSS-container, jar-NOUN SUFFIX

h. khní:nus 'I buy'
*k-hn*inu-s
1SG.AGT-buy-HABITUAL

i. ákskareʔ 'my girlfriend, boyfriend'
a*k-sk*ar-ʔ
1SG.POSS-friend of the opposite sex-NOUN SUFFIX

[8] *e*-Epenthesis II:

$$\emptyset \rightarrow \underset{\substack{|\\ \text{e}}}{\text{V}} \;/\; \underset{\substack{|\\ [-\text{low}]}}{\text{C}} \;\_\_\_\_\; \underset{\substack{|\\ \begin{bmatrix} \langle -\text{son} \rangle_a \\ \langle -\text{cont} \rangle_b \end{bmatrix}}}{\text{C}'}$$

Condition: a>b

(Note that stems that begin in a consonant cluster whose first element is *n, r,* or *w* condition both *e*-Epenthesis I [6] and *e*-Epenthesis II [8]. These stems must undergo *e*-Epenthesis II [8]; the reason for this will become clear in the discussion of stress.)

We know that the vowels in [5] and [7] are epenthetic because of the morphology; the consonant that conditions epenthesis is the initial segment of a stem, and the stem must be analyzed as beginning in a consonant rather than in the vowel *e* because the pronominal prefix alternants that occur are those that regularly occur with consonant stems, not those that occur with underlying *e*-stems (see, e.g. Michelson 1981).

Third, an epenthetic *e* breaks up word-final consonant plus ʔ clusters. Consonant plus ʔ clusters never occur on the surface in Mohawk (see note 3). Examples are given in [9], and the rule that inserts *e* in this environment is given in [10]. (Underlying word-final Cʔ clusters that receive an epenthetic *e* occur also in 5h, 5i, 5j, 5k, 7c, 7f, and 7i.) It is crucial to note that word-final Cʔ clusters must undergo [10] *e*-Epenthesis III rather than [8] *e*-Epenthesis II which also describes these clusters, since the word-final ʔ in Cʔ clusters is extrasyllabic. (Alternatively, the extrasyllabic condition in the environment of [8] must be abandoned and replaced by the condition that the consonant that triggers epenthesis must be followed crucially by another consonant.)

[9] **a.** ʌká:rateʔ 'I lay myself down'
ʌ-k-ara*t*-ʔ
FUT-1SG.AGT-lay oneself down-PUNCTUAL

b. rokú:toteʔ 'he has a bump on his nose'
ro-kut-o*t*-ʔ
MASC.SG.PAT-bridge of the nose-stand-STATIVE

c. ohnyʌ̀:tskwireʔ 'small branch'
o-hnyʌʔtskwi*r*-ʔ
NEUTER PAT-small branch-NOUN SUFFIX

[10] *e*-Epenthesis III:

$$\emptyset \rightarrow \underset{\substack{|\\ \text{e}}}{\text{V}} \;/\; \text{C} \;\_\_\_\_\; \underset{\substack{|\\ \begin{bmatrix} -\text{son} \\ -\text{cont} \\ +\text{low} \end{bmatrix}}}{\text{C}} \;\#$$

The forms in [5], [7], and [9], show an interesting interaction with stress (first pointed out in Michelson 1978). Stress regularly occurs on the penult in Mohawk. This is shown by the examples in [11], which do not contain any epenthetic vowels within the last two syllables of the word.

[11] **a.** kkétskwas 'I raise it'
k-ketskw-as
1SG.AGT-raise-HABITUAL

b. kataʔkeráhkhwaʔ 'I float'
k-ataʔkerahkw-haʔ
1SG.AGT-float-HABITUAL

c. katirútha? 'I pull it'
k-atirut-haʔ
1SG.AGT.-pull-HABITUAL

d. wakashé:tu 'I have counted it'
wak-ashet-u
1SG.PAT-count-STATIVE

e. kakʌʔroké:was 'I'm dusting'
k-akʌʔrokew-as
1SG.AGT-dust-HABITUAL

f. kerı́htha? 'I cook'
k-riht-haʔ
1SG.AGT-cook-HABITUAL

The Mohawk stress rule is stated in [12].

[12] Mohawk Stress Rule: At the right edge of the word, build a left-dominant branching foot (i.e., stress the penult).

Returning now to the examples that contain epenthetic vowels, when an epenthetic *e* occurs in a closed penult, as in [7d], [7e], and [7g], it is stressed. But when an epenthetic *e* occurs in an open penult, as in [1] or [5g], it is not stressed. In the latter case, the Mohawk Stress Rule does not count the epenthetic *e,* and stress occurs on the antepenult rather than on the penult. The Mohawk Stress Rule also ignores an epenthetic *e* that occurs in a final syllable before a word-final ʔ (and thus in a final closed syllable) as in [9]; these examples are also stressed on the antepenult. These epenthetic vowels are thus *weightless* with respect to stress.

It is possible for words to contain more than one epenthetic *e*. For example, in [7c] and [7f], as well as in [5h] through [5k], a weightless epenthetic *e* breaks up a word-final Cʔ cluster, and the resulting syllable is ignored by the Mohawk Stress Rule. Examples [7c] and [7f] contain a second epenthetic *e*; it occurs in a closed penult, not counting the final weightless syllable, and therefore it is stressed. The second epenthetic *e* in [5h] through [5k], on the other hand, occurs in an *open* syllable; therefore *both* instances of epenthetic *e* are weightless and ignored in determining the penult. Stress occurs on the fourth syllable from the end of the word in these examples.

Two stress-related phenomena also rendered opaque by an epenthetic *e* in an open syllable are Vowel Lengthening and Prothesis. Vowel Lengthening lengthens short vowels in stressed and open syllables; this rule is expressed in [13]. Stressed vowels that are lengthened occur in [11d] and [11e], where stress is indicated with an acute accent. (The stressed and lengthened vowels where stress is indicated with a grave accent are lengthened by a different rule and are distinguished from the acute vowels in having a falling pitch. See note 1.)

[13] Vowel Lengthening:

$\acute{V} \longrightarrow \acute{V}\text{:} \; / \; \underline{\quad\quad} \; CV$

Stressed open syllables are *not* lengthened however when the following syllable contains an epenthetic *e*, as in [5g], [5h], [5j], and [5k]. In these examples, the syllable that precedes the syllable that contains the epenthetic *e* behaves as if it were closed.

Prothesis [14] inserts an initial prothetic *i* into verb forms that contain only a single syllable (at the point when Prothesis applies). The examples in [15] all have an initial prothetic *i*.

[14] Prothesis:

$$\emptyset \rightarrow \underset{\substack{| \\ i}}{V} \; / \; \# \; \_\_ \; C_oVC_o\#$$

[15] **a.** íkyʌs — 'I put it'
k-yʌ-s
1SG.AGT-put-HABITUAL

b. íktats — 'I offer it'
k-tat-s
1SG.AGT-offer-HABITUAL

c. íkkets — 'I scrape it'
k-ket-s
1SG.AGT-scrape-HABITUAL

d. íseriht — 'Cook!'
s-riht-Ø
2SG.AGT-cook-IMPERATIVE

Prothesis applies even when one or more syllables of a verb contains an epenthetic *e* but there is only one *nonepenthetic* vowel as in [15d]. (Crucially, the epenthetic *e* in this example is a weightless vowel, which occurs in an open syllable; when the epenthetic *e* occurs in a similar example in a closed syllable, Prothesis does not apply; see 7e.) Once again, the epenthetic *e* does not count as (part of) a syllable when Prothesis applies. (Notice also that the stressed prothetic *i* in [15d], which is followed in the next syllable by an epenthetic *e,* is not lengthened by Vowel Lengthening.)

A very large number of morpheme-internal instances of *e* between a consonant and *r* (and between *w* and a following *y*) show the same behavior with respect to the Mohawk Stress Rule, Vowel Lengthening, and Prothesis as the epenthetic *e* in, e.g., [5g] and [5k]. Examples are given in [16]. It is more than likely that the vowels in these examples are the result of a historical epenthesis similar to the one described in *e*-Epenthesis I [6]. Synchronically, however, it is important to note that the *e* never alternates with Ø. I return to these examples in section 2.

[16] **a.** katoryà:neru 'I move fast'
k-atoryaˀn*e*ru-Ø
1SG.AGT-move fast-HABITUAL

b. wákeras 'it smells'
w-ak*e*ra-s
NEUTER AGT-smell-HABITUAL

c. wakátteru 'I'm dangerous'
wak-att*e*ru-Ø
1SG.PAT-be dangerous-STATIVE

d. tʌkyà:serʌˀ 'I will stack one on top of the other'
t-ʌ-k-yaˀs*e*rʌ-ˀ
DUALIC-FUTURE-1SG.AGT-stack-PUNCTUAL

e. yakóhterus 'she's scared'
yako-ht*e*ru-s
FEM.SG.PAT-be scared-HABITUAL

f. atkʌ̀:serʌ 'coaster, wedge'
Ø-atkʌˀs*e*rʌ-Ø
NEUTER AGT-support-NOUN SUFFIX

g. wakáweru 'I'm spilling it'
wak-aw*e*ru-Ø
1SG.PAT-spill-STATIVE

h. tewaréserus 'it boils, flows over'
te-w-ares*e*r-us
DUALIC-NEUTER AGT-boil, flow over-HABITUAL

i. ʌnékeri 'hay'
Ø-ʌnek*e*ri-Ø
NEUTER AGT-hay-NOUN SUFFIX

j. kenohkwáneraks 'I'm tying it in a bundle'
k-nohkwan*e*rʌk-s
1SG.AGT-tie in a bundle-HABITUAL

k. íkhnerʌks 'I tie something'
k-hn*e*rʌk-s
1SG.AGT-tie-HABITUAL

The data presented above show that an epenthetic *e* that occurs in a closed syllable is treated like any other syllable nucleus by the Mohawk Stress Rule, i.e. a penultimate *e* is stressed. But both an epenthetic *e* that occurs in an open syllable and the weightless *e* that occurs in examples like [16] do not behave as if they constituted a syllable nucleus. First, these instances of *e* are ignored by the regular rule of penultimate stress. Second, they do not create an open syllable when Vowel Lengthening applies. Third, forms that contain an epenthetic *e* exceptionally undergo Prothesis.

These facts may be handled by crucially ordering the three epenthesis rules given in this section with the Mohawk Stress Rule, Vowel Lengthening, and Prothesis. To derive the examples that contain an epenthetic *e* in an open syllable, the epenthesis rule that inserts *e* into open syllables (*e*-Epenthesis I [6]) is ordered after the Mohawk Stress Rule, Vowel Lengthening and Prothesis. The epenthesis rule that inserts *e* into word-final Cʔ clusters (*e*-Epenthesis III [10]) also must be ordered after the Mohawk Stress Rule, since this epenthetic *e* also is not counted in determining the penult (cf. the examples in [9]). In addition, this analysis requires either that the morpheme-internal weightless vowels be marked as exceptions with respect to Stress and Vowel Lengthening, or that the weightless vowels be synchronically inserted by *e*-Epenthesis I [6] (accordingly modified to insert epenthetic *e* morpheme-internally as well as at the relevant boundary). The latter alternative requires that we posit underlying representations for certain morphemes that never actually occur. Finally, the remaining epenthesis rule (*e*-Epenthesis II [8]), the rule that inserts vowels before clusters and therefore into closed syllables, must be ordered before the Mohawk Stress Rule so that an epenthetic *e* that occurs in a closed penult is correctly stressed. This analysis is summarized in [17].

[17] *e*-Epenthesis II [8]
Mohawk Stress Rule [12]
Vowel Lengthening [13]
Prothesis [14]
e-Epenthesis I [6]
e-Epenthesis III [10]

1.2. The Joiner

A second epenthetic vowel, an epenthetic *a* (the joiner), whose phonetic realization is identical to the phonetic realization of underlying /a/, is inserted between any two nonsyllabic segments at a boundary inside the verb base, e.g. between an incorporated noun root and a following verb root or between a verb root and a following derivational suffix such as the DISTRIBUTIVE or INSTRUMENTAL (see also Michelson 1988). Examples are given in [18]. The clusters into which the joiner is inserted are italicized in the segmented versions of the examples. Note that most of the two-consonant clusters and many of the three-consonant clusters broken up by the joiner occur elsewhere in Mohawk, both across morpheme boundaries and within morphemes, as shown by a comparison of the examples in [18i] and [18j] (see note 1 for the deletion of the underlying /ˀ/ in [18i]).

[18] a. tyeyaˀtakè:ru 'bodies are lying over there'
t-ye-yaˀ*t-k*ehru-Ø
CISLOCATIVE-FEM.SG.AGT-body-spread around-STATIVE

b. tekenʌyahríhthaˀ 'I break, smash stones'
te-k-nʌ*y-h*riht-haʔ
DUALIC-1SG.AGT-stones-smash-HABITUAL

c. kewʌnaˀshátsteˀ 'I mean what I say'
k-wʌ*n-ˀ*shatste-ˀ
1SG.AGT-voice-be strong-STATIVE

d. tehsaˀá:rarik 'Put the curtains together, close them!'
te-hs-aˀa*r-r*ik-Ø
DUALIC-2SG.AGT-curtains, net-put together-IMPERATIVE

e. kaná:waku 'in the swamp'
ka-na*w-k*u-Ø
NEUTER AGT-swamp-in-STATIVE

f. kerákwas 'I take it out of something'
k-*r-k*w-as
1SG.AGT–fill in-UNDOER-HABITUAL

g. tekahruwányu 'many objects put in your path'
te-ka-hru*w-n*yu-Ø
DUALIC-NEUTER AGT-put across-DISTRIBUTIVE-STATIVE

h. kathuwà:reks 'I go boating'
k-at-hu*w-h*rek-s
1SG.AGT-SEMI-REFLEXIVE-boat-push-HABITUAL

i. tekanakè:take 'two containers'
te-ka-nake*ʔt-k*e
DUALIC-NEUTER AGT-container-pluralizer

j. waʔtkashʌ́thoʔ 'I cried'
waʔ-*t*-*k*-ashʌtho-ʔ
FACTUAL-DUALIC-1SG.AGT-cry-PUNCTUAL

In the examples in [18], where the base can be segmented into smaller morphemes, we know that the joiner does not belong to either one of the adjacent morphemes because of the morphology. For example, we cannot analyze the joiner in [18b] as the initial segment of the verb root. This is because the verb root in [18b] can occur without the preceding incorporated noun root *-nʌy-* 'stones'. In this case the pronominal prefixes occur directly attached to the root, and the root takes the pronominal prefix alternants that occur with consonant-initial stems, not those that occur with *a*-stems, which would be the expected result if the *a* were the initial segment of the root. Thus we find the 1SG.AGT. form *tekhríhthaʔ* not **tekahríhthaʔ*.

A weightless *a* occurs also in the examples in [19], but as with the morpheme-internal weightless *e* in the examples in [16], we cannot analyze the stems in [19] synchronically into smaller units or morphemes.[5] It will be relevant for the analysis presented later that the weightless *e* in [16] and the weightless *a* in [19] both occur in identical environments, so that it is not possible to define distinctly the environment in which each vowel occurs. The weightless *a* is italicized in the segmented versions of the examples.

[19] a. oskú:taraʔ 'bark'
o-skut*a*r-aʔ
NEUTER PAT-bark-NOUN SUFFIX

b. onyátstaraʔ 'ribbon'
o-nyatst*a*r-aʔ
NEUTER PAT-ribbon-NOUN SUFFIX

c. otsiʔnéhtaraʔ 'bead'
o-tsiʔneht*a*r-aʔ
NEUTER PAT-bead-NOUN SUFFIX

d. okúhkwaraʔ 'nipple'
o-kuhkw*a*r-aʔ
NEUTER PAT-nipple-NOUN SUFFIX

e. kkwè:tarus 'I cut, slice it'
k-kweʔt*a*r-us
1SG.AGT-cut, slice-HABITUAL

f. tetyò:kara?s 'it's dark'
te-t-yo-?k*a*ra?w-s
DUALIC-CISLOCATIVE-NEUTER PAT-be dark-HABITUAL

The stress of forms that contain an epenthetic *a* is similar to those that contain an epenthetic *e*. When the joiner occurs in a closed penult, it is stressed; see the examples in [4] and in [18f]. When, on the other hand, the joiner occurs in an open penult, the antepenult is stressed, i.e. the Mohawk Stress Rule does not count the joiner in determining the penult; see the examples in [18d], [18e], and in [3]. Similarly, the examples in [19], which have a morpheme-internal weightless *a* in the penult, have antepenultimate stress. To derive both types of examples (18d and 18e as well as 19), we can assume one of two analyses. (1) The joiner is inserted at synchronically motivated boundaries by two rules. One rule, which is ordered before the Mohawk Stress Rule, inserts the joiner before morphemes that begin in a consonant cluster, thereby making the joiner eligible for stress. A second rule, ordered after the Mohawk Stress Rule, inserts the joiner before morphemes that begin in a single consonant (i.e. into open syllables). Morpheme-internal weightless *a* is marked as an exception to stress. (2) The same two rules of insertion are posited but in this alternative, the morpheme-internal weightless *a* is inserted by the second rule rather than being marked diacritically. In this case, the underlying clusters into which the weightless *a* is introduced must somehow be distinguished from the otherwise identical clusters which undergo *e*-Epenthesis.

The behavior of both the joiner and weightless *a* is different from that of weightless *e* in one important respect. While weightless *e* is ignored also by Vowel Lengthening, so that the vowel in a stressed and open syllable is not lengthened when the following syllable contains a weightless *e*, the joiner does condition Vowel Lengthening. For example in [18d] and [18e] the joiner creates the open syllable necessary for lengthening the short vowel in the preceding stressed antepenult.

This analysis, then, requires five distinct epenthesis rules: the three rules of *e*-epenthesis already discussed and two rules that insert the joiner, which are given in [20a]. To correctly derive the accent of forms that contain epenthetic vowels, the five epenthesis rules must be crucially ordered with respect to the Mohawk Stress Rule, Vowel Lengthening, and Prothesis. Further, either the morpheme-internal weightless vowels must be marked as exceptions to the relevant prosodic rules or they must be inserted by *e*-Epenthesis I and Joiner Insertion II. In the second alternative, however, each morpheme must be specified for the rule it undergoes, since the two rules insert vowels into identical clusters. The rules required are listed in [20b] in the order in which they must apply.

[20]. a. Joiner Insertion I:

Ø → V/C __ [C C
|
a

Condition: Applies at specified boundaries within the verb base

Joiner Insertion II:

Ø → V/C __ [C
|
a

Condition: Applies at specified boundaries within the verb base

b. Joiner Insertion I [20a]
e-Epenthesis II [8]
Mohawk Stress Rule [12]
Joiner Insertion II [20a]
Vowel lengthening [13]
Prothesis [14]
e-Epenthesis I [6]
e-Epenthesis III [10]

Notice that one consequence of this analysis is that Joiner Insertion II must refer to the same morphological restriction as Joiner Insertion I, i.e. the joiner occurs at specific boundaries within the verb base (e.g. between an incorporated noun root and a following verb root, between a verb root and most derivational suffixes).

The characteristic behavior of the joiner and epenthetic *e* is summed up in the chart in [21].

[21]

	joiner		epenthetic *e*		
	closed	open	closed	open	Cʔ#
Ignored by Stress	no	yes	no	yes	yes
Ignored by Vowel Lengthening	no	no	no	yes	—
Blocks Prothesis	—	—	yes	no	no

To conclude this section on the description of Mohawk epenthesis, I suggest the five observations in [22], which an analysis of epenthetic *e* and the joiner and their interaction with accentual phenomena will have to account for.

[22] a. Both the joiner and epenthetic *e* behave like underlying vowels when they occur before a sequence of two or more consonants (i.e. they count as a syllable nucleus with respect to Stress and Prothesis).

b. An epenthetic *e* that occurs word-finally in a closed syllable is weightless with respect to stress, while an epenthetic *e* that occurs word-medially in a closed syllable before a ʔ is not. For example in [7c] an *e* occurs in a word-medial *C*ʔ cluster and the *e* behaves like an underlying vowel; it is stressed. In [9], however, the *e* occurs in a word-final *C*ʔ cluster and the *e* is ignored by stress.

c. Epenthetic *e* does not trigger Vowel Lengthening, which lengthens short vowels in stressed open syllables, but the joiner does.

d. Epenthetic *e* (in open syllables) is invisible not only to Stress but also to Vowel Lengthening and Prothesis.

e. The environment in which morpheme-internal weightless *e* occurs is not phonologically distinct from the environment in which morpheme-internal weightless *a* occurs.

2. INVISIBILITY

An alternative to the solution presented in the previous section depends crucially on the following two assumptions. First, phonological representations consist of elements on two formally distinct tiers: a segmental tier and a timing tier. Not all theories that make such a distinction agree on the nature of the elements represented on the timing tier; in this paper, the elements C (syllable margin) and V (syllable peak) are used, according to the framework developed by Clements and Keyser 1983. Second, the two tiers are independent in the sense that (1) there need not be a one-to-one correspondence between elements on the segmental tier and elements on the CV-tier, and (2) it is possible to perform phonological operations—changes in distinctive feature values, deletions, insertions—on one tier without affecting the other tier. For example, long vowels are represented as a single set of segmental features associated to two V-slots, or units of timing, on the CV-tier. A rule of vowel shortening may delete one of the two V-slots, leaving the other V-slot and the associated segmental features intact. The purpose of this section is to show that epenthesis in Mohawk is best characterized in terms of such a theory and its assumptions. Specifically, it is argued here that the segmental features that identify the quality of the epenthetic vowel are epenthesized independently of the V-slot on the timing tier. This type of analysis has been previously proposed by other authors (e.g. Archangeli 1984) for other languages; these analyses have inserted V-slots first and then later provided the segmental features or melody for the empty V-slots by universal and language-specific default rules. The Mohawk data argue for an opposite procedure: first the segmental features are inserted and only later the corresponding V-slots. With respect to the Mohawk data, this is the only analysis that accounts for the observations made in [22] without requiring us to posit arbitrary diacritics.[6]

Given this general formulation of epenthesis, two separate rules are required to insert the segmental features of the epenthetic vowel: the first rule inserts the joiner, on the segmental or melody tier, into any consonant cluster that occurs within a base; the second rule inserts an epenthetic *e*, on the segmental or melody tier, between an oral consonant and a following (morpheme-initial) *n*, *r*, or *w* and between an oral consonant and a following extrasyllablic *k*, *t*, or *ʔ*. These two rules are stated in [23] and [24], respectively. In [23], the symbol *p* in the environment of the rule refers to any segmental matrix; this is necessary since, otherwise, the rule would not specify where exactly on the segmental tier the *a* is inserted.

[23] Joiner Insertion:

$$\emptyset \rightarrow a \,/\, \begin{array}{c} C] \\ | \\ P \end{array} \underline{\qquad} \begin{array}{c} [C \\ | \\ P \end{array}$$

Condition: applies before specified morphemes

[24] *e*-Epenthesis:

$$\emptyset \rightarrow e \,/\, \begin{array}{c} C \\ | \\ [-\text{low}] \end{array} \underline{\qquad} \left\{ \begin{array}{c} [C \\ | \\ [+\text{son}] \\ \\ C' \\ | \\ \begin{bmatrix} -\text{son} & \langle a \rangle \\ -\text{cont} & \langle b \rangle \end{bmatrix} \end{array} \right\}$$

Condition: a > b

These two rules insert the features that define *e* and *a* in all the environments in which they occur. I will call these *invisible* vowels to distinguish them from vowels associated with a V-slot in underlying representations. The two rules apply early, before the Mohawk Stress Rule. After the invisible vowels have been inserted by the rules in [23] and [24], three separate rules insert the V-slots to which the invisible vowels will link. The first rule, expressed in [25], inserts a V-slot over an invisible vowel whenever the invisible vowel precedes a sequence of at least two C-slots on the CV-tier. I make the assumption that the linking of the V-slot to the segmental matrix takes place automatically. I make the additional assumption that, by convention, a syllable node is generated as soon as the V-slot is inserted. V-insertion I [25] is ordered before the Mohawk Stress Rule so that, following automatic resyllabification, the invisible vowels are no longer invisible at the point when stress is assigned. This is shown by the derivation of [7e] in [26].

[25] V-Insertion I:

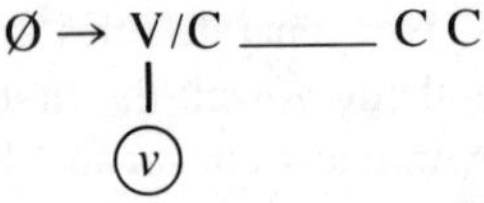

(ⓥ indicates a vowel without a timing slot)

[26] Derivation of sérhos (= 7e):

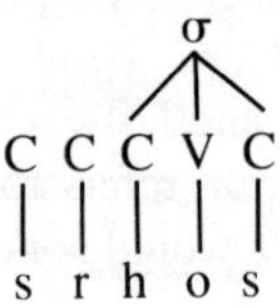

Syllabification

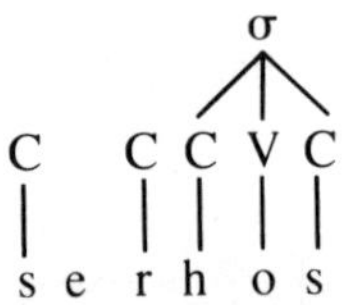

e-Epenthesis [24]

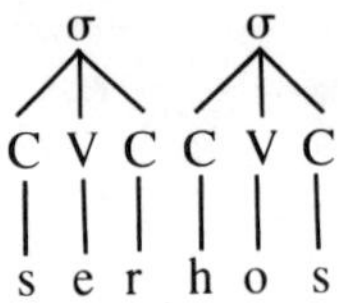

V-Insertion I [25]

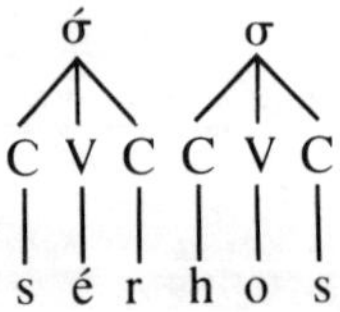

Mohawk Stress Rule [12]

The second rule that inserts a V-slot supplies a slot to instances of invisible *a* (the joiner) in all the remaining cases, i.e. when the *a* occurs in an open syllable. This second rule of V-slot insertion is ordered after the Mohawk Stress Rule but before Vowel Lengthening [13] to account for the fact expressed in [22c]: i.e. the joiner is invisible to stress but opens a preceding syllable so that Vowel Lengthening applies. The second V-insertion rule is given in [27], and the derivation of a representative form is given in [28]. Note that it is not necessary to repeat the environment of Joiner Insertion (i.e. / C] ____ [C) in the structural description of [27]; the timing slot can associate only with a previously unassociated vowel *a*.

[27] V-Insertion II:

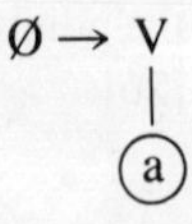

[28] Derivation of kaná:waku (= 18e):

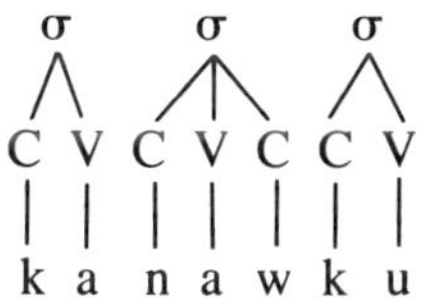

Syllabification

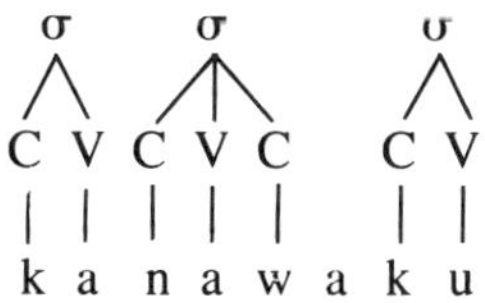

Joiner Insertion [23]

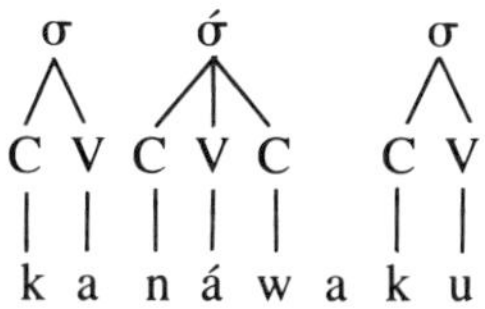

Mohawk Stress Rule [12]

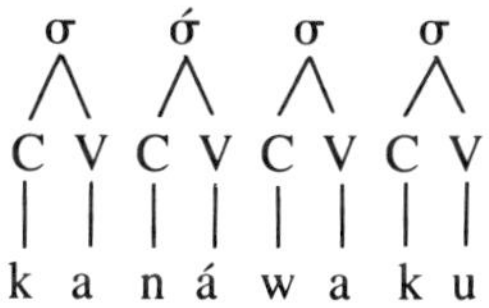

V-insertion II [27]; resyllabification[7]

kaná:waku Vowel Lengthening [13]

The third and final rule that inserts a V-slot inserts the slot over an invisible vowel *e* in all the cases not covered by the first rule [25]. This rule is ordered after the Mohawk Stress Rule, Vowel Lengthening, and Prothesis to account for [22b] and [22d]. A derivation is given in [30].

[29] V-Insertion III:

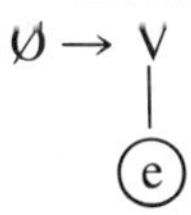

[30] Derivation of ʌká:rateʔ (= 9a):

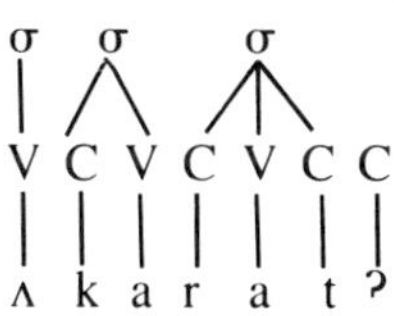

Syllabification

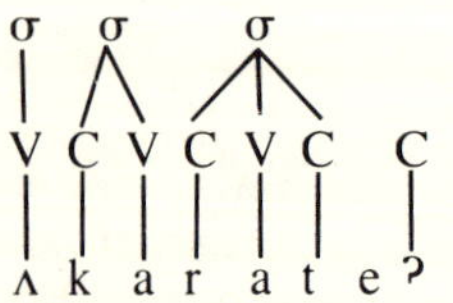

e-Epenthesis [24]

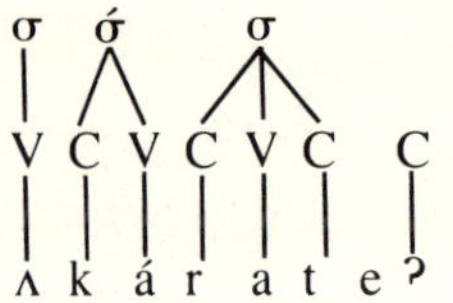

Mohawk Stress Rule [12]

ʌká:rateʔ Vowel Lengthening [13]

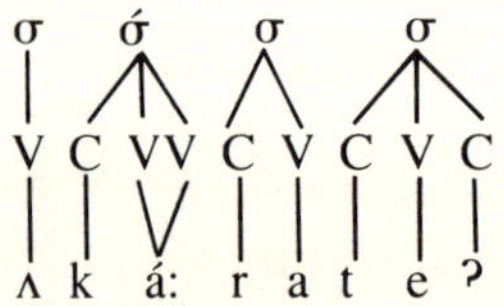

V-Insertion III [29]

The rules that are required in the invisibility analysis are listed in [31] in the order in which they must apply.

[31] Joiner Insertion [23]
e-Epenthesis [24]
V-Insertion I [25]
Mohawk Stress Rule [12]
V-Insertion II [27]
Vowel Lengthening [13]
Prothesis [14]
V-Insertion III [29]

Before going on to discuss the representation of morpheme-internal weightless vowels, I would like to point out three advantages of the analysis just presented over a rule-ordering analysis, as presented in section 1. First, a single rule inserts (the segmental features of) *e,* instead of the three rules under the rule-ordering analysis. Second, a single rule inserts (the segmental features of) *a,* thereby eliminating the need for duplicating the morphological restriction in the formal statement of the rules. Third, the different behavior of word-medial *Ceʔ* versus word-final *Ceʔ* with respect to stress, as noted in [22b], is handled without positing a separate rule just to account for the weightlessness of the word-final *Ceʔ* sequences. Finally, the problem pointed out in section 1 with respect to word-final *Cʔ* clusters, which meet the structural descriptions for two of the epenthesis rules but crucially must undergo only the later (poststress) one, disappears.

I think it is important to point out the problems with the alternative, more usual interpretation of epenthesis referred to earlier, i.e. the V-slot is inserted first and the segmental features are supplied later. There are several disadvantages to this approach. First, at least the following rules (informally stated) are required.

[32] *V-Insertion I* inserts a slot before any sequence of at least two consonants at a boundary within the base. It provides one of the slots that eventually is filled by the joiner.
V-Insertion II inserts a slot after a non-low consonant and before clusters of two consonants, except before *hC* or *sC*. It provides one of the slots that eventually is filled by an epenthetic *e*.
Mohawk Stress Rule [12].
V-Insertion III inserts a slot into all remaining consonant clusters that occur at a boundary within the base. It provides the second slot that eventually is filled by the joiner.
Vowel Lengthening [13]
Prothesis [14]
V-Insertion IV inserts a slot between a consonant and a following *resonant* or ˀ at a morpheme boundary. It provides the second slot that eventually is filled by an epenthetic *e*.
a-Epenthesis inserts the segmental features of the joiner (*a*) into V-slots that occur in the base but not into V-slots that occur before a stem.
e-Epenthesis inserts the segmental features of the vowel *e* into all remaining V-slots (i.e. those occurring before a stem).

Note that such an analysis requires one more rule, a fourth rule of V-insertion. Second, because the phonological environments of epenthetic *e* and the joiner partially overlap, it is not possible to predict which epenthetic vowel occurs solely on the basis of the phonological environment; therefore, such an analysis would require that one of the rules that supplies the features must repeat the morphological conditioning of the corresponding V-insertion rule. Third, as we will see later, this approach cannot be extended to account for nonepenthetic weightless vowels.

So far the analysis has involved epenthetic vowels that occur at a morpheme boundary and, therefore, have been argued to be synchronically inserted. Weightless vowels that occur within a morpheme never alternate with Ø (except as noted in note 4). Therefore, these *weightless* vowels are argued in this paper to be present in underlying representations.[8] However, as shown in the underlying representation of [16b] in [33], they are represented not as ordinary vowels, which consist of a segmental matrix and a corresponding V-slot, but rather as *invisible* vowels; invisibility in this case is interpreted to mean that only the segmental features are present, not the V-slot, which is supplied by the rules already discussed.

[33] Underlying representation of [16b] wákeras:

Since it is not possible to describe the environment in which the morpheme-internal epenthetic *e* occurs as distinct from the environment in which the morpheme-internal epenthetic *a* occurs, it is not clear how an alternative, in which the slots were inserted first and the appropriate vowel features later, could insert the specific vowel correctly in the appropriate environment without reference to diacritic features.

This analysis of invisible epenthetic vowels plus the V-slot insertion rules correctly derives the stress and vowel length of a rather complex, though relatively uncommon, type of paradigm. The examples in question involve morphemes with a morpheme-internal weightless *e* that is stressed in some forms of the paradigm but unstressed in other forms. In [34a] the stem *-ahsuter-* occurs before a consonant-initial suffix; therefore, the penultimate invisible *e* occurs in a closed syllable and is stressed. In [34b], on the other hand, the same stem occurs before a vowel-initial suffix; therefore, the penultimate invisible *e* occurs in an open syllable and is ignored by stress.[9]

[34] a. Derivation of tekahsutérhaʔ I splice, join together:

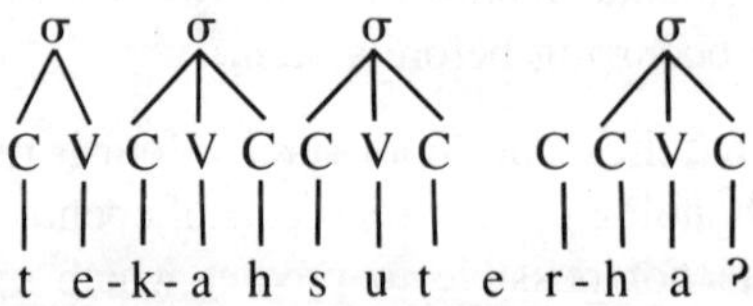

Syllabification

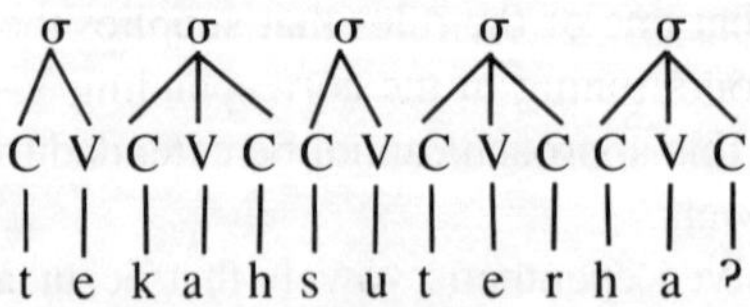

V-Insertion I [25]

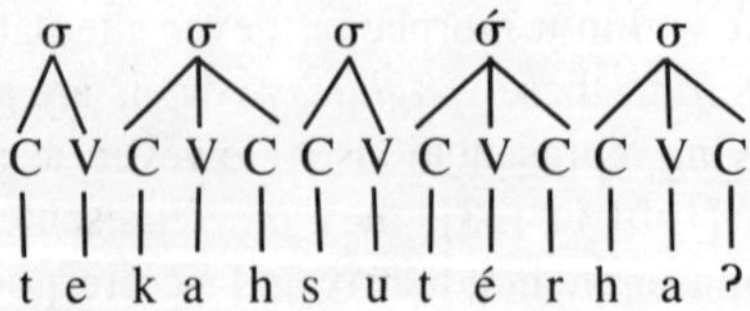

Mohawk Stress Rule [12]

n.a. Vowel Lengthening [13]

tekahsutérhaʔ

b. Derivation of tʌkahsúterʌʔ I will splice, join tog:

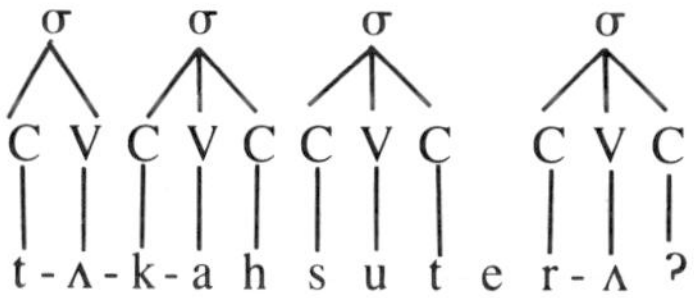

Syllabification

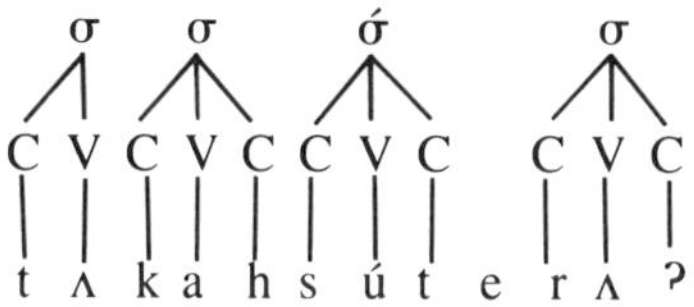

Mohawk Stress Rule [12]

n.a. Vowel Lengthening [13]

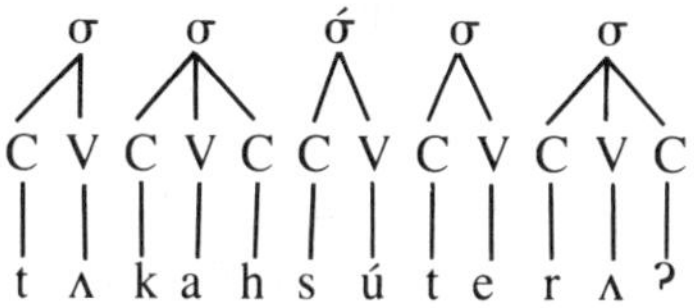

V-Insertion III [29]

Alternative theories, such as one that analyzes all epenthesis processes as the unitary insertion of a segmental matrix and a timing slot, as well as one that analyzes epenthesis as the insertion of an empty V-slot, require that stems such as *-ahsuter-* be marked with two diacritics, one for each of the epenthesis rules the stem undergoes.

3. DISCUSSION

In the previous section, it was argued that the interaction between weightless vowels in Mohawk and prosodic phenomena is most successfully treated in a theory in which it is possible to represent the segmental features of a vowel without necessarily positing a corresponding V-slot. Thus, synchronic rules of epenthesis in Mohawk were argued to consist of two independent processes: first, the features that identify the quality of the vowel are inserted on the segmental, or melody, tier; and second, the V-slot that gives the segment status as a syllable nucleus is inserted separately. This treatment accounts for the distinction between "full" vowels, which constitute a syllable nucleus, and weightless vowels, which do not form a syllable nucleus with respect to prosodic phenomena. The invisible vowels, whether synchronically inserted by epenthesis rules or already present in underlying representations, are analogous to floating tones in autosegmental analyses of tone; they may be interpreted as floating segments whose potential as a syllable nucleus is realized at different points in the derivation. This analysis of Mohawk epenthesis differs from recent analyses of epenthesis (e.g. Archangeli 1984) in that these insert the V-slot first and supply the segmental features later.

The Mohawk data bear on CV theory both in terms of an explanation for the function of epenthesis cross-linguistically and in terms of possible derivations within the theory. I will comment briefly on these two issues. First, most discussions of epenthesis have focused on epenthesis processes that function to break up nonoccurring sequences of consonants. For example, Lowenstamm and Kaye (1985) or Broselow (1982), in a more general study of the interaction of epenthesis and stress, have suggested that the insertion of an epenthetic segment may be predicted from the syllable structure of the language under investigation, i.e. the epenthetic segment occurs just in case the consonants cannot be correctly syllabified. The problem that Mohawk poses for these and similar analyses is that the insertion of the joiner is not strictly governed by syllable structure; the joiner occurs even when the cluster it breaks up occurs elsewhere, contrary to epenthetic *e*. Nevertheless, the joiner exhibits the same interaction with stress as does the epenthetic *e*. It might be possible to argue that at an early level of derivation (and word formation) syllable-initial CC clusters are not allowed in Mohawk so that the joiner also is inserted to produce a possible syllable. At a later level of derivation/word formation, certain clusters would be allowed at the beginning of a syllable, so that epenthetic *e* would be inserted only when the cluster is a nonoccurring one. In either case, CCC clusters would be eliminated before stress is assigned. However, there is no other evidence that the building of syllable structure operates in this way in Mohawk. (Other problems with such an analysis, such as morpheme-internal weightless epenthetic *e* and *a*, are not discussed here.)

Second, in earlier works involving nontonal phenomena (e.g. Clements and Keyser 1983), it was suggested that when an element on the timing tier is deleted, the associated melody segment also is deleted. Further, since epenthesis always involved the insertion of both slot and melody at the same time, floating melodies could never arise in derivations. However, nothing in the framework itself would rule out this possibility. Thus, it is interesting that, more recently, "floating" melodies have been posited in underlying representations (see Archangeli 1983; Shaw, this volume). This paper has suggested further that it is possible to insert just the melody analogous to a tonal autosegment in tonal analyses.

The analysis of epenthesis in Mohawk presented in this paper raises the possibility that it should be possible for different languages to exhibit two different types of epenthesis processes: (1) epenthesis rules that insert invisible vowels, which eventually receive a V-slot, versus (2) epenthesis rules that insert a V-slot, which eventually is filled by segmental features. If both types of epenthesis are possible, the two types should have different characteristics. As a preliminary distinction, I would suggest that the second type is motivated when the epenthesis is strictly syllable-conditioned, i.e. when the epenthetic vowel occurs just to break up nonoccurring consonant clusters. In this case, we do not expect the epenthesis rule to refer to morphological category or that the clusters broken up by the epenthetic vowel occur elsewhere in the language. Furthermore, it is likely that in the second case the language in question contains a single epenthetic vowel rather than two or more distinct qualities, as in Mohawk. The first type, on the other hand, is motivated by epenthesis processes, such as those in Mohawk, where there are several different epenthetic vowels, where the epenthesis rule(s) do not function strictly to break up nonoccurring consonant clusters. and where the environment cannot be expressed purely in terms of syllable structure. Thus, in Mohawk, the joiner occurs between any two consonants at a boundary in the base, whether or not the cluster occurs elsewhere in the language.

Lastly, the distinction between invisible segments and empty or unspecified slots should not be restricted to epenthesis processes (cf. e.g. LeSourd 1985).

4. SUMMARY

Both the epenthetic *e* and the joiner in Mohawk exhibit a complex interaction with accentual phenomena. When they occur in closed penults, they are stressed. When, however, they occur in open penults, they are *weightless,* or ignored by stress. Epenthetic *e* is weightless also when it breaks up word-final *Cʔ* clusters. Epenthetic *e* is ignored not only by stress but also by a rule that lengthens short stressed vowels in open syllables and by a rule that inserts an initial prothetic *i* into verbs that have fewer than two vowels. The joiner, on the other hand, does not block the vowel lengthening rule. Finally, both the weightless and the "full" epenthetic *e* occur in the same combinations of morphemes and in very similar (although not completely identical) phonological environments; this is true also of the joiner.

The analysis presented here inserts the melody segment independent of the timing unit (i.e. V-slot). Morpheme-internal vowels, whose historical source is probably epenthesis but that no longer alternate with Ø, are similarly represented in underlying representations as consisting only of a segmental feature matrix. V-slots are then supplied by three independent insertion rules, and the order of these rules with respect to the Mohawk Stress Rule, Vowel Lengthening, and Prothesis determines the behavior of the epenthetic or weightless vowels with respect to the relevant phenomena.

APPENDIX 1. E-EPENTHESIS BEFORE EXTRASYLLABIC C′

In this appendix, I briefly summarize the arguments for the extrasyllabic C′ condition for the insertion of (the segmental features for) epenthetic *e* (cf.

C_1 \ C_2	y	w	r	n	t	k	s	h	ʔ
y									
w								wh	
r	ry					rk		rh	
n	ny							nh	
t	ty				tt	tk	ts	th	
k	ky	kw			kt	kk	ks	kh	
s		sw		sn	st	sk		sh	
h	hy	hw	hr	hn	ht	hk	hs		
ʔ		ʔw	ʔr	ʔn	ʔt	ʔk	ʔs		

Mohawk CC Clusters

C_1 \ C_2	y	w	r	n	t	k	s	h	ʔ
y									
w									
r								rhy rhw	
n								nhy nhr	
t						tkw tky	tsh tsk tst tsn	thr thn ths thy thw	
k					kth	kkw	ksw ksh ksk kst	khn khr khw khs khy kht	
s				sny	sty sth	skw skt sky skk		shw shn shy shr	
h			hrh hry	hny hnh	hth htk hts hty	hkw hkh	hsk hst hsw hsy hsh		
ʔ		ʔwh		ʔny ʔnh	ʔth ʔty ʔtk ʔts	ʔkw ʔky ʔkt ʔkh ʔkk ʔks	ʔsw ʔst ʔsh ʔsk		

Mohawk CCC Clusters

Figure 1. CC and CCC Clusters in Mohawk.

[24]). It will be useful first to view Figure 1, which charts the CC clusters and CCC clusters that occur word-medially in Mohawk (see also Michelson 1983, 1988).

I will not be concerned here with an exact or elegant characterization of the possible sequences; I believe it is more important to determine the syllable affiliation of the consonants. (Generally, CC sequences may be defined as consisting of hC, ʔC, TC, Ry, Rh, wh where T = /k t s/ and R = /n r/. Negative conditions must then rule out *Cʔ, *tR, *kR, *tw, *sr, *hh, *ʔh.) The syllable membership of CC clusters is analyzed here as VC.CV (versus *V.CCV or *VCC.V), even though some of the CC clusters (e.g. all Cy clusters, th, kh) in the chart occur word-initially. This analysis is argued for mainly because of the rules regarding Vowel Lengthening [13], which lengthens a short stressed vowel in open syllables, i.e. when the stressed vowel precedes a CV sequence, but never when it precedes a CCV sequence. The analysis of clusters into V.CCV syllables would mean that Vowel Lengthening is conditioned by open syllables just in case the following syllable does not have a complex onset, a condition that seems unnatural.

The syllable membership of the medial consonant in the occurring CCC clusters is not crucial, and I know of no convincing evidence to decide between VC.CCV versus VCC.CV. (The CCC clusters that occur may be characterized generally as hCC, ʔCC, ChC, or CsC; further, no CCC cluster contains a CC cluster that does not occur independently.) In those cases where CCC clusters arise as the result of morpheme concatentation but where the CC cluster does not occur otherwise, an epenthetic *e* occurs to break up the clusters (i.e. CeCC) as described in section 1 (unless the cluster occurs at a boundary where the joiner occurs instead). Because the clusters broken up by an epenthetic *e* do not occur otherwise, I characterize the (medial) C before which the epenthetic vowel is inserted as extrasyllabic, or unassociated with any syllable (see also note 4).

APPENDIX 2. EXAMPLES THAT CONTAIN MORE THAN ONE EPENTHETIC VOWEL

A complete description of Mohawk epenthesis must include four additional types of examples, all of which contain two epenthetic vowels within the last four syllables of a word. These types are summarized in this section. I provide a sample derivation of the example in [36a].

[35] a. The antepenult contains the joiner, and the penult contains an epenthetic *e*. Examples are given in [36]. Stress is on the antepenultimate joiner, and the stressed vowel is short.

b. The antepenult and the ultima contain epenthetic vowels. The preantepenultimate syllable is stressed. There are two possibilities: (1) in [37] there is a joiner in the antepenult and an epenthetic *e* in the final syllable; (2) in [38] both the antepenult and the ultima contain an *e*. In addition, the derived stems *-raʔ-* 'approach' (*-r-ʔ-*, fill in -INCHOATIVE) and *-rahkw-* 'use' (*-r-hkw-*, fill in -INSTRUMENTAL) contain the joiner. They are given with the joiner since they represent the first layer of a complex derivation.

c. The penult contains the joiner, the ultima an epenthetic *e*. Stress is antepenultimate. Examples are given in [39].

d. Both the penult and the ultima contain an epenthetic *e*. The antepenult is stressed and lengthened. Examples are given in [40].

e. The antepenult contains a weightless *e* or *a*, and the penult contains the joiner. Stress is on the *penult*, which is not expected. Examples are given in [41]. The rules (of any analysis presented in this paper) predict that stress should occur on the antepenult (see Michelson 1981 or 1983 for derivations). In the invisibility analysis argued for in this paper, these examples can be handled by having V-insertion I [25] also insert a V-slot over an invisible *a* when the immediately preceding syllable contains an invisible *e* or *a*. Thus, the invisibility analysis produces the correct result, but without explaining *why* the stress is irregular in the way it is in these examples; however I know of no analysis that can explain the stress.

[36] a. orutákeri 'maple sap'
o-rut-k*e*ri-Ø
NEUTER PAT-tree, log-be liquid-STATIVE

b. ohnekákeri 'broth'
o-hnek-k*e*ri-Ø
NEUTER PAT-water-be liquid-STATIVE

c. kanatsyánerʌ 'it's fastened, tied to pegs'
ka-natsy-n*e*rʌ-Ø
NEUTER AGT-peg-tie-STATIVE

[37] a. yaʔkená:waraʔneʔ 'I approached the swamp'
y-aʔ-k-naw-raʔ-n*e*ʔ
TRANSLOC-FACTUAL-1SG.AGT-swamp-approach-PUNCTUAL

b. waʔkewʌ́:narahkweʔ 'I obey'
waʔ-k-wʌn-rahkw-ʔ
FACTUAL-1SG.AGT-voice-use-PUNCTUAL

[38] a. ʌ́kerahkweˀ 'I will use it as a container'
ʌ-k-rahkw-ˀ
FUT-1SG.AGT-use as a container-PUNCTUAL

b. tʌkarihwáweˀehsteˀ 'I'll put the subject forth, look into it, discuss it'
t-ʌ-ka-rihw-aw*e*ˀehst-ˀ
DUALIC-FUTURE-NEUTER AGT-matter-pierce-PUNCTUAL

c. ʌkenohkwánerʌkeˀ 'I will tie, bundle it'
ʌ-k-nohkwan*e*rʌk-ˀ
FUTURE-1SG.AGT-tie, bundle-PUNCTUAL

[39] a. wakhné:kareˀ 'I've put water into it'
wak-hnek-r-ˀ
1SG.PAT-water-fill in-STATIVE

b. ʌkkwè:tareˀ 'I cut, slice it'
ʌ-k-kweˀt*a*r-ˀ
FUTURE-1SG.AGT-cut, slice-PUNCTUAL

[40] a. turé:sereˀ 'it boiled, flowed over'
t-a-w-ares*e*r-ˀ
CISLOC-FACTUAL-NEUTER AGT-boil, flow over-PUNCTUAL

b. yʌ́:keweˀ 'I will get there'
y-ʌ-k-w-ˀ
TRANSLOC-FUTURE-1SG.AGT-arrive-PUNCTUAL

c. yó:tereˀ 'it's in the dish or glass'
yo-t-r-ˀ
NEUTER PAT-SEMI-REFL-fill in-STATIVE

[41] a. tekaˀnukserá:ke 'two onions'
te-ka-nuks*e*r-ke
DUALIC-NEUTER AGT-onion-pluralizer

b. skanyatará:ti 'one side of the lake'
s-ka-nyat*a*r-ti
ITERATIVE-NEUTER AGT-lake-be one side

[42] Derivation of orutákeri [36a]:

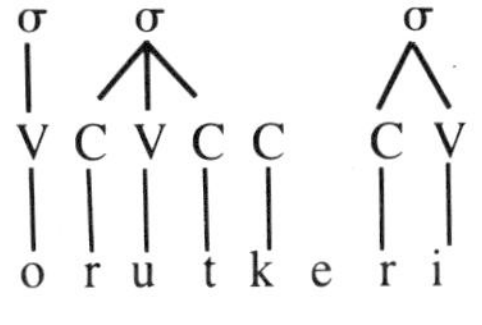

Syllabification

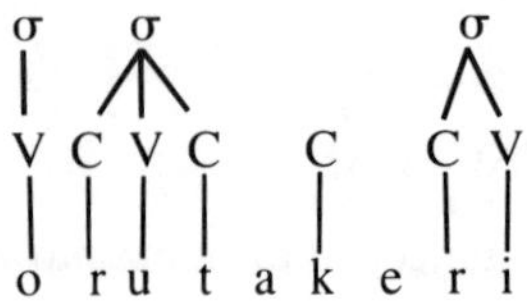

Joiner Insertion [23]

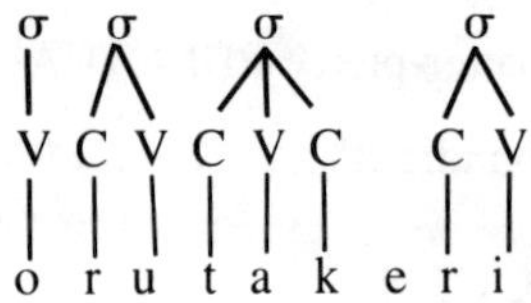

V-Insertion I [27]; Resyllabification

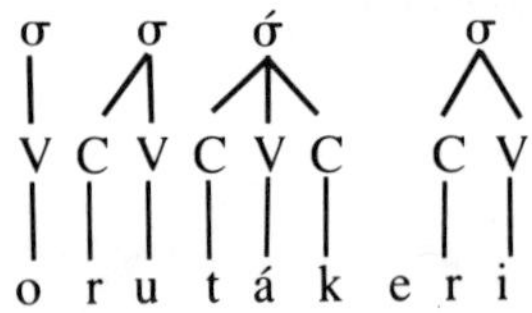

Mohawk Stress Rule [12]

n.a. Vowel Lengthening [13]

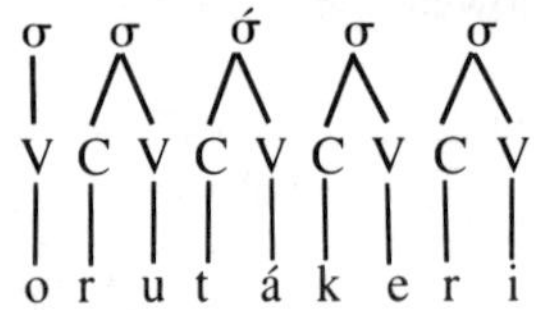

V-Insertion III [29]; resyllabification

NOTES

A substantially different version of this paper was presented at the Symposium on Canadian Native Languages in Theoretical Perspective, SUNY at Buffalo, March 15–16, 1985. I am indebted to Robin Barr, Harry Bochner, and Leo Wetzels for their comments on an earlier draft. I am especially grateful to Phil LeSourd, who read each of several drafts; without his suggestions many aspects of the analysis would not have the present form. I am solely responsible for any mistakes. Sadly both Mike and Catherine Norton passed away in 1988. I wish to express once again my deep appreciation of their knowledge and friendship.

1. Mohawk has three oral obstruent phonemes /k t s/, two laryngeal obstruents /h ʔ/, four resonants /n r w y/, four oral vowels /a e i o/, and two nasal vowels /ʌ u/ (phonetically [ʌ̃ ũ]). Voicing is not distinctive in the oral obstruents; basically they are voiced prevocalically. Stress is indicated by an acute accent, unless the stressed vowel has undergone one of two processes that replace *h* or ʔ with vowel length. In this case, the stressed and lengthened vowel has a (sharply) falling tone, and both stress and falling tone are indicated by a grave accent. (1) VhR → V̀:R (where R = resonant), (2) VʔC → V̀:C. In addition, a stressed and lengthened vowel that occurs before an intervocalic ʔ also has falling tone. Short stressed vowels never have falling tone.

The segmented versions of the examples do not necessarily correspond to underlying forms, nor is every example exhaustively segmented into morphemes. Examples are segmented mostly in an effort to provide the most precise description (phonological and morphological) of epenthesis in Mohawk. The abbreviation AGT stands for *agent,* PAT stands for *patient.*

2. Examples [2] and [4] are subject to a late, automatic rule that inserts *h* before *rh* and *nh*; thus they become *kéhrhaʔ* and *wakiʔtuhkwáhrhos,* respectively. This rule applies also to [7c] *séhrhos* and [34a] *tekahsutéhrhaʔ*.

3. However, not all instances of the vowel *e* in consonant plus *r* clusters (or in *Cʔ* clusters. see *e*-Epenthesis III) are epenthetic; sequences of *Cer* (and *Ceʔ*) where the *e* is underlying also occur. See Michelson 1981, 1983 for examples.

4. This rule was originally stated in Michelson 1981 as being conditioned by any extrasyllabic *r'* (both by a stem-initial *r'* and by a morpheme-internal *r'*), but only by a *stem-initial* extrasyllabic noncontinuant obstruent (*t* or *k*). Since then, I have come across additional data, where a *morpheme-internal* extrasyllabic obstruent (*t*) conditions *e*-epenthesis. These data are from Mithun 1977. For example, (page 34) *skáhkets* s-k-ahkt-s (ITERATIVE—1SG.AGT—go back—HABITUAL) versus *shóhktu* s-ho-ahkt-u (ITERATIVE—MASC.SG.PAT—go back—STATIVE); or (page 5) *tekshà:kets* te-k-shaʔkt-s (DUALIC—1SG.AGT—bend—HABITUAL) versus *tehoshà:ktu* te-ho-shaʔkt-u (DUALIC—MASC.SG.PAT—bend—STATIVE). See also Michelson (1988). The examples in [7] and the examples in this note indicate that *e*-Epenthesis II applies before extrasyllabic consonants *in derived environments,* i.e. the environment results from the concatenation of morphemes.

5. In Michelson (1983, 111), I suggested that one possible way to distinguish formally between the environment for *e*-epenthesis and the environment for *a*-epenthesis inside morphemes is to analyze the morphemes that contain an epenthetic *a* as two separate morphemes. For example, [19a] would be represented as *-skut-r-*. In this way, *a*-epenthesis could be sensitive to the presence of the boundary. The problem with such an analysis, as pointed out already in Michelson (1981, 111), is that the boundary is not synchronically motivated (and the historical facts are not terribly clear at present either).

6. The idea that segmental material may be inserted on the melody tier independently before the corresponding V-slot or C-slot on the timing tier was suggested independently in an early version of Wetzels (forthcoming), which has since been substantially revised. The idea that segments, and in particular vowels, may be represented in underlying representations (i.e. not as the result of epenthesis) on the segmental tier without a corresponding timing slot is not a new one, however. For example, Archangeli (1983) posits a vowel *a* that is not associated with a V-slot in the underlying representation of a particular suffix in Yawelmani; the *a* is realized only when a V-slot is epenthesized. See also Shaw (the preceding paper in this volume) for an underlying floating ʔ as well as underlying floating vowels. Of particular relevance for the analysis presented in this section is Hyman's (1985) theory of syllable weight and specifically his notion of "weightless" segments. Hyman argues (within a theory that assumes W(eight) U(nit)s) that phonetic epenthesis of vowels and consonants

involves the insertion of segmental features without a corresponding WU. I believe my analysis of Mohawk epenthesis supports this claim.

7. I have not indicated the metrical structure assigned by the Mohawk Stress Rule [12] in any of the derivations; thus, I point out here that the V-insertion rules in [27] and [29], which are ordered after stress, do not destroy the previously assigned metrical structure.

8. Note also (1) the *e* is never reduced to a schwa, and it is certainly never deleted; (2) speakers consistently write the *e* and have always done so.

9. Similar examples with a morpheme-internal weightless *a* do not exist.

REFERENCES

Archangeli, Diana. 1983. The Root CV-Template as a Property of the Affix: Evidence from Yawelmani. *Natural Language and Linguistic Theory* 1:347–84.

Archangeli, Diana. 1984. *Underspecification in Yawelmani Phonology and Morphology*. Ph.D. Diss., Massachusetts Institute of Technology.

Bonvillain, Nancy. 1973. *A Grammar of Akwesasne Mohawk*. The Mercury Series, Ethnology Division, paper no. 8. Ottawa: National Museum of Man, National Museums of Canada.

Broselow, Ellen. 1982. On Predicting the Interaction of Stress and Epenthesis. *Glossa* 16:115–32.

Chafe, Wallace L. 1977. Accent and Related Phenomena in the Five Nations Iroquois Languages. In *Studies in Stress and Accent,* Larry M. Hyman, ed., pp. 169–81. Southern California Occasional Papers in Linguistics, no. 4. Los Angeles: University of Southern California, Department of Linguistics.

Clements, G. N., and S. J. Keyser. 1983. *CV Phonology: A Generative Theory of the Syllable*. Linguistic Inquiry Monograph 9. Cambridge: MIT Press.

Hyman, Larry. 1985. *A Theory of Phonological Weight*. Dordrecht, Holland: Foris.

LeSourd, Phil. 1985. Accent and Syllable Structure in Passamaquoddy. Unpublished ms.

Lounsbury, Floyd. 1942. Phonology of the Oneida Language. Master's Thesis, University of Wisconsin.

Lowenstamm, Jean. 1981. On the Maximal Cluster Approach to Syllable Structure. *Linguistic Inquiry* 4:575–604.

Lowenstamm, Jean, and Jonathan Kaye. 1985. Compensatory Lengthening in Tiberian Hebrew. In *Studies on Compensatory Lengthening,* Engin Sezer and Leo Wetzels, eds., pp. 97–132. Dordrecht, Holland: Foris.

Michelson, Karin. 1978. Mohawk Epenthesis and Accent, paper presented at the 77th annual meeting of the American Anthropological Association, Los Angeles.

Michelson, Karin. 1981. Stress, Epenthesis and Syllable Structure in Mohawk. In *Harvard Studies in Phonology, Vol. II,* G. N. Clements, ed., Indiana University Linguistics Club, pp. 311–353.

Michelson, Karin. 1983. *A Comparative Study of Accent in the Five Nations Iroquoian Languages.* Ph.D. Diss., Harvard University.

Michelson, Karin. 1988. *A Comparative Study of Lake-Iroquoian Accent.* Dordrecht, Holland: D. Reidel.

Mithun, Marianne, ed. 1977. Iontenwennaweienstahkhwa' (Mohawk Spelling Dictionary). New York State Museum, Bulletin 429.

Mithun, Marianne. 1979a. Iroquoian. In *The Languages of Native America,* Lyle Campbell and Marianne Mithun, eds., pp. 133–212. Austin: University of Texas.

Mithun, Marianne. 1979b. The Consciousness of Levels of Phonological Structure. *International Journal of American Linguistics* 45:343–48.

Postal, Paul M. 1968. *Aspects of Phonological Theory.* New York: Harper & Row.

Shaw, Patricia A. 1985. The Complex Status of Complex Segments in Dakota. (this volume)

Wetzels, W. Leo. Forthcoming. The Timing of Latent Consonants in Modern French. In *Studies in Romance Languages,* Carol Neidle and Rafael A. Nunez Cedeno, eds., Dordrecht, Holland: Foris.

UNDERSPECIFICATION AND DERIVED-ONLY RULES IN SEKANI PHONOLOGY

Sharon Hargus

INTRODUCTION

The phonology of Sekani, an Athapaskan language spoken in British Columbia, provides support for the hypothesis that phonological representations are underspecified, as has been claimed in recent work on Lexical Phonology (Kiparsky 1982b; Archangeli 1988). Certain linkings between melody and skeleton must be absent in underlying representations in order to allow two rules to apply in nonderived environments. However, current underspecification theory does not systematically prohibit rules restricted to derived environments from applying to nonderived forms. Accordingly, I will propose that the way in which underlying feature values are selected must be modified to take into consideration the structural change of lexical rules restricted to derived environments.

The data that I will be discussing involve several rules in the stem phonology of Sekani.[1] Two of these rules, Nasalization and Diphthongization, must apply in the lexicon to nonderived forms, whereas two other rules, *a* Raising and *e* Raising, arguably are restricted to derived contexts. Since Diphthongization and Nasalization are clearly cyclic, lexical rules, their application to nonderived forms poses a potential problem for the Strict Cycle Condition, a problem that I argue can be avoided if they are reformulated as structure-building rules through the use of structural underspecification. However, the rule of *e* Raising would be predicted to apply in nonderived environments if underlying feature values are selected as is currently proposed by Archangeli (1988).

1. SOME RULES OF THE STEM PHONOLOGY OF SEKANI

1.1. Introduction to Sekani Phonology and Morphology

All of the data discussed in this paper are representative of the McLeod Lake, B. C., dialect, except where noted.

The surface segments of Sekani are as follows:

b	d	dz	dl	dž		g	gw	
(p)	t	ts	tl	tš		k	kw	
	t′	ts′	tl′	tš′		k′	k′w	ʔ
w̥		s	ł	(š)	ç	x		
w		z	l		y	γ		
m	n							h

Oral Vowels:			Nasal Vowels:			Tones:
i		u	į		ų	´ `
(I)						
e	ə	o	ę		ǫ	
	a			(ą)		

The segments shown in parentheses are rare. In the remainder of this paper, I will use a more practical orthography to represent some of these sounds:

ch	[tš]	j	[dž]
ch′	[tš′]	yh	[ç]
gh	[γ]	wh	[w̥]
ʔ	[ʔ]	sh	[š]
V	high tone vowel	V̀	low tone vowel

The vowel [I] is a lexical allophone of /ə/, occurring in place of [ə] after palatal consonants. I assume that [i] differs from [I] in terms of feature composition as follows:

$$\underset{\begin{bmatrix}+\text{high}\\-\text{back}\\+\text{tense}\end{bmatrix}}{[\text{i}]} \qquad\qquad \underset{\begin{bmatrix}+\text{high}\\-\text{back}\\-\text{tense}\end{bmatrix}}{[\text{I}]}$$

Thus the rule deriving [I] from /ə/ can be formulated as in [1]:

[1] 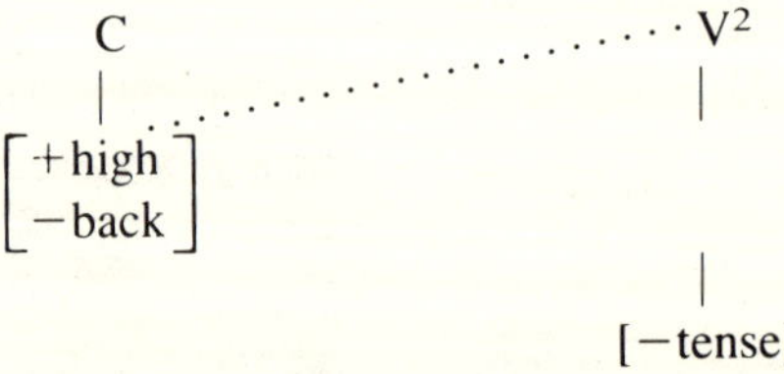

Since this rule has one lexically marked exception, [chəba] 'poplar', I assume that it applies in the lexicon.

Sekani verbal morphology is quite complicated. The verbal prefixes can be divided into thirteen position classes, listed in left-to-right order:

postposition (prefix position 1)
adverbial prefix (2)
incorporated stem (3)
distributive (4)
reversative, customary prefixes (5)
inceptive (6)
direct object (7)
nonsingular subject (8)
derivational, aspectual, and thematic prefixes (9)
conjugation prefix (10)
mode prefix (11)
subject (12)
classifier (13)

The stem is the rightmost element of the verb. The verb prefix positions have no theoretical status other than an indication of rule ordering among the word formation rules of Sekani.

The morphology of nouns and postpositions is less complex. The pronominal object of a postposition is marked with a prefix. Possessed nouns are marked with one of three possessive suffixes; if the possessor is pronominal, a possessive prefix occurs as well. Diminutive and augmentative suffixes also occur. Derived nouns may be formed by the attachment of one of three nominalizing suffixes to words of any major category: noun, verb, or postposition.

In glossing examples, I will be using certain abbreviations for various classes of morphemes:

adv	adverbial prefix
C	customary/habitual aspect
clf	classifier prefix
cnj	conjugation prefix
cont	continuative aspect
der	derivational prefix
hum	human

Imp	imperfective mode
mom	momentaneous aspect
nom	nominalizing suffix
O	object
Op	optative mode
per	perambulative prefix
Pf	perfective mode
pl	plural
psd	possessed noun suffix
Psr	possessor
rev	reversative prefix
S	subject
sg	singular
thm	thematic prefix
unsp	unspecified
voc	vocative

Some of these abbreviations refer to verb prefix morphology. Subscript numbers beneath prefix glosses in examples indicate to which verb prefix position the prefix belongs.

In the following discussion of Sekani phonology, I will assume the model of Lexical Phonology independently proposed by Pesetsky (1979), Strauss (see 1983), and Booij (1981), and further elaborated by Mohanan (1986), Kiparsky (1982b), and others. In this model, a subset of the phonological rules apply in the lexicon, interspersed cyclically with rules of word formation. This model was first applied to an Athapaskan language by Rice (1982), who proposed a level-ordered model of the Slave lexicon in which four levels can be distinguished. With certain modifications (see Hargus 1987, 1988), this model is also appropriate for Sekani.

Level 1:
stems
aspectual suffixes
possessive prefixes and suffixes
classifier prefixes (verb prefix position 13)

Level 2:
verb prefixes of positions 9–12

Level 3:
verb prefixes of positions 7–8

Level 4:
verb prefixes of positions 1–6
diminutive suffixes
nominalizing suffixes

A different approach to the lexical phonology of an Athapaskan language can be found in Speas (1984).

1.2. Nasalization

The Sekani rule of Nasalization is given in [2].

[2]

rime
Vn → V̨ / ___ ⁀(C)

Nasalization accounts for alternations like the following:

[3] **a.** [sətsònèʔ] 'my shit'
b. [tsǫ̀ʔ] 'shit'

The addition of the possessive suffix -[èʔ] prevents Nasalization from applying to the form in [3a]; compare the unsuffixed stem in [3b] with its surface nasal vowel. Additional examples of Nasalization are given in [4a] and [4b].

[4] **a.** /ts'e- nə -s - h -sit/
wake cnj 1sS clf
2 10 12 13 stem

[ts'e*n*əssit] 'I wake up O'

b. /ts'e- nə -h - sit/
wake cnj clf
2 10 13 stem

[ts'ęhsit] 'he, she wakes up O'

In the third person singular form [4b], the vowel of the conjugation prefix /nə/ has been deleted by a regular rule, and the remaining nasal consonant then undergoes Nasalization. The nasal consonant is preserved in the first person singular form [4a].

[5] **a.** / nə - tsəgh/
2sS cry
12 stem

[nətsəgh] 'you sg. cry'

b. /də -n- bə̀t/
der 2sS stomach
9 12 stem

[dįbə̀t] 'you sg. are hungry'

In [5b], the second person singular subject prefix loses its vowel when preceded by a vowel-final prefix of positions 7–11, feeding nasalization and another rule of *ə* Raising, given in [6]:

[6] ə → i / ___ [+nasal]

However, in [5a], the second person singular prefix is word-initial and thus does not undergo either the vowel deletion rule or Nasalization.

Nasalization applies in nonderived as well as derived environments, accounting for not only alternations like those above but also the largely complementary distribution of nasal vowels and syllable-final [Vn] sequences. However, there are a few contrasts between nasal vowels and syllable-final [Vn] sequences in Sekani, which I will now discuss. These [Vn] sequences pose varying degrees of difficulty for this abstract analysis of the nasal vowels.

1.2.1. Exceptions to Nasalization

The only regular class of exceptions to Nasalization are stems that end in /ən/.

Nasalization regularly applies to stem-final nasal consonants preceded by /i e u o/, as the following examples indicate:

[7]	[nǫ̀zę]	'skunk'
[8]	[ˀàtsų]	'grandmother' voc
[9]	[tlį]	'dog'
[10]	[ˀaht'ǫ]	'ammunition'

However, stems which end in [ən] or [In] regularly fail to undergo Nasalization:

[11]	[tə*n*]	'ice'
[12]	[sə̀*n*]	'star'
[13]	[dətl'ə*n*]	'sticky'
[14]	[yhI*n*]	'song'
[15]	[dəchI*n*]	'stick, wooden'

These data suggest that stem-final /ə/ blocks Nasalization. (Recall that the vowel [I] in [14]–[15] is an allophone of /ə/; cf. (1). In fact, this follows from a more general restriction on the distribution of [ə] in stems: [ə] does not occur in open-syllables stem-finally.[3] Given the filter in [16], Nasalization cannot apply to stem-final /ən/ because stem-final [ə̨] would result.

[16] * ə]   domain: level 1

Thus, it is not necessary to complicate the formulation of Nasalization in order to account for the preceding facts.

A few other instances of stem-final [Vn] sequences cannot be accounted for so neatly; they must be marked simply as exceptions to Nasalization. Some loan words, such as [17]–[18] contain surface nasal consonants where nasal vowels would be expected:

[17] [ga*n*dəl] 'candle'
[18] [ʔətsibalyà*n*] 'bald eagle'

Example [18] is a loan word from Carrier (Carrier Linguistic Committee 1974).[4] In addition to these loan words, a few stems that contain /on/ must be marked as exceptions to Nasalization.

[19] [ustò*n*] 'I hold O'
[20] [k'enəstò*n*] 'I'm broken, broke'
[21] [jo*n*] 'up here'

Note that the majority of /on/ stems regularly undergo Nasalization.

[22] [dətǫ] 'thick'
[23] [əsjǫ] 'he, she is old'
[24] [əsdǫ] 'I drink O'

The existence of exceptions to Nasalization in stems contrasts sharply with the situation found in the affixal morphology. No exceptions to Nasalization are found in the verbal prefixes or other affixes. (However, no surface instances of [ə̨] in the affixes are found either: the output of Nasalization in the verb prefixes undergoes *ə* Raising, as can be seen in [5b].) Thus exceptions to Nasalization are found only on Level 1.

So far, I have presented examples of surface stem-final [Vn]. Sequences of [Vn] that cannot be accounted for by the prohibition against stem-final [ə] must be listed as exceptions to Nasalization. In addition, one stem in Sekani poses a more serious threat to the analysis of Nasalization, in that it appears to contain a lexicalized output of Nasalization. In this stem, a nasal vowel occurs before the possessive suffix:

[25] -[chųèʔ] 'son'

Compare [3a]. To avoid the problem for Nasalization this stem creates, I suggested in Hargus (forthcoming) that this stem contains an empty stem-final consonant underlyingly: /chunC-èʔ/, since an empty stem-initial consonant that blocks an otherwise regular vowel deletion rule is well-motivated for another stem in Sekani.[5]

1.2.2. Domain of Nasalization

The fact that Nasalization has lexically marked exceptions suggests that it applies in the lexicon, rather than postlexically. Moreover, Nasalization feeds *ə* Raising, which is a lexical rule. There is additional evidence that Nasalization is a lexical rule. In Hargus (1985b) I argued that Nasalization is a cyclic, lexical rule on the basis of contrasts like the following:

[26] [sətsò*n*èʔ] 'my shit'

[27]	[seˀət'ǫ̀èˀ]	'leaves in my possession' (my (its) leaves)
[28]	[tsǫ̀azi]	'small piece of shit'

Nasalization has applied on the first cycle *after* possessive suffixation in [26], but on the first cycle *before* second cycle possessive suffixation in [27]. In [28], Nasalization must apply before the suffixation of the vowel-initial diminutive suffix -/azi/. The fact that Nasalization applies after the suffixation of some vowel-initial morphemes but before the suffixation of other vowel-initial morphemes indicates that the possessive suffix is a Level 1 affix and, thus, that Nasalization is a Level 1 rule.[6]

1.3. Diphthongization

The inventory of surface segments in Sekani includes five labio-velar consonants, each of which is exemplified as follows:

[29]	[sə*gw*ə̀t]	'my knee'
[30]	[də*kw*əs]	'he, she coughs'
[31]	[*k'w*əs]	'cloud'
[32]	[nà*w*ə̀t]	'he, she walks fast'
[33]	[*wh*əs]	'rose, thorn'

The segments [w] and [wh] are clearly labio-velars (/ghw xw/) at a more abstract level of representation, as discussed in Hargus (forthcoming). The late rule of Velar Loss accounts for the phonetic shape of these fricatives:

[34]
$$\begin{bmatrix} +\text{cont} \\ +\text{round} \end{bmatrix} \rightarrow \begin{bmatrix} -\text{high} \\ -\text{back} \\ +\text{anterior} \\ -\text{round} \end{bmatrix}$$

Labio-velars have a highly restricted distribution. They do not occur syllable-finally, unlike velars and other consonants. The majority of labio-velars in Sekani occur before the vowel [ə]. Labio-velars do not occur before the vowels [o] and [u], and surface forms in which labio-velars occur before [i e a] are extremely rare. Moreover, a corresponding gap in the distribution of velars also exists. Velar consonants that occur before [o] are very rare in Sekani. These distributional restrictions are summarized:

	o	ə	V ≠ ə, o
K	(Ko)	Kə	KV
Kw	*Kwo	Kwə	(KwV)

K = any velar

These restrictions on the distribution of labio-velars indicate that sequences of labio-velar + [ə] should not be taken at face value. Instead, such sequences should be derived from underlying velar + /o/ sequences by the following rule of Diphthongization, stated informally in [35]:

[35] o → wə / $\begin{bmatrix} \text{C} \\ \text{+high} \\ \text{+back} \end{bmatrix}$ ___

By positing a rule of Diphthongization, most of the labio-velars in underlying representations can be eliminated while the lack of velar + [o] sequences simultaneously is accounted for.

1.3.1. Domain of Diphthongization

Like Nasalization, Diphthongization is clearly a lexical rule, since its application feeds the Level 2–3 rule of *w* Vocalization. This latter rule is stated informally in [36]. For more information, see Hargus 1988.

[36] ghwə → u / $\begin{matrix} \text{V} \\ [-\text{round}] \end{matrix}$ ___

Vocalization applies to the optative prefix /gho/, after this prefix has undergone Diphthongization.

[37] /ghə-gho-tsəgh/
3pS Op cry
8 11

[wutsəgh] 'they cry' Op

	/ghə-gho-tsəgh/
Diphthongization	ghwə
w Vocalization	u
Velar rounding	ghw
ə Deletion	ϕ
Velar loss	w
	[wutsəgh]

(The rule of Velar Rounding will be discussed later.) As demonstrated in Hargus (1988), Diphthongization and Vocalization are cyclic, as well as lexical, rules.

1.3.2 Exceptions to Diphthongization

Limited alternations between [o] and [wə] after velars provide additional evidence for the velar + /o/ source of most surface labio-velars. These alternations indicate that Diphthongization has two systematic classes of exceptions. [1] /o/ is preserved before /ł/:

[38] a. /na -ghə-n -gǫt -*l*/
rev Prg 2sS crawl Prg
5 10 12

[naghįg*ol*] 'you sg. are crawling back'

cf. **b.** /k'è-na- n- gǫt - ts/
per C 2sS crawl C
2 5 12

[k'èngǫg*wə*ts] 'you sg. crawl around'

In [38a] and [38b], the root-final consonant /t/ in /gǫt/ 'crawl' is deleted before the alveolar aspectual suffixes /*l*] 'future' and /ts/ 'customary, perambulative'. [2] [ǫ] does not undergo Diphthongization:

[39] a. /gho-n- tsəgh/
Op 2sS cry
11 12

[wǫtsəgh] 'you sg. cry' Op

b. [*wə*tsəgh] 'he, she cries' Op

In [39a] the optative prefix /gho/ is prefixed to a form that contains the second-person singular subject prefix [n]. Following Nasalization, Diphthongization does not apply in this form. In [39b], Diphthongization is free to apply, because [o] is not nasal. The surface form of the optative prefix in [39a] is accounted for by the following rule of Velar Rounding:

[40] $$\begin{bmatrix} +\text{cont} \\ +\text{high} \\ +\text{back} \end{bmatrix} \rightarrow [+\text{round}] \ \% \ \_\_ \ [+\text{round}]$$

These blocking conditions on Diphthongization do not follow from more general principles of Sekani phonology. They must simply be incorporated into the rule of Diphthongization:

[41] $$o \rightarrow wə \ / \ \begin{bmatrix} \text{C} \\ +\text{high} \\ +\text{back} \end{bmatrix} \_\_ \ (\text{C}_1) \quad \text{where } \text{C}_1 \neq l \text{ and } o \neq [+\text{nasal}]$$

Like Nasalization, there are also exceptions to Diphthongization that are more idiosyncratic. One stem, −[gònè?] 'arm', contains a velar + [o] sequence that simply must be marked as an exception to Diphthongization. One prefix, [whə]− first-person plural object and possessive prefix, fails to obey the [ǫ] blocking condition on Diphthongization:

[42] /xo -nka- yə -nə -n -zən/
1pO P thm thm Pf want
1 7 9 11

[whį̨kayənį̨zən] 'he, she wants us'

The form *[whǫkayənį̨zən] is expected.[7]

1.3.3. Rule Ordering

We have seen that Diphthongization applies to the output of Nasalization, because of the [ǫ] blocking condition on Diphthongization. However, setting aside momentarily the correct formulation of the [o] + nasal blocking condition, another group of examples suggests that the rules apply in the order Nasalization–Diphthongization. There is a substantial number of stems of the shape labio-velar + [ən], an exhaustive list of which follows:

[43]	-[gwə̀n]	
	in [nį̨gwə̀n ts'ę̨lį̨ gàh]	'Iroquois Creek'
[44]	-[gwən]	'finger nail'
[45]	-[gwən]	'dry'
[46]	[kwə̀n]	'fire'
[47]	-[kw'ə̀n]	'burn'
[48]	-[wən]	'growl'

According to the preceding analysis of diphthongization, these forms are underlyingly velar + /on/. The final nasal consonant in these forms suggests that these stems are part of the systematic [ən] class of exceptions to Nasalization. Thus, if Diphthongization precedes Nasalization, their surface nasal consonants are easily accounted for:

[49]	/gon/ 'dry'
Diphthongization	gwən
Nasalization	—

Unfortunately, a substantially larger class of forms (eighteen in all, in my corpus) have stem-final surface velar + [ǫ(C)], which this order of the rules would predict surface as labio-velar + [ən]/[į̨C]. A few examples follow:

[50]	[kǫ]	'now, soon'
[51]	-[gǫ]	'crooked, dishonest' Imp
[52]	-[k'ǫ̀]-	'midget'
[53]	-[wǫ]	'kill pl. O'
[54]	-[k'ǫ̀h]	'burn, kindle' Imp
[55]	-[wǫh]	'for, on account of'

[56] [kǫh] 'housc'
[57] [ˀəts'əgǫ̀ˀ] 'dried meat'

If the rules apply in the order Diphthongization-Nasalization, these forms as well as forms like [39a] involving [ǫ] in prefixes must be listed simply as exceptions to Diphthongization. They cannot be accounted for under a revised blocking condition on Diphthongization, in which Diphthongization fails to apply before [n]; compare the [Kwən] forms. The contrast between -[gwən] 'dry' and -[gǫ] 'crooked' indicates that if Diphthongization is a synchronic rule, then either the forms like -[gwən] must be listed as exceptions to Nasalization or the forms like -[gǫ] must be listed as exceptions to Diphthongization.

The sheer numbers involved suggest that the rule order Nasalization-Diphthongization is to be preferred, since it requires less idiosyncratic marking of forms as exceptions to rules. If the rules apply in this order, the forms in [50]–[57] fall into a systematic class of exceptions to Diphthongization—those with [ǫ]; only -[gònèˀ] 'arm' must be listed as an idiosyncratic exception to Diphthongization. Of course, the forms in [43]–[48] must then be listed as exceptions to Nasalization, but these form a relatively smaller group of exceptions than those in [50]–[57].

1.4. e Raising

The structural description of *e* Raising is met in verbal roots ending in /e/ that are suffixed with the perfective aspect marker -/n/:

[58] V
[−back] → [+high] / ___ ⊤
[+nasal]

Some examples of this rule follow:

[59] **a.** /nà -sə -i -che -n/
cont cnj 1sPf dream cont:Pf
2 10 12

[nàsichį] 'I dreamed'

cf. **b.** [nàsche] 'I dream'

[60] **a.** /yighà -sə - n -ke -n/
across cnj 2sS travel by boat mom:Pf
2 10 12

[yighàsįkį] 'you sg. went across by boat'

cf. **b.** [yighàsįkèh] 'you sg. go across by boat'

1.4.1. e Raising Restricted to Derived Environments

Consider the following examples of stem-internal [ę]:

[61] [yhę̀*l*] 'trap'
[62] [dlęchow] 'rat'
[63] −[tsę̀*l*] 'handle compact O (uncontrol), Imp, Op
[64] −[xęh] 'thaw, melt O' Imp, Fut, Op
[65] −[xę̀l] 'roll O around'

If *e* Raising is restricted to derived environments, these forms will surface with [ę] as required. However, an alternative analysis of the domain of this rule is also possible: the perfective suffix is a reflex of Proto-Athapaskan *ŋ̈, a palatized velar nasal, whereas root-final [n] is a reflex of PA *n (Krauss & Leer 1981). If an additional synchronic nasal phoneme /ñ/ is posited, it is not necessary to assume that *e* Raising is restricted to derived environments: the structural description of the rule will not be met in nonderived forms, which lack the perfective suffix. However, since this contrast otherwise plays no role in the synchronic phonology of Sekani, I assume there is no such contrast between nasals in Sekani. Accordingly, *e* Raising is analyzed as a derived-only rule.

1.4.2. Domain of e Raising

e Raising is a rule of the stem phonology only. It does not apply to [ę] derived on Level 4:

[66] /k'e -n -tòn/
broke cnj
2 10 stem

[k'ętòn] 'he, she is broken'

[67] /ts'e -n -h -sit/
wake cnj clf
2 10 13 stem

[ts'ęhsit] 'he, she wakes up'

In the preceding examples, the Level 4 [e]-final prefixes *ts'e* and *k'e* are followed by the consonantal alternant of the Level 2 conjugation prefix. Although derived [ę] appears, it does not undergo *e* Raising. *e* Raising also does not apply to [ę] derived on Level 2 or 3:

[68]

/yidà	-də	̀n	-leh/
inside	wood	cnj	handle pl
2	9	10	stem

[yidàdę̀leh] 'he, she carries pl. wooden O inside'

[69]

/yə	-ghǫh-yə -	̀n	-h -	tsus/
3sO P	3sO	cnj	clf	handle cloth-like
1	7	10	13	stem

[yǫhyę̀htsus] 'he, she carries cloth-like O to O'

In [68] and [69], the [ę] is derived by the rule of *n*-Conjugation ə Fronting, which changes low tone [ə̨̀] to [ę]. This rule applies regularly to derived Level 2 [ə̨̀] and sporadically to derived Level 3 [ə̨̀]. Notice that *e* Raising does not apply to the output of this rule. The simplest explanation for this would be that *e* Raising shuts off after Level 1, but *e* Raising and *n*-Conjugation ə Fronting also could apply in counter–feeding order on Levels 2 and 3. *e* Raising then would shut off after Level 3.

The preceding data also indicate that ə Raising and *e* Raising should not be collapsed to a single rule of Raising:

[70]

$$\overset{\text{V}}{\begin{bmatrix}-\text{round}\\-\text{low}\end{bmatrix}} \rightarrow \begin{bmatrix}+\text{high}\\-\text{back}\end{bmatrix} \;/\; \underset{[+\text{nasal}]}{\underline{\quad}}$$

Since ə Raising applies on Levels 2 and 3, it must follow *n*-Conjugation ə Fronting (as predicted by the Elsewhere Condition). If e Raising did not turn off until after Level 3, *e* Raising and *n*-Conjugation ə Fronting would have to apply in counter–feeding order, as mentioned earlier. Then, the rules would have to apply in the following order on Levels 2 and 3:

[71] *e* Raising
n-Conjugation *ə* Fronting
ə Raising

The fact that *e* Raising and ə Raising are ordered differently with respect to another rule indicates that they cannot be collapsed.

1.5. *a* Raising

A third rule in Sekani raises the height of nasal vowels. Alternations between [a] and [ǫ] indicate that Sekani contains a rule of *a* Raising:

[72]

$$\text{a} \rightarrow \text{o} \;/\; \underset{[+\text{nasal}]}{\underline{\quad}}$$

These alternations are found in stems as well as in the Level 4 prefixes:

Stems:

[73] a. /che -nə -n -ʔa -n/
into water cnj Pf handle compact O mom:Pf
2 10 11 stem

[chenįʔ*ǫ*] 'he, she put compact O in the water'

b. [chęʔ*à*h] 'he, she puts compact O in the water'

[74] a. /dah- sə- n - ka - n/
up cnj 2sS handle contained O mom:Pf
2 10 11 stem

[dasįk*ǫ*] 'you sg. hung up contained O'

b. [dasįk*à*h] 'you sg. hang up contained O'

[75] a. /də -gha -n/
der hair Pf
9 stem

[dəw*ǫ*] 'he, she is hairy'

cf. **b.** /ʔə -gha -`ʔ/
unspPsr hair psd

[ʔəgh*à*ʔ] 'its hair'

Prefixes:

[76] a. /na -n - h -xęh/
rev 2sS clf melt, thaw
5 12 13

[n*ǫ*hxęh] 'you sg. thaw out O'

b. [n*a*sxęh] 'I thaw out O'

[77] a. /ʔa -n -h - sən/
adv Pf clf make
2 11 113

[ʔ*ǫ*hsən] 'he, she has O made'

b. /ʔ*a*ssən/ 'I have O made'

As is implicit from the formulation of this rule in [72], *a* Raising applies only to [ą] (or to [a] followed by syllable-final [n]). Compare [77c] and [77a]:

[77] c. /lə̀gàpi ʔa -nə -h -sən/
coffee adv 2sS clf make
2 12 13 stem

[lə̀gàpi ʔ*a*nahsən] ‘you sg. have coffee made’’[8]

In fact, there is little reason to prefer the formulation of *a* Raising in [72] over the formulation of this rule in [78]:

[78]

$$a \rightarrow o \;/\; \overset{\text{rime}}{\overbrace{\_\_\;n}}$$

However, one possible reason to prefer the formulation in [72] is that ə Raising and *a* Raising can then be collapsed into a general rule of Raising:

[79]

$$\overset{\text{V}}{\begin{bmatrix}+\text{back}\\ -\text{round}\\ \text{a low}\end{bmatrix}} \rightarrow \begin{bmatrix}-\text{a high}\\ \text{a back}\\ \text{a round}\\ -\text{low}\end{bmatrix} \;/\; \underset{[+\text{nasal}]}{\_\_}$$

Derived values of height, backness, and rounding are predictable from underlying lowness.

1.5.1. Rule Ordering

If *a* Raising is collapsed with *ə* Raising, it obviously must follow Nasalization. Otherwise, there is no evidence that *a* Raising cannot be formulated as in [78] and precede Nasalization.

Similarly, there is no evidence that *a* Raising and Diphthongization must apply in any particular order. Forms like [74a] suggest that Diphthongization does not apply to the output of *a* Raising; i.e. that these rules apply in counter–feeding order. However, as discussed in section 1.2, Diphthongization does not apply to [ǫ]. Thus, even if *a* Raising preceded Diphthongization, the output of *a* Raising would be unable to undergo Diphthongization.

Thus, the rules discussed so far apply in the following order:

[80] Nasalization
Diphthongization, *e* Raising, *a*/*ə* Raising

1.5.2. Domain of a Raising

Given the order in [80], there is no reason to assume that *a* Raising is a rule of the lexical phonology. In fact, it could be a postlexical rule that applies to all instances of lexically created [ą]. However, other data indicate that *a* Raising is not surface-true. [ą] is created by two lexical rules, and *a* Raising does not apply to these instances of [ą].

The first group of examples I will consider are forms that contain the human singular nominalizing suffix -[į] followed by one of the diminutive suffixes, -[azi] or -[azìįʔ]. Consider the following alternations:

[81] a. -/k'àh -į/
marry non:hum sg

-[k'àhį] 'spouse'

b. -/k'àh -į -azi/
marry nom:hum sg dim

-[k'àhązi] 'dear spouse'

[82] a. / tse -k'eh-į/
mountain on nom:hum sg

[tsek'ehį] 'Sekani person'

b. / tse -k'eh-į -azi/
mountain on nom:hum sg dim

[tsek'ehązi] 'dear Sekani person'

The vowel [ą] in [81b]–[82b] is created by the rule of Suffix Vowel Deletion (see Hargus 1988):

[83] V → Ø /] X __] V

This rule deletes the last vowel of a suffix before another vowel-initial suffix. If *a* Raising were a postlexical rule, it should apply to these instances of [ą]. However, the fact that it does not indicates that it is a lexical rule, since it must apply before Suffix Vowel Deletion.

A second group of forms that contain lexically created [ą] are those with the 'perambulative' construction prefixes *k'è* in adverbial prefix position 2 + *na* customary in position 5. (For more information about perambulatives see Hargus 1988). The *na* portion of this construction is actually present only in second person singular forms such as [84a]:

[84] a. /k'è- na- n - d be -h/
per C 2sS clf swim C
2 5 12 13 stem

[k'ènǫbeh] 'you sg. swim around'

In 1s, 3s, and 2p forms such as [84b]–[84d], the rule of Perambulative Reduction, stated informally in [85], applies.

[85] k′è-na → k′an / ___ [C] [(clf) stem

[84] **b.** /k′è- na- s -d be - h/
per C 1sS clf swim C
2 5 12 13 stem

[k′*ą*sbeh] 'I swim around'

c. /k′è- na- d - be - h/
per C clf swim C
2 5 13 stem

[k′ąbeh] 'he, she swims around'

d. /k′è- na- ah -d -be -h/
per C 2pS clf swim C
2 5 12 13 stem

[k′ąhbeh] 'you pl. swim around'

If *a* Raising were a postlexical rule, it should apply to the output of Perambulative Reduction. (I assume that Perambulative Reduction is a lexical rule, since it only applies to instances of the perambulative prefix *k′è* and not to other prefixes in the adverbial position such as *k′e* 'break'.) However, if *a* Raising is a lexical rule, ordered before Perambulative Reduction, then these data are easily accounted for.

1.5.3. Is *a* Raising Restricted to Derived Environments?

There is a gap in the distribution of [ą] in the lexical phonology of Sekani that suggests that the answer to this question may be no. Although there are many instances of nonnasal [a] in Sekani, only loan words contain instances of [ą] or [an]:

[86]	[wą̀dəldi]	'Friday'	(French *Vendredi*)
[87]	[ˀətsibaly*àn*]	'bald eagle'	(‹Carrier)
[88]	[g*an*dəl]	'candle'	(‹English?)

One way of accounting for the lack of [ą] and [an] would be to assume that *a* Raising applies in nonderived as well as derived contexts; that is, that non-alternating [ǫ] is to be regarded as /an/. Although this analysis immediately appears to be overly abstract, and will ultimately be rejected, in fact it would have certain advantages.

The main advantage is that the idiosyncratic exceptions to Nasalization and Diphthongization discussed in sections 1.2 and 1.3 need not be regarded as exceptional if *a* Raising applies to nonderived representations. Recall that the stem -[gònèˀ] 'arm' must be listed as an exception to Diphthongization, since it contains surface velar + [o]. The stems -[tòn] 'hold; break', [jon] 'up here', and all of the [Kwən] stems in [43]–[48] must be listed as exceptions to Nasalization. However, suppose that -[gònèʔ] 'arm' has the underlying representation -/gàn-èʔ/, where -/èʔ/ is one of the suffixes that marks possessed nouns. If *a* Raising is formulated to apply before syllable-final nasals as in [78] and Diphthongization and *a* Raising apply in counter–feeding order, then the fact that this stem does not undergo Diphthongization is easily accounted for:

[89]

	/gàn/
Diphthongization	—
a Raising	o
Possessive suffixation	gòn-èʔ

Next consider the exceptions to Nasalization. The surface distribution of [Vn] and [V̨] in stems is summarized:

	Vn	V̨
a	*an	*ą
o	(on)	ǫ
ə	ən	*ə̨
i	*in	į
e	*en	ę
u	*in	ų

Nonnasal [o] is fairly rare and, like [ə], does not occur in open syllables stem-finally. Moreover, outside of loan words and the systematic [ən] exceptions, the only stem-final [Vn] sequences are those that contain [o]. If nonalternating [ǫ] is /an/, then like derived /a-n/, such sequences will surface with nasal vowels (cf. [73a]–[75a]). Thus, stem-final [on] (and [wən] in the [Kwən] words) could be interpreted as /on/. With this move, the distribution of /o/ would be parallel to that of /ə/, and the prohibition against stem-final [ə] in [16] simply could be made more general, so that there are two vowels that do not occur stem-finally: /ə/ and /o/. Thus the [on] exceptions to Nasalization could be accounted for systematically, like the [ən] exceptions.

Positing the underlying representation /an/ for nonalternating instances of [ǫ] (and some instances of [on]) provides a principled account of the [on] and [wən] exceptions to Nasalization, as well as the single exception to Diphthongization. However, although this analysis does not require any additional rules, its attractiveness is short lived: a nonderived analysis of *a* Raising would create its own complexity in the form of an extra feature [tense] that is needed to avoid an ordering paradox.

Consider the order in which *a* Raising, Nasalization, and Diphthongization would have to apply in this analysis. The [ǫ] blocking condition on Diphthongization, now required only to account for velar + [ǫ] in prefixes, still establishes that Nasalization must precede Diphthongization and

Nasalization. (Recall that Diphthongization is blocked by [ǫ], but not by a syllable-final nasal.) Diphthongization must apply to the output of Nasalization in order to state the blocking condition correctly.

However, the form -/gànèʔ/ -[gònèʔ] 'arm' now establishes that Diphthongization and *a* Raising must apply in counter–feeding order:

	/gàn-èʔ/
Diphthongization	—
a Raising	o
	-[gònèʔ]
	/gàn-èʔ/
a Raising	o
Diphthongization	wə
	*-[gwə̀nèʔ]

This same form -/gàn-èʔ/ also indicates that *a* Raising must precede Nasalization. This stem is a suffixed root, containing the possessive suffix -[èʔ]. Since *a* Raising only applies before syllable-final nasals, *a* Raising must precede possessive suffixation. As seen earlier, possessive suffixation must precede Nasalization, which it bleeds. Thus, *a* Raising precedes Nasalization.

Notice that an ordering paradox has arisen, largely as a result of analyzing -[gònèʔ] 'arm' as -/gàn-èʔ/:

Nasalization precedes Diphthongization
Diphthongization precedes *a* Raising
a Raising precedes Nasalization

The only way to allow the rules to apply in the nonparadoxical order in [90] would be to assume that derived [o] (the output of *a* Raising) is somehow distinct from underlying /o/ (which undergoes Diphthongization).

[90] *a* Raising
Nasalization
Diphthongization

The motivation for assuming that Diphthongization precedes *a* Raising was the fact that Diphthongization does not apply to the output of *a* Raising in -[gònèʔ]. However, if underlying /o/ is distinct from the [o] that results from *a* Raising, as was once historically the case, then Diphthongization can be formulated so as not to apply to the output of *a* raising. Suppose /ə o/ are [−tense] and /a e u i/ are [+tense]. The output of *a* Raising would then be a [+tense, −low] vowel. Diphthongization merely would have to be revised so that it applies only to [−tense] vowels (only to /o/) in this analysis.[9]

The advantages and disadvantages of the nonderived and derived-only analyses of *a* Raising are summarized:

[91]

non-derived:	derived-only:
abstract representations /an/ required	no such representations required
feature [tense] required	[tense] not required
only loan words are idiosyncratic exceptions to Nasalization	[on], [Kwən] stems are exceptions to Nasalization
no idiosyncratic exceptions to Diphthongization	-[gònèʔ] 'arm' is an idiosyncratic exception to Diphthongization

The abstract analysis accounts for the facts more neatly but at the cost of abstract representations and an extra underlying feature. The nonderived analysis of *a* Raising accounts for the same facts by marking the forms as exceptions to phonological rules. Nonetheless, I believe that most phonologists would agree with Kiparsky (1973b) that abstractness in underlying representations should be constrained and that the abstractness required by the nonderived analysis of *a* Raising is excessive. Furthermore, as Kiparsky (1973b) has shown, even native forms may have to be marked as exceptions to phonological rules.

In fact, internal as well as external evidence suggests that the nonderived analysis is too abstract. First, the derived-only analysis eliminates an unnecessary, perhaps even paradoxical, ordering of the rules. Recall that in the nonderived analysis, *a* Raising had to precede possessive suffixation, and possessive suffixation, Nasalization. The abstract analysis requires explicit ordering of phonological and morphological rules, whereas in the derived-only analysis, it is possible to predict that morphological rules apply before phonological rules on the first cycle of a given level.[10]

Second, historical change has favored the derived-only analysis of *a* raising. In the Fort Ware dialect of Sekani (Hargus 1985), certain sound changes taking place indicate that [ǫ] from Proto-Athapaskan /*an/ has been completely reanalyzed as /on/. Sporadic nasalization of /*a/ is found in this dialect, particularly after alveolar consonants.[11] Thus, in one Sekani dialect, the application of *a* raising in nonderived environments has been reanalyzed completely out of the language.

All things considered, *a* Raising should be restricted to derived environments.

2. UNDERSPECIFICATION

In this section, I will explore the theoretical consequences of the preceding analysis, in which the lexical rules of Nasalization and Diphthongization must be allowed to apply in nonderived environments, while at the same time, other lexical rules, such as *e* Raising and *a* Raising, must be prevented from applying to nonderived forms. I will show that if some predictable structure is absent from underlying representations, Diphthongization and Nasalization may apply cyclically in nonderived environments, as required. However, I will also argue that the theory of underspecification proposed by Archangeli (1984) must be constrained so that derived-only rules are not allowed to apply in nonderived environments.

I begin this section with a short discussion of the motivation for the underspecification of underlying representations. This will require some discussion of the role of the Strict Cycle Condition as a constraint on abstractness, and the proposed derivation of the Strict Cycle Condition from the Elsewhere Condition (Kiparsky 1982b). Next, I show how Diphthongization and Nasalization can be reformulated as structure-building rules. Finally, I consider how underspecification theory must be modified so that *e* Raising and *a* Raising cannot apply to nonderived forms.

2.1. The Strict Cycle Condition

The Strict Cycle Condition was first proposed as a constraint on cyclic phonological rules by Kean (1974). One version of this principle is as follows:[12]

[92] *Strict Cycle Condition (Kiparsky 1982b):*

a. Cyclic rules apply only to derived representations.
b. Definition: A representation ϕ is derived with respect to rule R in cycle j if ϕ meets the structural description of R by virtue of a combination of morphemes introduced in cycle j or the application of a phonological rule in cycle j.

There are two kinds of motivation for the Strict Cycle Condition. Cyclic rules that apply in counter–feeding order are prevented from applying on earlier cyclic domains by the Strict Cycle Condition, thus preserving the counter–feeding order. In addition, the Strict Cycle Condition acts as a constraint on the abstractness of underlying representations. In this capacity, it supercedes the Revised Alternation Condition (Kiparsky 1973b), as first pointed out by Mascaró (1976); rules that must be restricted to derived contexts can be regulated by the Strict Cycle Condition, if they are cyclic. Since the hypothesis that lexical rules are cyclic is a major tenet of "classical" Lexical Phonology, the Strict Cycle Condition obviously plays a role in the theory of Lexical Phonology.[13] In the case of Sekani, it predicts that Nasalization and Diphthongization should be restricted to derived environments, since they are cyclic rules of the lexical phonology.

Recently, in a move that has had sweeping consequences, Kiparsky (1982b) proposed that the Strict Cycle Condition is not a primitive theoretical notion but in fact can be derived from the Elsewhere Condition (Kiparsky 1973a).

[93] *The Elsewhere Condition (Kiparsky 1984):*

Rules A, B in the same component apply disjunctively if and only if

a. The input of A is a proper subset of the input of B.
b. The outputs of A and B are distinct [i.e. do not specify contradictory feature values or structure—S.H.].

It is only necessary to assume that lexical items are "rules"—e.g. identity rules (L → L) or rules of lexical insertion (Ø → L)—in order to be able to predict that forms with lexically specified structure are in a disjunctive relation to rules that change structure; i.e. the derived-only (cyclic) rules are precisely those that override lexically specified structure.

To accommodate the growing body of evidence that certain metrical rules must apply on the first cycle to nonderived forms—e.g. the English Stress Rule (Hayes 1984)—Kiparsky (1982b) suggested that rules that build, rather than change, lexically specified structure are not regulated by the Strict Cycle Condition/Elsewhere Condition, since the outputs of such rules are not distinct from their inputs. Moreover, Kiparsky (1982b, 1985) has suggested that if underlying feature matrixes are unspecified for predictable features, then rules that assign redundant features also can be regarded as structure-building rules and are free to apply on the first cycle. Kiparsky (1985) has shown how this approach can provide a more insightful account of phonological rules and representations in a variety of languages. In the case of Sekani, the structure-building loophole suggests a way in which Nasalization and Diphthongization might be allowed to apply cyclically in nonderived environments after all.

Notice that the structure-building–structure-changing typology further predicts that only those rules formulable as structure-changing rules will turn out to be restricted to derived environments. As a notational consequence, brackets are no longer needed to indicate that a lexical rule is restricted to a derived environment: whether a rule obeys the derived-only restriction should be apparent from whether it is cyclic and from whether it overrides lexically specified structure. Thus, if the Sekani feature matrices are maximally underspecified, the derived-only rules of *a* Raising and *e* Raising ought to override lexically specified structure.

2.2. Diphthongization and Nasalization as Structure-Building Rules

Archangeli (1988) proposed that in a theory in which underlying representations are maximally underspecified, all predictable linkings between skeleton and melody are absent in underlying representations. Note that this is not prohibited by autosegmental theory: autosegments may be linked or unlinked underlyingly (Pulleyblank 1986). Moreover, this hypothesis suggests a way in which Diphthongization and Nasalization can be reformulated as structure-building rules.

The rule of Nasalization transfers the nasality of a syllable-final consonant onto a preceding vowel, suggesting that an autosegmental formulation of the rule is appropriate:

[94]

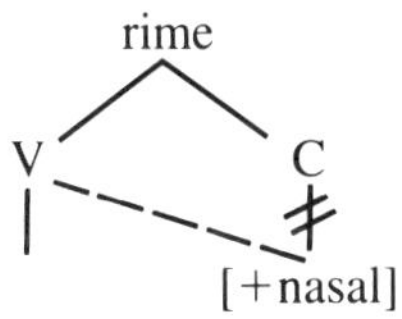

The need for Nasalization to apply in non-derived environments suggests that the link between the nasal autosegment and the consonant is absent in underlying representations. If the link is supplied by rule, then Nasalization can be regarded as a structure-building, rather than structure-changing, operation:

[95]

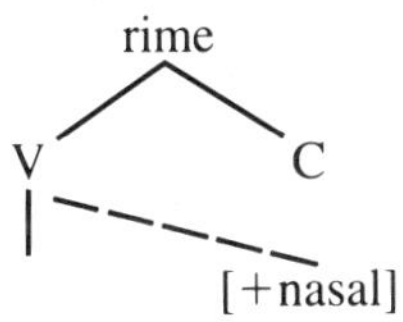

If the autosegment and consonantal slot are not underlyingly linked, then a second rule also is required to account for cases where Nasalization is blocked stem-finally (when bled by possessive suffixation or after /ə/), as well as where the nasal is not in the rime of a syllable:

[96]

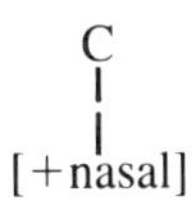

Of course, the two rules are correctly ordered by the elsewhere condition.

Next, consider Diphthongization. This rule transfers the rounding of /o/ to a preceding velar, leaving behind a vowel identical to /o/ in terms of height and backness but not rounding (i.e. [ə]). An autosegmental formulation of the rule will capture this generalization:

[97]

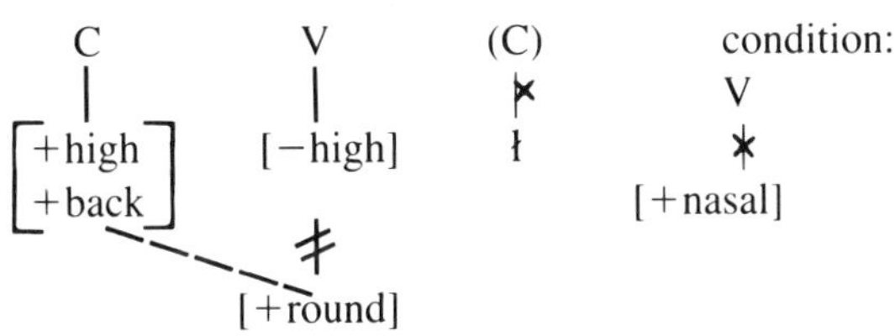

This rule can be transformed easily into a structure-building rule if the [+round] autosegment is not linked to the vowel slot underlyingly. Diphthongization simply links the [+round] autosegment to a preceding velar:

[98]

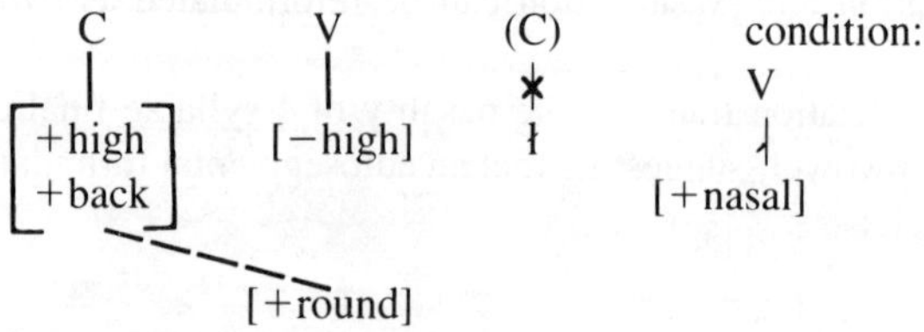

To account for cases in which no velar precedes /o/, an additional rule that links the [+round] autosegment to the vowel must be posited:

[99]

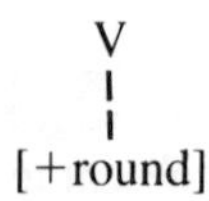

Clearly, this formulation of Diphthongization does not override lexically specified structure, since no linkings between V and the [+round] autosegment are posited for underlying representations in Sekani. As a structure-building rule, Diphthongization thus is free to apply to nonderived forms, as required.

In both revised formulations of Diphthongization and Nasalization, the autosegmental solution accounts for the absence of the autosegment on the vowel or consonant with which it is underlyingly associated as well as its attachment in phonetic forms to a preceding segment. For this reason, the autosegmental formalizations of these rules would be preferred anyway. Thus structural underspecification correctly predicts that Diphthongization and Nasalization may apply in the lexicon to nonderived forms, as required. However, notice that these formulations indicate that Archangeli's hypothesis, that all skeleton–melody linkings are absent underlyingly, is too strong. They suggest that only linkings for which there is some evidence of movement of an autosegment are absent underlyingly. Diphthongization is blocked by a following consonant that is linked to the features for [ł], as well as by [o] that is linked to a [+nasal] autosegment, indicating that some links must be present before Diphthongization applies. Although the latter link will be supplied by the rule of nasalization, the former must be present before Diphthongization applies to nonderived forms. This suggests that the link of C and [ł] is present underlyingly.

2.3. Underspecification of Underlying Features

So far, we have seen that the absence of some predictable structure in underlying representations has predicted correctly that Nasalization and Diphthongization may apply to nonderived forms. In this section, I will show how underspecification of underlying features fails to restrict *e* Raising to derived environments, as required. I will argue that the current algorithm for the selection of underlying features and feature values must be modified slightly to ensure that derived-only rules override lexically specified feature values.

Archangeli (1988) and Kiparsky (1985) pointed out that there are many possible ways to specify the underlying features and the values of those features. To remedy this, Archangeli suggested a number of constraints on the selection of the underlying feature matrixes, which I will now consider.

In Archangeli's theory, there are essentially no cross-linguistic predictions about the way in which underlying features are selected in any particular language: feature selection must be governed by language-specific considerations (which features are distinctive in the language), since, as pointed out by Archangeli, not all languages with n-vowel systems have the same n vowels in their inventory. However, the number of features that can appear in the underlying matrix is regulated by the universal principle in [100].

[100] *Feature Minimization Principle (Archangeli 1988):*

> A grammar is most highly valued when underlying representations include the minimal number of features necessary to make different the phonemes of the language.

The selection of underlying values of features likewise is governed by language-specific considerations, although here universal rules also play a role in the selection of values.

[101] *Alphabet Formation (Archangeli 1988):*

a. Given an opposition [aF]–[-aF] in environment Q in underlying representation, one value 'b' is selected as the matrix value for F in Q and the other value is specified by an automatically formed complement rule: [ ] → [-bF] / Q .

b. In the absence of language-internal motivation as selecting a value as the matrix value for a feature F, the value 'b' is selected as the matrix value where [ ] → [-bF] / Q is a member of the set of [universal—S.H.] default rules.

The motivation for part 2 of this algorithm is that a language that makes use of universal default rules as redundancy rules is simpler than one in which redundancy rules must be learned (Archangeli 1988). Thus, the value of a particular feature in an underlying representation is the opposite of the universally default value of that feature. What is absent from Alphabet Formation is a formalization of how values are 'selected' on the basis of language-specific evidence. Elsewhere, however, Archangeli suggests that language-specific evidence for the maximal underspecification of one particular vowel can be found in rules such as epenthesis or vowel harmony. If the vowel inserted by the epenthesis rule is maximally underspecified, the epenthesis rule can be more simply formulated because it is not necessary to complicate the rule with vowel melody features. Similar economy in rule formulation results from the maximal underspecification of the neutral vowel in harmony systems. The marking of values on other underlying features follows from the selection of one vowel as the maximally underspecified one.

There are some limitations of the algorithm in [101]: languages that lack epenthesis rules and harmony systems will have to rely solely on the (presently limited) inventory of universal default rules for the selection of underlying feature values, in the absence of other criteria for the selection of values. Moreover, if a language has two epenthesis rules that insert different vowels, the algorithm says nothing about which epenthesis rule indicates the maximally underspecified vowel. However, perhaps the most serious problem is the inherently limited predictive power of a theory that says "X is not universal; X is language-particular." By definition, such a theory is limited in the kinds of cross-linguistic predictions it can make. At best, universal algorithms for the selection of features and marking of values can be proposed, as Archangeli has done.

However, despite these limitations, let us now apply the theory proposed above to Sekani. The underlying feature matrix of the Sekani vowels follows.

[102]

	i	e	a	o	u	ə
[high]	+	−	−	−	+	−
[back]	−	−	+	+	+	+
[round]	−	−	−	+	+	−
[low]	−	−	+	−	−	−

According to the Feature Minimization Principle, the four values selected are more highly valued than any others for Sekani, since these features also are required to describe the consonant system. As a first step in paring away underlying values of these features, I note that Sekani has a rule of Epenthesis, which inserts a prothetic [ə] before a verb stem if no Level 2 or 3 prefixes are inserted by the morphology (see Hargus 1988 for more information). There is another indication that /ə/ is the default vowel in Sekani: rules that reduce /V-V/ sequences to [V] always delete [ə], if [ə] is one of the vowels in this sequence. If /ə/ is underlying featureless, then ə deletion can be formulated more economically as a rule that deletes skeleton positions. Thus, I erase the feature values for /ə/ and, accordingly, erase the same values of those features in the matrixes for the other vowels. This leaves us with the matrix in [103]:

[103]

	i	e	a	o	u	ə[14]
[high]	+				+	
[back]	−	−				
[round]				+	+	
[low]			+			

In Archangeli's theory, the missing features will be supplied by automatically formed "complement rules" (Archangeli 1988), which supply by rule the value of feature F that complements the value of F specified in underlying representations:

[104] [ ] → [−high]

[105] [ ] → [+back]

[106] [ ] → [−round]

[107] [ ] → [−low]

Thus, the fully specified vowel matrix of Sekani is completely predictable by complement rules and a universal redundancy rule in this theory.

However, consider what the matrix in [109] implies about the domain of *e* Raising. In this theory, neutralization rules may be formulated either as structure-building or structure-changing rules, depending on the choice of underlying features and feature values. The underlying feature matrices could be selected in a way that permits derived-only neutralization rules to apply in nonderived environments.

In fact, this is precisely the result of applying the preceding theory to Sekani. In the analysis of the vowels given in [109], /e/ is not specified for a value of the feature [high]. In this analysis, nothing would prevent *e* raising as formulated in [58] from supplying lexically unspecified feature values, thus allowing the rule to apply in nonderived contexts. In order to prevent *e* Raising from applying to nonderived forms, the underlying feature matrices must be selected in such a way that *e* Raising overrides the lexical specification [−high] for the vowel /e/. With this move, *e* Raising would be in a disjunctive relationship with lexical entries containing /en/. Thus, the Elsewhere Condition would prevent the rule from applying to nonderived forms, whose sequences of /e-n/ are not in a disjunctive relationship with the rule.

Thus, if /ə/ is the maximally underspecified vowel and /-/ is the value of [high] specified underlyingly, the following matrix will result:

Notice that following the application of the complement rule for [back], [+round] is predictable for /u/. Thus the correct value of [round] for /u/ can be supplied by the universal default rule in [108] proposed by Archangeli, which would apply after the complement rule for [back]:

[108] $[\ \ ] \rightarrow [\alpha\ \text{round}]\ /\ \underset{\begin{bmatrix}\alpha\ \text{back}\\ -\text{low}\end{bmatrix}}{\underline{\qquad}}$

(However, [+round] cannot be regarded as predictable for /o/; erasing [+round] on /o/ would cause /o/ and /ə/ to become nondistinct.) This results in the more economical matrix in [109]:

[109]

	i	e	a	o	u	ə
[high]	+				+	
[back]	−	−				
[round]				+		
[low]			+			

[110]

	i	e	a	o	u	ə
[high]		−	−	−		
[back]	−	−				
[round]				+	+	
[low]			+			

The specification [−high] can be removed from /a/, because [+low] vowels are universally [+high]:

[111] $[\ \ ] \rightarrow [-\text{high}]\ /\ \underset{[+\text{low}]}{\underline{\qquad}}$

However, [−high] cannot be removed from /o/, because this would fail to distinguish /o u/ underlyingly. Moreover, /u/ cannot be regarded as redundantly [+round], because this would fail to distinguish /u ə/ underlyingly.

[112]

	i	e	a	o	u	ə
[high]		−		−		
[back]	−	−				
[round]				+	+	
[low]			+			

Of course, given this new specification of the features, a different complement rule for [high] would be formed [114] and a special rule marking /ə/ as [−high] would be required [113]:

[113] $[\ \ ] \rightarrow [-\text{high}]\ /\ \underset{[-\text{round}]}{\underline{\qquad}}$

[114] $[\ \ ] \rightarrow [+\text{high}]$

Notice that *a* Raising is correctly predicted to apply in nonderived contexts in this analysis, but this is more or less an accident. If the feature [tense] had been selected underlyingly instead of [low] ([tense] must be introduced lexically to account for [I]), the underlying matrix in [115] would have resulted:

[115]

	i	e	a	o	u	ə
[high]	+				+	
[back]	−	−				
[round]				+		
[tense]			+			

Given this configuration, *a* Raising would have been permitted to supply values of the feature [low] in nonderived contexts.

The correct results can easily be obtained if derived-only rules are taken into consideration in selecting underlying features and values of features:

[116] If the structural change of a rule that is restricted to derived environments is [aF], then [F] must appear in the underlying feature matrix and only the value /-a/ can be marked on [F] in underlying representations.

This constraint on the selection of the underlying matrix will prevent features and values from being selected in a way that would allow derived-only rules to apply to nonderived representations.

3. CONCLUSION

Underspecification of underlying structure and features can be used to good advantage in the phonology of Sekani. However, contrary to the prediction of Archangeli (1988), not all conceivably predictable structure is absent in underlying representations, only linkings for which there is some evidence of autosegmental movement. In addition, the way in which underlying features and values of features are selected must be modified so that rules restricted to derived environments are not accidentally allowed to apply to nonderived representations.

NOTES

This paper is a revised version of Chapter 8 of my Ph.D. dissertation (Hargus 1985b). I would like to thank Glyne Piggott and Keren Rice for their comments on the version of this paper I delivered at the Buffalo conference. I also thank Bruce Hayes, Karin Michelson, Keren Rice, and Donca Steriade for their comments on earlier versions of this paper.

My research on Sekani has been generously supported by the British Columbia

Provincial Museum, Victoria; the National Museum of Man, Ottawa; the Arctic Institute of North America; the UCLA Graduate Division; the Jacobs Fund of the Whatcom Museum, Bellingham, Washington; the Wenner-Gren Foundation for Anthropological Research; and the Department of Indian and Northern Affairs, Prince George, British Columbia.

1. The name of the language is pronounced [sɛ́kəni].

2. I use a CV framework for the representation of the skeletal tier to aid the reader in interpreting representations such as that in [1]. In doing so, I am not making any theoretical claims about the preferred status of a CV skeleton as opposed to a featureless skeleton in the phonology of Sekani or of any other language.

3. A few examples of disyllabic stems in Sekani indicate that a syllable-final [ə] is permissible, as long as it is not stem-final:

[tl'ə̀ghəs]	'snake'
[hənə̀s]	'raft'

4. There is another, presumably native, word for 'bald eagle' in Sekani:

[ʔə -tsì -gày] 'bald eagle'
unspPsr head white

5. The nasal vowel in this stem is the reflex of the rarely attested Proto-Athapaskan nasal *[m/ŋʷ] (Krauss & Leer 1981, 70).

6. Actually, Nasalization is a rule that turns on at Level 1 and applies throughout the lexicon as well as postlexically. For a different analysis of Nasalization in a closely related Athapaskan language (in which the facts are crucially different), see Rice (in this volume).

7. In Fort Ware, this prefix is /xə/. This suggests that, historically, the McLeod Lake prefix did not have a [who] alternant.

8. The rule of *ə* lowering has applied in [77c]:

rime
/\
ə → a / __ h

9. In fact, in the Fort Ware dialect of Sekani (Hargus 1985), as well as in at least one dialect of closely related Beaver (Story 1979), these segments *are* distinct:

	McLeod Lake:	Ft. Ware; Beaver:
quality of underlying mid, round vowel	[o]	[U]
output of *a* Raising	[ǫ]	[ǫ]

(In Fort Ware, [U] is found only after velars; [o] occurs after other consonants.) The Sekani and Beaver vowels *ə o/U* are reflexes of the "reduced" Proto-Athapaskan vowels **ə U*, whereas *a e u i* are reflexes of the "full" Proto-Athapaskan vowels **a e u i* (Leer 1979).

10. However, this result runs counter to the prediction of Kiparsky (1982a) that the first rule of a given level is phonological, rather than morphological.

11. Compare the following forms, in which the McLeod Lake stem more closely represents the historically correct form:

McLeod Lake:	Fort Ware:
[sas]	[sąs] 'black bear'
[ʔəst*a*] 'father's brother'	[ʔəst*ą*] 'aunt's husband'
[nọd*a*]	[nụshd*ą*] 'lynx'
−[t*a*]	−[t*ą*] 'look at O' Imp
[ts*à*ʔ]	[tsàʔ], [ts*ą̀*ʔ] 'beaver'

12. Kiparsky (1985) proposed a different version of the Strict Cycle Condition; see also Shaw (1985).

13. A weakening of this hypothesis has been proposed in recent work on Lexical Phonology (Kiparsky 1985, Halle & Mohanan 1985).

14. [I] is not an underlying vowel, but values of the feature [tense] will have to be introduced lexically at some point. A rule that marks [tense] on vowels other than /ə/ will have to apply before the rule deriving [I] from /ə/ after palatals:

$$[\ ] \rightarrow [+\text{tense}] \ / \ \underline{\qquad} \begin{bmatrix} [-\overline{\text{back}}] \\ [+\text{round}] \\ [+\text{low}] \end{bmatrix}$$

Otherwise, the autosegmental formulation of this rule given in [1] would be impossible; a linear formulation in which the shared values of the palatal consonant and vowel are accidental would be required. However, the rule marking the default (-) value of [tense] need not apply before the rule which derives [I] from /ə/.

REFERENCES

Archangeli, Diana Bennett. 1988. *Underspecification in Yawelmani Phonology and Morphology*. New York: Garland Publishing.

Booij, Geert E. 1981. Rule Ordering, Rule Application and the Organization of Grammars. In *Phonologica 1980,* Wolfgang U. Dressler et al., eds., pp. 45–56. Innsbruck: Innsbrucker Beiträge zur Sprachwissenschaft, 36.

Carrier Linguistic Committee. 1974. *Central Carrier Bilingual Dictionary*. Fort St. James, B.C.: Author.

Halle, Morris, and K. P. Mohanan. 1985. Segmental Phonology of Modern English. *Linguistic Inquiry* 16:57–116.

Hargus, Sharon. 1985. The Surface Phonology of Fort Ware Sekani, with Recommendations for a Practical Orthography. Unpublished ms.

Hargus, Sharon. 1987. Infixation and Bracketing Erasure in Sekani. In Working Papers in Linguistics 9, Larry Kenton et al., eds. pp. 83–117.

Hargus, Sharon. 1988. *The Lexical Phonology of Sekani*. New York: Garland Publishing.

Hargus, Sharon. Forthcoming. Sekani Phonology. In *Contributions to Canadian Linguistics*. Ottawa: National Museum of Man.

Hayes, Bruce. 1984. *A Metrical Theory of Stress Rules*. New York: Garland Publishing.

Kean, Marie-Louise. 1974. The Strict Cycle in Phonology. *Linguistic Inquiry* 5:179–203.

Kiparsky, Paul. 1973a. Elsewhere in Phonology. In *A Festschrift for Morris Halle,* S. R. Anderson and P. Kiparsky, eds., pp. 59–76. New York: Holt, Rinehart and Winston.

Kiparsky, Paul. 1973b. Phonological Representations. In *Three Dimensions of Linguistic Theory,* Osamu Fujimura, ed., pp. 1–136. Tokyo: Institute for Advanced Studies of Language.

Kiparsky, Paul. 1982a. How are the Levels Linked? Unpublished ms.

Kiparsky, Paul. 1982b. Lexical Morphology and Phonology. In *Linguistics in the Morning Calm,* I.-S. Yange, ed., pp. 3–91. Seoul: Hanshin.

Kiparsky, Paul. 1984. On the Lexical Phonology of Icelandic. In *Nordic Prosody III: Papers from a Symposium,* C. C. Elert et al., eds. Umeå Universitet, Sweden.

Kiparsky, Paul. 1985. Some Consequences of Lexical Phonology. *Phonology Yearbook 2,* 85–138.

Krauss, Michael, and Jeff Leer. 1981. *Na-Dene Sonorants*. Alaska Native Language Center Research Papers, 5. Fairbanks: Alaska Native Language Center.

Leer, Jeff. 1979. *Proto-Athabaskan Verb Stem Variation. I: Phonology*. Alaska Native Language Center Research Papers, 1. Fairbanks: Alaska Native Language Center.

Mascaró, Joan. 1976. *Catalán Phonology and the Phonological Cycle*. Ph.D. Diss., Massachusetts Institute of Technology.

Mohanan, K. P. 1986. *Lexical Phonology*. Dordrecht: Reidel.

Pesetsky, David. 1979. Russian Morphology and Lexical Theory. Unpublished ms.

Pulleyblank, Douglas. 1986. *Tone in Lexical Phonology*. Dordrecht: Reidel.

Rice, Keren. 1982. On Stems and Lexical Phonology: An Athapaskan Example. Paper presented at Canadian Linguistics Association conference.

Rice, Keren. This volume. Vowel-Initial Suffixes and Clitics in Slave.

Shaw, Patricia. 1985. Modularisation and Substantive Constraints in Dakota Lexical Phonology. *Phonology Yearbook 2,* 173–202.

Speas, Peggy. 1984. *Navajo Prefixes and Word Structure Typology.* Cambridge: MIT Working Papers in Linguistics 7.

Story, Gillian. 1979. Problems of Interpretation in Beaver Phonemics. Unpublished ms.

Strauss, Stephen L. 1982. *Lexicalist Phonology of English and German.* (Publications in Language Sciences, 9) Dordrecht, Holland: Foris Publications.

VOWEL INITIAL SUFFIXES AND CLITICS IN SLAVE

Keren D. Rice

INTRODUCTION

In the Fort Nelson, British Columbia dialect of Slave, a northern Athapaskan language, there are a number of phonetically vowel-initial suffixes and clitics. One would predict that because these morphemes are all vowel-initial, they should pattern the same way with respect to all phonological rules. This is not the case. One set patterns as vowel-initial with respect to rules of vowel deletion, nasalization, and final consonant neutralization. A second set patterns as vowel-initial only with respect to vowel deletion. Finally, a third set patterns as vowel-initial with respect to nasalization and neutralization but not with respect to vowel deletion.

The facts regarding nasalization and neutralization can be accounted for in a theory of representations that distinguishes a timing tier from a melody tier (cf. Clements & Keyser 1983; Kaye & Lowenstamm 1985; Levin 1983, Marantz 1982). The morphemes that pattern as vowel-initial with respect to nasalization and neutralization have the same number of units on each tier while those that do not pattern as vowel-initial with respect to these rules are analyzed as having an underlying initial element on the timing tier that is not associated with a corresponding element on the melody tier. The patterning of these morphemes with respect to vowel deletion is accounted for by formulating the rule of vowel deletion so that it refers to adjacent elements on the melody tier, with adjacency on the timing tier being irrelevant. This paper thus lends support to the claim that the timing tier and the melody tier are independent levels of representation.

The third set of morphemes, those that pattern as vowel-initial with respect to nasalization and neutralization but not with respect to vowel deletion, can be shown to be clitics added to words only postlexically. The rule of vowel deletion is a morphologically conditioned rule, applying only to sequences of vowels in suffixes. Therefore, it does not apply in the environment of a clitic. This rule contrasts with the strictly phonologically conditioned rules of nasalization and neutralization. The fact that the rules of nasalization and neutralization are strictly phonological, while the rule of vowel deletion applies in a morphologically conditioned environment, follows from principles of lexical phonology, as proposed by Kiparsky (1985). Thus, this paper lends support to the claim that the domain of rules as lexical or postlexical is predictable based on universal principles.

In section 1, the vowel initial morphemes in Slave are presented. In section 2, the rules of vowel deletion, nasalization, and final consonant neutralization are discussed. An analysis is given in section 3.

1. SOME MORPHOLOGY—THE VOWEL-INITIAL FORMS

In this section the phonetically vowel-initial forms are surveyed. All the morphemes included in this section interact phonologically with their host and are treated by at least some, but not necessarily all, phonological processes as vowel-initial.

1.1. -é Possessive

The suffix *-é* is attached to the possessed noun in a possessive construction and indicates that the noun is alienably possessed. Some examples of nouns with the possessive suffix are given in [1].[1] The hyphen in front of the possessed forms indicates that these forms must be preceded by a possessor, either a possessive prefix or a noun. The possessive suffix is italicized.

[1]	Nonpossessed Form:	Possessed Form:	
	tu	-tu*é*	'water'
	meeh	-meez*é*	'knife'
	ts'ah	-ts'ad*é*	'hat'
	shį	-yin*é*	'song'[2]
	ʔe	-ʔe*ė́*	'coat'

1.2 *-i* Nominalizer

The nominalizer *-i* is illustrated in the examples in [2] through [5].[3] The [a] forms show a verb and the [b] forms the corresponding nominalization with the suffix *-i*. The nominalizer is italicized.

[2] a. ts'eʔáh 'one eats'
ts'e- unspecified subject + ʔáh 'eat'
b. ts'eʔáhl*i* 'one who eats'
ts'eʔáhl 'one eats' + -i nominalizer

[3] a. tethehchúh 'clothlike object is spread out'
te- 'spread out' + the- conjugation + h- classifier + chúh 'clothlike object is located'
b. dechįtée k'e tethehchudh*i* 'rug, linoleum, floor covering'
dechįtée 'floor' + -k'e 'on' + tethehchudh 'clothlike object is spread out' + -i nominalizer

[4] a. dahthela 'plural objects are located above'
dah- 'above' + the- conjugation + -la 'plural objects are located'
b. méh yú dahthelai 'clothespin'
méh 'with it' + yú clothes' + dahthela 'plural objects are located above' + -i nominalizer

[5] a. déhkéts'įtlah 'one goes up'
déhké- 'up' + ts'e- unspecified subject + ne- conjugation + -tlah '1, 2 go'
b. méh déhkéts'įtlad*i* 'ladder'
méh 'with it' + déhkéts'įtlad 'one goes up' + -i nominalizer

1.3. Tense, Mode, and Aspect

A number of postverbal morphemes in Slave indicate tense, mode, and aspect. Some examples of vowel-initial postverbal morphemes are given in [6] through [14]. The tense/mode/aspect morphemes are italicized.

[6] íle negative
hejį 'she, he sings'
hejin*íle* 'she, he does not sing'

[7] égųh past
hejin*égųh* 'she, he sang'

[8] éhł*eh* past habitual
hejin*éhłeh* 'she, he used to sing'

[9] ésįi future probability
hejin*ésįi* 'she, he will probably sing'

[10] élį yes/no question
hejin*élį* 'is she, he singing'

[11] íhzǫ 'always'
hejin*íhzǫ* 'she, he always sings'

[12]	oli hejin*oli*	futurc 'she, he is going to sing'
[13]	úh hejin*úh*	'when' 'when she, he sings'
[14]	e ojin*e*	future 'she, he is going to sing'

These tense/mode/aspect morphemes appear to be clitics rather than suffixes. Zwicky and Pullum (1983) suggest several characteristics that differentiate lexical inflection from cliticization. One criterion they propose is that of analyzability. According to this criterion, in cliticization the clitic and host are readily analyzable, while they may not be in inflection. This is the case in Slave. The tense/mode/aspect forms illustrated in [6] through [14] are easily distinguished from their host. There also are tense/mode/aspect affixes in Slave, found within the verb complex as prefixes. The forms of these affixes depend on a number of different factors and they are not always readily analyzable. A second criterion proposed by Zwicky and Pullum is selectivity. Clitics, they propose, are not highly selective of host, while affixes can be. The Slave tense/mode/morphemes under consideration here are free in their combinations with verbs, whereas the tense/mode/aspect affixes within the verb show co-occurrence restrictions. A third criterion for distinguishing clitics from lexical inflection has to do with idiosyncratic exceptions. The tense/mode/aspect forms are regular throughout a paradigm, as expected of clitics. The tense/mode/aspect affixes within the verb exhibit a variety of idiosyncracies. The tense/mode/aspect morphemes in question in this paper thus appear to be clitics, added to verbs postlexically, whereas the suffixes are lexically part of the verb.

1.4. *-ah* Diminutive

There are a number of different diminutive forms in Slave, one of which is *-ah*. *-ah* is a non-category determining suffix that can attach to both nouns and verbs without affecting category. As a noun suffix, it generally has the meaning of a small one or a species similar to that of the noun but smaller. The examples in [15] show *-ah* suffixed to noun stems. The suffix is italicized.

[15]	**a.**	tu tu*ah*	'water' 'small water, pond'
	b.	tsá tsá*ah*	'beaver' 'small beaver, young beaver'
	c.	deeh deeh*ah*	'river' 'creek'

d. nǫ́da	'wild cat (any kind, particularly lynx)'
nǫ́da*ah*	'domestic cat'
e. digah	'wolf'
digah*ah*	'coyote'

The examples in [16] show *-ah* as a verb suffix. In [16a], the verb stem is /-tsedl/ 'be small' followed by a suffix *-e*. In [16b], the verb stem is /-nédh/ 'be long.'

[16] a. ʔaetsédle	'it is small'
ʔaetsédl*ah*	'it is very small'
b. nenéh	'it is long'
nenéh*ah*	'it is a little bit long'

Some facts suggest that *-ah* is a suffix rather than a separate word. First, the meaning of noun-*ah* is not necessarily predictable from the meaning of the parts. It often means 'small', as in the examples in [15a–15c]. However, other meanings are possible, as in [15d] and [15e]. Second, phonologically it is part of a noun or verb. This can be seen by the fact that it triggers the rule of vowel deletion, a rule that deletes the first of two adjacent suffix vowels in suffixes. This rule is discussed in section 2. Vowel deletion occurs only within a word, never between words. If the diminutive *-ah* were a separate word, it would present the only case where vowel deletion applies between words.

2. THE INTERACTION OF VOWEL-INITIAL MORPHEMES WITH PHONOLOGICAL RULES

In this section, the patterning of the vowel-initial morphemes presented in section 1 will be examined with respect to three phonological rules, vowel deletion, nasalization, and neutralization.

2.1. Vowel Deletion and Morpheme Ordering

Vowel-vowel sequences are permitted across morpheme boundaries within a word in Slave when one of the vowels is a stem vowel. When both vowels are suffixes, the first of the two vowels must delete.

First, consider the circumstances under which vowel-vowel sequences are permitted. When a vowel-final stem is followed by a vowel-initial suffix or clitic, vowel-vowel sequences are found, as shown in the examples in [17] through [20]. Example [17] shows the possessive suffix *-é,* [18] the nominalizer *-i,* [19] the diminutive *-ah,* and [20] tense/mode/aspect forms. The italicized sequences represent a stem vowel followed by a suffix or, in the case of [20], a clitic.

	Nonpossessed:	Possessed:	
[17] a.	tu	-t*ué*	'water'
b.	mee	-m*eeé*	'clothing'[4]
c.	sa	-z*aé*	'month, sun'[5]

[18] a.	sǫ́ts'edę́ya	'it is tied around the neck'
	sǫ́ts'edę́y*ai*	'necklace'
b.	náte	'she, he dreams'
	nát*ei*	'one who dreams, prophet'
c.	uits'edi	'one whistles'
	méh uits'ed*ií*	'whistle' (noun)
[19] a.	tsá	'beaver'
	ts*áa*h	'young beaver'
b.	tthee	'rock'
	tth*eea*h	'small rock'
[20]	uits'edi	'one whistles'
	uits'ed*ií*le	'one does not whistle'

In [17] through [20], the first of the two italicized vowels is in a stem and the second is in a suffix or clitic. Both vowels remain.

When a vowel-initial stem follows a vowel-final word, where the first vowel is either the vowel of a stem or the vowel of a suffix attached to a stem, both vowels appear phonetically. In [21], an example is given of a vowel-initial stem.[6]

[21] -undie 'older brother'

When this stem is preceded by a vowel-final lexical item, where the final vowel is part of either a stem or a suffix, both vowels remain. Vowel deletion thus does not apply across word boundaries, and therefore it never deletes the final vowel, stem or suffix, of a word before a following vowel-initial word. This can be seen in the forms in [22].

[22] a.i.	dene̜	'person, man'
a.ii.	den*e* *u*ndie	'Brother (in church)'
b.i.	ʔehtsíe	'grandfather'
b.ii.	ʔehtsí*e* *u*ndie	'grandfather's older brother'
c.i.	ʔamá	'mother'
c.ii.	ʔam*á* *u*ndie	'mother's older brother'

The final vowels of the words in [22ai] and [22bi] are suffixes,[7] a noun stem formative of the form *-e*. The final vowel in [22ci] is a stem vowel. Examples

[22a] and [22b] thus show suffixed forms preceding a vowel-initial stem; [22c] shows a stem vowel preceding a vowel-initial stem. In both cases, vowel sequences remain.

The conclusion can be drawn that when two vowels, one of which is a stem vowel,[8] are adjacent in a compound or suffixation structure both vowels appear phonetically.

I will now turn to cases where both vowels in a sequence of vowels belong to suffixes. When a vowel-final suffix is adjacent to a vowel-initial suffix, it is not obvious phonetically that two suffixes are present because the vowel of the first suffix always deletes when the second suffix is vowel-initial. A number of examples illustrating this deletion are discussed below.

The examples in [23] are possessed nominalizations. The first example of each pair shows a nominalized verb and the second its possessed form. Both suffixes, *-i* nominalizer and *-é* possessive, are present in the underlying representation of the possessed nominalization. Not both these suffixes are phonetically present, however; the vowel of the nominalizer is deleted. The underlying presence of the nominalizer is suggested by its occurrence in the nonpossessed form and by the morphological fact that the possessive suffix attaches only to nouns. Given this, the suffix *-i* nominalizer must be present in order for possessive suffixation to occur and must be deleted preceding the vowel initial suffix *-é* possessive in the forms in [23].

[23] *-i* Nominalizer + *-é* Possessive:

a.	méh ʔįhts′ǫ ts′eneh*i*	'telephone'
	-méh ʔįhts′ǫ ts′eneh*é*	'telephone' (possessed form)
b.	ʔedehtl′éh híchudh*i*	'photograph'
	-ʔedehtl′éh híchudh*é*	'photograph' (possessed form)

The examples in [24] show possessed and possessed diminutive forms.

[24] *-é* Possessive + *-ah* Diminutive:

a.	tu	'water'
	-tué	'water' (possessed form)
	-túah	'pond' (possessed diminutive form)
b.	meeh	'knife'
	-meezé	'knife' (possessed form)
	-méezah	'small knife, pocket knife' (possessed diminutive form)

As in the possessed nominalizations, the vowels of both suffixes are not both present phonetically in the possessed diminutives. Only the vowel of the diminutive suffix actually surfaces. Given this, one can propose that the possessive suffix is inside of the diminutive suffix. There are two pieces of evidence for this claim. First, ordering facts suggest that the possessive occurs inside the diminutive. In the data in [25], the suffixes *-é* possessive and *-cho* augmentative are present.

[25] *-é* Possessive + *-cho* Augmentative:

-tué	'water' (possessed form)
-tuécho	'lake' (possessed form)

Here the consonant-initial suffix, *-cho,* clearly follows the vowel-final suffix *-é.* The augmentative and diminutive function similarly in Slave, suggesting that the correct order of affixation indeed is possessive followed by augmentative. Second, when a consonant intervenes between two vowels, both suffixes are phonetically transparent, as shown in the data given in [25]. If the diminutive preceded the possessive, both suffixes should occur phonetically since the diminutive is consonant-final. One would expect the possessed form of [24a], 'pond', to be *[-tuahé], an incorrect form. Phonological facts thus also suggest the ordering possessive–diminutive.[9]

The examples in [26] show nominalized forms and their corresponding diminutives.

[26] *-i* Nominalizer + *-ah* Diminutive:

a.	dechįtée k'e tethehchúdhi	'rug'
	dechįtée k'e tethehchúdhah	'small rug'
b.	méh k'enáʔets'ehtsili	'washing machine'
	méh k'enáʔets'ehtsilah	'small washing machine'

In the diminutive forms, the vowel of the nominalizer is deleted. The ordering of the nominalizer inside the diminutive is supported in several ways. Most obvious is the fact that if they occurred in the opposite order, the vowel-initial nominalizer would follow the consonant-final diminutive and both should occur phonetically, giving the phonetic form *-*ahi*. Another fact that supports this ordering of morphemes is the order of the nominalizer and augmentative. As the data in [27] illustrate, when the augmentative suffix *-cho* is present, the ordering of affixes is clearly nominalizer followed by augmentative.

[27] *-i* Nominalizer + *-cho* Augmentative:

-dechįtée k'e tethehchúdhi	'rug, floor covering' (possessed form)
-dechįtée k'e tethehchúdhicho	'large rug, floor covering' (possessed form)

In these forms the ordering of the possessive and nominalizer suffixes before the augmentative suffix is transparent, since both suffixes are phonetically present. Given that the augmentative and diminutive function similarly in Slave, one would expect that, since the augmentative follows the nominalizer, the diminutive also will follow the nominalizer. Other arguments based on the phonological rules of nasalization and neutralization also support this ordering. These rules are discussed in sections 2.2 and 2.3, respectively.

In order to account for the fact that when two suffix vowels are adjacent only one of the vowels actually appears phonetically, a rule of vowel deletion is necessary. This rule deletes the first of two adjacent suffix vowels. The possessive, nominative, and diminutive suffixes are all regular with respect to vowel deletion. This rule is stated formally in [28].[10]

[28] *Vowel Deletion:*
V → Ø / X] __] V X = stem

The examples shown so far involve vowel deletion with the possessive, nominalizer, and diminutive suffixes only. When the tense/mode/aspect clitics are considered, a different pattern is found. With these forms, vowel deletion fails to occur, as shown in [29].

[29] **a.** hejinol*ií*le 'she, he will not sing'
hejin 'she, he sings' + oli future + íle negative
b. ojin*eí*le 'she, he is not going to sing'
ojin 'she, he will sing' + e future + íle negative
c. hejinol*ié*lį 'will she, he sing?'
hejin 'she, he sings' + oli future + élį question marker
d. ojin*eé*lį 'is she, he going to sing?'
ojin 'she, he will sing' + e future + élį question marker

When two vowels in tense/mode/aspect clitics are adjacent, vowel deletion does not occur.

The diminutive also can occur with the tense/mode/aspect clitics, with the diminutive inside the clitics. Vowel deletion is not applicable, since the diminutive is consonant-final. An example of this ordering is given in [30a], where both the diminutive *-ah* and the yes/no question marker *éli* are present. In [30b], a tense/mode/aspect morpheme follows the augmentative *-cho*. Here, two vowels are adjacent, but vowel deletion fails to occur.

[30] **a.** ˀaetsédlahélį 'is it a little small?'
b. necháchoélį 'is it really big?'

In this section, two different things have been shown.[11] First, the linear order of morphemes following the stem is as shown in [31].

[31] stem—nominalizer—possessive—diminutive—tense/mode/aspect

Second, vowel deletion applies to a sequence of vowels when both belong to suffixes. It does not apply across word boundaries or when the second vowel belongs to a vowel-initial tense/mode/aspect clitic. Thus, the possessive, nominalizer, and diminutive suffixes pattern as a group with respect to vowel deletion and the tense/mode/aspect clitics form a set on their own.

2.2. Nasalization

There are both oral and nasalized vowels phonetically in Slave. However, all nasalized vowels can be derived from underlying oral vowel-nasal sequences, allowing the elimination of nasalized vowels from the underlying inventory of sounds.

A rule of nasalization is motivated by alternations such as those shown in [32] through [34]. When the nasal is in the coda of the syllable, nasalization occurs. When it is syllable-initial, nasalization does not occur.

In [32], examples of the alternation between nasalized and oral vowels are shown with the possessive suffix. When this suffix is not present, a nasalized vowel occurs. When the vowel-initial suffix is added, nasalization does not occur.

[32] *Possessive Construction:*

	Nonpossessed Form:	Possessed Form:	
a.	shį	-yiné	'song'
b.	tę	-tené	'ice'
c.	tsǫ́	-tsóné	'excrement'
d.	dechį	-dechiné	'wood, stick'
e.	kǫ́	-kóné	'fire'

In [33], alternations between nasalized vowels and oral vowels are shown, with the nasalized vowel appearing word-finally in a verb form and the oral vowel occurring when the nominalizer is present.

[33] *Nominalizer:*

a. theʔǫ — 'sg. object is located'
thátsʼehʔoni — 'chewing tobacco'
thá- 'mouth' + tsʼe- unspecified subject + h- classifier + ʔon 'singular object is located' + −i nominalizer

b. tsʼehtsį — 'one makes'
méh kǫ́tué tsʼehtsini — 'malt'
méh 'with it' + kǫ́tué 'alcohol' + tsʼehtsin 'one makes' + -i nominalizer

c. dékʼǫ — 'it burns'
ʔekʼa dékʼoni — 'candle'
ʔekʼa 'fat' + dékʼon 'it burns' + -i nominalizer

When a vowel-initial tense/mode/aspect clitic follows a nasal, nasalization does not apply, as expected since the nasal is not in a coda. In each pair of data in [34], the first line shows a form with a nasalized vowel and the second line a form with an oral vowel and a tense/mode/aspect clitic.

[34] *Tense/Mode/Aspect:*

a.	hejį	'she, he sings'
	hejiníle	'she, he does not sing'
b.	nehtsį	'you sg. make'
	nehtsinélį	'do you sg. make?'

In all the examples in [32] through [34], nasalization takes place when the nasal is word-final. Nasalization actually occurs in a more general environment, whenever the nasal is syllable-final. This can be seen in several different structures. First, in the compound forms in [35], the first item of the compound ends in a nasal and nasalization takes place, since the nasal is syllable-final.

[35]

a.	dechį	'wood, stick'
	dechįtene	'wooden box'
	dechin 'wood' + tene 'box'	
b.	tsǫ́	'excrement'
	tsǫ́kǫ́é	'toilet'
	tsón 'excrement' + kǫ́é 'house'	

Second, nasalization occurs before the consonant-initial augmentative suffix *-cho,* as shown in [36].

[36]

a.	kǫ́	'fire'
	kǫ́cho	'big fire'
b.	tę	'ice'
	tęcho	'large ice, glacier'

Third, nasalization also applies within the verb prefix complex. For example, the second-person singular subject prefix has two forms, [ne] and nasalization, depending on which level the preceding lexical material is. These two forms are illustrated in the data in [37].

[37]

a.	nejį ne- second-person singular subject + -jin 'sing'	'you sg. sing'
b.	dįjį de- inceptive + ne- second person singular subject + -jin 'sing'	'you sg. start to sing'

In [37a], the second person singular subject has the form [ne], whereas in [37b] it surfaces as nasalization on the prefix *de-*. In this second case, the vowel of the subject morpheme deletes, leaving a nasal. This nasal gets syllabified into the coda of the preceding syllable. A second rule, which is not relevant to the discussion here, raising, also applies in [37b]. These forms show that nasalization is a very general rule, occurring whenever the nasal is in the coda of the syllable.

These alternations between nasalized and oral vowels can best be accounted for by a rule of nasalization, as shown in [38].

[38] Nasalization:

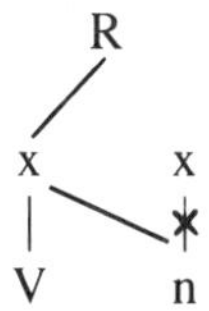

The rule states that when a vowel is followed by a nasal in the rhyme of the same syllable, the nasal delinks from its timing unit, indicated by 'x,' and relinks with the timing unit to its left, ultimately giving a nasalized vowel.

So far, it has been shown that when *-é* possessive, *-i* nominalizer, and the tense/mode/aspect clitics follow a nasal consonant, nasalization is blocked. This is to be expected because in these cases, the structural description of nasalization is not met. While in the representation in [39a] nasalization is predicted to occur, in one like [39b], the nasal forms the onset of the second syllable and thus nasalization is blocked.

[39] a.

b.

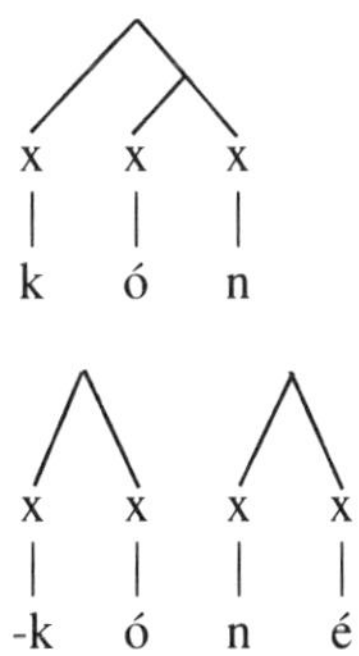

Given that the diminutive suffix *-ah* patterns with the possessive and nominalizer with respect to vowel deletion, exhibiting regular vowel-initial behavior, a reasonable expectation is that it also patterns with them with respect to nasalization. Thus, one would expect, given that *-ah* begins with a vowel phonetically and conditions vowel deletion, that it would block nasalization. As the data given in [40] show, this is not the case. When *-ah* is present, nasalization unexpectedly occurs. In the data in [40], nonsuffixed forms, possessed forms, and diminutive forms are given for several nasal-final stems. The nasalized vowel is present in the nonsuffixed form, as expected, and the oral vowel in the possessed form, also as expected. Unexpectedly, the nasalized vowel also is present in the diminutive form.

[40]	Nonpossessed Form:	Possessed Form:	
a.	kǫ́	-kóné	'fire'
	kǫ́ah		'small fire'
b.	tsǫ́	-tsóné	'excrement'
	tsǫ́ah		'small excrement'
c.	shį	-yiné	'song'
	shįah		'small song'
d.	tę	-tené	'ice'
	tęah		'small ice'

In section 4, a solution will be sought for the unexpected occurrence of nasalization when the diminutive suffix is present. Before turning to this solution, however, a second rule that separates *-ah* diminutive from the rest of the vowel-initial forms will be examined.

2.3. Neutralization

In Slave, all stem-final consonants neutralize to [h] syllable-finally. In syllable-initial position, several different stem-final consonants are found: [h], [d], [l], [z], and occasionally [dl]. Alternations between [h] and a consonant are illustrated in [41] for the possessive suffix, in [42] for the nominalizer suffix, and in [43] for some of the tense/mode/aspect forms.

[41]	*Possessive Suffix:*	
a.	ts'a*h*	'hat'
	-ts'a*d*é	'hat' (possessed form)
b.	mį́*h*	'net'
	-mį́*l*é	'net' (possessed form)
c.	dee*h*	'river'
	-dee*z*é	'river' (possessed form)

[42]	*Nominalizer:*	
a.	déhkéts'įtla*h*	'one goes up'
	déhkéts'įtla*d*i	'ladder'

b. ˀek'enáˀets'ehtsi*h* — 'one washes'
méh yú k'enáˀets'ehtsi*l*i — 'washing machine'

[43] a. duhtla*h* — 'I will go'
duhtla*d*éhsįi — 'I will probably go'
b. náˀenehge*h* — 'I am sewing'
náˀenehge*z*éhłe — 'I used to sew'

The examples in [41] through [43] all illustrate neutralization occurring word-finally. This rule actually occurs whenever a consonant is syllable-final. There are several sources of evidence for this environment for the rule. First, distributional facts suggest this environment. No consonant other than [h] ever occurs in syllable-final position in Slave. Second, when consonant-final words such as those given in [41] occur as the first member of a compound and are followed by a consonant-initial item, neutralization occurs, as shown in [44].

[44] mį́*h*tl'ųlé — 'rope for fishnet'
mį́l 'net' + tl'unl 'rope' + -é possessive

Neutralization also occurs when a consonant-final item occurs preceding the augmentative suffix -cho, as illustrated in [45].

[45] ts'a*h*cho — 'cowboy hat'
ts'ad 'hat' + -cho augmentative

Finally, neutralization applies in the prefix complex of verbs. The vowel of the conjugation prefix the- is deleted in the third person form of a verb under certain conditions that are not relevant to the discussion here. The remaining consonant is resyllabified into the coda of the preceding syllable and is neutralized to [h]. An example is given in [46].[12]

[46] a. ˀedé*th*įk'é — 'you sng. shot yourself'
ˀede- + reflexive + the- conjugation + ne- second person singular subject + -k'é 'shoot'
b. ˀedé*h*k'é — 'she, he shot herself, himself'
ˀede- reflexive + the- conjugation + -k'é 'shoot'

In the third-person form given in [46b], the vowel of the conjugation prefix is deleted and the remaining *th* becomes [h] by neutralization.

Like nasalization then, neutralization occurs when the consonant is syllable-final and fails to occur when the consonant is syllable-initial. This rule is shown in [47]. The rule changes a consonant in the coda of a syllable to [h].

[47] Neutralization:

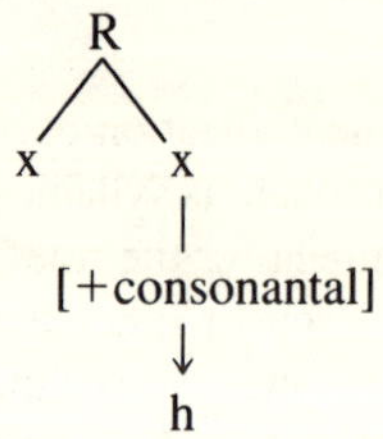

If resyllabification applies automatically following the attachment of a vowel-initial suffix, then neutralization is prevented, as shown in the examples in [41] through [43].

Unexpectedly, neutralization does occur in the context of the diminutive suffix. In this, as in nasalization, the diminutive stands apart from the other vowel-initial forms. Its unexpected application is illustrated in [48]. The forms on the first line of each pair show the free and possessed forms and on the second line the diminutive and the possessed diminutive.

[48]	Nonpossessed form:	Possessed form:	
a.	tée*h*	-tée*l*é	'mat'
	tée*h*ah	-tée*l*ah	'small mat'
b.	mį*h*	-mį*l*é	'net'
	mį*h*ah	-mį*l*ah	'small net'
c.	ts'a*h*	-ts'a*d*é	'hat'
	ts'a*h*ah	-ts'á*d*ah	'small hat'
d.	łu*h*	-lu*z*é	'spoon'
	łu*h*ah	-lú*z*ah	'small spoon'

In the diminutive form, neutralization occurs despite the fact that the diminutive suffix is apparently vowel-initial.[13] In the possessed diminutive form, however, neutralization does not apply. As is shown in the data in [24], the possessive suffix occurs inside of the diminutive. Therefore, the final consonant of the stem is syllabified into the onset of the syllable with the possessive suffix as nucleus. Vowel deletion then occurs after the addition of the diminutive suffix, leaving the stem-final consonant in an onset. This is illustrated in the derivation of [48b] in [49]. I assume cyclic application of phonological rules.

[49]

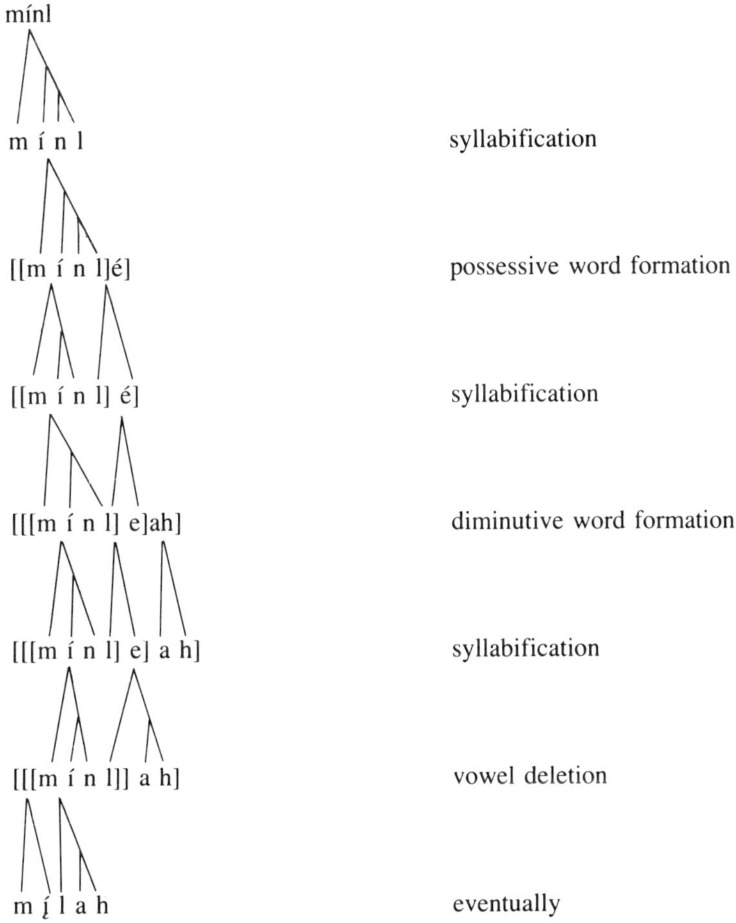

In diminutive nominalized forms, neutralization also does not apply, as shown by data given in [26], repeated in [50].

[50] **a.** dechįtée k′e tethehchúdhi 'rug'
dechįtée k′e tethehchúdhah 'small rug'
b. méh k′enáˀets′ehtsili 'washing machine'
méh k′enáˀets′ehtsilah 'small washing machine'

If the nominalizer is added prior to the diminutive, the failure of neutralization to apply in these forms can be accounted for in a similar way to that required for the possessed diminutive forms illustrated in [49]. The final consonant of the stem, *dh* in [50a] and *l* in [50b], becomes onset of the syllable containing the vowel of the nominalizer as nucleus. When neutralization later applies, this stem-final consonant is already in an onset and thus the structural description of neutralization is not met.

2.4. Summary

The class of morphemes that pattern in some way as vowel-initial fall into three groups. (1) Vowel deletion occurs but nasalization and neutralization do not occur (*-é* possessive, *-i* nominalizer). This group is the fully regular one, patterning as vowel-initial with respect to nasalization, neutralization, and vowel deletion in that nasalization and neutralization are blocked and vowel deletion applies. (2) Vowel deletion, nasalization, and neutralization all occur (*-ah* diminutive). This suffix is regular with respect to vowel deletion but unexpectedly triggers nasalization and neutralization, even though it apparently does not provide the necessary syllable structure. (3) Vowel deletion, nasalization and neutralization all fail to occur (tense/mode/aspect clitics). This group is regular with respect to nasalization and neutralization but irregular with respect to vowel deletion.

3. A SOLUTION

The problem presented in section 2 is that all the apparently vowel-initial morphemes do not pattern as a group with respect to various phonological rules. A solution to this paradox is to assign different representations to the different vowel-initial forms. These facts can be accounted for if the morphemes that do not allow nasalization and neutralization are given representations such as in [51a] and the diminutive, which does allow these rules to apply, is given the representation in [51b].

[51] a.
```
X        X        X X X
|        |        | | |
é        i        í l e
```
b.
```
X X X
  | |
  a h
```

First, the morphemes that pattern as if they were vowel-initial with respect to nasalization and neutralization will be looked at; then the diminutive, which patterns as vowel-initial with respect to vowel deletion, will be examined.

3.1. Syllabification, Nasalization, and Neutralization

The possessive, nominalizer, and tense/mode/aspect clitics consist of exactly the number of units on the timing tier as there are segments on the melody tier, as in [51]. In order to look at how these representations can be used to account for the patterning of these forms, it is necessary to outline a theory of syllabification. I assume a theory of syllabification along the lines of that proposed by Steriade (1982). A phonological representation, consisting of a string of timing units (indicated here by x's) and a melody tier, is subject to a rule that assigns syllable structure. The maximal syllable in Slave is CVC and all syllables contain a nucleus. The nucleus is part of the rhyme, which may or may not have a coda. The minimal syllable is shown in [52a] and the maximal syllable in [52b].

[52] a.

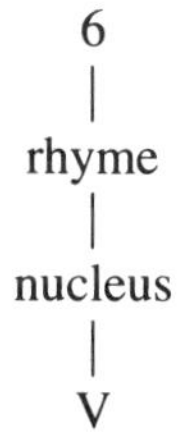

b.

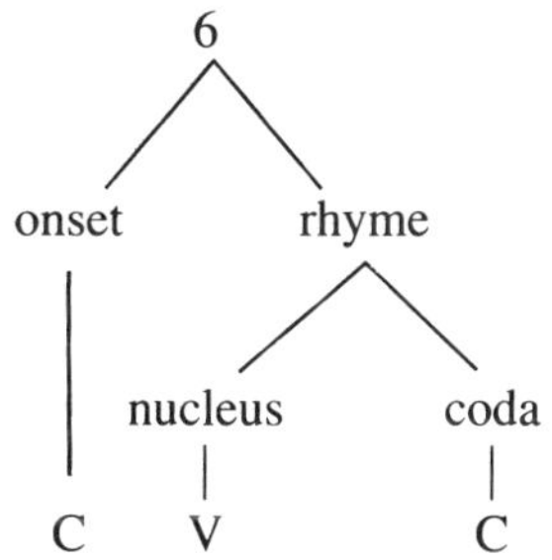

When word formation occurs, if a morpheme is added with no timing unit that can be syllabified into the onset, then resyllabification occurs, if possible, moving a timing unit and its melody from the coda of the previous syllable into the empty onset, as shown in [53].

[53]

Thus, an onset will contain a timing unit x if it possibly can.

To return now to the Slave morphemes in question, assume they have the representations shown in [51]. Consider, first, the suffix *-é* possessive. When this suffix is added to a consonant-final stem, the consonant originally syllabified in the first syllable can be resyllabified into the second syllable, yielding a filled onset. This is illustrated in [54] for the word *-kóné* fire (possessed form).

[54]

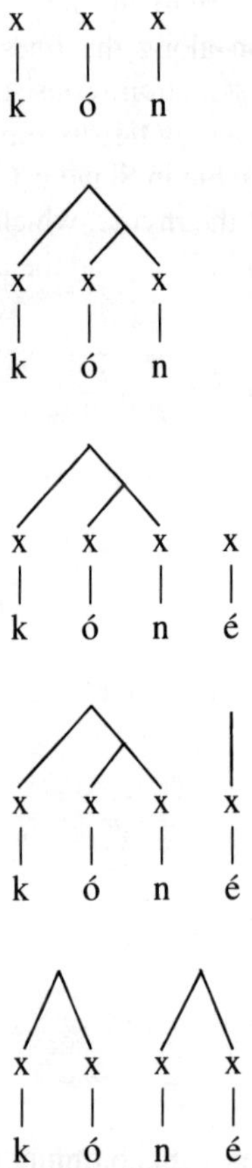

syllabification

possessive word formation

syllabification

resyllabification

The *n* of the first syllable moves into onset position in the second syllable. In the nonpossessed form, /kón/, resyllabification cannot occur and the structural description of nasalization is met.

The nominalizer is similar. A partial derivation for the verbal part of *méh déhkéts'įtladi* 'ladder' is shown in [55].

[55]

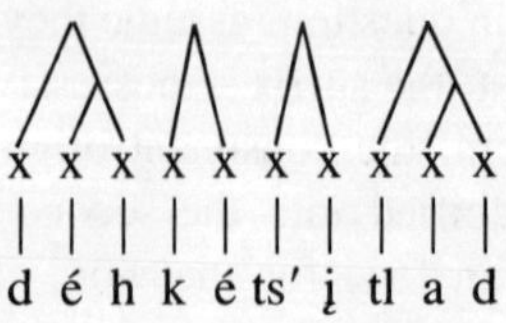

word formation and syllabification

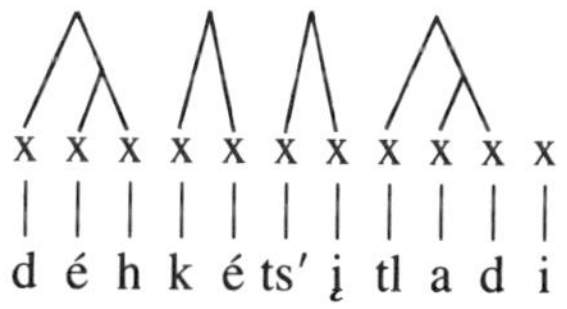

nominalization

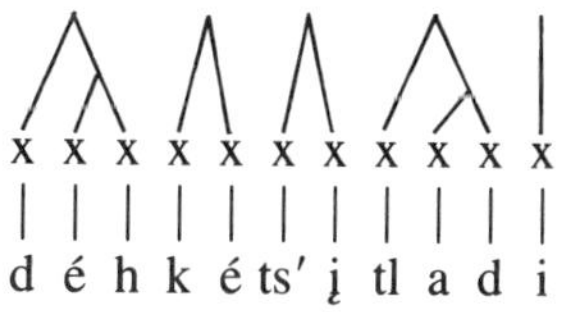

syllabification

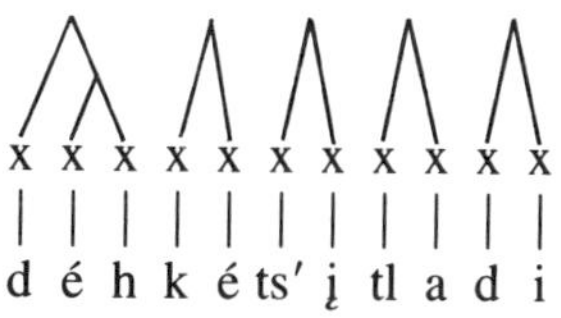

resyllabification

In the verb form *déhkéts'įtlah* 'one goes up', resyllabification does not occur and neutralization can apply.

Now consider the suffix *-ah*. Suppose that this suffix has a representation with an empty timing unit for the onset, as shown in [56].

[56]

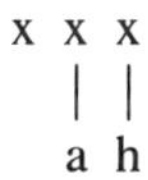

Because an onset point exists, resyllabification fails to occur when this suffix is present: the onset position is filled. Nasalization and neutralization thus can apply since their structural descriptions are met. This is illustrated in the derivation in [57] for nasalization with the word *-kónah* 'small fire (possessed form)' and in [58] for neutralization with the word *-téelah* 'small mat (possessed form)'.

[57]

syllabification

diminutive formation

syllabification

[58]

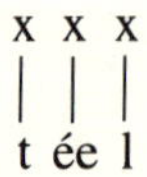

syllabification

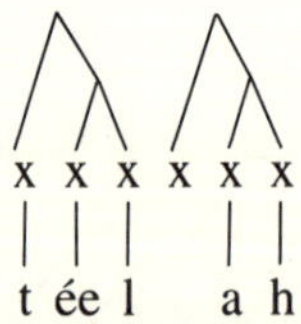

diminutive formation

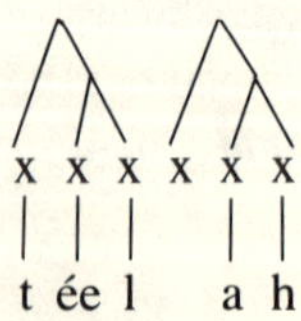

syllabification

Resyllabification does not occur because there is a timing unit in the onset of the final syllable, so the structural descriptions of the rules of nasalization and neutralization are met and the correct forms result.

By using a different representation for the diminutive form than for the other vowel-initial forms, it is possible to account for the fact that nasalization and neutralization occur only before the diminutive. This morpheme itself has an extra timing unit that constitutes an onset, blocking resyllabification and thus allowing both nasalization and neutralization to apply.

3.2. Vowel Deletion

So far, it has been shown that by giving the diminutive a different type of representation from the other vowel-initial forms, the facts of nasalization and neutralization can be accounted for. The vowel deletion facts still have to be considered. The diminutive patterns with the true vowel-initial suffixes, the possessive and nominalizer, with respect to vowel deletion. Consider the representations in [59], where the vowels themselves are on a tier distinct from that of the timing units.

[59] a.
```
X X X  X X  X X
| | |  | |  | |
h í ch u dh i é
```
cf. [23b]

b.
```
X X X X X X X
| | | |   | |
k ó n é   a h
```
cf. [40a]

In these representations, there are adjacent vowels on the melody tier. In [59a] these vowels are adjacent on both the timing and the melody tiers, while in [59b] the timing units of *e* and *a* are not adjacent but the vowels themselves are. If the rule of vowel deletion requires adjacency on just the melody tier, then vowel deletion is expected in both forms in [59]. The rule of vowel deletion is formulated in [60]. I assume here that vowel melody features are marked by the presence of the feature [−consonantal] on the melody tier.

[60] Vowel Deletion:

```
      X
      |
[−consonantal] → Ø /___ [−consonantal]
```

This rule will delete a vowel and its timing unit when it is adjacent to another vowel on the melody tier. Since the environment of the deletion rule does not require that the vowels in question be adjacent on the timing tier but only on the melody tier, the extra timing unit present in a form like [59b] does not block the rule from applying.

The rule of vowel deletion does not affect vowels in the tense/ mode/ aspect clitics. This fact can be accounted for if the clitics are added to the verb after the rule of vowel deletion turns off. The representations solution is consistent with this analysis. Suppose that the grammar is organized into levels as shown in [61].

[61] Level 1 (lexical): possessive, nominalizer, diminutive
Level 2 (postlexical): tense/mode/aspect

Vowel deletion applies at Level 1 and then turns off, accounting for the fact that it fails to apply when tense/mode/aspect clitics are involved. Nasalization and neutralization, on the other hand, follow all word formation, applying only after all segments are syllabified. This accounts for the fact that they do not apply with the true vowel-initial forms but do apply with the diminutive, which is not truly vowel-initial.

3.3. The Placement of the Phonological Rules—Predictions from Lexical Phonology

In the previous section it was shown that the model of the grammar shown in [61] makes correct predictions about the interaction of phonology and morphology if the rules of nasalization and neutralization can occur after all word formation and if the rule of vowel deletion can turn off before the tense/ mode/ aspect clitics enter into word formation. In this section, I will address the question of whether this ordering is predicted by principles of lexical phonology or whether it must be stipulated. The rules of nasalization and neutralization are considered first, followed by consideration of the rule of vowel deletion.

While nasalization and neutralization can follow all word formation processes and yield correct phonetic forms, must they follow all word formation? If these rules are predicted by principles of lexical phonology to apply immediately on Level 1, it will be difficult to block their application in forms to which the tense/mode/aspect clitics are added postlexically. In this case, the rules of nasalization and neutralization must not apply but their structural description is met until the clitics are added postlexically. If the rules of nasalization and neutralization must apply immediately, then they should apply in the verbs with the tense/mode/aspect clitics. In this section, I will show that not only must these rules be postponed until the postlexical component of the grammar to predict the actually occurring forms in Slave, principles of lexical phonology predict that they indeed must be postponed until this point. If these two phonological rules are lexical, then violations of the principle of structure preservation and the Strict Cycle Condition arise. The rules in fact are predicted to be postlexical.

First, once the different representations for vowel initial suffixes are introduced, nasalization and neutralization become completely regular.[14] They apply whenever the nasal or consonant is in the coda and fail to apply otherwise. Nasalized and oral vowels are totally in complementary distribution; apparent surface counterexamples arise only because some morphemes have no segment filling an onset position. This also is true with respect to neutralization. Exceptions are only apparent, arising from the existence of morphemes such as the diminutive with empty onsets. The rules thus apply without exception and across the boards without regard to word-internal structure. These are characteristics, according to Kiparsky (1985), of postlexical rather than lexical rules.

These rules not only show characteristics of postlexical rules but also are predicted to be postlexical by the universal principles of structure preservation and the Strict Cycle Condition. First, consider the rule of nasalization. This rule introduces nasalized vowels. All nasalized vowels in Slave are derived by this rule and, thus, are not present in the lexicon. The principle of structure preservation predicts that nasalized vowels should arise only postlexically, since there are not any nasalized vowels in the lexicon. Nothing special need be said about nasalization if it does apply postlexically, as this domain of application is predicted. Its application in the lexicon, on the other hand, would be the marked situation.

Neutralization also is predicted by the principles of lexical phonology to be postlexical. Kiparsky (1985) proposed that in the lexicon all levels except perhaps the final are cyclic. All phonological rules that apply on a cyclic level must be cyclic. While it cannot be demonstrated for Slave that the levels of the lexicon indeed are cyclic, I will assume with Kiparsky that it is part of universal grammar that nonfinal lexical levels are cyclic and that, therefore, the rules that apply on them apply cyclically. These rules thus are subject to the Strict Cycle Condition, applying only in derived environments. In examining the question of what can create a derived environment, Kiparsky (1985) proposed that structure-building rules such as syllabification rules do not create a derived environment for the application of later phonological rules.

The Slave rule of neutralization is a rule that applies in derived environments only in the sense that it is dependent on the structure-building rule of syllabification that applies to create part of its structural description. Otherwise, it applies in a nonderived environment: it involves neither juxtaposition of morphemes nor an environment created by prior application of a non-structure-building rule. Given this, neutralization should not apply in the lexicon since its application would violate the Strict Cycle Condition. The only place that this rule can apply then is postlexically.

Within the assumptions of lexical phonology then, both nasalization and neutralization are predicted to apply postlexically. The representations analysis proposed in this paper allows just this characterization of these rules.

The rule of vowel deletion, unlike the rules of nasalization and neutralization, is predicted to be a rule of the lexical phonology. This rule makes crucial reference to word-internal structure, only applying between two suffixes. It obeys the Strict Cycle Condition: it only applies in derived environments, namely in environments derived through the juxtaposition of morphemes. It also is structure preserving, as single vowel sequences are found in the lexicon. There is no reason for it to be blocked from applying as soon as it structural description is met.

Based on empirical arguments, the rules of nasalization and neutralization in Slave have been shown to apply in the postlexical component of the grammar, following the syllabification of a clitic with its host, while vowel deletion must apply lexically but not postlexically. Two principles of lexical phonology, structure preservation and the Strict Cycle Condition, predict exactly these domains for these three rules.

4. SUMMARY

Suffixes that are apparently vowel-initial fall into two sets in Slave. One set exhibits true vowel-initial behavior with respect to the rules of nasalization, neutralization, and vowel deletion. The second set has a dual nature: they are vowel-initial with respect to vowel deletion but not with respect to nasalization and neutralization. These morphemes are vowel-initial on the melody tier but have an extra unit on the timing tier. A third set of morphemes also is vowel-initial but fails to provide the environment for vowel deletion. These morphemes are clitics rather than suffixes, being added to the verb postlexically. The representations proposed for these morphemes provide an example showing the independence of the timing and melody tiers. These different representations also allow an analysis consistent with assumptions of lexical phonology for predicting the domains of phonological rules to be either lexical or postlexical; these principles predict that the rules will apply in exactly the domains that they must apply in to account for the alternations found in Slave. Support, is thus lent to the inclusion of these principles in universal grammar.

NOTES

This research was funded by the British Columbia Provincial Museum and by the Friends of the British Columbia Provincial Museum. Many thanks to them, and many thanks to the many people from Fort Nelson, British Columbia, who worked with me to give me data for this paper. I owe a great debt of gratitude to Leslie Saxon and Sharon Hargus for their careful reading and many comments on earlier versions of this paper. Many thanks also to Karin Michelson for her very careful editing. Problems, of course, remain mine.

1. Note the following orthographic symbols: ch = [č], dh = [δ], th = [θ], tth = [tθ], gh = [γ], sh = [š], ee = [e], e = [ϵ], V̨= nasalized vowel, V́ = high tone vowel.

2. Voicing alternations between voiced and voiceless continuants are found, with voiced continuants occurring following another syllable and voiceless continuants appearing word-initially. See Rice (1986) for details.

3. See section 3 for discussion of the neutralization rule that operates in the (a) forms in these data.

4. Recall that orthographic ee is a single segment [e].

5. Many phonetic facts are suppressed here. The possessive suffix tends to assimilate in quality to a preceding non-high vowel.

6. That this stem is vowel-initial rather than glottal stop-initial can be seen by examining possessive forms. The first person singular possessive prefix has the form *se-* before a consonant-initial stem. This is illustrated in [ia]. In [ib] and [ic], it is shown that when a stem begins with a glottal stop, the first person singular prefix also is *se-*, as expected.

[i] a.	setthí	'my head'
b.	ʔelá	'boat'
	seʔeláé	'my boat'
c.	ʔudáa	'jackfish'
	seʔudáá	'my jackfish'

Before a vowel-initial stem, the vowel of the prefix is deleted. This is shown by the form in [ii].

[ii]	sundie	'my older brother'
	/se + undie/	

/undie/ thus is a vowel-initial stem, since it allows prefix vowel deletion, a rule that does not apply when a consonant-initial stem is present.

7. The word *dene* 'person, man' historically consists of a noun stem **ne* with a prefix *də-*. The final vowel does not pattern as a stem vowel in Slave but has been reanalyzed as a suffix. A number of phonological arguments suggest this. First, in stems, the vowel *e* (phonetic [ɛ]) must be in a closed syllable; it occurs in an open syllable only in affixes. If *dene* were an unsuffixed form, it would be a counterexample to this generalization. Second, as is discussed in section 3, vowel deletion does not occur when a stem vowel is involved. The possessed form of this word is *-dené,* with vowel deletion, suggesting again that *-e* is a suffix. Thus, from phonological evidence it seems clear that the historical stem vowel of **ne* has been reanalyzed as the suffix.

8. Recall from note 6 that when the first of two adjacent vowels is in a prefix, that vowel deletes.

9. When the possessive suffix *-é* and the diminutive suffix *-ah* are present, the vowel of the possessive is deleted. However, its high tone remains and this tone appears on the stem vowel. Because tones reassociate to the left in Slave, the fact that the tone of the possessive suffix occurs on the stem vowel further supports the ordering of possessive inside diminutive.

10. See Hargus 1985 for some discussion of the complexities of vowel deletion.

11. The nominalizer and tense/mode/aspect clitics do not co-occur.

12. The underlying representations given here have been simplified so that irrelevant morphology is not indicated. See Rice (in press) for details of verb morphology.

13. It has been suggested to me that the diminutive is actually a clitic rather than a suffix. Evidence discussed in section 1 argues against this analysis. Furthermore,

because the diminutive does not pattern like the vowel-initial clitics with respect to vowel deletion, two levels of postlexical clitics would be required to account for the patterning of vowel deletion.

14. In this note, I will point out several forms that appear to be counterexamples to this claim.

Hargus (1985) argues that nasalization must be a cyclic rule in Sekani. The argument for this comes from doubly possessed nouns. Certain nouns in Slave and other Athapaskan languages are inalienably possessed, requiring a prefixal or nominal possessor. To show possession of these nouns by other than their natural owner, a double possessive construction is used, as in [i].

[i]	**a.** ˀeghú ˀe- unspecified possessor + ghu 'tooth' + ´ possessive	'a tooth'
	b. seˀeghú se- 'my' + ˀe- unspecified possessor + ghu 'tooth' + ´ possessive	'a tooth of mine (in my possession)'

If there is no possessive suffix on the inalienably possessed noun, one occurs on in the double possessive construction, as shown in [ii].

[ii]	**a.** ˀet'oh ˀe- unspecified possessor + t'oh 'nest'	'a nest'
	b. seˀet'ohé	'a nest of mine'

The problem pointed out by Hargus is that when a nasal-final noun is in a doubly possessed construction with the suffix *-é,* nasalization still occurs, as in [iii].

[iii]	**a.** ˀet'ǫ́	'leaf'
	b. seˀet'ǫ́é	'my leaf'

This, she argues, shows the need for the cycle, with the following derivation.

[iv]	t'ón	
	[ˀe[t'ón]]	possessive word formation
	[ˀe[t'ǫ́]]	nasalization
	[se]ˀe[t'ǫ́]]é]	possessive word formation

If nasalization is noncyclic, **seˀet'óné* would result.

This same form occurs in Slave. However, other nasal-final stems pattern differently. For instance, in the following form the cyclic hypothesis makes the wrong prediction.

[v]	ˀetthę́	'meat'
	seˀetthéné	'my meat'

Clearly the same explanation will not account for both of these forms. If [iiib] is the anomaly, then there is no evidence for the cyclicity of nasalization. If [v] is the anomaly, then one might propose that resyllabification is blocked by a double bracketing]].

In a number of words, nasalized vowels occur before another vowel. Some of these are shown in [vi].

[vi]	**a.** kų́e	'house'
	b. -lį́é	'dog'
	c. t'ahsį́i	'something'
	d. k'álalį́i	'willow buds'

In (via), a stem formative suffix *-e* occurs. The possessive *-é* is found in [vib] and a suffix *-i* in [vic] and [vid]. The facts in [via] and [vib] can be accounted for if the underlying representations for the roots (nonsuffixed forms) are of the following form.

[vii]

When the suffix is added and syllabification occurs, the following forms arise.

[viii]

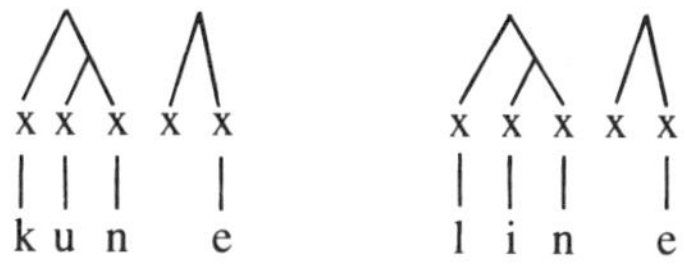

The *n* will stay in the first syllable and nasalization will occur. This same analysis is also available for the form in [iii].

Examples (*vic*) and (*vid*) have the suffix *-i*. While this is historically the nominalizer, it is nonproductive with these forms today. These forms appear to have the following representations after syllabification.

[ix]

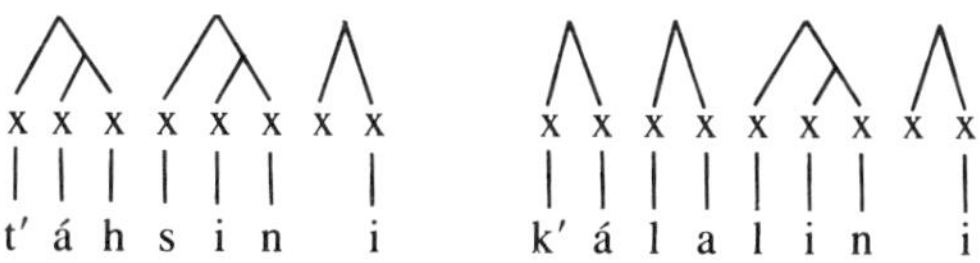

The extra onset point blocks resyllabification, allowing nasalization to apply. Interestingly, there is historical evidence supporting this proposal. In the Hare dialect of Slave, the nominalizer is *-yi* instead of *-i*. In Fort Nelson, this "consonant-initial" form is retained in frozen forms, but it is restructured to vowel-initial in its productive use. See Rice (in press) for discussion.

REFERENCES

Clements, G. N., and S. J. Keyser. 1983. *CV Phonology: A Generative Theory of the Syllable*. Linguistic Inquiry Monograph 9. Cambridge: MIT Press.

Hargus, S. 1985. *The Lexical Phonology of Sekani*. Ph.D. Diss., University of California, Los Angeles.

Kaye, J., and J. Lowenstamm. 1985. Compensatory Lengthening in Tiberian

Hebrew. In *Studies on Compensatory Lengthening*. E. Sezer and L. Wetzels, eds., Dordrecht, Holland: Foris Publications.

Kiparsky, P. 1985. Some Consequences of Lexical Phonology. *Phonology Yearbook 2*, pp. 85–138.

Levin, J. 1983. Reduplication and Prosodic Structure. Unpublished ms.

Marantz, A. 1982. Re Reduplication. *Linguistic Inquiry* 13:435–82.

Rice, K. 1986. The Environment for Continuant Voicing in Some Athapaskan Languages. Paper presented at the Milwaukee Morphology Conference.

Rice, K. in press. *A Grammar of Slave (Dene)*. Mouton Language Library. Berlin: Mouton de Gruyter.

Steriade, D. 1982. *Greek Prosodies and the Nature of Syllabification Processes*. Ph.D. Diss., Massachusettes Institute of Technology.

Zwicky, A., and G. Pullum. 1983. Inflection versus cliticization: English *n't*. *Language*, 59:502–13.

ARTICULATORY AND ACOUSTIC CORRELATES OF PHARYNGEALIZATION: EVIDENCE FROM ATHAPASKAN

Eung-Do Cook

INTRODUCTION

It is well known that a particular distinctive feature may have more than one articulatory or acoustic correlate, or conversely, a given articulatory gesture or acoustic impression may be attributable to more than one distinctive feature. For example, the feature [flat], as it was originally proposed by Jakobson, Fant, and Halle (1952), was supposed to be realized by one of three different secondary articulations; namely, labialization, velarization, and pharyngealization, which are mutually exclusive of a given phonological system. While neither the claim about the distribution of these secondary articulations nor the distinctive feature [flat] itself is a serious issue nowadays, the phonetic mechanism involved in pharyngealization has attracted considerable attention ever since the proposal by Stewart (1967) for a feature involving the position of the tongue root, i.e. [advanced tongue root] or [ATR].

Phonological study also is concerned with the relationship between phonological segments or features in a sequence. I am particularly interested here in how a given distinctive feature or a set of features interacts with another feature or set of features; i.e. how a distinctive feature is implemented by different articulatory means or has different acoustic effects in different phonological contexts. Note that I am not concerned about what is known as phonotactics or sequential constraints nor about general phonological processes, most of which are assimilatory. The best analogy I may draw from segmental phonology is what is umlaut for vowels is palatalization for consonants ([+high] and [−back] being the most relevant distinctive features for both processes), although the phonetic implementation of whatever distinctive feature is associated with pharyngealization is much more complex than what is involved in umlaut and palatalization. The relationship between the distinctive feature involving pharyngealization and its phonetic correlates will not be adequately determined until more details are known of its articulatory (physiological) and acoustic characteristics.[1]

The proposal for a distinctive feature, such as [ATR] referring to the tongue root position, [wide] or [expanded] referring to the pharyngeal cavity, is based on the well-documented articulatory mechanism for which there is little difference from language to language. But the same is not true of what appear to be acoustic correlates of pharyngealization, which include pitch, phonation type/voice quality, voicing, and tensity. While I am unable to offer unequivocal evidence for the establishment of a particular distinctive feature for pharyngealization or all of its acoustic correlates, a new set of data from Athapaskan will add another dimension to the ongoing research and eventually contribute to the resolution of the complex problem; i.e. the phonological relationship of pharyngealization vis à vis other distinctive features in a system as well as the possible range of articulatory and acoustic correlates as manifested on the synchronic level and in diachronic processes.

This paper is organized as follows. Sections 1 and 2 are concerned with the tongue root feature as applied to the analysis of West African vowel harmony and Mon-Khmer register. It will be shown how the so-called voice qualities (phonation types) are correlated with two sets of harmonic vowels on the one hand and two voice registers on the other. Section 3 shows that the two voice qualities in Jalapa Mazatec (of the Popolocan family in Mexico), which are similar to those in Mon-Khmer and African languages, are not attributable to pharyngealization but to laryngealization. Section 4 shows how an analysis involving two syllable types (fortis versus lenis) in British Columbia Athapaskan, such as Babine and Carrier,[2] contributes to our knowledge of the tongue root feature. Finally, Section 5 offers a brief discussion of a number of phonetic effects of pharyngealization, as revealed in both synchronic and diachronic processes in different languages, and the significance of the tongue root feature as applied to the analysis of seemingly unrelated phonological phenomena.

1. VOWEL HARMONY IN WEST AFRICAN LANGUAGES

The recent phonetic studies of the West African languages, particularly those by Stewart (1967), Ladefoged (1968), and Lindau (1974) have offered convincing evidence that the phonetic mechanism for the well-known vowel harmony in such languages as Twi, Fante, Igbo, and Akan, etc. is the position of the tongue root. For one set of vowels, the tongue root is advanced widening the pharyngeal cavity, and for another set, the tongue root is retracted narrowing the pharyngeal cavity. Using the feature [ATR], Stewart (1967) presents the two sets of Akan vowels.

[1] Akan vowels

a. Advanced Tongue Root ([+ATR]): i, e, ɜ, o, u.

b. Retracted Tongue Root ([−ATR]): ɪ, ɛ, a, ɔ, ʊ.

Such terminological preferences as *Wide* (Ladefoged 1972) and *Expanded* (Lindau 1978) to *Advanced Tongue Root* suggest that the crucial articulatory correlates for the feature in question is the relative width of the pharyngeal cavity, which is controlled primarily by the relative tongue root position. But, an important question that still remains unanswered is whether the phonological contrast is basically bilateral or multilateral. At least three different tongue root positions can be readily recognized: neutral, advanced, and retracted. In most languages, however, phonological contrast is between the neutral (normal) tongue root position and the retracted tongue position (pharyngealized), although in some Mon-Khmer languages the contrast may be between the neutral and the advanced tongue positions.[3] In any case, I shall be concerned in this paper with the pharyngeal cavity narrowed by the retracted tongue root; i.e. pharyngealization.

Another phenomenon often associated with the two categories of vowels is the so-called phonation types or voice qualities. Sapir (1931) observed in Gweabo, a West African language of the Niger-Congo family, a 'muffled' voice quality in one set of vowels and a 'bright' quality in another set. These two voice qualities or phonation types are essentially identical to what Berry (1955) and Tucker (1936) observed in other West African languages. The correlation between the vowel qualities and voice qualities (phonation types) can be summarized as follows:

[2]	**a.** [+ATR/+wide]:	i e ɜ o u	dull, breathy, muffled
	b. [−ATR/−wide]:	ɪ ɛ a ɔ ʊ	bright, tight, creaky

It is not clear what phonological function the phonation types play in the West African languages, but contrastive function of the similar phenomena is well established in the Mon-Khmer languages.

2. VOICE REGISTERS IN THE MON-KHMER LANGUAGES

Apparently inspired by Stewart's analysis of Akan vowel harmony, Gregerson (1976) introduced the tongue root feature in the Mon-Khmer languages in order to describe two contrastive syllable types, which are characterized by two distinct phonation types or voice qualities as well as vowel qualities. These two types of syllables are known (after Henderson 1952) as registers or voice registers. According to Gregerson (1976, 1980), the phonetic basis for these contrastive syllable types is the tongue root: the retracted tongue root for the first register and the advanced (or perhaps neutral) tongue root for the second register. In Rengao, according to Gregerson (1980), there are five vowel qualities, each of which is distinguished by the tongue root feature/pharyngeal cavity, just like the two sets of vowels in Akan and other West African languages.[4]

[3] Rengao Vowels:

a. Advanced Tongue Root (second register): i, e, ə, o, u.
b. Retracted Tongue Root (first register): ei, ɛ, a, ɔ, ou.

Furthermore, each of the two sets characterized by the pharyngeal cavity is mutually exclusive of the other in a given word, i.e. there are two sets of harmonic vowels just as in the West African languages. What is more remarkable is the articulatory and acoustic correlates of the two registers in Mon-Khmer, which is summarized by Gregerson as follows:

[4] Mon-Khmer Registers:

Register:	Initial C:	Voice quality (phonation):	Vowel quality:	Pitch:
First RTR	surds ([−voiced])	clear normal tense	more open on-glided	higher
Second ATR	sonants ([+voiced])	deep breathy relaxed	close centering diphthongs	lower

Putting aside the initial consonant, which will be taken up shortly, the first register is characterized by the more open and lower vowel qualities and higher pitch as well as the clear normal voice quality (phonation type), whereas the second register is characterized by the higher and closer vowel qualities, lower pitch, and the deep breathy phonation type. Considering the tongue root feature as the phonetic basis for the two contrastive syllable types, Gregerson calls the first register "retracted tongue root prosody" and the second register "advanced tongue root prosody." Consequently, Gregerson recognizes only five instead of ten vowels for Rengao, where pharyngealization (i.e. retracted tongue root) or the lack of it is taken to be a prosodic feature whose domain is the word. This treatment of the pharyngeal feature is consistent with the view that the registers primarily distinguished by phonation types are *contrastive,* which of course means that the open and close vowel qualities are ancillary and incidental to the syllable type, i.e. prosody.

To put it in terms of autosegmental phonology, the pharyngeal cavity feature constitutes an autosegmental tier.

A much more interesting phonetic correlate of the Mon-Khmer registers is the diachronic developments in the environment of voiced versus voiceless syllable initial consonants. The initial consonant in [4] refers to the original (written) consonant: voiceless for the first register (RTR) and voiced for the second register (ATR). It is well documented that vowels occurring in syllables with originally voiceless initials have become more open, lower, and/or tense, while originally voiced syllable initials have induced no such vocalic change, e.g. (Diffloth 1982):

[5] **a.** *gɔk → kɔk
b. *kɔk → kak

As will be shown shortly, a synchronic analogue of this diachronic relationship between the initial consonant type and the vowel quality is found in the Athapaskan languages of British Columbia. It is particularly interesting to note the close relationship between the pharyngeal mechanism and the laryngeal mechanism (voicelessness, higher pitch), observed among languages that are related neither genetically nor geographically. Before presenting Athapaskan material, I shall briefly comment on Jalapa Mazatec, where it appears that the three distinct phonation types have nothing to do with the pharyngeal cavity/tongue root feature.

3. VOICE QUALITIES IN JALAPA MAZATEC

According to a recent paper by Kirk, Ladefoged, and Ladefoged (1984), the syllable phonology of Jalapa Mazatec is quite complex. It has "three contrastive pitch levels and glides between them."[5] Nasalization is phonemic for vowels. In addition to these, this language "makes use of three contrastive types of phonation," which are exemplified by the following.

[6]	Phonation type:	Modal [V]:		Creaky [V̰]:		Breathy [V̤]:	
	Examples	[ja^{1}]	'tree'	[ja̰^{2}]	'he carries'	[ja̤^{2}]	'he wears'
		[nt^{h}æ^{3}]	'seed'	[ndæ̰^{3}]	'arse'	[ndæ̤^{3}]	'horse'

Where 1, 2, and 3 mark tone.

Where the normal type of voiced vowel is called *modal voice*, the authors attempt to define phonological representations of creaky voice and breathy voice. Putting details aside, they conclude that breathy voice is represented by /h/ in the context (C)C__V, and creaky voice by /ʔ/ in the context (C) C , e.g.
[+voice]

[7] a.	Creaky voice:	/nˀu^{1}/	[nṵ̃^{1}]	'vine'
	ʔ/(C)C_V	/kˀã^{2}/	[kã̰^{2}]	'alone'
b.	Breathy voice:	/mhæ^{2}/	[mæ̤^{2}]	'he wants'
	h/(C) C _V [+voice]	/jha^{2}/	[ja̤^{2}]	'he wears'

In addition to these synchronic accounts of creaky voice and breathy voice, an analogous diachronic account is given for the emergence of the breathy type from disyllabics as illustrated by the following examples.

	Disyllabic: Proto-Mazatec *(C)CvdV.hV		Monosyllabic: Mazatec (C)CvdhV(V)		
[8] a.	*me^{3}he^{2}	——————→	/mhæ^{2}/	[mæ̤^{2}]	'he wants'
b.	*nt^{y}a^{4}hu^{4}	———→ ntiho ——→	/ndhio^{3}/	[ndi̤o̤^{3}]	'stone'

Given these analyses, voice quality of phonation type has nothing to do with pharyngealization, but it is clearly attributable to laryngealization: /ʔ/ for creaky voice and /h/ for breathy voice, the latter of which is essentially identical to the case of the second register in Mon-Khmer and the former to the creaky vowel of Tsmishian (Dunn & Hays 1983) and the constricted vowel of Proto-Athapaskan (see Krauss 1978; Cook 1981). Needless to say, the three phonation types in Jalapa Mazatec are not contrastive at the phonemic level where they are represented by laryngeals.

4. FORTIS AND LENIS TYPES OF SYLLABLE IN BABINE AND CARRIER

Babine, an Athapaskan language of interior British Columbia, closely related to Carrier, has a typical Athapaskan phonemic inventory. It has a core obstruent system with three sets of occlusive obstruents (plain, aspirated, and glottalized) and two sets of nonocclusive obstruents (voiceless and voiced). One bilabial *b*, two nasals *m* and *n*, and laryngeals ʔ and *h* are peripheral members of the consonantal system. The vocalic system consists of the most typical qualities of a five vowel system plus schwa. As far as the segmental inventories are concerned, there is nothing of particular interest. However, Story (1984), in her most illuminating study of Babine phonology, observes a very interesting phonological process by which the consonants are divided into two natural classes: the fortis class and the lenis class. The fortis class includes the aspirated and glottalized occlusives, voiceless continuants and laryngeals, and the lenis class consists of the remaining consonants, i.e. the plain occlusives, nasals, and voiced continuants. With this classification in mind, the Babine consonants are arranged as in [9].

[9] Babine Consonants:

a.	b	d	dl	dz	g/dž	G	Gʷ	
b.		t	tł	ts	k/tš	q	qʷ	
c.		t′	tł′	ts′	k′/tš′	q′	q′ʷ	ʔ
d.			ł	s	x	x̣	x̣ʷ	h
e.	m	n	l	z	y	γ	w	

Fortis class: b, c, d.
Lenis class: a, e.

This fortis-lenis classification of Babine consonants is based on the vowel allophony. According to Story, each of the six vowel phonemes has a higher allophone (closed) and lower allophone (open) following a lenis syllable initial and a fortis syllable initial, respectively. The two vowel qualities conditioned by the two classes of initial consonants are summarized in [10].

[10]	**a.** Lenis syllable:	i	e	æ	o	u	ə
	b. Fortis syllable:	ẹ	ɛ	a	ɔ	ọ	ʌ
		1	2	3	4	5	6

One might be tempted to define the alternating vowel qualities for each of the six vowel phonemes in terms of tongue height or tenseness, as some Africanists attempted to describe the two sets of harmonic vowels in the West African languages. But, Story points out that [ẹ] of /i/ is lower and more back than [e] of /e/ and [ọ] of /u/ is lower than [o] of /o/, which clearly indicates that the characteristic of the two alternating vowel sets cannot be described adequately only in terms of the two tongue features, namely tongue heights and tongue positions (front versus back). Although Story does not make reference to the retracted tongue root or pharyngealization or to voice qualities, I have no doubt in my mind from my experience with "flattened" vowels in Chilcotin (see Cook 1983) and "retracted vowels" in Interior Salish (see Cook 1985), that the phonetic basis for the vowel quality in the fortis syllable is the retracted tongue root–narrowed pharyngeal cavity. Then, it is clear that what is described for Babine in terms of fortis-lenis syllable types is analogous to what is described in terms of first and second registers for Mon-Khmer. Not surprisingly, Story also observed that pitch is lower for the lenis syllable and higher for the fortis syllable. The phonetic correlates of the two types of syllables are now summarized in [11].

	Syllable type:	Initial C:	Vowel quality:	Pitch:
[11]	**a.** [+RTR]	fortis	open, lower	higher
	b. [−RTR]	lenis	close, higher	lower

The vocalic alternations observed in Babine are not restricted to the phonetic level (allophonic); the same principle is observed on the phonological level (morphophonemic) as well as in diachronic processes. As shown in [10], each of the six Babine vowel phonemes has two mutually exclusive allophones occurring in the fortis syllable and lenis syllable, respectively. Taking those given in [10a] as underlying, the six vowel phonemes of Babine are *i, e, a, o, u,* and *ə*. Of these vowel phonemes, *i, e,* and *a* constitute two sets with *e* being a member of either set in the phonologically conditioned morphophonemic alternations exemplified in [12].

[12] a.	e/a:	b-en	'his mother'	s-an	'my mother'
		b-eq'əy	'his aunt'	s-aq'əy	'my aunt'
b.	i/e:	b-ini	'his brain'	s-eni[sɛni]	'my brain'
		bə-zi	'his belt'	se [sɛ]	'belt'
		s-γi	'my grease'	xe [xɛ]	'grease'

It is understandable why schwa is not involved in a similar alternation, but strangely there is no u/o alternation, e.g. *b-undi* 'his older brother' **b-ondi* and *s-undi* 'my older brother' **s-ondi*. It is clear, however, that the alternating vowel heights are conditioned by the same initial consonant classes. These synchronic morphophonemic alternations must be vestiges of more general diachronic processes, which Story calls *F-mutation* (lowering by fortis initials) and *L-mutation* (raising by lenis initials). The following examples illustrate how the four Proto-Athapaskan full vowels have developed into Babine by F-mutation and L-mutation. Notice that PA high vowels are F-mutated, and PA low vowels are L-mutated.

[13] a. F-mutation:

	F-initial		L-initial (no change):	
PA *i → Babine əy	səy[6]	'I'	-dis	'turn'
	ts'əy	'canoe'	-ni	'say'
PA *u → Babine o	to	'water'	nu	'island'
	ɬod	'scab'	-γu	'tooth'
	tɬ'oɬ	'rope'	-yuɬ	'blow'

b. L-mutation:

	L-initial		F-initial (no change):	
PA *e → Babine i	-di	'horn'	ɬes	'flour'
	-γis	'egg'	qe	'foot'
	dzin	'day'	t'es	'charcoal'
PA *a → Babine e	-de	'lip'	tsa	'beaver'
	-le	'hand'	-ˀad	'wife'
	ye	'louse'	sa	'sun'

Assuming now Story's term fortis–lenis is interchangeable with tense–lax, consider what features are necessary to specify the five sets of Babine consonants as well as the vocalic alternations. If [tense] is used to specify the fortis–lenis classes of consonants, sets (b), (c), and (d) are specified as [+tense] as against other sets that are [−tense]. Putting nasals aside, no other feature is necessary to distinguish (d) from (e), but another feature is required to distinguish phonemically (b) from (c), since both are [+tense]. As far as phonemic opposition is concerned either [aspiration] or [glottalization] may be chosen, but in either case, voicing is redundant.

5. SUMMARY AND DISCUSSION

The choice of tense–lax feature for Babine is significant not only for the description of Babine phonology, but also for general theoretical considerations, since this feature still remains poorly understood despite the amount of research and discussion it has been accorded. One of the important works dealing with this feature is Kim's study (1965) of Korean stops, whose three-way phonemic opposition is quite comparable to that of Babine and Athapaskan in general. While the plain and aspirated series are essentially identical in the two languages, the third series in Korean phonetically is not quite the same as the glottalized series of Babine. Nonetheless, "tensity is the primary feature" for Korean, Kim concludes, as it is for Babine, demonstrated by the phonological processes of all levels both in synchronic and diachronic processes.

More recently, subsequent to the proposal for the tongue root feature–pharyngeal cavity, it has been questioned whether the pharyngeal cavity feature (tongue root) may replace the tensity feature, i.e. whether these two features have the same phonetic mechanism (see Halle & Stevens 1969; Lindau 1974). For Babine, tensity has two different effects on the vowel: for the phonological (i.e. morphophonemic) alternation, it simply means lowering the tongue height from high to mid or from mid to low; for the phonetic (i.e. allophonic) alternation, it means retracting the tongue root, which automatically lowers the tongue height. Since lowering the tongue height does not necessarily retract the tongue root, the tongue root feature is necessary to describe the vowel allophony. The diachronic changes and synchronic alternations of Babine vowels conditioned by syllable-initial tense consonants suggest the following sequence of events: first the tense consonants encouraged the tongue height to be lowered (diachronic process), then the lowering effect was further intensified to push back the tongue root (synchronic pharyngealization). Viewed in this way, tensity has two very closely related phonetic correlates that do not have the same phonetic mechanism.

I have already commented on the similarity between the registers (phonation types) of Mon-Khmer and the fortis-lenis syllable types of Babine. Diffloth (1982) makes the following statement about the historical developments of Mon-Khmer registers:

> Several of its languages have contrastive phonation types, usually clear voice vs. breathy voice, accompanied or not by pitch contrasts. Several more languages used to have such register contrasts in the past, which have now given way to tone or aspiration contrasts, as in standard Thai, or to vowel distortions, as in the case of Khmer.

If this sequence of events indeed is a reality of the Southeast Asian languages, part of this diachronic process, which Thai has undergone, is reversed in Babine, where it was shown that the tense-lax contrasts in Babine consonants have given way to two types of syllables that are virtually identical to Mon-Khmer registers with alternating vowel qualities and pitch levels. Although Story does not mention phonation types, she mentions the difference of pitch level in the two types of syllables: lower for the lenis syllable and higher for the fortis syllable. Considering this fact, it is quite conceivable that the fortis syllable has a tense voice and lenis syllable a lax voice, which is observed in many Mon-Khmer languages (Gregerson 1976). As mentioned earlier, syllable initial voiceless consonants in Mon-Khmer cause the lowering of vowels. According to Diffloth, the initial consonants that ''distorted'' vowel qualities include not only the voiceless stops but also implosives. He questions why the voiceless stops and implosives that are *voiced* constitute a natural class. From what is observed in Babine and from Kim's analysis of Korean (the third series of which are apparently similar to the implosives of the Southeast Asian languages), it is obviously the tensity, rather than voicing, of the consonants which may be voiceless, aspirated, or implosive.

Returning now to Babine and Carrier, these languages are very closely related and were considered until recently dialects of one language. These two languages have virtually identical inventories of vowels and consonants, and the consonants of Carrier also constitute two natural classes exactly as the Babine consonants do, with the exception of /ʔ/, which belongs to the lenis class in Carrier but to the fortis class in Babine. This subclassification of Carrier consonants, however, is not motivated by any allophonic variations of vowels but by pitch variations. No significant vowel allophony has been reported on Carrier, but according to Story (1986), ''in analogous environments, the pitch of a syllable with a fortis onset is higher than the pitch of a syllable with a lenis onset.'' The correlation between the initial consonant type and pitch level is obvious not only in these two Athapaskan languages but also in the Mon-Khmer languages, as discussed earlier. Considering the phonetic characteristics of the initial consonants, i.e. tense/lax, voiceless/voiced, aspirated/unaspirated, glottalized/plain, etc., and pitch level, it is quite obvious that the laryngeal mechanism is involved in this correlation. What is not obvious, however, is the behavior of /ʔ/. Why does it belong to opposite classes in Babine and Carrier—two very closely related languages? Also, in final position, /ʔ/ has left opposite effects in different Athapaskan languages, developing into high tone in some languages and low tone in others. A similar phenomenon, known as tonal flip-flop, is observed in other languages, but no plausible explanation is available. The pharyngealization of Babine vowels is obviously a synchronic analogue of the diachronic vocalic distortion of Mon-Khmer, which suggests that the tensity of initial consonants may constitute a necessary but not sufficient condition for the pharyngealization of vowels, as witnessed in Babine and Carrier. But then, what constitutes a sufficient condition? The interaction between the laryngeal mechanism and pharyngeal mechanism probably holds a key to the right answer.

NOTES

I wish to thank Stephen R. Anderson for information on further references and John J. Colarusso, Jr., who has probably done the most extensive research on pharyngealization, for copies of his work, including his dissertation entitled ''The Northwest Caucasian Languages: A Phonological Survey,'' Harvard University, 1975. One of the highlights of Colarusso's study is the proposal for a distinctive feature, [constricted pharynx] (CP), which is required, along with [advanced tongue root] (ATR), to account for the phonemic contrasts of Ubykh velars and uvulars. From this study, however, it is difficult to determine what systematic correlation obtains for the Northwest Caucasian languages between pharyngealized consonants and vocalic qualities, which is one of the main concerns of this paper.

I gratefully acknowledge the support of the Calgary Institute for the Humanities, of which I was an Annual Fellow while working on the final version of this paper.

1. See Halle (1983) for a theoretical model that is an explicit attempt to determine the precise relationship between a distinctive feature and its articulatory correlate(s).

2. The consonants of Chilcotin, another Athapaskan language in British Columbia, include subclasses based on the tongue root feature, whose affects on vowel allophony are virtually identical to those of Babine; see Cook (1983).

3. See Gregerson (1976). Gregerson does not interpret the phenomenon as I have, but what he calls *abnormal auditory impression* (phonation type) is due to either the advanced tongue root position in some language or retracted tongue root position in others.

4. Each of the two diagraphs in [3b] apparently represents a phonetically complex but phonemically simple vowel. Gregerson (1976) does not offer an explicit phonetic description of these vowels, but from what I know of the pharyngealized vowels in other languages, these vowels must have an on-glide; i.e. [^{e}i̯] and [^{o}u̯].

5. I might hazard a guess that ''glides between them'' probably means contour tones, falling and rising from and to any two level tones.

6. The phonological status of /əy/ is somewhat ambiguous. Story (1984, 35–40) states that [ʌ^{i}], which represents /əy/ in the fortis syllable, derives from Proto-Athapaskan ''*i occurring in open stem syllables or in stem syllables with syllable-

final ʔ, h, or x. . ." Diphthongs with an off-glide are extremely rare; more frequently found in other Athapaskan languages are [ᵊi], or [ᵊe] with an on-glide, which are interpreted phonemically as monophthongs /i/ and /e/, respectively. Where an off-glide occurs following a full vowel, however, as in [aⁱ], [eⁱ], and [aᵘ], the glides in the phonemic interpretations (/ay, ey, aw/) are considered as true consonants, not only because /y/ frequently alternates with /ž/, but also /y/ and /w/ pattern as the voiced counterparts of /š/ and /xʷ/, respectively. See Cook (1977) for further discussion.

REFERENCES

Berry, J. 1955. Some Notes on the Phonology of the Nzema and Ahnta Dialects. *Bulletin of the School of Oriental and African Studies* 17:160–65.

Colarusso, J., Jr. 1975. The Northwest Caucasian Languages: A Phonological Survey. Ph.D. Diss., Harvard University.

Cook, E.-D. 1977. Syllable Weight in Three Northern Athapaskan Languages. *International Journal of American Linguistics* 43:259–68.

Cook, E.-D. 1981. Athapaskan Linguistics: Proto-Athapaskan Phonology. *Annual Review of Anthropology* 10:253–73.

Cook, E.-D. 1983. Chilcotin Flattening. *Canadian Journal of Linguistics* 28:123–32.

Cook, E.-D. 1985. Pharyngealization in the Northwestern Languages. Paper presented at 24th Conference on American Indian Languages. Washington, D.C. December.

Diffloth, G. 1982. Proto-Mon Registers: Two, Three, Four . . .? *Proceedings of the Eighth Annual Meeting of the Berkeley Linguistics Society* 8:148–57.

Dunn, J., and R. A. Hayes. 1983. Tsimshian Uvular Syllables. *International Journal of American Linguistics* 49:46–63.

Gregerson, K. 1976. Tongue-Root and Register in Mon-Khmer. In *Austroasiatic Studies, Part I,* P. Jenners, et al., eds., pp. 323–69. Oceanic Linguistics Special Publication no. 13. Honolulu: University of Hawaii.

Gregerson, K. 1980. Pharynx Symbolism and Rengao Phonology. Unpublished ms.

Halle, M. 1983. On Distinctive Features and Their Articulatory Implementation. *Natural Language and Linguistic Theory* 1:91–104.

Halle, M., and K. N. Stevens. 1969. On the Feature "Advanced Tongue Root." MIT. *Quarterly Progress Reports* 94:209–15.

Henderson, E. J. A. 1952. The Main Features of Cambodian Pronunciation. *Bulletin of the School of Oriental and African Studies* 14:149–74.

Jakobson, R., C. G. M. Fant, and M. Halle. 1952. *Preliminaries to Speech Analysis.* MIT Acoustic Laboratory Technical Report no. 13.

Kim, C.-W. 1965. On the Autonomy of the Tensity Feature in Stop Classification (with Special Reference to Korean Stops). *Word* 21:339–59.

Kirk, P. L., P. Ladefoged, and J. Ladefoged. 1984. Phonological Representation of Breathy and Creaky Voice in Jalapa Mazatec. Paper presented at the Annual Meeting of the American Anthropological Association, Denver, Colorado.

Krauss, M. E. 1978. Athapaskan Tone. Unpublished ms.

Ladefoged, P. 1968. *A Phonetic Study of West African Languages*. 2d ed. Cambridge: Cambridge University Press.

Ladefoged, P. 1972. Phonological Features and Their Phonetic Correlates. *Journal of the International Phonetic Association* 2:2–12.

Lindau, M. 1974. The Feature Advanced Tongue Root. In *Third Annual Conference on African Linguistics*, E. Voeltz ed. Bloomington: Indiana University Press.

Lindau, M. 1978. Vowel features. *Language* 54:541–63.

Sapir, E. 1931. Notes on the Gweabo language of Liberia. *Language* 7:30–41.

Stewart, J. M. 1967. Tongue Root Position in Akan Vowel Harmony. *Phonetica* 16:185–204.

Story, G. 1984. *Babine and Carrier Phonology: A Historically Oriental Study*. Summer Institute of Linguistics and University of Texas at Arlington.

Story, G. 1986. A Preliminary Report on the Nature of Central Carrier with a Section on Verb Prefix Tonomechanics. Unpublished ms.

Tucker, A. N. 1936. The Function of Voice Quality in Nilotic Languages. In *Proceedings of the Second International Congress of Phonetic Sciences*, D. Jones and D. B. Fry, eds., pp. 125–28. Cambridge: Cambridge University Press.

Part Two

THE MORPHO-SYNTAX OF COMPLEX VERBAL MORPHOLOGY

AGREEMENT IN DOGRIB: INFLECTION OR CLITICIZATION?

Leslie Saxon

INTRODUCTION

A number of proposals have been made about the syntactic structure of sentences containing verbs marked with pronominal agreement when there is no lexical NP in the sentence corresponding to the agreement morphology. Thus, for the Dogrib sentence [1],

[1] Done nà*se*nįįht'ih.
person ls-3-PF-punch
'A person punched me.'

where the italicized *se-* is first person singular non-subject agreement, syntactic analyses like those in [2] and [3] might be put forward.

[2] [$_S$ [$_{NP}$ done] [$_{VP}$ [$_{NP}$ se-] [$_V$ nànįįht'ih]]]

[3] [$_S$ [$_{NP}$ done] [$_{VP}$ [$_{NP}$] [$_V$ nàsenįįht'ih]]]

Examples [2] and [3] differ in whether the object NP node is considered to be empty in the syntactic component of grammar. I call [2] the *incorporation analysis*. According to this type of analysis, the NP node is considered to be filled at S-structure, though its contents is incorporated into the verb at a later stage of the derivation of the sentence. The analysis of Breton in Anderson (1982) is this type of analysis.[1] I call [3] the *empty category analysis*. According to this analysis, the object NP node is considered to be empty throughout the syntactic derivation of the sentence.[2]

As will be shown in the next section of this paper, the empty category analysis of Dogrib poses a problem for Government–Binding Theory (Chomsky 1981; 1982), specifically for the principle of the Functional Determination of Empty Categories. The following section explores the possibility of adopting the incorporation analysis for non-subject NPs in Dogrib. Adopting this analysis, it is possible to avoid the problem alluded to previously. Although morphological facts initially support the incorporation analysis, conflicting syntactic facts will be presented that lead to rejecting it. Next, the sentences under discussion will be shown to indeed contain syntactic NP nodes problematic for Functional Determination. Assuming the Projection Principle, the NPs that are empty under the empty category analysis will be shown to be arguments, that is, they will be shown to have theta roles associated with them. In the final section of the paper, a solution to the problem is presented, the rejection of the Functional Determination of Empty Categories as a principle for the classification of empty categories. Instead, I propose that empty categories are inherently specified for the features previously determined contextually, namely [±anaphor] and [±pronominal], just as they may be inherently specified for features of person, number, etc. This conclusion thus matches conclusions reached by Brody (1984) and Safir (1984), who both argue for the abandonment of the principle of Functional Determination.

1. THE PROBLEM FOR THE FUNCTIONAL DETERMINATION OF EMPTY CATEGORIES

In this section, the empty category analysis of Dogrib is assumed. In the Government–Binding Theory, lexical pronouns are inherently specified as having either the features [+pronominal, −anaphor] or [−pronominal, +anaphor]. English *it* is a lexical pronominal; *themselves* is a lexical anaphor. The features [±pronominal] and [±anaphor] are attributed to phonologically empty NPs by another mechanism, the Functional Determination of Empty Categories (Chung 1982, after Chomsky 1982, 84). According to this principle, the details of which are shown in [4], these features of empty categories are determinable from context.

[4] *The Functional Determination of Empty Categories:*

a. If $[_{NP}\ ]$ is locally bound by an element in a non-theta position, then it is [−pronominal].
   (i) If [−pronominal] and A-bound, then [+anaphor]. (NP-trace)
   (ii) If [−pronominal] and A′-bound, then [−anaphor]. (variable)

b. If [$_{NP}$] is free or locally bound by an element in a theta position, then it is [+pronominal].
   (iii) If [+pronominal] and governed, then [−anaphor]. (pro)
   (iv) If [+pronominal] and ungoverned, then [+anaphor]. (PRO)

Once the features of empty NPs have been defined according to [4], the empty NPs are subject to the binding theory.

Functional Determination works to the extent that the empty category types it defines are mutually exclusive. If empty category types in certain contextual positions are not mutually exclusive, the system fails. The following Dogrib data will show that empty categories of either of two types may occur in any non-subject position. One solution to this problem is suggested in the section to follow, but eventually the principle of Functional Determination will be rejected altogether.

The Dogrib sentences in [5]–[9] contain empty categories, according to the empty category analysis.

[5] [$_{NP}$] nàˀedìik'è nàwìt'ah.
store ld-PF-go
'We've been to the store.'

[6] K'àowoh [$_{NP}$] ˀǫ̀gorèhde.
boss lp-3-PF-fire
'The boss fired us.'

[7] ˀeyi ts'ǫ̀ǫko [$_{NP}$] naxįts'ǫ̀ kàretla ha.
that old woman 2p-to 3-IMP-go out Fut
'That old woman will come out toward you.'

[8] John mbeh t'à [$_{NP}$] ˀedèhgo.
knife with Refl-3-PF-stab
'John stabbed himself with a knife.'

[9] ˀeyi done [$_{NP}$] ˀedets'ǫ̀ naìch'o.
that person Refl-to 3-IMP-be angry
'That guy is angry at himself.'

To submit these empty NPs to the binding theory, we need to determine their features of [±pronominal], [±anaphor]. With the assumption that an empty category in the subject position in Dogrib is governed by Inflection, not shown in [2] or [3], then under [4.b.iii], the empty category in [5] is defined as [+pronominal, −anaphor], or small *pro,* being free. With these features determined, it is simple to check that this empty category meets the requirements of the Binding Theory. Assuming that the empty categories in [6] and [7] are governed by the verb *ˀǫ̀gorèhde* and the postposition *naxįts'ǫ̀,* respectively, these nonsubject empty categories also fall under [4.b.iii] and are defined as small *pro,* [+pronominal, −anaphor]. Being free in their governing categories, these NPs also meet the requirements of the Binding Theory.

The problem arises with examples like [8] and [9]. Assuming that the empty categories in [8] and [9] are governed by the verb *ˀedèhgo* and the postposition *ˀedets'ǫ̀* respectively, each of these empty categories also falls under [4.b.iii], being governed and locally bound by an element in a theta position (namely, the subject in each sentence). They thus are defined as [+pronominal, −anaphor]. This result proves problematic when we come to the Binding Theory: the empty categories, defined as pronominals under Functional Determination, are not free in their governing categories but are bound. In fact, the only pure anaphors defined by the Functional Determination of Empty Categories are NP-trace: reflexive-type anaphors are predicted not to exist as empty categories. Yet in Dogrib and in other languages, for example Chamorro (Chung 1982), empty reflexive-type anaphors are permitted in any position under which they are sanctioned by the binding theory. These positions naturally overlap with positions in which empty pronominals (small *pro*) are permitted.

2. IS THERE A MORPHOLOGICAL SOLUTION?

Now, it could be coming clear how the incorporation analysis might dissolve the problem just noted for the Functional Determination of Empty Categories. If NP positions, especially non-subject NP positions, are not assumed to be empty but instead to be filled by syntactic pronouns, then the Functional Determination of Empty Categories is not involved in the specification of their features, and no problem arises. I will show now that even in a model with a fairly restricted view of what may qualify as a word-formation process outside of the lexicon, there is considerable initial plausibility on morphological grounds for treating non-subject agreement in Dogrib as pronoun incorporation, or cliticization, as I will refer to it henceforth.

Examples [10] and [11] show how [7] and [8] would be represented under the incorporation analysis.

[10] [ˀeyi ts'ǫ̀ǫko [$_{PP}$ [$_{NP}$ naxį-] -ts'ǫ̀] kàretla ha]

[11] [John mbeh t'à [$_{NP}$ ˀede-] [$_{V}$ -`hgo]]

There are no empty categories in these structures, hence no challenges to the principle of Functional Determination.

Under the assumption that the post-syntactic incorporation of pronouns is restricted to processes of cliticization,[3] can we justify calling the incorporated pronouns clitics on morphological grounds? As I will show, non-subject agreement in Dogrib has quite different morphological properties from subject agreement. Measured against Zwicky and Pullum's (1983) dichotomy between morphological processes of cliticization and inflection, non-subject agreement shows the morphological characteristics of cliticization, while subject agreement shows the characteristics of inflection.

Consider first Zwicky and Pullum's criterion of analyzability. According to this criterion, Zwicky and Pullum claim that only morphemes entering into word-formation processes in the lexicon (inflectional morphology, in their terminology) may be realized by polysynthetic forms. Instances of cliticization, in contrast, always involve structures readily analyzable into clitic and 'host'. Let's compare, then, Dogrib first-person singular subject forms in [12] with nonsubject forms in [13].

[12] shè*h*tį — 'I'm eating'
wh*i*da — 'I'm sitting'
wek'èrezhǫ — 'I know it'
*è*hch'è — 'I got mad'

[13] nà*se*nįįht'ih — 'he punched me'
xa*se*rehtǫ — 'he's teaching me'
*s*aʔį — 'he saw me'

Subject agreement, in [12], has the quality of inflection by Zwicky and Pullum's criterion: the form of the morpheme depends on such factors as verb class, conjugation, and aspect, and hence may be called polysynthetic. Non-subject agreement, in [13], has the quality of cliticization: here, the agreement element is identified easily and is not dependent in form on its host's morphological properties.

By Zwicky and Pullum's criterion of selectivity of 'host', Dogrib subject and non-subject agreement differ also. Subject agreement is restricted to verbs. Non-subject agreement is not so restricted, occurring on verbs, as in [13], and also on postpositions and nouns, marking objects and possessors, as in [14].

[14] *se*gha — 'for me'
*se*ts'ǫ — 'from me'
*se*gàh — 'beside me'

*se*mǫ — 'my mother'
*se*mbeė — 'my knife'
*se*kwį — 'my grandchild (male speaking)'

According to Zwicky and Pullum, it is typical of inflection to be highly selective of its host and not typical of cliticization.

Subject and non-subject agreement in Dogrib also differ in a third respect relevant to Zwicky and Pullum's criteria. Zwicky and Pullum claim that inflectional affixes may show idiosyncratic exceptions, whereas clitics should exhibit no irregularities. In Dogrib, in addition to the many paradigms of subject agreement that arise as a result of the polysynthetic character of subject agreement, there are a few cases of truly exceptional forms containing subject agreement, such as those in [15]:

[15] a. ʔareh*sį* 'I say'
cf. ʔa*di* 'he says', etc., for non-first-singular forms
b. ʔekǫ̀ nàweh*sà* 'I'd go there'
cf. nàwe*zhà* 'he would go' etc., for non-first-singular forms

The italicized verb stems *-sį* and *-sà* in [15] are used exclusively for first person singular forms; the stems *-di* and *zhà* are used for all others. Such exceptional forms do not exist in paradigms of non-subject agreement—all such forms are regular.

In summary, it seems that, by Zwicky and Pullum's criteria, subject agreement in Dogrib results from word-formation processes in the lexicon (in their terminology, inflectional processes); non-subject agreement, in contrast, has properties more typical of cliticization, word-formation processes that are post-syntactic.

Although the morphological evidence of Dogrib non-subject agreement suggests an incorporation analysis of non-subject pronouns in this language, syntactic evidence rules out such an analysis. The morphological differences between subject and non-subject agreement are not matched by the syntactic differences predicted according to the model of the interaction of morphology and syntax suggested by Zwicky and Pullum or by Anderson's model.

According to Zwicky and Pullum's model, clitic structures result from the combination of syntactic units in the syntactic component of grammar; inflectional structures result from the combination of morphological units in the word-formation component of grammar. Clitics, then, but not inflectional elements, are predicted to have independent syntactic status at some level of syntactic structure. In the case of clitic *pronouns,* these clitics will correspond to syntactic noun phrases. It therefore is predicted under this view of clitics that a clitic and a full lexical NP filling the same grammatical function cannot both occur in a single structure. If the two did co-occur, it would be equivalent to the case of two full lexical NPs filling a single function, within Government–Binding Theory a violation of the Theta Criterion (Chomsky 1981) and also disallowed in other syntactic theories. In the case of inflectional pronouns, the same dependence between morphology and syntax is not predicted. Thus, whether or not an inflectional pronoun occurs within a word in a sentence is predicted to have no bearing on syntactic properties of the structure. If a full lexical NP does co-occur with an inflectional pronoun representing the same grammatical function, the inflectional pronoun is considered to be an indication of grammatical concord.

From the classification of Dogrib subject agreement as inflection and non-subject agreement as cliticization, a prediction about the syntax of structures containing these elements follows: it is predicted that subject agreement may co-occur with a subject noun phrase, but non-subject agreement may not co-occur with a non-subject noun phrase.

As the examples in [16]–[19] show, this prediction does not hold up. Thus, [16] shows subject agreement and a subject NP co-occurring; this we predict is possible. However, [17] shows non-subject agreement co-occurring with a direct object NP; [18] shows it co-occurring with a postpositional object NP; and [19] with a possessor NP. (NP and agreement are italicized.)

[16] *Tłı̨chǫ̀* tłı̨ t'à mbehchı̨ k'*ets'e*dlì.
Dogrib dog by sled 1p-IMP-slide
'We Dogribs pull sleds using dogs.'

[17] ʔayìiha *cheko* *go*ihtà ?
why boy 3p-3-IMP-count
'Why is she counting the boys?'

[18] ʔası̨̀ nàìdì k'èèzhǫ *nı̨* xàrè *ne*ts'ǫ̀ goı̨nde ?
Q doctor 2s self 2s-to 3-PF-speak
'Did the doctor speak to *you* specifically?'

[19] *John* *we*mǫ ʔèya elı̨.
3-mother sick 3-IMP-be
'John's mother is sick.'

The syntactic evidence of [16]–[19], which show a lack of contrast between subjects and non-subjects, therefore weighs against the conclusions reached on the basis of morphology. On the basis of the syntactic evidence, both subject and non-subject agreement must be classified as inflectional, that is, resulting from word-formation processes of the lexicon and not of a post-syntactic word-formation component. Therefore, despite (morphological) appearances, the problem of the Functional Determination of Empty Categories cannot be solved by appealing to a morphological solution such as is represented by the incorporation analysis.[4]

3. EMPTY CATEGORIES AND THETA ROLES

There seems to be one more potential route to take to avoid the conclusion of the first section of this paper. If there were no non-subject NP node in the syntactic structure of [8], for example, then the principle of Functional Determination could be maintained. So the question arises, within Government–Binding Theory, on what basis do we decide whether a clause contains an empty node? The existence of empty categories in this theory depends on the Theta Criterion (Chomsky 1981, 36) and the Projection Principle (Brody 1984, 374), which can be stated as in [20].

[20] *Theta Criterion:*

Each argument bears one and only one theta role, and each theta role is assigned to one and only one argument.

Projection Principle:

If A theta-marks B (B a category or a position) at some level, then A theta-marks B at all levels.

By these principles, [21] contains two empty NPs at all syntactic levels, since the subject of [21], 'I', bears the theta role Agent, and the object, 'it', bears the theta role Patient.

[21] $[_{NP}$] $[_{NP}$] whihtsį.
1s-PF-make
'I made it.'

With respect to the reflexive examples [8] and [9], the question arises, Do these clauses really have two arguments bearing separate theta roles? Does [8] have the problematic structure shown earlier (repeated here),

[8] John mbeh t'à $[_{NP}$] ˀedèhgo.
knife with Refl-3-PF-stab
'John stabbed himself with a knife.'

or is *ˀedèhgo* a verb like the English *self-destruct* or *self-pollinate,* assigning only one theta role in clauses containing it? The evidence of the following examples favors the analysis in which two theta roles are assigned in each case.

[22] Mbò į̀hchih, nemǫ chi gha, nemba chi gha.
meat 2s-IMP-take 2s-mother too for 2s-sister too for

Nį ˀedegha chi mbò į̀hchih.
2s Refl-for too meat 2s-IMP-take

'Take meat, for your mother and for your sister. Take meat for *yourself* too.'

[23] Dàtlǫ geret'è netà. Nį chi ˀedexè
how many 3p-IMP-be 2s-IMP-count 2s too Refl-with

ˀįtà wenawįndi ìle sǫ̀.
U-2s-IMP-count 2s-OPT-remember Neg Prohib

'Count how many there are. Don't forget to count in *yourself* too.'

From the interpretations represented in the glosses of [22] and [23], it seems that arguments bearing the theta roles of Benefactive [22] and Patient [23] are being contrasted in these examples rather than arguments bearing the Agent theta role. From the possibility of these interpretations, I can only assume that such non-subject argument positions also exist in the more commonplace cases, such as [8] and [9].[5]

Nothing remains, then, but an evaluation of the principle of the Functional Determination of Empty Categories, since (try as we might) it is impossible to escape the conclusion that empty reflexive-type anaphors exist, as in [8] and [9], and that the Functional Determination principle is unable to characterize them as such.

4. REJECTING FUNCTIONAL DETERMINATION

As mentioned previously, the principle of the Functional Determination of Empty Categories depends on the mutual exclusivity in any one context of the categories it defines. The principle fails on two accounts to define the range of empty categories in Dogrib. First, it fails to provide for the case of a pure anaphor of the reflexive rather than the NP-trace type; and second, even if such a type were defined, it would not be distinguishable by context from empty pronominals, since in Dogrib either an empty anaphor or an empty pronominal may occur in non-subject positions.

The principle of the Functional Determination of Empty Categories has been the topic of works by Brody (1984) and by Safir (1984). Both of these researchers argue that the principle of Functional Determination is in some respects wrong and in some respects redundant. Safir shows that some empty categories must be considered to be both variables and pronominals, a situation not permitted by [4]. He suggests treating empty NPs just like lexical pronouns: empty *and* lexical pronouns each have inherent features and each are inserted freely into syntactic structures. Principles such as the Binding Theory, the ECP, as well as the Theta Criterion and the Projection Principle, rule out many of the generated structures as ungrammatical. Brody shows in considerable detail how this is possible.[6]

This paper provides another argument against the maintenance of the Functional Determination of Empty Categories as an independent principle of grammar. In place of the Functional Determination, I propose the following for Dogrib: the empty NPs in [5]–[7] are specified inherently with the features [+pronominal, −anaphor]; those in [8] and [9], and [22] and [23], with the features [−pronominal, +anaphor]. The [+pronominal, −anaphor] empty NPs thus are identical to the small *pro* of Italian; the [−pronominal, +anaphor] empty category is an empty reflexive-type pure anaphor. Brody and Safir each assume that no such empty category exists. My arguments up to now, I hope, have shown that their assumption is wrong. I will attempt to show now that the whole snow fort does not collapse under the weight of this new assumption.

There would seem to be a problem distinguishing the newly introduced empty anaphor, which can be called 'little *ana*', from the category previously recognized as [−pronominal, +anaphor], NP-trace. Brody and Safir each assume, for example, that a [−pronominal, +anaphor] empty category cannot have an independent theta role. This assumption does not seem to depend on any principle but instead ensures that any [−pronominal, +anaphor] empty category is NP-trace. Contrary to Brody and Safir, I have to assume that little *ana* does bear an independent theta role. Nothing prevents empty categories in general from bearing theta roles—both PRO and *pro* do. It seems ad hoc therefore to assume that little *ana* cannot. *Ana* and NP-trace thus are distinguished by the fact that *ana* may head a chain but NP-trace may not. It is possible to further distinguish *ana* from NP-trace. As is shown in Saxon (1984b), the binding theory is entirely redundant with respect to NP-trace. Other principles, such as the ECP, the Theta Criterion, and Case Theory limit its distribution. (Bouchard discusses this, too, in his 1982 dissertation.) Thus, it is possible to take the position that NP-trace is undefined with respect to the features [±anaphor] and [±pronominal], since nothing but the binding theory refers specifically to these features.

If this move seems radical, it can be compared to the move made by Brody and Safir in their treatment of variables, previously considered to be [−pronominal, −anaphor] empty categories. Both Brody and Safir urge that variables, unlike other empty categories, should continue to be contextually defined, for instance by the definition in [24] (Safir 1984, 631):

[24] *Variable:*

X is a variable if it is locally A′-bound and in an A-position.

Safir argues convincingly that the property of being a variable cuts across other classifications of NPs: thus, either empty NPs or lexical NPs, and either pronominal or non-pronominal NPs can be variables. The remarks earlier about NP-trace suggest that, like variables, NP-traces stand apart from true anaphors and pronominals, which are arguments, in consequence of bearing theta roles.[7]

I should say something also about the so-called identification hypothesis or Taraldsen's generalization, the idea that empty categories of a certain type must be 'identified' by agreement.[8] By this hypothesis, Italian has little *pro* but English does not, because only in Italian do verbs show agreement rich enough that an empty NP can be identified by it. I have introduced little *pro* and little *ana* in positions in Dogrib not available for little *pro* in Italian. By the identification hypothesis, this should be possible only if there is agreement in Dogrib rich enough to identify little *pro* and little *ana*. It happens that Dogrib does have a very rich agreement system and, indeed, in most cases the features of the empty NPs *are* recoverable from agreement.

In summary, if Brody's and Safir's conclusions about the redundancy and error of the principle of Functional Determination can be agreed with, this paper adds further support to their conclusion by presenting evidence that there is an empty category type in Dogrib, little *ana,* which *in principle* cannot be defined by Functional Determination. It has been shown that by giving up the Functional Determination as an independent principle and acknowledging that empty categories may have inherent specifications for the features [±anaphor] and [±pronominal], the properties of little *ana* can be accounted for. It has been shown that this assumption may make some changes in our conception of NP-trace necessary. It has been shown also, however, that these changes do not alter the theory in any very revolutionary way.

NOTES

The fieldwork that lies behind this paper was supported financially by the National Museum of Man (Ottawa) contract no. 1630-1-469. I would like to thank the following people and acknowledge their help and encouragement: my principle consultants in Rae-Edzo and Yellowknife, Vital Thomas, Alice Mackenzie and Elizabeth Mackenzie, and also Sandra Chung, Donna B. Gerdts, Geoffrey K. Pullum, and Keren Rice.

1. Compare also the somewhat similar suggestions involving incorporation or infixation in Baker (1985) and Speas (1986).

2. Another possibility follows the proposal of Hale (1983) for Warlpiri. I do not consider this proposal here at all, but see Saxon (1984a; 1986), and compare Speas (1986).

3. Note that this assumption about what can be incorporated is not the same as that assumed by Anderson (1982), Baker (1985), or Speas (1986).

4. There are strong morphological arguments against an incorporation analysis, in addition to the syntactic argument just presented. For example, noun compounds formed in the lexicon may contain subconstituents marked with subject *or* non-subject agreement. Consider (i) and (ii):

[i] łiwe ts'edè dzę̀ę̀
fish one IMP eat day
'Friday' (lit. 'one-eats-fish day')
[ii] goghò kàle dǫ̀ǫ̀
one-tooth 3-IMP-take out person
'dentist' (lit 'he-takes-out-one's-teeth person')

These compounds show the subject and non-subject inflectional affixes *ts'e-* and *go-*, both glossed 'one; unspecified human'. According to an analysis in which subject agreement is a lexical process but non-subject agreement is not, (i) is predicted to be possible but (ii) is not.

This form of argument is due to Keren Rice. See Rice (1985; this volume) for morphological arguments from Slave against incorporation-type analyses. See also Rice (1983) for an analysis of Athapaskan morphology in the framework of lexical phonology and morphology (Kiparsky 1982). In this framework, the similarities and differences between Athapaskan subject and non-subject agreement follow from the organization of the lexicon into levels with distinct phonological and morphological properties.

5. Note my implicit assumption that a distinct argument (the subject NP) is associated with the Agent theta role. This need not be taken as an assumption: examples can be found parallel to [22] and [23], in which the argument bearing the Agent theta role receives a contrastive interpretation. For example,

[i] John ʔedegha mbò ìhchih; nį chi ʔedegha mbò į̀hchih.
Refl-for meat 3.-IMP-take 2s too Refl-for meat 2s-IMP-take
'John is taking meat for himself; you too take meat for yourself.'

From a comparison of [22] and [i], it seems clear that in these examples the listener, 'you', is associated with two theta roles, Agent and Benefactive, and therefore, by the Theta Criterion, with two argument positions, subject and object of *gha*, 'for'.

The point is perhaps even clearer in the case of the Dogrib disjoint anaphor. As is argued in Saxon (1984b; 1986), Dogrib possesses a disjoint anaphor, an NP that has the usual syntactic distribution of anaphors and the somewhat less usual semantic property of indicating an individual disjoint in reference from its syntactic antecedent. In [ii], the empty category is a disjoint anaphor. *Ye-* marks agreement with this NP.

[ii] Jim [$_{NP}$] yegha mbò ìhchih.
DA-for meat 3-IMP-take
'Jim is taking meat for her.'

In this example, 'Jim' bears the theta role Agent, and the referent of the empty category (anyone but Jim) bears the theta role Benefactive. With the disjoint anaphor, the *self-destruct* question does not arise, since the syntactic antecedent of the anaphor and the anaphor itself do not refer to the same individual.

6. Jaeggli (1984) also argues for the abandonment of the principle of the Functional Determination of Empty Categories. Like Brody and Safir, Jaeggli shows that the principle allows for the possibility of some empty NP positions being defined either as variables or as *pro*. As with Brody or Safir, then, according to Jaeggli, empty categories must be understood as having inherent properties and as occurring freely in syntactic structures, where they are subject to general principles limiting the occurrence of NP types. Diverging from the other researchers, however, Jaeggli argues that the NP can be either a variable or a pronominal but not both. For views contrary to Jaeggli's on this point, see Brody (1984) and Safir (1984) on 'PRO-gates'; Georgopoulos (1985) on variables in Palauan; and section 3, where I assume that the reflexive empty NP is both an anaphor and a variable, being A′-bound by the topic *nį*, 'you'.

7. This distinction was suggested to me by Sandra Chung.

8. As is well known, the correlation between 'rich agreement' and the possibility for empty NPs is far from exact. For some discussion, see Chung (1984).

REFERENCES

Anderson, S. R. 1982. Where's Morphology? *Linguistic Inquiry* 13:571–612.

Baker, M. 1985. *Incorporation: A Theory of Grammatical Function Changing*. Ph.D. Diss., Massachusetts Institute of Technology.

Bouchard, D. 1982. *On the Content of Empty Categories*. Ph.D. Diss., Massachusetts Institute of Technology. (Published in 1984 under the same title, Dordrecht, Holland: Foris Publications.)

Brody, M. 1984. Contextual Definitions and the Role of Chains. *Linguistic Inquiry* 15:355–80.

Chomsky, N. 1981. *Lectures on Government and Binding*. Dordrecht, Holland: Foris Publications.

Chomsky, N. 1982. *Some Concepts and Consequences of the Theory of Government and Binding*. Linguistic Inquiry Monograph 6. Cambridge: MIT Press.

Chung, S. 1982. On extending the Null Subject Parameter to NPs. In *Proceedings of the First West Coast Conference on Formal Linguistics,* D. P. Flickinger, et al., eds., pp. 125–36. Stanford: Stanford Linguistics Association.

Chung, S. 1984. Identifiability and Null Objects in Chamorro. *Proceedings of the Tenth Annual Meeting of the Berkeley Linguistics Society*. Berkeley: University of California. pp. 116–30.

Georgopoulos, C. 1985. Variables in Palauan Syntax. *Natural Language and Linguistic Theory* 3:59–94.

Hale, K. 1983. Warlpiri and the Grammar of Non-Configurational Languages. *Natural Language and Linguistic Theory* 1:5–47.

Jaeggli, O. 1984. Subject Extraction and the Null Subject Parameter. *Northeastern Linguistics Society* 14:132–53.

Kiparsky, P. 1982. Lexical Morphology and Phonology. In *Linguistics in the Morning Calm,* I. S. Yang, ed. Seoul: Hanshin.

Rice, K. 1983. Epenthesis in the Athapaskan Languages and the Linking of Levels. Presented at the Annual Meeting of the Canadian Linguistics Association, Vancouver, British Columbia.

Rice, K. 1985. On the Placement of Inflection. *Linguistic Inquiry* 16:155–61.

Rice, K. This volume. On Bracketing Paradoxes in Slave.

Safir, K. 1984. Multiple Variable Binding. *Linguistic Inquiry* 15:603–38.

Saxon, L. 1984a. Control and Agreement in Dogrib. In *ESCOL '84: Proceedings of the First Eastern States Conference on Linguistics,* G. Alvarez et al., eds., pp. 128–39. Columbus: Ohio State University.

Saxon, L. 1984b. Disjoint Anaphora and the Binding Theory. In *Proceedings of the Third West Coast Conference on Formal Linguistics,* M. Cobler, et al., eds., pp. 242–51. Stanford: Stanford Linguistics Association.

Saxon, L. 1986. *The Syntax of Pronouns in Dogrib.* Ph.D. Diss., University of California, San Diego.

Speas, M. 1986. *Adjunctions and Projections in Syntax.* Ph.D Diss., Massachusetts Institute of Technology.

Zwicky, A., and G. K. Pullum. 1983. Inflection versus Cliticization: English *n't. Language* 59:502–13.

DISJOINT REFERENCE IN A 'FREE WORD ORDER' LANGUAGE

Ann Grafstein

INTRODUCTION

This paper is concerned with the realization of the universal principle of obligatory Disjoint Reference (DR) in the Algonquian language, Ojibwa. Ojibwa is a language with a highly flexible surface word order accompanied by a rich system of inflectional and derivational morphology. The morphology plays the primary role in encoding the thematic structure of sentences in Ojibwa.

The term *nonconfigurational* recently has been used to characterize languages exhibiting a particular cluster of grammatical properties. For our purposes, the most important of these properties are free word order and the extensive use of null anaphora (see Hale 1981; 1982; 1983). I have argued (Grafstein 1984) that the grammatical characteristics of Ojibwa suggest that it fits nicely within this class of languages.

Following Hale (1982), I assume that the free word order characteristic of nonconfigurational languages results from context-free lexical insertion under categorially unspecified terminal nodes in a syntactic phrase marker. These terminal nodes receive their category labels by virtue of upward percolation of the features of the lexical items inserted under them. It follows from this conception of the phrase structure of nonconfigurational languages that there is no canonical linear ordering among words in a phrase marker. The linear order of the words in a phrase marker is identical to that of the words in the surface sentence. It also follows from this notion of context-free lexical insertion under categorially neutral terminal nodes that no categorial slots exist independent of lexical insertion; that is, there are no base-generated empty categories.[1]

Within the Government-Binding (GB) Theory (Chomsky 1981; 1982), the principle of Disjoint Reference is expressed as principle B of the binding theory: a pronominal is free in its governing category. In this paper, I claim that the principle of DR, as formulated within the GB theory, is not applicable to languages like Ojibwa.

I would like to stress that this claim does not constitute a challenge to the universality of principle B. I assume, in fact, that for every language there is some principle that stipulates the conditions under which a pronominal is interpreted as disjoint in reference from other arguments. However, the particular way in which this principle is instantiated may be expected to vary to some extent across languages, depending on certain typological characteristics of the language in question. In this paper, a principle of DR for Ojibwa is proposed that is consistent with the primacy of the morphology in encoding thematic structure and that, at the same time, accounts in a unified way for an otherwise disparate set of data.

Before proceeding, it would be helpful to know some of the general grammatical characteristics of Ojibwa relevant to the analysis proposed here. First, nouns in Ojibwa, as in all Alogonquian languages, are divided into two grammatical gender classes: animate and inanimate. As will be shown presently, this gender distinction interacts with Ojibwa's verb classification system.

Second, following Bloomfield (1957), Algonquianists generally recognize two main classes of verbs: transitive and intransitive.[2] Intransitive verbs contain anaphoric reference to one argument (normally, the argument which will be referred to as agent), while transitive verbs are marked for agreement with two arguments (normally, the arguments which will be referred to as agent and theme). Within each of these two main classes, verbs are further sub-classified according to the gender of their arguments. Animate Intransitive (AI) verbs take animate arguments, while Inanimate Intransitive (II) verbs take inanimate arguments. Transitive Animate (TA) verbs, on the other hand, take animate themes, while Transitive Inanimate (TI) verbs take inanimate themes.

Finally, obviation is one of the most salient characteristics of all Algonquian languages. Obviation is a process whereby noncoreferential third persons are morphologically distinguished from one another when they appear in the same sentence. It is obligatory when the third persons appear either within the same clause or within a possessive expression; otherwise, it is optional. Obviation is marked not only on nouns but also on verbs with obviative arguments. Examples of the use of obviation are given in [1] and [2]. In both

[1a] and [2a], in which there is only one third person, there is no obviation marking, whereas in [1b] and [2b], one of the two third persons is marked obviative. The suffix *-an* attached to animate nouns indicates obviation.

[1] a. gi-gi:-ba:škizwa: mo:zw
2-PAST-shoot moose
'you shot a moose'

b. Mary o-gi:-ba:škizwa:-an mo:zw-an
3-PAST-shoot-OBV moose-OBV
'Mary shot a moose'

[2] a. ni-da:nis niba:-w
1-daughter,sleep-3
'my daughter is sleeping'

b. John o-da:nis-an niba:w-an
3-daughter-OBV sleep-OBV
'John's daughter is sleeping'

It also would be helpful to outline some relevant aspects of my theoretical approach to Ojibwa grammar, as discussed in Grafstein (1984). First, the lexical entry for each noun stem and verb stem includes a specification of its argument requirements; that is, the number of arguments that are later obligatorily or optionally associated with the noun form or verb form in the syntactic phrase marker. This specification will be referred to as the stem's Argument Structure (AS) (cf. Williams 1981). Nouns are assumed to have arguments in order to account for the possibility of possessive expressions: in such cases, the possessor is taken to be the argument of the possessed noun.[3]

Within this analysis, each argument listed in the AS of a stem is linked with a particular thematic role in the sense of Jackendoff (1972). I would like to emphasize that no theoretical status is attributed to the particular thematic roles to which arguments are linked. My concern is with the purely formal assignment of thematic roles to nominal arguments in the general sense of Chomsky (1981). For terminological convenience, however, the traditional names for thematic roles (e.g., agent, theme, goal, etc.) will be used.

Finally, as proposed in Grafstein (1984), the thematic structure of a sentence in Ojibwa is determined by a combination of inherent properties of the stem and the inflectional affixes attached to it. *All* affixation processes—derivational and inflectional—take place in the lexicon, so that the lexicon generates a set of fully inflected words. The inflectional affixes attached to lexical items encode the feature composition of each of its arguments. A noun in a phrase marker is interpreted as a particular argument of a lexical item when its features match the features attributed to that argument by the relevant affixes.

Consider, for example, a sentence with an intransitive verb form such as

[3]. It should be noted that, in both [3] and [4], each permutation is an example of a possible word order, although in each case the [a] sentences seem to represent the preferred word order.

[3] a. mawi- w ǰi:ǰi:š
cry- 3 baby
'the baby is crying'
b. ǰi:ǰi:š mawi-w

Mawi- 'cry' is an AI verb stem. As has been shown, this means that it is specified lexically as taking one animate argument. The inflectional affix *-w* indicates that the argument of the verb form is a third person. Since *ji:ji:š* is a third-person animate noun, it is interpreted as the argument of *mawiw.*

The interpretation of sentences with transitive verbs is somewhat more complex. *Nosine:w* in [4] is a TA verb stem. This means, as noted earlier, that it is marked lexically for taking two arguments and that its theme is animate. The inflections attached to transitive verb stems encode properties of particular arguments. Because of this, it is possible to determine which noun is associated with which argument role. Consider, for example, the sentences in [4].

[4] a. animoš o-nosine:w-a:-an bo:žẽs-an
dog 3-chase-3-OBV cat-OBV
'the dog is chasing the cat'
b. bo:žẽs-an o-nosine:w-a:-an animoš
c. o-nosine:w-a:-an bo:žẽs-an animoš

The affix *-a:,* which is attached to the verb form, is known as a TA theme sign. It indicates that the *theme* argument is a third person. The obviative marker following the theme sign indicates that the theme argument also is obviative. Now, the prefix on a TA verb form refers to the argument that is *not* referred to by the theme sign. So, in [4], the prefix *o-* indicates that the agent argument is a third person. Since *bo:žẽs-an* is marked obviative, it is interpreted as the theme. This leaves the nonobviative *animoš* to be interpreted as agent. From these examples, it can be seen that the thematic structure of an Ojibwa sentence is interpreted on the basis of the morphology of its constituents rather than on the basis of their linear position in a syntactic phrase marker.[4]

1. THE ABSENCE OF ANAPHORS IN OJIBWA

Having made these introductory remarks, I would now like to consider why the Binding Theory is not the appropriate statement of the principle of DR for Ojibwa. The Binding Theory, as outlined in Chomsky (1981; 1982), is concerned essentially with characterizing the anaphoric and distributional properties of three classes of nominal expressions: anaphors, pronominals, and R-expressions. Their properties are predicted by the following three conditions, which make up the Binding Theory (Chomsky 1981, 188):

[5] a. An anaphor is bound in its governing category[5].
b. A pronominal is free in its governing category.
c. An R-expression is free.

Only anaphors and pronominals, then, are subject to conditions that stipulate that they must be bound in certain contexts. For this reason, condition C will not be discussed.

Turning first to Condition A, I claim that Ojibwa does not have a class of nominal expressions that properly can be termed *anaphors*. The class of anaphors is considered to consist of lexical anaphors (reflexives such as *herself* and reciprocals such as *each other*) and NP-trace. NP-trace arises as a result of NP movement rules. Since nonconfigurational languages like Ojibwa are assumed to have no movement rules in their grammars (see Hale 1981; 1982), the question of NP-trace can be safely dismissed and attention turned to the lexical anaphors.

Although there are structures in Ojibwa that receive a reciprocal or reflexive interpretation, this interpretation does not arise as a result of a reciprocal or reflexive NP appearing in an argument position. Instead, certain verb forms are interpreted reciprocally whereas others are interpreted reflexively because of the morphology of their respective verb stems. Examples of verb forms interpreted reciprocally and reflexively are shown in [6] and [7] respectively.

[6] a. ni-gizi:bi:gin-idi-min
1-wash-REC-1PL
'we are washing each other'
b. gizi:bi:gin-idi-w-ag
wash-REC-3-PL
'they are washing each other'

[7] a. gizi:bi:gin-idizo-w
wash-REFL-3
'he is washing himself'
b. ni-gizi:bi:gin-idizo-min
1-wash-REFL-1PL
'we are washing cach ourselves'

As shown in [6], the reciprocal affix is *-idi-* and as shown in [7] the reflexive affix is *-idizo-*.

If reciprocals and reflexives in Ojibwa were realized as lexical anaphors, as they are in English, then the inflections that appear on the verb form in constructions such as [6] and [7] presumably would encode properties of two arguments: the anaphor and its antecedent. In fact, however, the verb forms in

[6] and [7] are intransitive (AI) verb forms. As already indicated, AI verb stems are specified in the lexicon as taking only *one* obligatory argument. Furthermore, the inflectional affixes attached to AIs encode properties of only *one* argument.

As one indication that the forms in [6] and [7] actually are AIs, the set of inflectional endings found on verbs, which are indisputably AIs (shown in [8]), can be compared with those found on reflexives and reciprocals (shown in [9]).

[8] AI Inflectional Endings:

1	0	11−min[6]
2	0	12−min
3	−w	22−m
obv.	−w−an	33−w−ag

[9]

Reflexives	Reciprocals
1 nigizi:bi:ginidizio	—
2 gigizi:bi:ginidizo	—
3 gizi:bi:ginidizo-*w*	—
OBV. gizi:bi:ginidizo-*w-an*	—
11 nigizi:bi:ginidizo-*min*	nigizi:bi:ginidi-*min*
12 gigizi:bi:ginidizo-*min*	gigizi:bi:ginidi-*min*
22 gigizi:bi:ginidizo-*m*	gigizi:bi:ginidi-*m*
33 gizi:bi:ginidizo-*w-ag*	gizi:bi:ginidi-*w-ag*

Notice that the endings are identical in each case.

If my claim that there are no lexical anaphors is correct, then no formulation or interpretation of principle A is relevant in determining the well-formedness of structures that are interpreted reflexively or reciprocally in Ojibwa. The principle of DR that will be formulated provides a principled explanation for why reflexive and reciprocal interpretations can be derived only from intransitive verb forms—verb forms in which inflections encode properties of only one argument.

2. PRONOMINALS IN OJIBWA

Consider Condition B. Ojibwa does not have a set of phonetically realized personal pronominal arguments.[7] Rather, obligatory arguments not associated with overt noun forms are interpreted as associated with the features encoded by the affixes, which refer to the argument in question. These features receive an interpretation analogous to that of overt pronouns in languages that have them. This can be demonstrated by comparing the sentences in [10] and [11].

[10] a. gi:-bangišin-w abino:ǰi:š
PAST-fall-3 child
'the child fell'

b. gi:-bangišin-w
PAST-fall-3
'he' or 'she' fell'

[11] a. gi:-bangišin-w-ag abino:ǰi:š-ag
PAST-fall-3-PL-child-PL
'the children fell'

b. gi:-bangišin-w-ag
PAST-FALL 3-PL
'they fell'

It can be seen that the affixes attached to the [b] forms, which do not have overt arguments, parallel precisely those attached to the [a] forms, which do have overt arguments. In [10a] and [11a], feature matching proceeds in a straightforward manner. *Bangišin-* 'fall' is an AI verb stem that takes an obligatory animate argument. The inflectional affix *-w* in [10a] indicates that this argument is a third person. Since *abino:ǰi:š,* 'child', is both animate and a third person, it is interpreted as the argument of the verb form. In [11a], the affix *-w* once again indicates that the verbal argument is a third person, and the affix *-ag* indicates that the argument is plural. Since *abino:ji:šağ,* 'children', is an animate third-person plural, it is interpreted as the argument of the verb form.

Consider the [b] forms. These are both perfectly well-formed sentences, even though there is no overt noun form in either case. The Theta Criterion (Chomsky 1981) stipulates that, in a well-formed sentence, the argument requirements of verbs are satisfied. We must assume, therefore, that the argument requirement of *bangišin-* in [10b] and [11b] is satisfied by something other than an overt noun form. It is my claim that when no overt noun form is present, an argument requirement is interpreted as being satisfied by an argument bearing the features encoded by the relevant affixes. These features are interpreted just as if they were lexical pronouns, except that they have no syntactic realization.

At first glance, it might appear that the most plausible analysis of pronominal interpretation in Ojibwa would be to treat pronominally interpreted features as instances of the *pro,* which occurs in the so-called *pro*-drop languages like Spanish and Italian (see, for example, Chomsky 1981; 1982). *Pro* is basically a phonologically null pronominal that, under certain conditions, can replace a lexical subject. We can say informally that *pro* can occur in languages in which overt agreement marking on verbs is sufficiently "rich" to license the dropping of a lexical subject.

It should be emphasized that *pro* occupies a particular slot in a syntactic phrase marker—the subject slot. If phonologically null arguments in Ojibwa are assumed to be instances of *pro,* then it must be assumed that they occupy particular positions in the syntactic phrase marker. This assumption, however, would be inconsistent with the conception of Ojibwa as a nonconfigurational language. As noted earlier (see the introduction), in nonconfigurational languages lexical items are freely inserted under category-neutral terminal nodes, resulting in free word order. The phrase structure positions occupied by lexical items, then, correspond to their surface linear order. If there are no phrase structure positions generated independently of lexical insertion, then there can be no phrase structure nodes that dominate phonologically null (or empty) categories. The conception of Ojibwa as a nonconfigurational language precludes the option of analyzing the pronominal interpretation in Ojibwa in terms of *pro*. Rather, it is assumed that there simply are no pronouns in Ojibwa and that a nonovert argument does not occupy a slot in the syntactic phrase marker. In the absence of overt noun forms, the argument requirements of verbs are satisfied by features attributed to the relevant argument in accordance with the morphology of verb forms. As already indicated, these features are interpreted exactly as are lexical pronouns in languages that have them.[8]

The absence of lexical pronouns in Ojibwa, of course, has an important implication for the role of Condition B of the Binding Theory. If there are no lexical pronouns in Ojibwa that occupy particular N slots in phrase markers, then there can be no syntactic structures to which Condition B of the Binding Theory can apply.

3. THE PRINCIPLE OF DISJOINT REFERENCE

Nevertheless, like lexical pronouns, pronominally interpreted features in Ojibwa have the property of DR; that is, under certain conditions, these 'pronominals' must be interpreted as noncoreferential with other arguments. Since there are no lexical pronouns, the feature composition of a pronominal is known exclusively from the morphology of the verb form or noun form of which it is an argument. In the case of third-person pronominals the presence or absence of an obviative affix determines whether that pronominal is interpreted as coreferential or noncoreferential with a nonobviative third person elsewhere in the sentence. If an affix indicates that the pronominal is obviative, then it is interpreted as noncoreferential with any nonobviative third person in the string, as is illustrated in [12].

[12] John o-wa: bam-a:-an
3-see-3-OBV
'John$_i$ sees him$_j$'

If the objective affix were not attached in [12], we would have the ill-formed string in [13].

[13] *Johno-wa:bam-a:
3-see-TA-3
'John$_i$ sees him$_i$'

In [13], the absence of the obviative affix on the verb form indicates that its pronominal argument is coreferential with the nonobviative *John*.

Now the affixes attached to any transitive verb form with a pronominal argument obligatorily indicate that the argument is disjoint in reference from the other argument of the verb form. There is, for example, no combination of affixes in Ojibwa which can be attached to transitive verbs to derive readings equivalent to *'you see you' or *'I see us.' In addition, we have seen that a reflexive or reciprocal interpretation can be realized only as an *intransitive* (AI) verb form. Taken together, these two facts suggest that there is a constraint on the argument structure of transitive verb forms in Ojibwa such that no two arguments of a transitive verb may corefer. This constraint, I believe, is essentially the principle of DR in Ojibwa, which I formulate as [14].

[14] The obligatory arguments within the AS of a lexical item must be assigned distinct features for person.

This constraint makes interesting predictions concerning some otherwise puzzling data. First, it correctly predicts that structures interpreted reflexively or reciprocally surface as intransitive rather than transitive verb forms. If such structures surfaced as transitive verb forms with two obligatory arguments, then both arguments would be assigned nondistinct features for person, in violation of [14].

Second, this principle predicts certain otherwise unexplained facts about obviation. It was noted earlier that obviation is obligatory when the third persons occur within the same clause or within a possessive expression. These are precisely the contexts in which DR is obligatory; that is, when both third persons are arguments of the same lexical item.

That obviation is obligatory when the third persons appear within the same clause is illustrated by the difference in grammaticality between [12] and [13]. Similarly, the difference in grammaticality between [15a] and [15b] demonstrates that obviation is obligatory within possessive expressions containing two third persons.

[15] a. John o-da:nis-an
3-daughter-OBV
'John's daughter'

b. *John o-da:nis

When the nominals are not arguments of the same lexical item, [14] makes no predictions whatsoever. Under these circumstances, then, obviation should be optional. Thus, both [16a, 16b] and [17a, 17b] in fact are well formed.

[16] **a.** animoš o-gike:nda:n [bo:žẽs ga:zo-d]
dog 3-know cat hide-3
'the dog knows that the cat is hiding'
b. animoš o-gike:nda:n [bo:žẽs-an ga:zo-ini-d]
dog 3-know cat-OBV hide-OBV-3
'the dog knows that the cat is hiding'

[17] **a.** Mary o-gi:-oǰi:ma:-an John o-gosis-an
3-PAST-kiss-OBV 3-son-OBV
'Mary kissed John's son'
b. Mary o-gi:-oǰi:ma:-an John-an o-gosis-ini
3-PAST-kiss-OBV OBV-son-FURTHER OBV[9]
'Mary kissed John's son'

It is of interest to note that the dichotomy between obligatory and optional obviation has posed somewhat of a puzzle for scholars concerned with the study of Algonquian languages. Traditionally, Algonquianists have tended to view obviation as a principle of Algonquian discourse rather than as a principle of Algonquian sentence grammar.[10] This approach to obviation predicts that within a particular span of discourse, only one animate third person can be nonobviative; the rest must be obviative. The optional absence of obviation within a given stretch of discourse is seen as an exception to this otherwise valid principle of discourse (Bloomfield 1957, 32).

Given the principle of DR formulated in [14], however, we do not have to stipulate that obviation is obligatory in certain contexts and optional in others. The precise contexts in which obviation is optional or obligatory follow directly from this general principle of Ojibwa grammar. In [12] as opposed to [13], for example, both arguments of the transitive verb are assigned distinct features for person.[11] Thus, [14] predicts that [12] is well formed in contrast to [13]. Similarly, in [15a], the argument of the possessed noun (i.e., the possessor, *John*) and the possessed noun (i.e., *-da:nisan*) both are assigned distinct features for person, in contrast to [15b], in which they are not. Hence, the ill-formedness of [15b] is predicted by [14].

Consider [16] and [17]. The optionality of obviation in these contexts also is consistent with [14]. In [16], *animoš* and *bo:žẽ:s* are not arguments of the same lexical item. *Animoš* is an argument of the matrix verb, while *bo:žẽ:s(-an)* is an argument of the embedded verb.

Finally, in [17], *Mary* is an argument of the verb whereas *John* is an argument of the possessed noun. Therefore, they are not arguments of the same lexical item. Hence, obviation marking on *John* is optional. Since [14] makes no predictions when the third persons in question are not part of the same lexical item, obviation is not obligatory in these cases.

The principle of DR proposed in this section imposes a distinctness condition on the sets of features that can be attributed to the arguments of a single lexical item. It accounts in a principled, unified way for certain apparently unrelated facts about Ojibwa. First, it predicts that only intransitive—not transitive—verb forms can be interpreted reflexively or reciprocally. Second, it distinguishes between the contexts of obligatory and optional obviation. Obviation is obligatory when the third persons are within the argument structure (that is, they are arguments) of the same lexical item; otherwise, it is optional.

4. CONCLUSION

I have argued in this paper that there is no class of nominal expressions in Ojibwa that can be properly termed *anaphors* or *pronouns*. As a consequence of the absence of anaphors and pronouns in Ojibwa, the Binding Theory, as formulated in Chomsky (1981; 1982), is not applicable to Ojibwa. Nevertheless, as has been seen, there is a principle of Disjoint Reference in Ojibwa; that is, there are conditions under which arguments must be disjoint in reference from other arguments.

In section 3, I formulated a principle of DR for Ojibwa that captures these conditions. This formulation is consistent with the assumption that the principle of DR is not a property of the grammars of particular languages. Rather, it is stipulated in universal grammar (UG) that all languages have some version of this principle. At the same time, an examination of Ojibwa shows that the precise formulation of the principle of DR is not stipulated in UG. Presumably, the way in which this principle is instantiated in particular languages is subject to parametric variation and is linked to other grammatical characteristics of the language in question.

The formulation of the principle of DR that I have proposed for Ojibwa is consistent with the universality of this principle and, at the same time, reflects the primacy of the morphology in encoding thematic structure in Ojibwa. The analysis developed here implies that there is an interaction between the appropriate statement of universal linguistic principles and aspects of language typology.

NOTES

The data on which this analysis is based were collected in part during the course of field work conducted on a group of Ojibwa dialects known as Algonquin. The specific dialects in question are those spoken in Winneway River and Rapid Lake, both in northwestern Quebec. Much of the analysis presented here also is based on research conducted on the variety of Ojibwa spoken in Kenora, Ontario. I am grateful, of course, to the many native consultants who were willing to share their language with me.

1. See Hale (1981, postscript) and Hale (1982) for details. See also Grafstein (1984) for a detailed articulation of this approach with respect to Ojibwa.

2. I omit reference to the so-called pseudo-transitive and pseudo-intransitive verbs discussed, for example, in Bloomfield (1957).

3. The assumption that nouns can take arguments is not unique to my analysis. See, for example, Williams (1981) who also makes this assumption.

4. For a more complete account of how thematic structure is encoded in Ojibwa, see Grafstein (1984).

5. The notion of 'governing category' is defined in terms of syntactic configurations. It has been argued (see Hale 1982) that the minimally hierarchical phrase structure that characterizes nonconfigurational languages does not allow for a nontrivial application of the principle of government. If this is correct, then the domain of application of the binding conditions, in any case, would have to be reformulated for nonconfigurational languages like Ojibwa. See Grafstein (1984, Chapter 4) for a more complete discussion.

6. The numbers *11* and *12* refer to the first-person plural exclusive and the first-person plural inclusive, respectively. The first person plural exclusive is used when the addressee is excluded as a participant, and the inclusive form is used when the addressee is included as a participant.

7. Ojibwa actually does have a set of personal pronouns, but they do not function as verbal arguments. Their primary function is to signal emphasis or, in combination with demonstrative pronouns, deixis. For example, the sentence *wi:n a:koziw,* where *wi:n* is the third-person singular pronoun, means something like 'him, he is sick.'

8. See Bailin and Grafstein (1985) for a discussion of the theoretical implications of null anaphora in nonconfigurational languages.

9. The term *further obviative* refers to the second of two obviatives, normally to a noun possessed by an obviative third person.

10. See, for example, Bloomfield (1957), Hockett (1966), and Wolfart (1973); see also Grafstein (1984) for a critique of this approach to obviation.

11. The reader may have noticed that I assume obviation to be a person feature. In so doing, I am not claiming that the obviative is some kind of fourth person, as has sometimes been maintained (see, for example, Frantz 1966). I think that what justifies treating obviation as a person feature is that it functions in a similar way to other person features in distinguishing the referent of the argument to which it refers from the referents of other arguments in the same sentence. In this sense it functions differently from the singular/plural distinction. *I* and *us,* for example, differ only in

that *I* is singular and *us* is plural. Their referents *intersect*. A nonobviative and an obviative third person, on the other hand, are *disjoint* in reference.

REFERENCES

Bailin, A., and A. Grafstein. 1985. Configurationality and the Theta-Criterion. *The McGill Working Papers in Linguistics/Cahiers Linguistiques de McGill* 2, no. 2:1–11.

Bloomfield, L. 1957. *Eastern Ojibwa: Grammatical Sketches, Texts, and Word Lists*. Ann Arbor: University of Michigan Press.

Chomsky, N. 1981. *Lectures on Government and Binding*. Dordrecht, Holland: Foris Publications.

Chomsky, N. 1982. *Some Concepts and Consequences of the Theory of Government and Binding*. Linguistic Inquiry Monograph 6. Cambridge: MIT Press.

Frantz, D. 1966. Person Indexing in Blackfoot. *International Journal of American Linguistics* 32:50–58.

Grafstein, A. 1984. *Argument Structure and the Syntax of a Non-Configurational Language*. Ph.D. Diss., McGill University.

Hale, K. 1981. On the Position of Walpiri in a Typology of the Base. Bloomington: Indiana University Linguistics Club.

Hale, K. 1982. Preliminary Remarks on Configurationality. In *NELS 12*, Amherst, Mass.: Graduate Student Linguistic Association, pp. 86–96.

Hale, K. 1983. Warlpiri and the Grammar of Non-Configurational Languages. *Natural Language and Linguistic Theory* 1:5–47.

Hockett, C. 1966. What Algonquian Is Really Like. *International Journal of American Linguistics* 32:59–73.

Jackendoff, R. 1972. *Semantic Interpretation in Generative Grammar*. Cambridge: MIT Press.

Williams, E. 1981. Argument Structure and Morphology. *The Linguistic Review* 1:81–114.

Wolfart, H. C. 1973. *Plains Cree: A Grammatical Study*. Transactions of the American Philosophical Society. New Series - Volume 63, part 5. Philadelphia: American Philosophical Society.

ARGUMENT STRUCTURE AND THE MORPHOLOGY OF THE OJIBWA VERB

Glyne L. Piggott

INTRODUCTION

Ojibwa is a nonconfigurational language. As is typical of such languages, it has a relatively free word order and a rich system of affixes. The richness of the system of affixes is most strikingly revealed in the composition of verb forms; by comparison, affixation on nouns is quite limited. An indication of the role of affixes is provided by the following two sentences.

[1] a. nigi:wa:bama: mo:z 'I saw a moose'
ni-gi:-wa:bam-a: mo:z
1-past-see-3 moose

b. nigi:wa:bamig mo:z 'The moose saw me'
ni-gi:-wa:bam-igw mo:z
1-past-see-3 moose

Superficially, the only formal difference between these two sentences is in the endings of the verbs; the verb in sentence [1a] has the suffix *-a:* where [1b] has *-igw*. This difference, however, is correlated with what might be viewed as the grammatical function of the NPs in the sentences; the noun *mo:z* must be interpreted as 'object' in [1a] but as 'subject' in [1b]. The order of words is largely irrelevant, for well-formed sentences with the meanings indicated in [1] would result from reversing the word order.

The irrelevance of word order and the importance of affixes are further revealed in the following data. The sentences in [2] all mean 'John saw his (own) dog'.

[2] **a.** John ogi:wa:bama:n odayan
John o-gi:-wa:bam-a:-an o-day-an
John 3-past-see-3-obv 3-dog-obv
b. John odayan ogi:wa:bama:n
c. ogi:wa:bama:n John odayan
d. odayan ogi:wa:bama:n John

In contrast the following all mean 'John's dog saw him (John)'.

[3] **a.** John ogi:wa:bamigo:n odayan
John o-gi:-wa:bam-igw-an o-day-an
John 3-past-see-3-obv 3-dog-obv
b. John odayan ogi:wa:bamigo:n
c. ogi:wa:bamigo:n John odayan
d. odayan ogi:wa:bamigo:n John

From the data just cited, it should be obvious that the appropriate interpretation of sentences is determined largely by the nature of the affixes on verbs and nouns. This paper outlines an approach to the analysis of the Ojibwa verb that illuminates the properties of certain affixes and underlines their crucial role in the morphosyntax of Ojibwa. A major part of the study focusses on the function of the personal affixes such as *ni-* (first person), *ki-* (second person) and *o-* / *-w* (third person) as these interact with the class of affixes represented by *-a:* and *-igw*. I show how certain principles, especially the Theta Criterion (Chomsky, 1981), determine how these verbal affixes function. My analysis also provides a basis for understanding the traditional classification of verb stems in Ojibwa and other Algonquian languages.

This paper is organized roughly as follows. It begins with a presentation of a fairly traditional description of features of the Ojibwa verb. This is followed by a brief review of basic assumptions about lexical structure with reference to the representation of Ojibwa verb forms. I then look at certain instances of affixation in terms of the role of affixes in encoding properties of arguments and show how the morphology of different verb forms can be explained. Finally, some of the implications of the analysis both for a grammar of Ojibwa and for the theory of grammar are explored.

1. BACKGROUND

Ojibwa, like other Algonquian languages, assigns nouns to one of two grammatical classes, traditionally identified as animate and inanimate gender. The nouns in [4a] are animate and those in [4b] are inanimate. The meanings of the forms in the different classes indicate that the distinction is not semantically based.[1]

[4] a. Animate (AN):	b. Inanimate (IN):
akik 'pail'	ona:gan 'cup'
a:gam 'snowshoe'	makizin 'shoe'
ogima: 'leader'	ǰi:ma:n 'boat'
miši:min 'apple'	makak 'box'
miskomin 'raspberry'	ode:himin 'strawberry'

One of the indicators of the different classes is the way in which plural is marked. The plural of animate nouns is formed by affixation of the suffix *-ag* (or one of its morphophonemic variants), while the corresponding suffix for inanimate nouns is *-an* (or one of its variants). Another indicator is the different forms a verb takes when it appears in construction with nouns of different classes.

1.1. Intransitive Verbs

Consider the difference between [5a] and [5b].

[5] a. bi:nizi akik 'The pail is clean'
b. bi:nad ona:gan 'The dish is clean'

The two verb forms *bi:nizi* and *bi:nad* are determined by the classes of the nouns of which they are predicated, *akik* being animate and *ona:gan* inanimate. To interchange these forms would result in ungrammatical sentences. Traditionally, a form such as *bi:nizi* is classified as an animate intransitive (AI) verb, because it requires an animate subject, while *bi:nad* is an inanimate intransitive (II) verb, because its subject must be inanimate.[2]

The two verb forms in [5a] and [5b] obviously share a common root. Thus, the function of indicating whether a form is AI or II can be readily assigned to the endings. Bloomfield and others label these endings *finals* (F) and categorize those that appear on intransitive verbs into two types. The ending *-izi* on the verb form *bi:nizi* [5a] is an AI-final and *bi:nad* [5b] contains the II-final *-ad*. The general assumption is that such finals are added to what might be called roots to form verb stems, selectionally marked for the type of noun with which they may co-occur. The form of an AI or II verb stem is not entirely predictable from the root, since there is more than one final for each category. Moreover, the affixation of an AI-final such as *-izi* does not always correlate with the affixation of II-final *-ad*. The list of intransitive verb stems given in [6] shows the different finals and how they are paired.

[6] *Intransitive Stems:*

AI	II	
ni:nim-izi	ni:nim-ad	'be weak'

oza:w-izi	oza:w-a:	'be brown'
zo:ng-izi	zo:ng-an	'be strong, firm'
zak-iz-o	zak-id-e:	'burn'
ago:ǰ-in	ago:d-e:	'hang'
bangiš-in	bangis-in	'fall'[3]
maškawaǰ-i	maškawad-in	'be frozen'
we:na:ǰ-iw-i	we:na:ǰ-iw-an	'be pretty'

In addition to pairs of intransitives, such as those in [6], several verbs show no difference betweeen the AI and II stems and a few show suppletion. Examples of the latter are listed in [7] and of the former in [8].

[7] AI	II	
aya:	ate:	'be in a place'
mindido	miča:	'be big'

[8] AI/II	
bi:goška:	'be broken'
žo:biška:	'be bent'
mo:škine:	'be full'
zi:gise:	'spill'
biska:bi:	'return'

Verb stems such as those in [6], [7], and [8] may undergo further affixation. The first person [1] prefix *ni-* and the second person [2] prefix *ki-* may appear before AI stems.[4] Affixes marking tense also may be prefixed; they always follow the personal prefixes. It is interesting to note that the third person [3] prefix *o-* does not occur before intransitive verb stems. The traditional analysis assumes that the presence of a third person subject is marked by a suffix *-w*, which may follow either an AI or an II stem.[5] A number of other suffixes also may follow finals. These include various aspectual markers and personal suffixes that indicate agreement with a plural subject. The suffixes that follow finals are generally classified as inflectional. An intransitive verb form may contain the following components, though each is not present in every form.

[9] PERSON + TENSE + X + FINAL + PERSON + ASPECT + NUMBER

The schema in [9] does not capture all the possible affixes in an intransitive verb form. The component represented as X may contain several affixes in addition to a basic verb root. However, such affixes do not figure in the analysis of verbs provided in this study.

1.2. Transitive Verbs

Transitive verbs show a distinction comparable to that shown by the intransitives in [5]. The relevant distinction is reflected in [10].

[10] **a.** niwa:bama: akik 'I see a pail'
b. niwa:banda:n ona:gan 'I see a dish'

The standard description of Ojibwa follows Bloomfield (1946; 1957) in attributing the difference between the verb forms in [10] to the fact that transitive verbs must be marked for agreement with their objects. The sentence in [10a] requires a verb called a transitive-animate (TA) verb (*niwa:bama:*) because the object is an animate noun, while the transitive-inanimate (TI) verb (*niwa:banda:n*) in [10b] is required by the presence of an inanimate noun as object.

The TA verb *niwa:bama:* is analyzed as containing a root *wa:b* 'see' and a final *-am,* which form a TA verb stem *wa:bam* 'see something animate'. This is restricted to occurring only when the object of the verb is an animate noun. The TI verb *niwa:banda:n* is traditionally regarded as containing a separate and distinct final *-and,* added directly to the root. However, this analysis is rejected by Piggott (1979), who argued that the TI stem should be derived from the TA stem by affixation of a morpheme *-d.* The function of this affix will be discussed later. It is sufficient to note here that in the TI verb form in [10b], the suffix *-d,* is followed by a final *am.* Thus, the pair of verb stems in [10] is *wa:bam* (TA) and *wa:bam-d-am* (TI). The suffix *-d* appears in many but not all TI stems; its appearance, however, is not entirely unpredictable. It is determined by the particular TA-final to which it is attached. As might have been guessed from the situation with intransitives, there are several TA-finals. Examples of TA stems and the corresponding TI ones are given in [11] and [12]. The examples in [11] contain the suffix *-d,* while those in [12] do not.

[11]	TA	TI	
a.	wa:b-am	wa:b-am-d-am	'see'
b.	apag-in	apag(i)-d-am[6]	'throw'
c.	gike:n-im	gike:n-d-am	'know'

[12]	TA	TI	
a.	mak-aw	mak-am	'find'
b.	onz-w	onz-am	'boil'
c.	we:b-in[7]	we:b-in-am	'abandon'

Piggott (1979) proposes that, in the derivation of TI stems, the suffix *-d* normally is attached to TA stems containing the finals *-am, -in*<1>, *-im,* or the causative final *-ih.* It normally does not follow the TA-finals *-aw, -w* and *-in*<2>. The finals *-im* and *-in*<1> are subject to truncation, in the sense of Aronoff (1976), before the suffix *-d.* Notice also that the finals *-aw* and *-w* in [12a] and [12b] also undergo truncation, the context being before the final *-am.* Thus, a TI stem like *gike:n-d-am* [11c] is really derived from *gike:n-im-d-am* and a stem like *mak-am* [12a] is really derived from *mak-aw-am.*[8]

It is generally recognized that there are more morphological patterns involving pairs of transitive verbs than those shown in [11] and [12]. The patterns represented in [13] are quite common. The first column contains TA stems and the second the corresponding stem that occurs when the object is an inanimate noun.

[13]	TA	TI	
a.	bi:n	bi:-d-o:	'bring'
b.	wan-ih	wan-ih-d-o:[9]	'lose'
c.	biskiš-im	biskis(i)-d-o:	'bend'
d.	bi-m	bi-m-o:	'remove'
e.	na:n	na:-d-i	'fetch'

The stems in the 'TI' column have not been traditionally classified as TI stems. Bloomfield (1957) considered these to be members of a class of pseudo-transitive verbs. He assumed that TI stems should contain the final *-am,* which is present in all of the TI forms shown in [11] and [12]. None of the forms in the second column of [13] has this affix. I argued against the traditional analysis in Piggott (1979) on the grounds that any typological distinction between TI forms in [11] and [12] and the forms identified in (13) as TI would be purely arbitrary. Apart from the difference in finals the verbal morphology makes no other distinction between these forms. Such a difference does not necessarily signal a typological difference, since it is recognized that a number of different finals may mark a particular type. For example, there are several AI-finals, and we have just recognized several TA-finals. It would be reasonable to expect that there would be several TI-finals, if there is a distinct category of TI stems. Following this reasoning, the TI forms in [11] and [12] and the second column forms in [13] must be recognized as one type.

The problem that the traditional description of Ojibwa verbs attempts to handle by labelling arises as a result of the recognition that the finals that appear in the second column forms in [13] are identical to AI-finals. The finals *-o:* and *-i* appear in AI stems such as the following

[14]		
	bimibat-o:	'run'
	onwa:t-o:	'be noisy'
	wa:b-i	'see'
	maw-i	'cry'
	namadab-i	'sit'

Since the verb stems in second column of [13] contain elements characteristic of intransitive verbs (i.e. AI-finals), it was felt that they could not be classified as true transitives. However, since they occur with nouns as objects, they could not be seen as true intransitives either. Hence, a category of pseudo-transitives was recognized.

The second column forms in [13], which obviously are related to TA stems, are not the only Ojibwa verbs that have AI-finals but may appear in sentences with nouns as objects. A fairly significant number of verbs show such behavior and are not related to TA stems. Consider the data in [15].

[15]	**a.** gimo:di	'He steals'
	b. ni-gimo:di-n ji:ma:n	'I steal a canoe'
	c. o-gimo:di-n-an miši:min-an	'He steals an apple'

The verb forms in [15] are based on the stem *gimo:di* 'steal' which contains the AI-final *-i*. Sentences [15b] and [15c] clearly show that this verb may take either an inanimate noun as an object (*ǰi:ma:n*) or an animate one (*miši:min*). Given the data in [15] and the second column forms of [13], it is obvious that the presence of an intransitive verb final does not entail that the verb cannot take a noun as an object.

The occurrence of data such as [15] does not mean that the second column forms of [13] are not members of a special class of verbs. The verb in [15] could be just another member of this class, the defining properties of which are (a) that they contain AI-finals and (b) that they function like transitives (i.e. they take nouns as objects). This is the position taken in the traditional analysis; the verb *gimo:di* 'steal' in [15] is regarded as a pseudo-transitive. However, there is convincing evidence that even stems like the ones in [11] and [12], which are classified as TIs, contain a final that is identical to one that appears on AI verb stems. For example, all the AI stems in [16] contain the final *-am*.

[16]	bo:n-am	'lay (an egg)'
	asosod-am	'cough'
	wi:sa:ge:nd-am	'suffer'
	ode:nd-am	'be jealous'

The TI final *-am* recognized in [11] and [12] cannot be distinguished from the final in [16] on either phonological or morphological grounds. Moreover, some TI stems seem to function both as transitives and as intransitives. Consider the following data.

[17]	**a.** gike:ndam	'He knows'
	b. gike:ndam a:kozid animoš	'He knows that the dog is sick'
	c. ogike:nda:n a:diso:ka:n	'He knows the legend'

The verb *ogike:nda:n* in [17c], which consists of the third person prefix *-o,* the stem *gike:ndam,* and a suffix *-n,* is typically TI, whereas *gike:ndam* in [17a] is AI in form and function. Notice that third person subject is marked by the prefix *o-* in [17c] but not in [17a]; the third person form of an AI verb never has a prefix.

The observations made so far point to the obvious conclusion that every TI verb form contains an AI-final. Thus, the TI forms in [11] and [12] and the second column forms of [13] cannot be treated as different classes. The position taken in Piggott (1979) goes even further. There I argued that AIs and TIs should not be treated as fundamentally different types of verbs. The verbal morphology offers no support for such a distinction.

Ojibwa verbal morphology does indicate, however, that the TA verb constitutes a distinct type. There is a set of affixes, called *theme-signs* (TS), that may appear only with TA stems. These affixes are *-a:*, *-igw*, *-i*, and *-ini*. The following data give some idea of their distribution.[10]

[18] **a.** niwa:bama:g — 'I see them'
ni-wa:b-am-a:-ag
1-see-F-TS-3Pl

b. niwa:bamigo:g — 'They see me'
ni-wa:b-am-igw-ag
1-see-F-TS-1Pl

c. kiwa:bamimin — 'You see us'
ki-wa:b-am-i-min[11]
2-see-F-TS-1Pl

d. kiwa:baminim — 'I see you (plural)'
ki-wa:b-am-ini-m
2-see-F-TS-2Pl

Notice that the forms of the verb in [18a] and [18b] differ in the identity of the theme-sign, and the thematic roles of the participants are reversed. These theme-signs traditionally have been described as having the following functions: (a) *-a:* indicates third person object and is called the *direct theme-sign;* (b) *-igw* indicates third person subject and is called the *inverse theme-sign;* (c) *-i* marks second person subject when first person is object; (d) *-ini* marks first person subject when second person is object. As the data in [18] show, the theme-signs may be followed by suffixes that mark agreement for number. Affixes with various aspectual functions may also follow the theme-signs.

1.3. Verbal Inflectional Categories

The Ojibwa verb forms discussed so far would appear in declarative main clauses. Verbs that appear in interrogative sentences and subordinate clauses are inflected quite differently. Traditional Ojibwa grammar, therefore, distinguishes a set of *independent* forms that occur in declarative clauses from the set of *conjunct* forms that appear in interrogative and subordinate clauses. One of the most noticeable differences between the two sets of forms is that personal prefixes do not occur in conjunct verb forms. Distinctions for person is marked only by suffixes. It is may be noted that an identical set of conjunct suffixes is added to AI and TI verbs, indicating that the verbal morphology often treats these types in a similar manner.

Verbs in the independent paradigm as well as those in the conjunct paradigm differentiate four aspectual types. Traditional descriptions recognize the *preterite, dubitative,* and *preterite-dubitative* aspects. The preterite roughly refers to events completed in the past, the dubitative indicates nonevidential or doubtful occurrences, and the preterite-dubitative combines the meanings of the first two. The fourth aspectual type, called the *indicative,* is considered to be 'unmarked' for aspect. This paper will focus on properties of indicative forms in the independent paradigm. However, the basic principles of the proposed analysis should generalize readily to all aspects in both the independent and the conjunct paradigms.

The observations made in the preceding sections draw attention to some typically Algonquian features that must be accounted for: (a) The morphologically marked classification of verbs is not between transitives and intransitives but between verbs that must take animate objects (TAs) and those that do not have this restriction. (b) The TI verbs, which are derived from TAs, occur with inanimate objects but pattern morphologically with verbs that cannot take objects. (c) The personal prefixes and the theme-signs interact to ensure proper assignment of thematic roles in transitive clauses containing TA verbs. Illumination of these features of the Ojibwa verb can be provided in the theoretical framework to be sketched.

1.4. Theoretical Framework

My analysis of Ojibwa verbs is situated in the framework of Government-Binding (GB) Theory (Chomsky 1981). GB theory assumes a set of universal principles that must hold in every grammar under the appropriate conditions. The morphology of the Ojibwa verb offers an interesting perspective on the way in which certain principles may be manifested in a grammar. Of particular interest are the Projection Principle and the Theta Criterion. The Projection Principle requires that the properties of lexical items hold at all levels of grammar. This principle is of direct relevance to the way in which distinctions of transitivity are encoded in Ojibwa. There are different formulations of the second principle, the Theta Criterion, in the literature, but its essentials may be expressed as follows:

[19] *Theta Criterion:*

> Each obligatory argument bears one and only one theta-role and each theta-role is assigned to one and only one argument.

The analysis to follow will try to define the conditions under which the Theta Criterion holds in Ojibwa.

The position taken in this paper is influenced primarily by the concept of argument structure elaborated in Williams (1981a) and by the analysis of Ojibwa developed by Grafstein (1984). Williams defines the argument structure of a lexical item as "a labelled listing of the arguments that a lexical item can have." Following Grafstein, it is assumed that the lexical entry of an Ojibwa verb contains a specification of the number of arguments it may take, each argument being associated with a particular thematic role such as agent (A), theme (Th), goal (G), etc. I argue that certain verbal affixes assign features to arguments, thereby identifying them (in a sense to be made precise later). The morphology of a verb form is largely determined by which of the arguments in an argument structure is identified and by the number of identified arguments. It appears that the number of identified arguments may range from zero to a maximum of two.

Certain assumptions about lexical representations also inform this analysis of the Ojibwa verb. The model of word structure outlined in Selkirk (1982) and further elaborated in Walsh (1985) is accepted as essentially correct. Affixes and roots are regarded as lexical entries. Each lexical entry contains information about its subcategorization and its category membership. As indicated earlier, it is also assumed that each lexical item is specified for the arguments that it may take. Affixes and roots are inserted into structures generated by a set of word structure rules. The set of representations, the set of word structure rules, and a set of principles together account for all the well-formed words of a language. Fully affixed words are inserted into syntactic structures.

Among the set of principles that govern word structure are the principles of X-bar theory. A basic claim of this theory is that constructions are headed. Words, like phrases, therefore are assumed to have heads. The location of the head of a word seems to be parametrically determined. Languages like English define the head by a rule proposed first by Williams (1981b) and modified by Selkirk (1982, 20) as follows:

[20] *Right-Hand Head Rule (revised):*

In a word-internal configuration

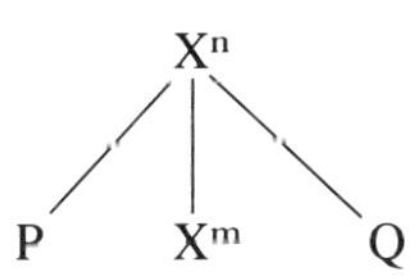

where *X* stands for a syntactic feature complex and where *Q* contains no category with *X*, X^m is the head of X^n.

The head of a word transmits its properties to the entire word by means of *Percolation* (Selkirk 1982, 21).

[21] *Percolation:*

If a constituent α is the head of a constituent β, α and β are associated with the identical set of features (syntactic and diacritic).

Ojibwa provides some support for the right-hand head rule (RHHR). There are denominal verbs and deverbal nominals, both of which are formed by suffixation. These are illustrated in [22] and [23], respectively.

[22] **a.** ogima: 'leader, chief'
b. ogima:wi 'be a leader, chief'

[23] **a.** nagamo 'to sing'
b. nagamowin 'song'

Examples of [22b] and [23b] have the structures shown in [24a] and [24b], respectively.

[24] **a.** **b.**

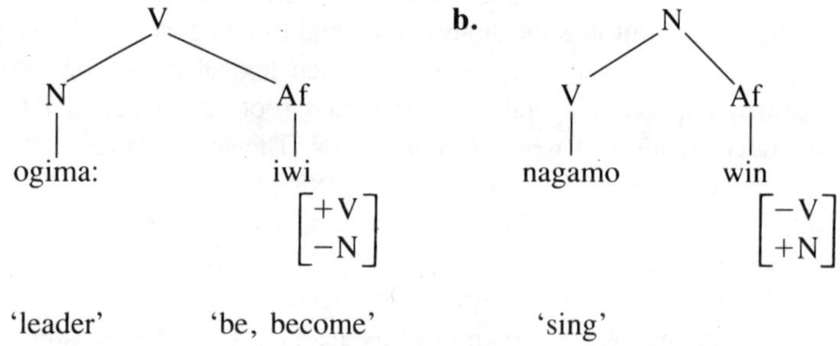

The hypothesis that Ojibwa is right-headed figures prominently in the analysis of verbs.

2. LEXICAL PROPERTIES OF OJIBWA VERBS

In GB theory, lexical items must be specified for the thematic roles they may assign to noun phrases. As indicated earlier, I follow Williams (1981a) in assuming that this specification is in the form of a labelled listing of arguments (i.e. an argument structure). The argument structure of some basic verb roots of Ojibwa is given in [25], using a formalism adapted from Hale (1983) and Grafstein (1984).

[25] bi:n (x-Th) 'clean'
wa:b (x-A) 'see'
gimo:d (x-A, y-Th) 'steal something'
mi: (x-A, y-Th) 'give something'

Generally, verb roots are lexically specified for at least one argument, but some verbs have no argument structure, such as the weather verbs *gimiwan* 'rain', *no:din* 'be windy' and *zo:gipo* 'snow'.

2.1. The Finals

Roots such as those in [25] must, of course, be followed by finals. In sections 1.1 and 1.2, it was observed that finals are often differentiated between those that indicate that the verb takes an animate noun as 'object' and those that distinguish between animate and inanimate 'subjects' of intransitive verbs. The latter can be accounted for by assuming that some intransitive finals are specified [+animate] and others [−animate]. If finals are treated as heads, then, as required by the Right-hand Head Rule [20] and the Percolation Principle [21], the specification [± animate] becomes a feature of the verb. The feature is assigned to the argument structure of the verb. Thus, the derived argument structures of the AI verb *bi:nizi* [5a] and the II verb *bi:nad* [5b] are as shown in [26a] and [26b], respectively.

[26] a. bi:n-izi (x[+animate]-Th) 'be clean'
b. bi:n-ad (x[−animate]-Th) 'be clean'

Some intransitive verbs such as those cited in [8] are not differentiated for the gender of their arguments. A verb such as *mo:škine:* 'be full' [8] can be predicated of either an animate or an inanimate noun. Such verbs may be accounted for by assuming a set of intransitive finals that lack lexical specification for gender. Hence, neither [+animate] nor [−animate] is assigned to the argument structure of the derived verb. The argument structure of *mo:škin* would be as in [24a] and would be unchanged in the derived intransitive verb [27b].

[27] a. mo:škin (x-Th) 'full'
b. mo:škin-e: (x-Th) 'be full'

As pointed out in section 1.1, there are several AI- and II-finals, and the combination of a given final with a particular root does not appear to be predictable. This would indicate that each root is lexically subcategorized by the finals that may be attached to it. A root such as *wa:b* 'see' is lexically specified as taking the AI-final *-i*, whereas a root like *bi:n* 'be clean' is subcategorized by the finals *-izi* (AI) and *-ad* (II). A different pair of intransitive finals *-izi* (AI) and *-an* (II) subcategorizes a root such as *zi:w* 'be sour', whereas the pair *-izi* (AI) and *-a:* (II) subcategorizes *miskw* 'red'. Although the affixation of specific finals to specific roots does not appear to be predictable, certain patterns can be discerned. For example, the AI-final *-izi* is affixed only to verb roots with the argument structure (x-Th). In comparison, the finals *-i*, *-o:*, and *-am* are affixed only to roots whose argument structures contain the specification (x-A), requiring that the x-argument be linked to the thematic role of agent.[12] Examples of the latter are cited in [14] and [16]. This restriction on the appearance of AI-finals *-i, -o:,* and *-am* will figure prominently in the analysis of the TI verbs given later.

Roots also are subcategorized by transitive finals. However, unlike intransitive finals, there is no pairing of transitive finals. The set of transitive finals is restricted to those that form TA stems, see [11], [12], and [13]. Thus, a root like *gike:n* 'know' is subcategorized by the final *-im* and *we:b* 'abandon' by the final *-in*⟨2⟩. Normally, only one TA-final may be attached directly to a given root. However, there are cases in which a particular root may be followed by more than one final. Consider the following data.

[28]	**a.** dakw	'hold'
	b. dakw-in(2) [dakon]	'hold something (animate)'
	c. dakw-im [dakom]	'hold in one's teeth something (animate)'
[29]	**a.** ze:g	'afraid, frighten'
	b. ze:g-ih	'frighten something (animate)'
	c. ze:g-im	'frighten by using one's mouth something (animate)'

The TA final in [28c] and [29c] *-im* has a fairly clearly identifiable meaning 'by use of mouth', whereas the final *-ih* derives causative verbs.

Often, the meaning of roots is modified not by finals but by other types of affixes to which finals then are attached. A typical situation is the following set of TA stems, all involving the root *ga:nd* 'push' or one of its morphophonemic variants.

[30]	**a.** ga:nd-in	'push something animate'
	b. ga:nd-ah-w	'push with instrument something (animate)
	c. ga:nǰ-ibi-n	'push with hands something (animate)'
	d. ga:ns-ikk-aw	'push with foot something (animate)'
	e. ga:nǰ-iwe:b-išk-aw	'push roughly with foot something (animate)'

Notice, for example, that in [30b] the instrumental suffix is followed by the TA final *-w*, and in [30e] there are two prefinal suffixes, each of which adds something to the meaning of the root.

Returning now to the characterization of the lexical properties of finals, it is obvious that TA-finals modify the argument structure of the roots to which they are affixed. For example, the derivation of the TA stem *wa:bam* 'see something animate' from a root such as *wa:b* as represented in [25b] involves the addition of an argument. This type of modification, however, is not peculiar to this derivation. It is possible to maintain that the derivation of a TA stem by the addition of a final always involves the addition of an argument. Moreover, the argument invariably is [+animate]. These facts may be accounted for readily by assuming that every TA-final actually has an argument structure containing an argument linked to a particular thematic role. Thus, the final *-am* would have the argument structure shown in [31a] and the argument structure of *wa:bam* 'see something (animate)' is as in [31b].

[31] **a.** -am (y[+animate]-Th)
b. wa:bam (x-A, y[+animate]-Th)

I assumed earlier that finals are heads of verb stems. Given this assumption, the argument structure of a TA final must be inherited by the verb. The result of argument inheritance is revealed most clearly when a TA-final is added to a root whose argument structure contains more than one argument. For example, the final *-in*⟨1⟩ has the following specification: (y[+animate]-Th). This suffix may be attached to roots such as *bi:* [32a] or *mi:* [33a].

[32]	**a.**	bi: (x-A)	'bring'
	b.	bi:-in[bi:n] (x-A, y[+animate]-Th)	'bring something (animate)'
[33]	**a.**	mi: (x-A, y Th)	'give something'
	b.	mi:-in [mi:n] (x-A, y-Th, y[+animate]-Th)	

The stem *bi:n* [32b] means 'bring something (animate)', but *mi:n* [33b] means 'give something to someone, something (animate)'. If the representation in [33b] is derived by the affixation of the final *-in* to the root *mi:,* it clearly is problematic. It is not consistent with the meaning of the TA stem *mi:n* 'give something to someone', and it implies that there could be two arguments of the verb both functioning as themes. The problem of [33b] can be resolved by assuming a general convention that changes this representation to the one in [34].

[34] mi:n (x-A, y[+animate]-G, z-Th) 'give to someone (animate) something'

The required adjustment to argument structure reflected in [34] would entail that the argument introduced by the TA-final must assume the role of goal. Other affixes that may be added to the TA stem may refer to this argument but not to the lexically specified (y-Th) argument, now identified as (z-Th). The latter cannot influence the morphology of the TA verb.

The convention just introduced also is needed to account for the argument structure of benefactive verbs derived from TI stems (ultimately from TA stems). These verbs contain the TA-final *-aw,* which has the argument specification (y[+animate]-Th). The claim that the argument introduced by this TA-final normally is a theme supported by TA stems such as those in [35].

[35]	no:nd-aw (x-A, y[+animate]-Th)	'hear something (animate)'
	we:pid-aw (x-A, y[+animate]-Th)	'hit something (animate)'
	mak-aw (x-A, y[+animate]-Th)	'find something (animate)'
	bizind-aw (x-A, y[+animate]-Th)	'listen to something (animate)'

When this final is added to a TI stem such as *bi:d-* (x-A, y-Th) 'bring something', the derived argument structure must be adjusted to provide for the benefactive interpretation. Note the set of forms in [36].

[36]	bi:n (x-A, y[+animate]-Th)	'bring something (animate)'
	bi:-d-o: (x-A, y-Th)	'bring something'
	bi:-d-aw (x-A, y[+animate]-G, z-Th)	'bring to someone (animate) something'

Later discussion will clarify the relationship between the TA and TI forms of the verb and the derivation of benefactives from the latter.

It should be apparent from what has been said so far that, apart from being subcategorized by finals, Ojibwa verb roots have no inherent lexical features that distinguish transitive from intransitive verbs. Roots that are lexically specified as having only one argument may take both intransitive and transitive finals. Thus, a root such as *ze:g* 'afraid, frighten' [29a], which has a single argument (x-Th), may form an intransitive verb *ze:g-izi* 'be afraid' or may be followed by TA-finals as shown in [29b] and [29c]. Similarly, the root *wa:b* 'see' is subcategorized by both the AI-final *-i* and the TA-final *-am,* yielding the intransitive verb *wa:bi* 'see' and the transitive verb *wa:bam* 'see something (animate)'. Even a root like *iž* 'go, come' may be part of an intransitive stem (*iža:* 'go, come') or a transitive stem (*iža:m* 'go, come to someone (animate)').

Further evidence that transitivity in Ojibwa cannot be associated strictly with the number of lexically specified arguments of a root is provided by cases such as *gimo:d* (x-A, y-Th) 'steal something' [25]. This root combines with the AI-final *-i* and the resulting stem *gimo:di* may be inflected in the same way as an AI stem such as *wa:bi* 'see' or *bi:nizi* 'be clean', each of which is specified as having only one argument. Typical inflections for first, second, and third person forms, singular and plural, are shown in [37].

[37]	**a.** 'see':	**b.** 'steal':
1	ni-wa:b(i)	ni-gimo:d(i)[13]
2	ki-wa:b(i)	ki-gimo:d(i)
3	wa:bi-(w)	gimo:di-(w)
1p	ni-wa:bi-min	ni-gimo:di-min
2p	ki-wa:bi-m	ki-gimo:di-m
3p	wa:bi-w-ag	gimo:di-w-ag

In each of these forms only one argument is referred to by the prefix and/or the suffix. Conjunct verb forms, which appear in subordinate clauses and wh-questions, also show no distinction between stems like *gimo:di* and those like *wa:bi.*

Although *gimo:di* patterns morphologically with verb stems that have only one argument, there are at least two reasons for recognizing that the argument structure of the root *gimo:d* contains two lexically specified arguments. First, this root may be followed by certain TA finals. When a TA final is affixed, the resulting verb may take three NPs as arguments. For example, the TA final *-im,* the applicative suffix, may be added to *gimo:d* producing a verb stem *gimo:dim.* This stem clearly has the argument structure (x-A, y[+animate]-G, z-Th) and the meaning 'steal something from someone (animate)', as is shown by the sentences in [38].[14]

[38] **a.** nigi:gimo:dima: bi:ye:n miši:minan
ni-gi:-gimo:d-im-a: bi:ye:n miši:min-an
1-past-steal-F-3 Peter apple-obv
'I stole an apple from Peter.'
b. nigi:gimo:dima: bi:ye:n ǰi:ma:n
'I stole a canoe from Peter.'

Note, however, that in these sentences the form of the verb is not determined by the gender of either *miši:min* 'apple' (animate) or *ǰi:ma:n* 'canoe' (inanimate), each of which bears the role of theme.

The second reason for recognizing two arguments in the root *gimo:d* is that this would explain why the stem *gimo:di* may appear in sentences in which there are NPs that must be interpreted as bearing the role of theme. Such sentences, already cited as [15b] and [15c], are repeated in [39].

[39] **a.** ni-gimo:di-n ǰi:ma:n 'I steal a canoe'
b. o-gimo:di-n-an miši:min-an 'He steals an apple'

The correct interpretation of these sentences can be provided only if the verb has two arguments. These arguments have to be inherent to the root, since none of the affixes attached to the root introduces an argument. Indeed, in some dialects of Ojibwa, there is no difference between the form of the verb when there is an overt NP theme and that when there is no overt theme. For example, in the Algonquin dialects of Northwestern Quebec, the following sentences may be encountered.

[40] **a.** gimo:di 'He steals'
b. gimo:di ǰi:ma:n 'He steals a canoe'
c. gimo:di miši:minan 'He steals an apple'

Verb forms such as those cited in [39] and [40], of course, are the type traditionally classified as pseudo-transitive. They generally exhibit the morphology of intransitive verbs but may appear in transitive constructions. An understanding of the basis for the difference between the pseudo-transitive and the transitive animate (TA) verb can be found in the difference in argument structure, which reflects the difference in derivational history. Consider the representation of a TA stem such as *wa:bam* and a stem such as *gimo:di.*

[41] wa:b-am (x-A, y[+animate]-Th) 'see something (animate)'
gimo:d-i (x[+animate]-A, y-Th) 'steal something'

The important difference is that the y-argument of TA verbs is marked for gender but not that of pseudo-transitive verbs. This is a direct consequence of the fact that every TA-final adds a y-argument that is specified [+animate]. This difference between TA and pseudo-transitive verbs introduces a distinction important for the morphology and semantics of Ojibwa verb forms, namely, the difference between an identified and an unidentified argument. I propose the following characterization of the principle of argument identification.

[42] *Argument Identification:*
An argument is identified if it is marked for gender
(i.e. [±animate]).

Given the analysis developed so far, there are only two sources of identified arguments. Certain intransitive finals mark an x-argument for gender, and TA finals add y-arguments marked [+animate]. It is now possible to capture what pseudo-transitive verbs like *gimo:di* 'steal something' have in common with AI verbs with *wa:bi* 'see'. Both types lack an identified y-argument. The principle of argument identification plays an important role in the analysis of the Ojibwa verb, and it will be considered in more detail in the following sections.

2.2. The Derivation of TI Stems

Earlier I said that the verbal morphology indicates that the transitive-inanimate (TI) verbs, derived from TA stems, are the same type as AIs and pseudo-transitives. In simple declarative sentences, the TIs take the same affixes as the pseudo-transitives and, in subordinate clauses, an identical set of affixes is added to AIs, TIs, and pseudo-transitives. Among the set of common conjunct endings are the following:

[43]	Singular		Plural
1	-(y)a:n	1p	-(y)angw(incl.)
2	-(y)an	1p	-(y)a:ng(excl.)
3	-d/-g	2p	-(y)e:gw
3(obv)	-ini-d	3p	-wa:-d

Each of the suffixes or combination of suffixes just cited indicates agreement with only one argument. If the morphology of a verb reflects properties of its argument structure, then it must be shown that the argument structure of TI verbs is not like that of TA verbs but like that of AIs and/or pseudo-transitives.

The argument structure of a verb must determine, to some extent, the syntactic contexts in which the verb is found. The following data illustrate the range of occurrence of TI verbs in simple declarative clauses. The stem involved is *gike:ndam* 'know something', which is derived from the TA stem *gike:nim* 'know something (animate)'.

[44] **a.** nigike:ndam 'I know'
b. nigike:nda:n a:diso:ka:n 'I know the legend'
c. nigike:ndam/nigike:nda:n a:kozid animoš 'I know that the dog is ill'

Notice that the suffix *-n* is added to the stem when there is an overt NP-theme [44b]. This can be analyzed as the same suffix that appears in pseudo-transitives such as that in [39a]. Thus, the form of TI verbs and the constructions in which they appear are directly comparable with pseudo-transitive verbs. This would be consistent with the following representation of the argument structure of the TI stem *gike:ndam* (cf. [41]).

[45] gike:ndam (x[+animate]-A, y-Th) 'know something'
gike:n-im-d-am
know—F(TA)—d—F(AI)

Consider, now, how the representation in [45] would be derived. The addition of the suffix *-d* to the TA stem has the effect of removing the identification from the y-argument. Minimally, this would entail the deletion of the feature [+animate] and yield a representation such as [46].

[46] gike:n-im-d (x-A, y-Th)

The form in [46] is not a possible Ojibwa verb stem, since the suffix *-d*, lacking categorial features, cannot be a head. A proper stem may be derived by the addition of a final. The affixation of the AI-final *-am* serves the function of deriving the well-formed stem in [45] from [46].

Recall, now, the observation made earlier that every TI stem contains one of the three AI-finals: *-am, -o:,* and *-i.* These finals may be attached only to roots that contain an argument specified as (x-A). An interesting feature of TA verbs, and indeed a constraint on the well-formedness of these verbs, is that there must be an x-argument associated with the theta-role agent (A). Thus, it is appropriate that the derivation of TI verbs from TA stems would involve the affixation of finals that may only be attached to roots with the specification (x-A).

Although every TI stem must contain one of the three finals just cited, they do not all undergo affixation of *-d*. In Piggott (1979), I argued that there are two patterns of derivation: one involving the affixation of *-d,* the other the affixation of zero (Ø). The latter should be construed as an instance of zero-derivation, however this is captured formally. The process of zero-derivation has the same function as the affixation of *-d,* the removal of the specification [+animate] from the y-argument of a TA stem. The following data give some idea of the derivation of the TI stem *bimo:* 'remove something'.

[47]	bi (x-A) →	'remove'
	bi-m (x-A, y[+animate]-Th) →	'remove something (animate)'
	bi-m-Ø (x-A, y-Th) →	'remove something'
	bi-m-Ø-o: (x[+animate]-A, y-Th)	'some animate agent remove something'

Given the patterns of derivation proposed for TI stems, it follows that the TI verb will always have the following argument structure.

[48] *Argument Structure of TI Verb:*
(x[+animate]-A, y-Th)

The specifications in [48] also are appropriate to the pseudo-transitives. Actually, considering only the argument structure of the verb, there is no distinction to be made between pseudo-transitives and TI verbs. Therefore, these verbs should be expected to behave similarly, and they do. As is recognized even in the traditional analysis of Ojibwa in Bloomfield (1957), some TA verbs (e.g. *na:n* 'fetch something (animate)') are paired with pseudo-transitives (e.g. *na:di-n* 'fetch something (inanimate)') rather than with TIs. Hence, TIs and pseudo-transitives were considered to occupy similar syntactic slots. In terms of the analysis proposed here, those morphological features shared by TIs, pseudo-transitives, and AIs simply mark the presence of a single *identified* argument in the argument structure of a verb.

If the ending *-d,* which is added to some TA stems in the derivation of the corresponding TIs, merely changed the gender specification of the y-argument from [+animate] to [−animate], the proposed account of the morphology of TI verbs would be untenable. A change in the gender specification of the y-argument from [+animate] to [−animate] would not change the status of this argument as determined by the principle of argument identification [42]. Fortunately, there is fairly good evidence that the suffix *-d* should not be considered to mark the presence of an inanimate noun as theme. First, there are sentences such as [44a], where the TI verb occurs but there is no NP-theme. The TI verb may also occur when the verb has a sentential complement, as is the case in sentence [44c].

Additional support for the claim the suffix *-d* does not identify an argument as [−animate] comes from the derivation of benefactive verbs. As shown by the forms in [36], the TI stem *bi:do:* 'bring something' contains the suffix *-d,* but so does the benefactive verb *bi:daw* 'bring something to, for someone'. If the suffix *-d* did identify an argument as [−animate], it would entail that the NP-theme of benefactive constructions should be restricted to an inanimate noun; and this is not the case, as is shown by sentences such as those in [49c and 49d].

[49]	**a.** nibi:na: akik	'I bring a pail'
	b. nibi:do:n ona:gan	'I bring a cup'
	c. nibi:dawa: bi:ye:n akikon	'I bring for Peter a pail'
	d. nibi:dawa: bi:ye:n ona:gan	'I bring for Peter a cup'

Animate nouns such as *akik* 'pail' or inanimate nouns such as *ona:gan* 'cup' may occur quite freely as themes of benefactive verb. Notice that the form of the verb in [49c] and [49d] is not determined by the gender of the theme.

The analysis developed so far has focused on those morphological features that are common to AIs, TIs, and pseudo-transitive verb forms. They all contain finals that identify an x-argument, and they lack identified y-arguments. They are distinguished from TA verbs, which not only require that there be at least two arguments but also that the y-argument must be identified. However, some differences among AIs, TIs, and pseudo-transitives merit direct comment. The difference between AIs and the pseudo-transitives is obvious. The former take only one argument, while the latter have two arguments in their argument structure and may (but need not) occur in constructions in which both arguments are realized. As indicated by the forms in [39], in at least some dialects of Ojibwa, the presence of an NP-theme requires the affixation of the suffix *-n* to pseudo-transitive verbs in simple declarative sentences.

The differences between pseudo-transitives like *gimo:di* 'steal' and TIs also merit comment. One obvious difference is the fact that pseudo-transitives may take animate nouns as themes but TI verbs cannot. Thus, while [39b] is well formed, the following is an unacceptable sentence.

[50] *obi:do:nan miši:minan 'He brings an apple'

This difference between TIs and pseudo-transitives can be related to the derivational history of TIs. A principle analogous to Blocking (Aronoff 1976) may be invoked. Since all TIs have corresponding TAs that must take animate nouns as themes, this principle would prohibit the appearance of a TI verb in a syntactic context in which its base, the TA verb, may also occur. This principle may be expressed as follows:

[51] A verb containing an unidentified y-argument may not assign its theta-role to an NP specified as [+animate] if it is related to a verb with an identified ([+animate]) y-argument.

Another difference between TIs and pseudo-transitives is not explained so readily. Recall that pseudo-transitives may appear in well-formed sentences such as [15a] *gimo:di* 'he steals', in which there is no morphological indication that the theme has been assigned to an NP; the suffix *-n* is lacking. It appears that the theta-role of the y-argument has not been assigned. If TIs always manifest the same behavior as pseudo-transitives, there should be evidence that TI verbs do not have to assign the theta-role of the y-argument.

This appears to be the case for a number of TI stems, such as *bizindam* 'listen to something', *no:ndam* 'hear something', and *gike:ndam* 'know something', as indicated by the following data.

[52]	nibizindam	'I listen'
	nino:ndam	'I hear'
	nigike:ndam	'I know'

However, stems such as *wa:bandam* 'see something', *bi:do:* 'bring something', and *na:di-* 'fetch something' do not seem to occur in sentences equivalent to those in [52]. The sentences in [53] have not been attested in Ojibwa, but those in [54] are well formed.

[53]	*niwa:bandam	'I see'
	*nibi:do:	'I bring'
	*nina:d[i]	'I fetch'
[54]	niwa:banda:n	'I see it (inanimate)'
	nibi:do:n	'I bring it (inanimate)'
	nina:din	'I fetch it (inanimate)'

The status of forms like those in [53] require further investigation. If they are unacceptable in all dialects of Ojibwa, a possible explanation to be pursued is that some derived TIs are lexically marked as requiring affixation of *-n* in first and second person forms. This possibility is suggested by the fact that, in most of the Algonquin dialects of Ojibwa, forms such as those in [52] do not occur. The equivalent forms are given in [55].

[55]	nibizinda:n	'I listen, I listen to it (inanimate)'
	nino:nda:n	'I hear, I hear it (inanimate)'
	nigike:nda:n	'I know, I know it (inanimate)'

Notice that each of the forms in [55] is ambiguous. The nature of the ambiguity suggests that the presence of the suffix *-n* does not mean that the theta-role of the y-argument has been assigned to an NP. Acceptance of this possibility would permit us to maintain the position that is implicit in our concept of an unidentified argument, namely, that such arguments do not have to assign their theta-roles. This would entail that even TI forms like those in [54] are ambiguous with a form like *nina:din* [54] meaning either 'I fetch' or 'I fetch it (inanimate)'. A verb like *nigimo:d[i]*, cited earlier, also is ambiguous. It means either 'I steal' or 'I steal something'.

It should be emphasized that the ambiguity of a form such as *nigimo:d[i]* is not to be attributed to semantics of the root per se but is a consequence of the fact that the root *gimo:d* contains two arguments. Some support for this position comes from the behavior of the verb *wi:sini* 'eat'. This verb contains only one lexically specified argument and the form *niwi:sin[i]* means 'I eat'.

It cannot mean 'I eat it (inanimate)'. The form with the latter meaning is *nimi:jin*. This is because there is a stem *mi:ǰi* 'eat something' with the argument structure (x[+animate]-A, y-Th). This accounts for the well-formedness of [56a] but the unacceptability of [56b].

[56] **a.** nimi:ǰin wi:ya:s 'I eat meat'
b. *niwi:sinin wi:ya:s 'I eat meat'

Notice that both *wi:sini* and *mi:ǰi* contain the AI-final *-i*.

To summarize the account of Ojibwa verbal morphology provided so far, the following features should be kept in mind. The class of affixes called *finals* subcategorizes the verbal roots and partly determines the argument structure of derived verb stems. All transitive finals are specified as inherently having an identified [+animate] argument, while intransitive finals may only modify the argument structure of a root by adding gender specification to an argument. The analysis of the function of finals illuminates the traditional distinctions of verb types recognized in Algonquian languages and explains why AIs, TIs, and pseudo-transitives manifest similar morphological characteristics. The distinctness of the TA verb stem also emerges clearly, for this is the only type in which there is an identified y-argument. I turn next to an analysis of the function of the personal affixes and the theme-signs, which should further illuminate the structure of TA verb forms.

2.3. Theme-Signs and Personal Affixes

I earlier introduced a set of affixes attached to Ojibwa verb forms in declarative sentences to mark person. These are the prefixes *ni-* (first person = 1), *ki-* (second person = 2) and *o-* (third person = 3). In addition, there is a suffix *-w* that also marks third person. The prefix *o-* may occur only when the verb contains two or more arguments, and the suffix *-w* is attached whenever the verb contains only one argument. The latter normally will be an AI or II verb. However, in some dialects the suffix *-w* also is affixed to all pseudo-transitives and TI forms. By contrast, in other dialects, the prefix *o-* is added to a pseudo-transitive verb when the theta-role of the unidentified y-argument has been assigned to an NP, whereas the suffix *-w* occurs when the y-argument has not assigned its theta-role to an NP.

The personal affixes have a function similar to that of finals; each assigns a feature to an argument. When a personal affix is added to a TI, AI, or psuedo-transitive stem, it assigns the relevant specification for person to the x-argument. This would yield representations such as those that follow.

[57] ni-ze:giz[i] (x[+animate, 1]-Th) 'I am afraid'
ze:gizi-(w) (x[+animate, 3]-Th) 'He is afraid'

The addition of a personal affix to a TA stem, on the other hand, may result in the assignment of a specification to either of two arguments.

[58] **a.** ni-wa:bam-a: (x[1]-A, y[+animate, 3]-Th)
'I see him, it (animate)'
b. ni-wa:bam-ig(w) (x[3]-A, y[+animate, 1]-Th)
'He sees me'

In [58a], the x-argument is specified as first person, whereas, in [58b], the y-argument is so specified. Notice that, in the representation of argument structure in the TA forms, the x-argument is specified only for person and not for gender. This is characteristic of TA verb forms. I propose that the specification of an argument for person may have the same effect of identifying the argument as does the specification for gender. The principle stated in [42] may be revised accordingly as follows.

[59] *Argument Identification:*

An argument is identified if it is marked for person or gender ([±animate]).

The concept 'marked for person' requires explication. I take the position that any argument specified as first person or second person is 'marked for person'. In addition, an argument specified as third person is 'marked for person' if and only if either the prefix *o-* or the suffix *-w* marks person. The significance of these qualifications should emerge more clearly in the discussion to follow shortly. For the time being, we may note from the representations in [58] that arguments may be specified for person either by means of a personal affix or by addition of a theme-sign. I claim that an argument is not 'marked for person' if it is specified as third person by a theme-sign.

The specification of an argument for person has considerable significance for my analysis of the assignment of theta-roles in Ojibwa. A principle fundamental to this analysis may be stated as

[60] *Theta-Role Assignment:*

An identified argument must assign its theta-role to an NP.

Obviously, Principle [60] is, in part, an instantiation of the Theta-Criterion in Ojibwa. It would entail that the y-argument of a TA stem being specified [+animate] must transmit its theta-role to an NP. However, principle [60] is mediated by another principle, which requires that only arguments that are specified for person may assign their theta-roles. Accordingly, [60] may be revised by adding a second clause as in [61].

[61] *Theta-Role Assignment:*

An identified argument must assign its theta-role to an NP; an argument may assign a theta-role to an NP iff it is specified for person.

The principle [61] is basic to an understanding of the morphology of TA verb forms, especially the occurrence of theme-signs.

There are four theme-signs that may be attached to TA verbs in declarative sentences. These have been identified earlier as *-a:*, *-igw*, *-i*, and *-ini*. The data in [18] give some idea of the distribution of these theme-signs, but it is now possible to give a more precise statement of their meaning and function. The theme-signs *-a:* and *-igw* both assign the specification third person to an argument, while *-i* and *-ini* assign the specification first person to an argument. The distribution of each is quite clear.

[62] *-i* specifies the y-argument as 1st person.
-ini specifies the x-argument as 1st person.
-a: specifies the y-argument as 3rd person.
-igw specifies the x-argument as 3rd person.

The theme-signs *-i* and *-ini* are restricted, in simple declarative sentences, to constructions in which the other argument is second person; *-a:* and *-igw* occur in other constructions.

Given this characterization of the meaning and distribution of each of the theme-signs and assuming the empirical correctness of the Mirror Principle (Baker, 1985; Grimshaw, 1986), the verbs in [58a] and [58b] must be represented as in [63a] and [63b], respectively.

[63] a.

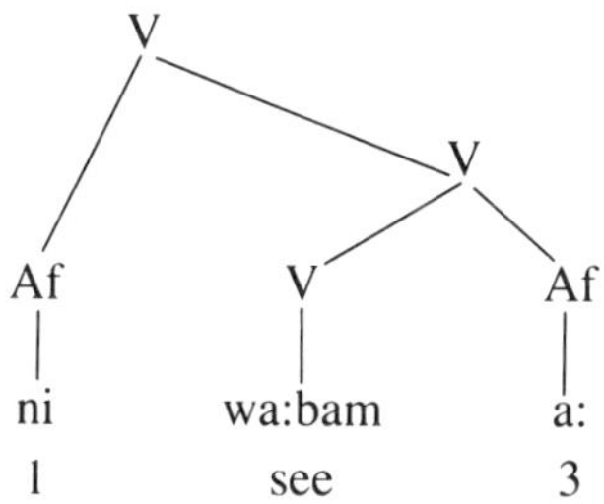

(x[1]−A, y[+animate], 3]−Th)
'I see him'

b.

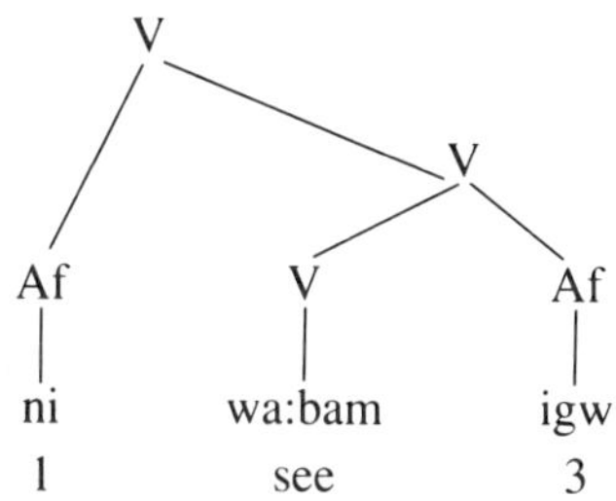

(x[3]−A, y[+animate, 1]−Th)
'He sees me'

Forms like *kiwa:bam(i)* 'you see me' and *kiwa:bamin(i)* 'I see you' would be represented as in [64a] and [64b], respectively.

[64] a.

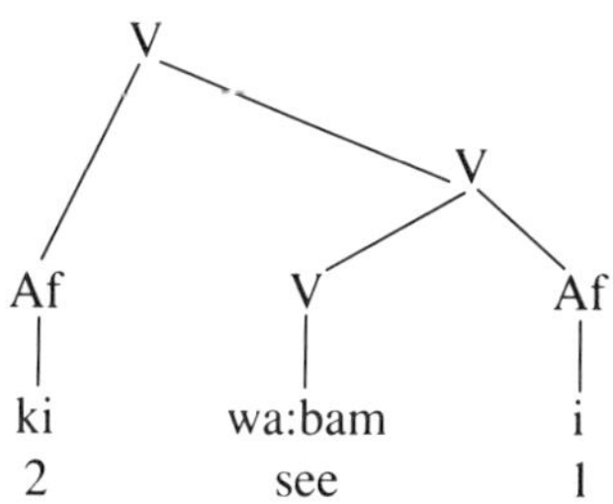

(x[2]−A, y[+animate, 1]−Th)

b.

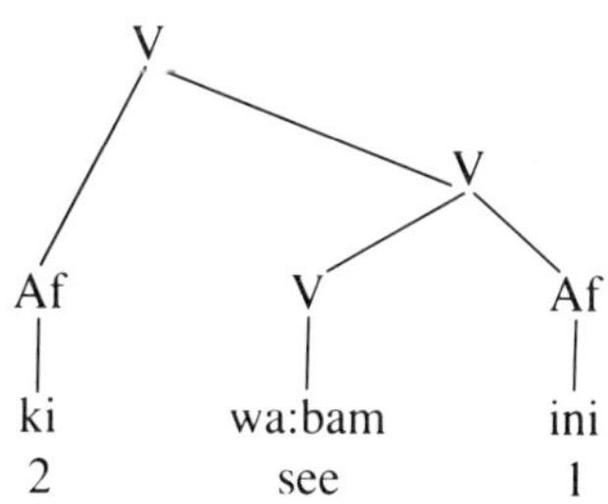

(x[1]−A, y[+animate, 2]−Th)

Notice that the representations in [63] and [64] follow directly from the characterization of theme-signs given in [62]. The personal prefixes must be attached directly to the TA stem.

The proposals just outlined explain why theme-signs occur in TA verb forms. After addition of personal affixes to verb stems, TA verbs may have two identified arguments. Since both arguments must assign theta-role to NPs and may do so only if they are specified for person, according to principle [61], there must be at least two ways to specify arguments for person. Theme-signs and personal affixes are the two elements that fulfill such a function.

It may be recalled that the unidentified y-argument of a TI or pseudo-transitive verb does not have to assign its theta-role to an NP and, therefore, does not have to be specified for person. However, nothing that has been said so far excludes the possibility that this argument might be specified for person by a personal affix. Allowing for such a possibility would lead to the prediction that theme-signs could be attached to pseudo-transitive and TI stems, and we know that this cannot happen. To block this undesirable option a constraint such as the following is proposed.

[65] A y-argument may be marked for person if it is [+animate].

A constraint such as this would seem to be necessary in order to account for some curious gaps in the types of sentences that may occur in Ojibwa. For example, sentences with the following meanings are not possible.

[66] He stole me.
I will steal you.
You stole me.

For such sentences to have equivalents in Ojibwa, the y-argument of the stem *gimo:di* (x[+animate], y-Th) would have to be marked for person, even though it is not specified for gender.

A fundamental feature of the analysis developed so far is the distinction between an identified and an unidentified argument. It has been proposed that the former must assign its theta-role to an NP, while the latter, though present in the argument structure of a verb, does not have to assign its theta-role to an NP. Since the latter does not have to assign its theta-role, verbs with unidentified y-arguments may appear in sentences in which there are no NP-themes, as illustrated by(40a). However, the presence of unidentified arguments must be recognized if we are to account for the fact that pseudo-transitive verbs appear in constructions in which both agents and themes are realized. The NP-theme of a pseudo-transitive verb manifests all the features of the NP-theme of a transitive-animate (TA) verb. Compare the data in [67] with those in [68].

[67]	ni-gimo:di-n-an miši:min	'I steal an apple'
	ni-gimo:di-n-ag miši:min-ag	'I steal apples'
	o-gimo:di-n-an miši:min-an	'He steals an apple, apples'

[68]	ni-wa:bam-a: miši:min	'I see an apple'
	ni-wa:bam-a:-ag miši:min-ag	'I see apples'
	o-wa:bam-a:-an miši:min-an	'He sees an apple, apples'

In addition to the possibility that arguments may not be identified, Ojibwa morphology requires recognition of the possibility that arguments may be absorbed. Certain affixes clearly have the power to prevent arguments from transmitting their theta-roles to NPs. One such affix is the suffix *-ige:*. This ending may be added either to a TA stem or to the stem modified by the 'detransitivizing' suffix *-d,* resulting in AI stems such as those illustrated below [69b and 69c].

[69]	**a.** dakom	'bite something (animate)'
	b. dakonge:	'He bites people'
	c. dakonǰige:	'He bites things'

The TA stem *dakom* has the argument structure (x-A, y[+animate]-Th). Neither of the derived AI stems may take an NP-theme. Consequently, in the process of derivation, the y-argument of the TA stem has been deprived of the power to transmit its theta-role. This may be captured formally by associating with the suffix *-ige* the capacity to absorb the theta-role of the y-argument. This would result in representations such as those that follow.

[70]	dakom-ige: (x-A, y[+animate])	'bite people'
	dakom-d-ige: (x-A, y)	'bite things'

Since the y-argument in each of the stems in [70] bears no thematic role it can never be realized by an NP.

A second example of argument absorption is provided by the affixation of a suffix *-m* to certain AI stems. This suffix seems to be restricted to stems that contain the argument structure (x-A).[15] The verb form produced by addition of this suffix has been traditionally described as having an indefinite actor. Consider the following.

[71]	**a.** nagamo	'he sings'
	b. nagamom	'there is singing'
[72]	**a.** mi:nikwe:	'he drinks'
	b. mi:nikwe:m	'there is drinking'

Neither [71b] nor [72b] may appear in constructions with an NP-agent. Therefore, one must assume that the addition of the suffix *-m* has resulted in the absorption of the thematic role of agent.[16]

The account of argument absorption that I propose would entail that a form such as *nagamom* [71b] have a dummy argument [x] that lacks specification for a thematic role. There is a bit of evidence that this may be the right characterization. These verbs take the same suffixes when they appear in subordinate clauses as do inanimate intransitive (II) verbs; the latter are marked for agreement with one inanimate NP-argument.

3. IMPLICATIONS

The analysis of Ojibwa verbal morphology presented in this paper certainly has implications not only for other aspects of Ojibwa grammar but also for the theory of grammar. I will touch briefly on some of these, focussing first on other properties that Ojibwa grammar must have to be consistent with my characterization of argument structure, the role of various affixes and the internal structure of verb forms.

Consider, first, the role of finals as heads of verbs. According to the definition of heads in the Right-hand Head Rule [20], all verb finals must be lexically assigned to the category verb (+V, −N). Consequently, a more accurate representation of the finals *-izi* and *-aw*, for example, would be as in [73a] and [73b], respectively.

[73] **a.** -izi ([+animate], [+V, −N])
b. -aw ((y[+animate]-Th), [+V, −N])

Verbs would obtain their categorial features from affixes with representations such as these. Since every verb must contain a final, there would be no need to assume that the roots to which finals are attached are lexically assigned to the category verb. Indeed, roots in Ojibwa and in other Algonquian languages might be considered to be lexically unspecified for category membership. Consistent with such a position would be cases in which formatives function as either verbal or nominal roots. One such case is the entry *miskw*. The addition of a nominal final produces a noun *miskwi* 'blood', but affixation of AI and II finals produces the verbs *miskozi* and *miskwa:* 'be red'. These are just three of several derived verbs and nouns based on the root *miskw*. Many other Ojibwa roots exhibit a similar pattern.

Let us turn, next, to the consequences of a principle such as Theta-role Assignment [61]. The instantiation of this principle in a sentence such as [74] is obvious.

[74] Bill mo:zon ogi:wa:bama:n
Bill mozw-an o-gi:-wa:b-am-a:-an
Bill moose-obv 3-past-see-animate-3-obv
'Bill saw a moose'

Recall that the verb stem *wa:bam* has the argument structure (x-A, y[+animate]-Th). *Bill* bears the theta-role of the x-argument and *mo:zon* is assigned the role of the y-argument.[17] However, in the following sentences, not every theta-role is assigned to an overt NP.

[75] a. mo:z nigi:wa:bama: 'I saw a moose'
mozw ni-gi:-wa:b-am-a:
moose 1-past-see-animate-3

b. ogi:wa:bama:n 'He saw him'
o-gi:-wa:b-am-a:-an
3-past-see-animate-3-obv

Principle [61] can only be satisfied if the structure of [75a] contains an NP that bears the theta-role of the x-argument of the verb and if [75b] contains two NPs to which the theta-roles of the x- and y-arguments are assigned. These considerations justify representations such as those in [76a] and [76b] for sentences [75a] and [75b], respectively.

[76] a. [NP e] mo:zw ni-gi:-wa:b-am-a: 'I saw a moose'
I moose 1-past-see-animate-3

b. [NP e] [NP e] o-gi:-wa:b-am-a:-an 'He saw him'
He him 3-past-see-animate-3-obv

The empty NP ([NP e]) in [76a] bears the theta-role of the x-argument and each of the empty NPs in [76b] receives a theta-role from the verb.

An analysis of Ojibwa that postulates empty NPs is viable only if there are general principles that constrain the appearance of such empty categories. One such principle is obviously the Theta Criterion. One clause of this principle may be expressed as follows.

[77] *The Theta Criterion (first clause):*

Every NP-argument must bear one theta-role.

The Theta Criterion ensures that empty NPs may be posited only where they may receive a theta-role from a verb. One additional constraint imposed by Ojibwa grammar is the following.

[78] *The Empty Category Condition:*

An empty NP must be licensed by an argument that is specified for person.

Condition [78] ensures that sentences such as the following are ill-formed.

[79] a. *Bill gi:wi:sini 'Bill ate something'
Bill [NP e] gi:-wi:sini-w
Bill past-eat-3

b. *nigi:gimo:d 'I stole something'
[NP e] [NP e] ni-gi:-gimo:di
I 1-past-steal

The verb *gi:wi:sini* in [79a] contains only one argument, which must be assigned to *Bill*. On the other hand, the verb *nigi:gimo:d(i)* in [79b] contains two arguments, but only one of these is specified for person. Hence, only one of the two empty NPs in [79b] would be licensed. Implicit in the analysis is the claim that, for most dialects of Ojibwa, the y-argument of pseudo-transitive verbs, which is unidentified, could not license an empty NP. It also is the case that an argument whose theta-role has been absorbed could not license an empty NP, but this could be derived from the fact that an absorbed argument has no theta-role to assign to any NP.

The principles cited so far also illuminate the structure of the so-called passive construction in Ojibwa. Sentences such as those in [80] traditionally are regarded as passives.

[80] **a.** mo:z gi:wa:bama: — 'A moose was seen'
mozw gi:-wa:b-am-a:
moose past-see-animate-3

b. nigi:wa:bamigo: — 'I was seen'
ni-gi:-wa:b-am-igw-o:
1-past-see-animate-3-F(AI)

The argument structures of the verbs in [80a] and [80b] are as in [81a] and [81b], respectively.

[81] **a.** gi:-wa:bam-a: [x-A, y[+animate 3]-Th)
b. ni-gi:-wa:bam-igw-o: [x[3]-A, y[+animate, 1]-Th)

In [81a] the y-argument is identified and, according to principle [61], it must assign its theta-role to an NP. The x-argument is not specified for person and, therefore, cannot license an empty NP. The structure of [80a] must, consequently, contain only one NP, which must be the theme. This would yield the passive interpretation. The account of the passive in [80b] is less straightforward. The x-argument of [81b] is specified as third person by the theme-sign *-igw*. Crucially, however, it is not *marked* for person. Therefore, the x-argument does not have to assign a theta-role to an NP. The sentence [80b] could be represented as [82].

[82] [NP e] ni-gi:-wa:b-am-igw-o:
I 1-past-see-animate-3-F

Since the y-argument is identified, it must assign a theta-role to an NP. The empty NP in [82] would bear the role of theme. This would force the passive interpretation of sentence [80b].

The analysis of Ojibwa passives depends crucially on the assumption that an unidentified argument is not required to assign a theta-role to an NP. This assumption would appear to be incompatible with the theta-criterion as it is generally understood. We already have claimed that one clause of this principle, expressed as in [77], holds in Ojibwa; it is the second clause, formulated in [83], that seems to be violated by Ojibwa.

[83] *The Theta Criterion (second clause):*

Every theta-role must be assigned to an NP-argument

The problem may be placed in perspective by focussing on the analysis of sentences containing pseudo-transitive verbs. Some of these, already encountered, are repeated in greater detail.

[84] a.	nimi:nikwe:			'I drink'
	[NP e]	ni-mi:nikwe:		
	I	1-drink		
b.	nibi: nimi:nikwe:			'I drink water'
	[NP e]	nibi:	ni-mi:nikwe:	
	I	water	1-drink	

According to our analysis, the argument structure of the verb *nimi:nikwe:* in both of these sentences is the same, i.e. (x[1]-A, y-Th). Yet, in [84a], the theta-role of the y-argument is not assigned, although in [84b], the theta-role must be assigned, if the NP *nibi:* is to receive a theta-role. I propose to deal with the problem by postulating that the second clause of the Theta Criterion is parameterized and that the proposed principle of Theta-role Assignment [61] really is the Ojibwa instantiation of that second clause. Such proposal would allow the theta-role of an unidentified argument to remain unassigned. However, it would not explain why the theta-role of the y-argument must be assigned in sentences such as [84b].

A solution to the problem of theta-role assignment is contained in the procedure for matching arguments to NPs described by Grafstein (1984) and in a suggestion by Lisa Travis (personal communication). It requires that the mechanism of theta-role assignment be divided into two parts. One part is the familiar process of a verb assigning a theta-role to an NP, and the second part involves a process of checking the argument structure of a verb by an NP to find an appropriate theta-role. In Ojibwa, for verbs that must assign their theta-roles, there always must be NPs that match the identified arguments. In contrast, arguments that do not have to assign their theta-roles to NPs will assign these roles only when there are NPs that match these arguments. According to this proposal, the assignment of theta-roles is not really optional for some verbs, since a theta-role always must be assigned when there is an NP that matches the argument bearing the theta-role.

It now should be obvious how theta-role assignment would be handled in cases such as those in [84]. In [84a], the theta-role of the x-argument is assigned to the empty NP, since this argument, being identified, must assign its theta-role. However, the y-argument does not have to assign its theta-role, and there is no NP match for this argument. The sentence is well formed, even though the theta-role of the y-argument is unassigned. On the other hand, in [84b], the NP *nibi:* matches the y-argument and must receive its theta-role from this argument. These cases contrast with one such as [56b], which is ill-formed because the NP *wi:ya:s* 'meat' is not matched with an argument and cannot be assigned a theta-role.

4. SUMMARY

I have elaborated an analysis of parts of the verbal morphology of Ojibwa that deepens our understanding of what various verbal affixes signify. Finals, personal affixes, and theme-signs clearly have been shown to modify argument structure in various ways. The analysis proposed in this paper leads to some fairly interesting claims about the distribution of empty categories in Ojibwa and about the instantiation of the Theta Criterion. Since Ojibwa is very much like other Algonquian languages, the analysis should be taken as applicable to other members of the family. More important, the implications for the theory of grammar implicit in the idea of parameterizing the Theta Criterion should not be overlooked. It appears that the Ojibwa distinction between unidentified and identified arguments is equivalent to the more familiar distinction between optional and obligatory arguments. My proposal about theta-role assignment with respect to unidentified arguments should be extended to optional arguments wherever these are recognized.

NOTES

This paper draws on several years of research on Ojibwa. It has benefited from collaboration with a number of people, foremost among these being Ann Grafstein and several native consultants. The latter include Sam Osawamick and Edna Manitowabi of Wikwemikong (Ontario), Shirley Batt from Kenora (Ontario), Daniel Rogers and Gordon Simpson from Winneway River (Quebec), Jacob Wawatie from Lac Rapide (Quebec), and Annette Smith from Maniwaki (Quebec). My research on Ojibwa has been supported generously by grants from the Social Sciences and Humanities Research Council of Canada, the most recent being Research Grant No. 410-82-0891.

1. The claim that the classification is not semantically based is supported by the fact that a noun may be classified as animate in one dialect but as inanimate in another. For example, in some Western dialects, the noun *asin* 'stone' is animate, but in the Odawa dialect it is inanimate.

2. For the time being, I will continue to use the terms *subject* and *object* as these have been traditionally used, but these functional categories are not considered to be

categories in a grammar of Ojibwa and will play no role in the analysis outlined in this paper.

3. This pair of intransitive stems has phonetically identical finals. However, evidence that they are fundamentally different finals is provided by the fact that the AI-final causes palatalization of the preceding consonant but the II-final does not.

4. Ojibwa, like other Algonquian languages, distinguishes an exclusive first person plural form that excludes the addressee as a referent from an inclusive first person plural that signals that the addressee is included. The former would contain the personal prefix *ni-* and the later the prefix *ki-*.

5. This suffix is deleted word-finally by a regular phonological process.

6. The vowel shown in parenthesis is regarded as epenthetic.

7. This TA-final is phonetically identical to the TA-final in [11b]. However, they are different finals, and this is reflected in their phonological behavior. The final in [11b], henceforth referred to as *-in*⟨1⟩, causes palatalization of a preceding *d* (e.g. *bo:giǰ-in* 'fart on something (animate)' from the root *bo:gid-*), while the final in [12c], henceforth *-in*⟨2⟩, does not have such an effect (e.g. *nawad-in* 'grab something (animate)'.

8. There is some additional data to show that (a) the derivation of TI stems involves the affixation of the suffix *-d* to TA stems and (b) the truncation phenomena obey the restrictions just outlined. The pair of stems meaning 'shoot with an arrow' is *bim-w* (TA) and *bim-w-d-am* (TI). This is the only case that I know of where the suffix *-d* appears after the final *-w*. Notice that the truncation of the final does not occur, since the suffix *-d* cannot trigger truncation of the final *-w*.

9. The sequence $h + d$ is realized phonetically as [t].

10. The phonetic realization of these affixes is affected by processes that delete word-final short vowels and glides.

11. Instead of the theme-sign *-i:*, some Ojibwa dialects have *-iži* and others have *-iši*.

12. Denny (1983; 1985) also has argued that the distribution of finals is not entirely unpredictable.

13. The segments shown in parenthesis are not realized phonetically (see note 10).

14. I use the label *goal* (G) to cover a range of roles including benefactives and other relational or associative functions, many of which are identified with the meaning of an applicative suffix. Terms like *agent* and *theme* must also be construed broadly. For example, the role causer is subsumed under the label *agent*.

15. The equivalent suffix in the Algonquin dialects is *na:niwan*.

16. The capacity of affixes to absorb theta-roles is not peculiar to Ojibwa. The English suffixes *-er* and *-ee* have similar functions.

17. For discussion of how NPs receive the appropriate theta-roles, see Grafstein (1984).

REFERENCES

Aronoff, M. 1976. *Word Formation in Generative Grammar.* Linguistic Monograph 1. Cambridge: MIT Press.

Baker, M. 1985. The Mirror Principle and Morphosyntactic Explanations. *Linguistic Inquiry* 16:373–415.

Bloomfield, L. 1946. Algonquian. In *Linguistic Structures of Native America,* H. Hoijer, et al., eds., pp. 8–129. New York: Viking Fund Publications in Anthropology 6.

Bloomfield, L. 1957. *Eastern Ojibwa.* Ann Arbor: University of Michigan Press.

Chomsky, N. 1981. *Lectures on Government and Binding.* Dordrecht, Holland: Foris Publications.

Denny, J. P. 1983. Semantics of Abstract Finals in Algonquian Transitive Inanimate Verbs. *Canadian Journal of Linguistics* 28:133–48.

Denny, J. P. 1985. Semantic Verb Classes and Abstract Finals. In *Papers of the 15th Algonquian Conference,* W. Cowan, ed., pp. 241–71. Dept. of Linguistics, Carleton University, Ottawa.

Grafstein, A. 1984. *Argument Structure and the Syntax of a Non-Configurational Language.* Ph.D. Diss., McGill University.

Grimshaw, J. 1986. A Morphosyntactic Explanation for the Mirror Principle. *Linguistic Inquiry* 17:745–50.

Hale, K. 1983. Warlpiri and the Grammar of Non-Configurational Languages. *Natural Language and Linguistic Theory* 1:5–47.

Piggott, G. 1979. Verb Classification in Ojibwa. *Montreal Working Papers in Linguistics* 12:149–86.

Selkirk, E. 1982. *The Syntax of Words.* Linguistic Monograph 7. Cambridge: MIT Press.

Walsh, L. 1985. *The Nature of Morphological Representations.* Ph.D. Diss., McGill University.

Williams, E. 1981a. Argument Structure and Morphology. *Linguistic Review* 1:81–114.

Williams, E. 1981b. On the Notions "Lexically Related" and "Head of a Word." *Linguistic Inquiry* 12:245–74.

THE MORPHOSYNTAX OF ESKIMO CAUSATIVES

John T. Jensen

Alana Johns

INTRODUCTION

Eskimo has been considered a language that poses problems for the Lexicalist Hypothesis (Chomsky 1970), which restricts word formation to the lexicon. Smith (1982a; 1982b), for example, claims that syntactic operations such as passive and antipassive crucially interact with derivational affixations. Grimshaw and Mester (1985), on the other hand, defend the lexicalist hypothesis with respect to the data of Eskimo within Lexical Functional Grammar (LFG) (Kaplan & Bresnan 1982), which allows lexical rules to manipulate grammatical functions.

We will argue for an alternative lexicalist analysis that does not require lexical rules of the type used in Lexical Functional Grammar but relies on the argument structure of lexical items (including affixes)[1] and the mechanism of feature percolation (Lieber 1983). In addition, we propose the Theta-feature Criterion, which restricts the number of theta roles of any given type that may be assigned by a lexical item. The result is a simple system that accounts for the relevant facts within the Lexicalist Hypothesis in a principled way without appealing to operational rules within the lexicon (as does LFG) or derivational morphology applying in the syntax (as does Smith 1982a; 1982b).

To begin, we will illustrate some of the properties of simplex sentences in Eskimo.[2] Sentence [1] shows an intransitive sentence in which the verb agrees only with the absolutive NP. Sentence [2] shows a transitive sentence in which the verb agrees with both an ergative agent and with an absolutive theme.[3]

[1] arnaq ani-vuq
woman(abs) go out-3sg
'The woman is going out'

[2] arna-up angut aktuq-paa
woman-erg man(abs) touch-3sg/3sg
'The woman is touching the man'

The sentences in [3] demonstrate more complex verb forms having the suffix *-juma-* 'want'.[4] In [3a] *-juma-* is attached to an intransitive verb, and the resulting complex verb remains intransitive and agrees only with an absolutive NP. In [3b] *-juma-* is attached to a transitive verb. The verb remains transitive and agrees with both the absolutive theme and the ergative agent. Notice that the subject of 'want' is identical to the subject of the stem verb. With *-juma-* there can be no violation of this restriction; [3c] is ungrammatical. To say 'The woman wants the man to go out' a different affix, *-(r)qu-* 'want' or 'tell' is needed, as in [3d].

[3] a. arnaq ani-juma-vuq
woman(abs) go out-want-3sg
'The woman wants to go out'

b. arna-up angut aktu-ruma-vaa
woman-erg man(abs) touch-want-3sg/3sg
'The woman wants to touch the man'

c. *arna-up angut ani-juma-vaa
woman-erg man(abs) go out-want-3sg/3sg
'The woman wants the man to go out'

d. arna-up angut ani-qu-vaa
woman-erg man(abs) go out-tell-3sg/3sg
'The woman tells the man to go out' or 'The woman wants the man to go out'

Similarly, causative expressions are formed with suffixes, as is shown in the sentences in [4].

[4] a. nutara-up arnaq ani-ti-taa
child-erg woman(abs) go out-cause-3sg/3sg
'The child made the woman go out'

b. nutara-up arna-mut angut aktuq-ti-taa
child-erg woman-all man(abs) touch-cause-3sg/3sg
'The child made a woman touch the man'

In [4a] the causative morpheme *-tit-*, which is a member of the class of affixes referred to as double transitive, is attached to an intransitive verb. The result is a transitive verb that agrees with two NPs, the ergative 'causer' and the absolutive theme of the stem 'to go out'. In [4b] the causative suffix is attached to a transitive verb. The result is again transitive, and as in [4a], the agreement is with the 'causer' and with the theme of the stem 'touch'. In particular, note that the verb does not agree with the agent of the stem 'touch', which appears in an oblique case, the allative.

1. PREVIOUS ANALYSES

Woodbury (1977a, 313) provides a rule of equi NP deletion in order to account for examples such as (3a–3b). The rule is given in [5].

[5] *Equi NP Deletion:*

Join a clause and its complements to form a simplex clause.
Conditions:
(a) $I_{\text{subord. cl.}}$ is coreferent with $I_{\text{matrix cl.}}$
(b) The verb of the matrix clause is an equi subject verb.
Side Effects:
(a) $I_{\text{subord. cl.}} \rightarrow \emptyset$
(b) $II_{\text{subor. cl.}} \rightarrow II_{\text{matrix cl.}}$
(c) The verb of the subordinate clause is adjoined to the left of the verb of the matrix clause.
where I = subject, II = object, subord. = subordinate, cl. = clause

Smith (1982a, 167) gives a similar analysis, which is depicted in [6].

[6] a.

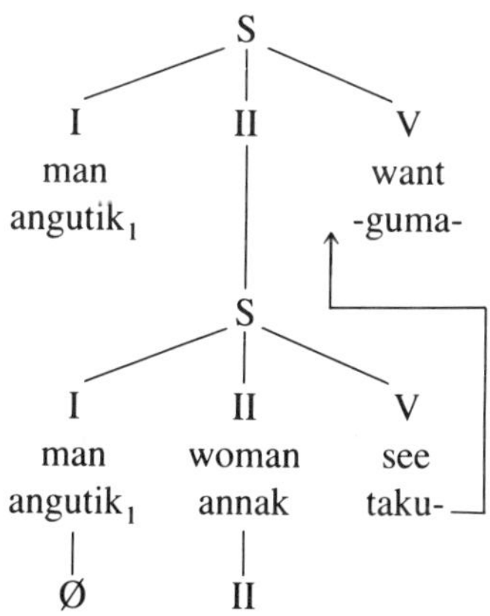

b.

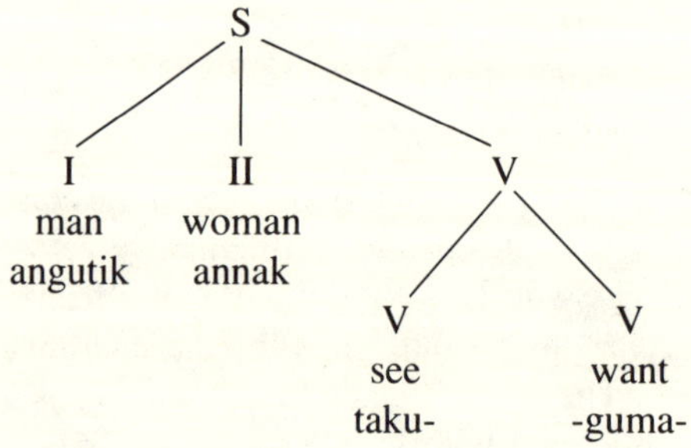

c. angutik-p annak taku-guma-vaa
man-erg woman(abs) see-want-3sg/3sg.
'The man wants to see the woman'

The example in [6a] shows the underlying representation and the effects of clause union upon it. As can be seen, the embedded S is the direct object (II) of the higher S. Equi NP deletion applies, eliminating the lower of the coindexed subjects (I). In the final form, [6b], the lower verb *taku-* 'see' has adjoined to the higher verb *-guma-* 'want', and the stranded lower object *annak* has become the object of the higher complex verb. The output is [6c]. Both the analysis of Smith and that of Woodbury imply that a great deal of syntax is involved in the formation of words in Eskimo. If this were so, then the Lexicalist Hypothesis would have to be abandoned.

Grimshaw and Mester (1985) take a different approach to examples like [3a–3b]. They assume that, since these complex verbs are words (see Sadock 1980), their derivation must take place within the lexicon. They make use of the mechanisms of LFG to get the correct results. In their analysis, the morpheme *-juma-* 'want' is an affix that assigns a subject role and that triggers obligatory binding and deletion of the subject of the verb stem to which it attaches. This entire process forms what they term a lexical rule, which is given in [7].

[7] Grimshaw and Mester, The *-guma-* Rule:
Add x, bind.

The *-guma-* rule relies on the assumption that the added argument must be a subject. One might think that this information must be part of the lexical entry of *-guma-*, since there are other morphemes in Eskimo that, in Grimshaw and Mester's framework, would add an argument assigned the object function.[5] Grimshaw and Mester discuss this question in footnote 13 of their paper. They argue that the subject status of the added argument can be predicted from its thematic role. The deletion of the lower subject occurs as a result of what they term the *Functional Uniqueness Principle,* which prohibits any verb from having more than one argument in any particular grammatical relation. The lower subject deletes, therefore, because the two subjects are bound by the *-guma-* rule and because the verb may not have two subjects. One of the benefits of their approach is that they need not stipulate that the direct object of the lower verb must become the direct object of the derived verb, as Smith and Woodbury must do. This is because Grimshaw and Mester are not dealing with full clauses, but with morphemes. This approach does not contradict the Lexicalist Hypothesis, since the rules that account for the data are lexical rather than syntactic.

Woodbury (1977a, 312) treats examples such as [4], where the affix *-tit-* 'cause' is attached to an intransitive and a transitive verb, with a rule of clause union, given in [8].

[8] *Clause Union:*

Join a clause and its complement to form a simplex clause.
Condition:
The matrix verb is of the class of double transitive verbal suffixes.
Side effects:
(a) $\text{erg}_{\text{subord. cl.}} \rightarrow \text{chômeur}_{\text{matrix cl.}}$
(b) $\text{abs}_{\text{subord. cl.}} \rightarrow \text{abs}_{\text{matrix cl.}}$
(c) The verb of the subordinate clause is adjoined to the left of the verb of the matrix clause.
(d) The matrix clause chômeur is marked with the allative case suffix.

Smith (1982a) gives a similar account of [4a] but not of [4b], since it appears that the affixation of double transitive affixes to transitive stems is not acceptable to all speakers of Labrador Inuttut (personal communication to Grimshaw and Mester). Johnson (1980) reports that such examples are found readily in the Rankin Inlet dialect, which is a close neighbor of the dialect discussed in this paper.[6] They also are to be found in Greenlandic Eskimo, as discussed by Woodbury. The unacceptability of constructions like [4b] for native speakers of Labrador Inuttut, therefore, is the exception rather than the rule.

Grimshaw and Mester do not present an analysis of [4b] since their description is of Labrador Inuttut. They do present a lexical rule (1985, 11) to account for examples such as [4a], and this is given in [9].

[9] Grimshaw and Mester, The *-kqu-* Rule:
Add x, reassign GF
(GF = Grammatical Function)

In [9], the name of the rule contains another double transitive affix *-kqu-* 'order, want', which works the same as *-tit-* in [3d]. This rule has an affix add an argument, which is assigned subject function. The Functional Uniqueness Principle will not allow the verb to have two subjects. Deletion occurs only under a binding relation, and the double transitive affixes do not bind the embedded subjects; they reassign their grammatical function. The reassignment of grammatical function occurs according to "some hierarchy of grammatical relations with Subject highest, Object next, and Indirect Object lower still" (p. 10). In essence then, these lexical rules are a restricted type of syntactic rule, since they refer to grammatical relations below the word level and manipulate them (e.g. reassign grammatical function).

2. OUR ANALYSIS

The approaches as outlined commit us either to word formation within or after the syntax, or to syntactic rules within the lexicon. We reject this weakening of the Lexicalist Hypothesis and will adhere to a strong version of it. In keeping with the modular approach to syntax, we assume that the lexicon and the syntax are separate components, each with its own properties. All word formation takes place in the lexicon. Affixes are attached to stems in accordance with their subcategorization frames and other properties. Features of stems and affixes, including argument structure, determine the features of the words of which they are a part. We assume the percolation conventions given in [10].

[10] *Percolation Conventions:*

a. Features of an affix must percolate to the mother node.

b(i). Features of a stem percolate unless features of an affix conflict.

b(ii). Theta-features of verbal morphemes do not percolate to a nominal mother.

Convention [10a] ensures that the lexical features of affixes take precedence over those of stems; in effect, this is a restatement of Lieber's convention II (cf. Lieber 1983, 253). Convention [10bi] is a restatement of Lieber's convention III. We are assuming that the ability to assign a particular theta-role to an argument is a lexical feature of the verb or affix (see Johns 1984b and Zubizarreta 1985). We shall call these *theta-features.*[7] Our restatement is designed to extend Lieber's convention III to include percolation of theta-features. In Lieber's discussion, conflict occurs when contrary category features could potentially percolate from a stem and an affix attached to it, e.g. *standard* [−V] + *ize* [+V] → *standardize* [+V], where the feature [+V] of the affix takes precedence over the feature [−V] of the adjectival stem. Condition [10bi], in conjunction with the Theta-feature Criterion in [11], will prevent the percolation of a theta-feature in a stem where the affix percolates the same feature. We propose the Theta-feature Criterion as a refinement of the latter half of the Theta Criterion of Chomsky (1981, 36), which states that "each theta role is assigned to one and only one argument."

[11] *Theta-feature Criterion:*

No word can assign more than one instance of a given type of theta role.

The Theta-feature Criterion prohibits a lexical item from assigning two identical types of theta roles, e.g. two agents.[8]

Under convention [10bii] thematic roles of a verb stem cannot percolate to the mother node when a nominalizing affix is attached.[9] The final theta-features that manage to percolate to the highest word node represent the arguments which are syntactically realized, in the terminology of Zubizarreta (1985). An argument is syntactically realized iff it bears a grammatical relation, e.g. subject or object, to the predicate that assigns it a theta role. The mere fact that a theta-feature does not percolate to the word level does not mean that the theta role cannot be expressed. Therefore, a theta-feature prevented from being syntactically realized can still be lexically[10] realized in the form of an adjunct phrase. So the English derived nominal *destruction* does not inherit the theta-features that assign the theme and agent roles syntactically. However, the theme and agent roles may be expressed semantically in adjunct phrases as in *the destruction of the city by the barbarians*. Those arguments in Eskimo that are lexically but not syntactically realized will appear in a oblique case, i.e. a case other than ergative and absolutive, which are the syntactic cases, and will not agree with the verb.[11] The cases on the oblique arguments correspond roughly to the semantics of these arguments. Johnson (1980, 15) notes that "the choice of a case marker for an oblique object is influenced by semantic roles, in contrast to purely grammatical cases such as ergative and absolutive." We will not discuss which of the two syntactically realized arguments is the subject and which the object.[12]

We do not require rules that internalize or externalize arguments (Williams 1981 and Zubizaretta 1985) or ones that manipulate grammatical relations within the word (Grimshaw and Mester 1985). In our treatment, words are formed in the lexicon by concatenation of morphemes, following their subcategorization and other properties. The results of the interaction follow from general principles of percolation.

We can illustrate the concatenation of morphemes and the operation of feature percolation with some examples. In [12], the intransitive agreement marker is attached to a verb that assigns a theme role (T). Since the affix assigns no thematic role, the theme role of the stem percolates freely. In [13], a transitive agreement marker is attached to a verb that assigns both a theme and an agent role (A). Both theta-features percolate, since the affix has no argument structure of its own.

[12] arnaq ani-vuq
woman(abs) go out-3sg
'The woman is going out'

```
     T
    / \
  ani  vuq
   T   3sg
'go out'
```

[13] arna-up angut aktuq-paa
woman-erg man(abs) touch-3sg/3sg
'The woman is touching the man'

```
       T, A
      /    \
  aktuq     paa
  T, A      3sg/3sg.
'touch'
```

The affix *-juma-* 'want' has usually been treated as if it were a verb with its own theta-features. This can be seen in the discussion earlier of Woodbury (1977), Smith (1982a; 1982b), and Grimshaw and Mester (1985). This assumption forces an analysis where there is coreference between the two subjects, followed by deletion of the embedded subject, to ensure that the complex verb has only one subject in surface structure.

We treat *-juma-* 'want' as an auxiliary or modal affix with no argument structure of its own. The theta-features of the verb stem to which it attaches percolate freely through the affix without addition or modification. In this sense, affixes of this type can be said to be transparent to percolation. Some support for this position comes from the data in [14] and [15].

[14] **a.** aullaq-tuq
leave-3sg
'He is leaving'

b. aulla-ruma-juq
leave-want-3sg
'He wants to leave'

[15] **a.** imaaq-tuq
fall into the water-3sg
'He falls into the water'

b. imaa-rumaaq-tuq
fall into the water-might-3sg
'He might fall into the water'

The affix *-juma-* 'want' in [14b] is similar to, and is probably contained within, the morpheme *-jumaaq-* 'might' or 'probably will' in [15b]. Schneider (1972, 118) makes reference to this property of affixes like *-juma-* 'want': ". . . ce sont des sortes de verbes AUXILIAIRES: vouloir, devoir, pouvoir. . . ." Finally, we note that these morphemes differ from the English 'want' in that they cannot attach to nominal stems (what is referred to as noun incorporation).

[16] a. *iglu-juma-vunga
house-want-1sg
'I want a house'

b. iglu-qaq-punga
house-have-1sg
'I have a house'

The ungrammaticality of [16a], as contrasted with the grammaticality of [16b], results from subcategorization properties of the affix *-juma-* 'want' rather than from any language-specific prohibition against noun incorporation, since this is quite common, as in [16b]. This fact is predicted if *-juma-* 'want' is a modal but not if it is a verbal affix. In [17], we show an intransitive verb to which *-juma-* 'want' is attached.

[17] arnaq ani-juma-vuq
woman(abs) go out-want-3sg
'The woman wants to go out'

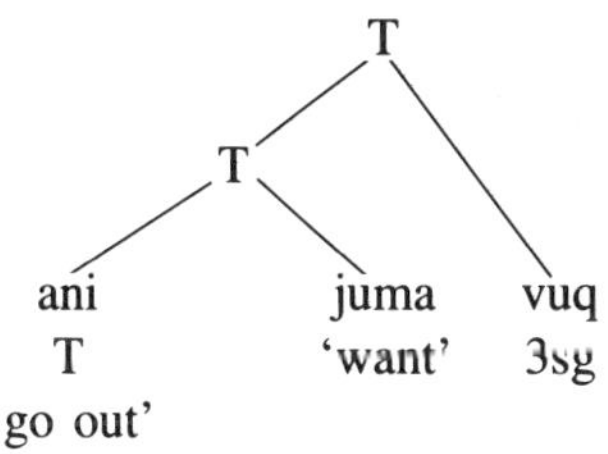

Since, in our analysis, this affix has no theta-features of its own, the theme role of the stem will percolate freely. Similarly, in [18], the theta-features (theme and agent) of the transitive verb *aktuq-* 'touch' percolate freely through the affix *-juma-* 'want'.

[18] arna-up angut aktu-ruma-vaa
woman-erg man(abs) touch-want-3sg/3sg
'The woman wants to touch the man'

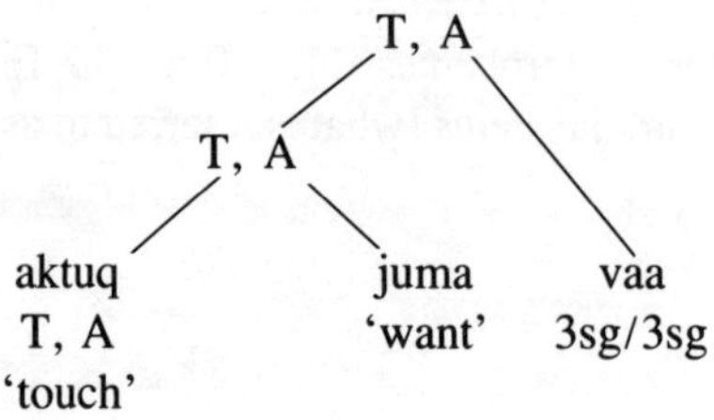

In contrast to *-juma-*, the causative morpheme *-tit-* has a theta-feature that assigns an agent role. In [19] we illustrate the attachment of the causative *-tit-* to an intransitive verb.

[19] nutara-up arnaq ani-ti-taa
child-erg woman(abs) go out-cause-3sg/3sg
'The child made the woman go out'

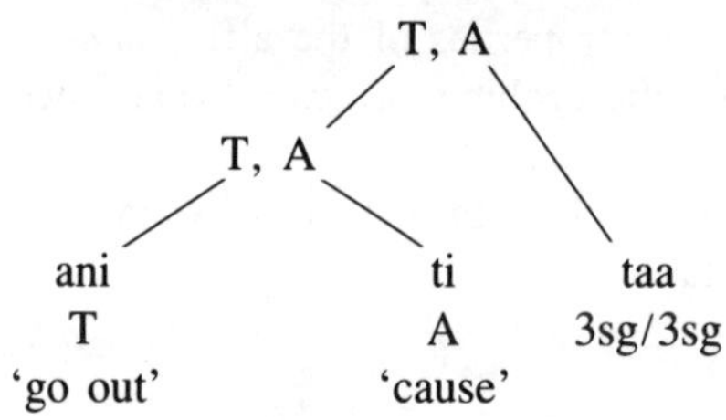

Since the causative morpheme assigns an agent role, this feature must percolate. The intransitive verb stem *ani-* 'go out' carries the theta-feature theme, which also will percolate. Convention [10bi] is not violated since the two features percolated are of distinct types. The result is a derived transitive verb with transitive agreement marking. In [20], we show the more complex case, where causative *-tit-* is attached to a transitive verb.

[20] nutara-up arna-mut angut aktuq-ti-taa
child-erg woman-all man(abs) touch-cause-3sg/3sg
'The child made the woman touch the man'

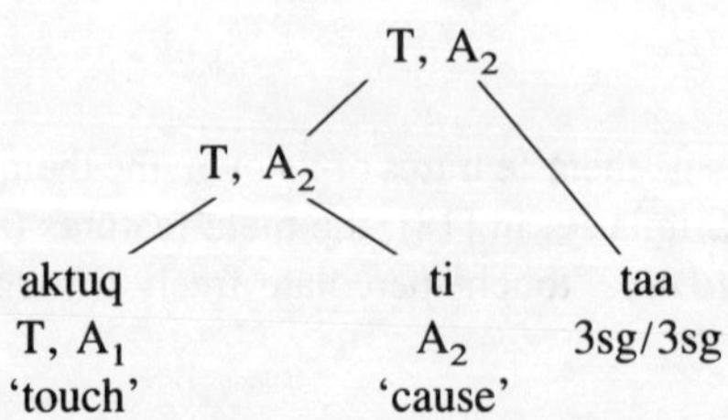

In [20], both the causative affix and the verb stem carry the theta-feature agent. By percolation convention [10a], the agent role of the affix (A_2) must percolate. Percolation convention [10bi] allows only the theme role of the verb stem to percolate. The agent role of the verb stem conflicts with the agent role of the affix by virtue of the Theta-feature Criterion and, therefore, cannot percolate. The result is a transitive verb that agrees with the causer in the ergative case and the theme of the stem 'touch' in the absolutive case. The lower agent of the stem 'touch' (A_1) does not agree with the verb (it is not syntactically realized) and appears in the allative case.

3. PASSIVE AND ANTIPASSIVE

In the previous section, we have shown that two affixes analyzed as syntactic rules can be easily treated within a lexical account using only lexical principles. In this section, we will demonstrate that two additional affixes, which have long been treated as syntactic rules, also are amenable to a lexical analysis. Moreover, the lexical account of these affixes is more in keeping with the properties of Eskimo and shows the relation between what appear to be syntactic rules and certain nominalizing affixes. In [21a], we see a simple transitive construction with the agent in ergative case and the theme in absolutive case. The corresponding sentence in [21b] shows a verb containing the morpheme *-tau-*, which traditionally is called the *passive morpheme*. We see that, in this construction, only the theme agrees with the verb. The agent is in an oblique case, in this instance the ablative. In [21c], we have a verb containing the morpheme *-si-*, which traditionally is called the *antipassive*. In this construction, only the agent agrees with the verb. The theme is in an oblique case, this time the comitative.

[21] a. arna-up angut kunik-paa
woman-erg man(abs) kiss-3sg/3sg
'The woman kissed the man'

b. angut arna-mit kunik-tau-vuq
man(abs) woman-abl kiss-pass-3sg
'The man was kissed by the woman'

c. arnaq angum-mik kunik-si-vuq
woman(abs) man-comit kiss-antipassive-3sg
'The woman kissed a man'

The two morphemes *-jau-* and *-si-* have been viewed as performing syntactic operations, the former involving movement of the direct object to subject position with subsequent demotion of the original subject, and the latter as detransitivizing the verb, thus demoting the direct object (for analyses along this line, see Woodbury 1977[13], Smith 1982a; 1982b, and Marantz 1984). As syntactic rules, these morphemes pose a problem for the Lexicalist Hypothesis. Grimshaw and Mester (1985, 4–5) allow rules of this type in the lexicon. Their rules of passive and antipassive are given in [22].

[22] Passive:
S → OBL
O → S
OBL CASE = $_c$ dative

Antipassive:
O → OBL
OBL Case = $_c$ instrumental

Where S = subject, O = object, and OBL = oblique

We argue that such rules constitute a violation of the Lexicalist Hypothesis, since they involve manipulations of grammatical relations. We propose to adhere to the Lexicalist Hypothesis by restricting the lexicon to principles of interaction, such as the percolation conventions and Theta-feature Criterion described earlier. Consequently, we must provide an alternative analysis. We argue that these morphemes carry lexical features and are not signals of syntactic operations. They appear to be syntactic operations only because of the combination of the lexical properties of the affix with those of the stem. In our analysis, the passive morpheme *-jau-* contains the lexical property of assigning the role theme, and the antipassive morpheme *-si-* assigns the role agent.[14] We view these morphemes as similar to the English nominalizers *-ee* and *-er* as in [23].

[23] murder-ee (*-jau-*)
murder-er (*-si-*)

These morphemes differ from the English ones in that they must be analyzed as also containing a predicative 'be'. This is quite straightforward for *-jau-*, since it is a combination of the morpheme *-jaq-* plus the copula *-u-* 'be'.[15] Before we discuss the combined effects of the nominalizer and the copula, let us first examine the evidence in [24] and [25], which supports our contention that the passive and antipassive contain nominalizers.

In [24], we see that the addition of *-jaq-* to verb stems produces nominals similar to those produced by the addition of the morpheme *-ee* in English, meaning 'that which underwent an action'.[16]

[24] *-jaq-:*

a.	kunik-paa	'He kisses her'
	kuni-gaq	'the one who is kissed'
b.	ikajuq-tuq	'He is helping'
	ikaju-gaq	'the one who was helped'

c.	titiraq-tuq	'He is writing'
	titira-gaq	'that which was written'

In [25], the addition of *-ji-* (in our analysis the morpheme *-si-* without the copula function) closely parallels the effects of the English nominalizer *-er,* meaning 'the one who performed an action'.

[25] *-ji-:*

a.	kunik-paa	'He kisses her'
	kunik-ti	'kisser'
b.	ikajuq-tuq	'He is helping'
	ikajuq-ti	'helper'
c.	titiraq-tuq	'He is writing'
	titiraq-ti	'writer' or 'clerk'

In [26], we see that these constructions can take possessive affixes, which confirms their nominal status.

[26] kunik-ti-ga 'my kisser'
kiss-er-my

The example in [27] shows that, although the theme argument of the verb stem *ikajuq-* 'help' cannot be realized syntactically, it can still be lexically realized in the comitative case.

[27] nutarar-mik ikajuq-ti ani-vuq
child-comit help-er go out-3sg
'The helper of the child is going out'

That arguments of verbs contained within nominals cannot be realized syntactically is a direct result of Percolation Convention [10bii]. Note that the same blocking of syntactic realization can be seen in the so-called antipassive in [28]. Even the case marking of the oblique theme argument is the same *-mik* (comitative) that we saw in [27].

[28] Saali Piita-mik aktuq-si-juq
Sally(abs) Peter-comit touch-antipass-3sg
'Sally touched Peter'

In [29] through [31], we again see the similarity between the effects of the nominalizer and the alleged rule, in this case the passive *-jau-*. In [29], we have a simple transitive sentence with the agent *Peter* in ergative case and the theme *nanuq* in absolutive case. [30] is a Greenlandic example (gloss ours) from Fortescue (1984).

[29] Piita-up nanuq kapi-vaa
Peter-erg bear(abs) stab-3sg/3sg
'Peter stabbed the bear'

[30] nanuq Piita-mit tuqu-taq
bear(abs) Peter-abl kill-ee
'The bear killed by Peter'

[31] nutaraq arna-mit ikaju-gau-vuq
child(abs) woman-abl help-pass-3sg
'The child was helped by the woman'

In [30], the verb has the theme nominalizer *-jaq-* attached. The agent of the verb is lexically realized in ablative case. This is the same case as that found on the displaced agent in the passive construction in [31]. It is important to realize that the NPs in absolutive case in [28], [30], and [31] do not get their theta roles from their respective verb stems, but from the theta-features of the nominalizing affix. In our analysis, the morphemes *-jau-* and *-si-* carry theta-feature which must be coindexed with identical theta-features carried by the verb stems to which they attach. We assume that these morphemes cannot assign semantic roles on their own, as the causative affix can. This may be a result of the fact that these morphemes do not add any meaning to the verb but merely change the category of the phrase. In [32], we give our analysis of these nominalizers.

[32] a. $[A_i]_N$ 'kisser' (from [20a])

kunik ti_N
T, A_i A_i

b. $[T_i]_N$ 'helpee' (from [19b])

ikaju gaq_N
T_i, A T_i

In [32a], the nominalizer *-ti-* 'er' attaches to the verb stem *kunik-* 'kiss' and binds the agent of *kunik-*. The theta-feature of the affix percolates to the mother node but the theta-features of the stem cannot percolate, due to convention [10bii]. Since only the theta-feature not bound by the affix may be lexically realized, we must assume that the binding of the two identical roles prevents lexical realization of the bound theta-feature blocked within the verb stem. In [32b], we give a similar analysis for the morpheme *-jaq-*, where only the theme role of the affix will percolate to the mother node.

Recall that the passive morpheme *-jau-* is composed of not only *-jaq-* but the predicative affix *-u-*, which has the meaning 'X is a ____', as in [33].

[33] *-u-* 'be' or 'X is a ____':

arna-u-vunga
woman—be—1sg
'I am a woman'

What is predicated of X can either be a basic nominal, as in [33] or a derived nominal, such as those produced by the affixation of the nominalizers *-jaq-* and *-ji-*. In [34], we see that the addition of the predicative morpheme to the derived nominal correctly produces the results of the syntactic rules passive and antipassive.

[34] a.

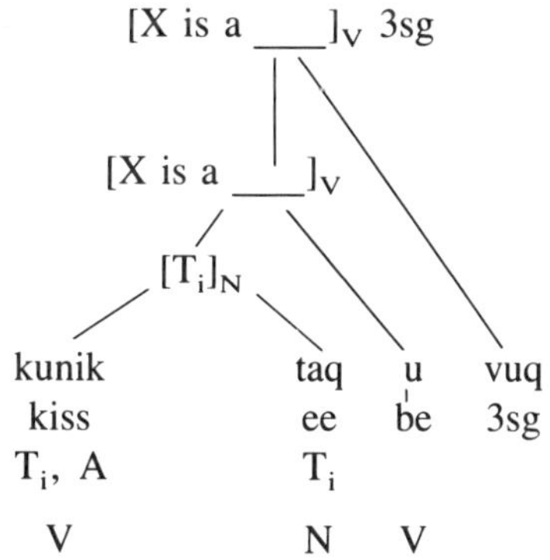

kunik-tau-vuq
'He was kissed'
(Literally: 'He is a kissee')

b.

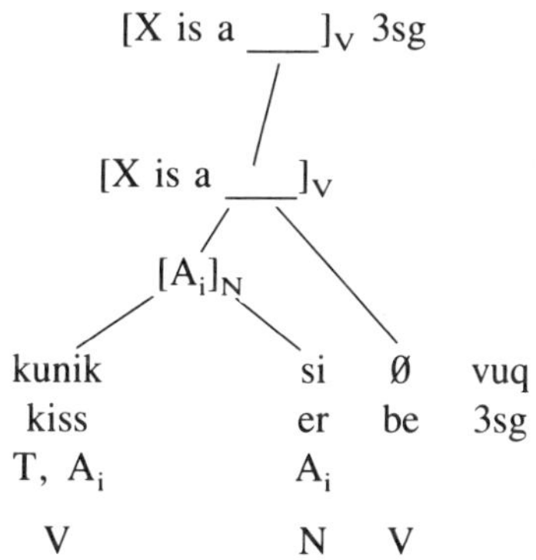

kunik-si-vuq
'He kissed someone'
(Literally: 'He is a kisser')

Notice that, in both examples in [34], the nominal blocks the percolation of the theta-features of the stem verb to the node dominating the predicative 'be'. Thus, X does not inherit any theta-feature from the nominal that is predicated of it. This is to be expected, since when regular nominals, as 'woman' in [33], are predicated of X, they do not transmit theta-features. This follows from the nature of copulas. Only X will percolate to the higher node to agree with the verb. Note that, in [34b], we posit a null morpheme 'be'. In fact, we consider the morpheme *-si-* to represent simultaneously both the nominalizer *-ji-* and a copula.

The example in [35a], at first glance, would seem to be a counterexample to the predictions of the Theta-feature Criterion [11], since the verb agrees with both 'the child', the agent of the cause affix, and 'the woman', the agent of the touching.

[35] **a.** nutara-up arnaq anguti-mik aktuq-si-ti-taa
child-erg woman(abs) man-comit touch-er(be)-cause-3sg/3sg
'The child made the woman touch the man'

b.

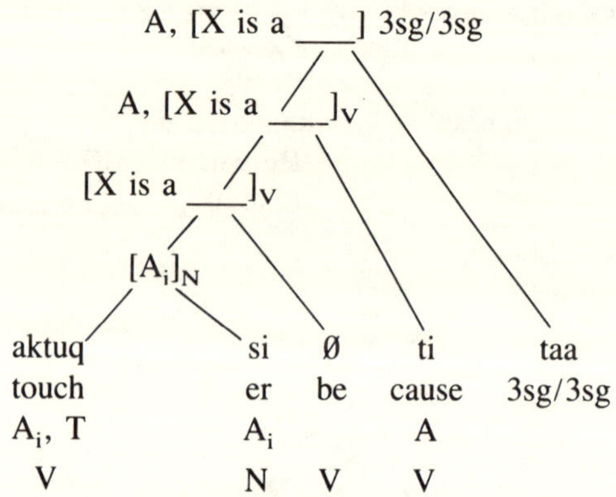

Literally: 'The child made the woman be a toucher of the man'

If it were the case that two agents agree with the verb, this would run counter to the Theta-Feature Criterion [11], which says that no word can assign more than one instance of a given type of theta role. However, when we examine the structure produced by our analysis, we see that X—not the agent of the stem—agrees with the verb. The agent role of the stem never percolates outside the noun. So sentence [35b] is more literally 'The child made the woman be a toucher of the man'. In the literal translation, it is clear that 'the woman' does not receive a thematic role any more than it does in the sentence 'The child made the woman be a doctor'. Finally, in [36], we see that the same analysis can be easily made for a construction containing the nominalizer *-jaq-*.

[36] **a.** nutara-up angut arna-mit aktuq-tau-ti-taa
child-erg man(abs) woman-abl touch-ee-be-cause-3sg/3sg
'The child made the man be touched by the woman'

b.

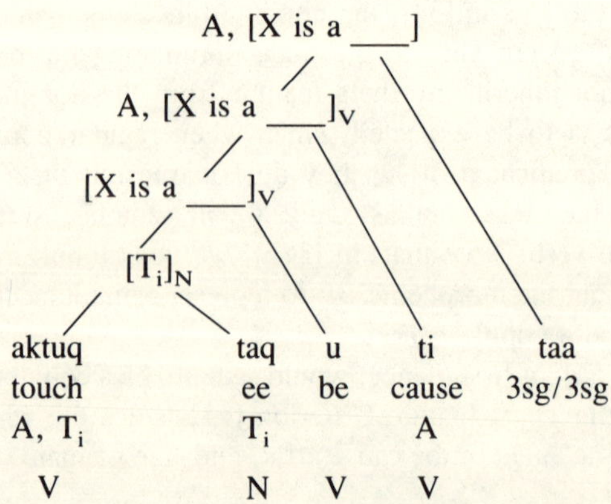

Literally: 'The child made the man be a touchee of the woman'

Compare [36] with [20], which is a true example of double theta-features on the highest node resulting from percolation.

4. CONCLUSION

In this paper, we have outlined an approach to a theory of lexical syntax by providing analyses of a number of constructions in Eskimo that have been thought to be syntactic rules operating within the word.[17] The analyses we have provided are based on principles that are needed independently to account for lexical properties of affixational morphology. Percolation Conventions are needed to account for word formation in general. The Theta-feature Criterion is a general restriction on verb stems. It is not without motivation that we defended the Lexicalist Hypothesis. The grammar can be simplified by restricting each component to a particular set of principles. The introduction of rules into a lexicon that already has Percolation Conventions results not only in two rather disparate systems within a component but also makes for redundancy where both systems can handle the same phenomena. This approach also is in keeping with the current trend away from rule-governed systems in favor of representations and principles (see Bennis and Koster 1985).

We have argued that the best way to account for the complex verb derivation in Eskimo is through the interaction of lexical features (specifically theta-features) within the word. We have shown that there is reason to believe that the morpheme *-juma-* 'want' is more like a tense or modal morpheme than the morpheme *-tit-* 'cause', and that this can be used to explain the different effect that each affix has in the derivation of the complex verb. We also have argued that there is evidence from the grammar of Eskimo that the morphemes called *passive* and *antipassive* are morphemes with theta-features, and that these theta-features account for the rule-like appearance of constructions that contain morphemes like *-jau-* and *-si-*.

NOTES

We wish to thank the organizations whose financial support made it possible to write this paper. These include the Northern Research Scientific Training Grants and the Rector's Fund, administered by the University of Ottawa, as well as the Social Sciences and Humanities Research Council of Canada.

1. Following Williams (1981), we take the argument structure of lexical items to be simply a list of thematic roles that the item can assign in the syntax. An internal argument is one where the lexical item is a sister of the argument. An external argument is assigned via predication. These are roughly equivalent to the traditional concepts of subject and object, but see Williams (1984) for important distinctions.

2. The data presented in this paper was provided by Basil Kiblakoot, a native speaker of Inuktitut, from Baker Lake, Northwest Territories, Canada. It is consistent with other dialects with the exception of Labrador Inuttut, which prohibits the attachment of certain affixes to transitive stems (to be discussed later).

3. For brevity, we have omitted the indicative and the participial moods from the morpheme-by-morpheme translations. The intransitive mood markers are *-vu(q)-* (indicative), and *-ju(q)-* (participial). The transitive mood markers are *-va(q)-* (indicative), and *-ja(q)-* (participial). These forms are found after stems ending in vowels; after consonants indicative forms begin with /p/, and participial forms begin with /t/ (or /g/).

4. The form *-juma-* appears after stems ending in a vowel, *-guma-* after velars, and *-ruma* after uvulars.

5. See Woodbury (1977b) for examples of the morpheme *-ut-*.

6. These affixes have an added complication in that at times they can be glossed as 'let' rather than 'cause'. With the 'let' translation, the preferred syntax is lower agent in absolutive case and lower theme in oblique comitative case. We believe that this alternative can be explained by an analysis where the subject of 'let' is not an agent; however, further research is necessary.

7. The issue of the range of theta-role types is far from settled. While this question deserves serious attention, we will not attempt to resolve it here.

8. This criterion also resembles the functional uniqueness principle of Lexical Functional Grammar. However, the Functional Uniqueness Principle rules out a lexical item from having more than one subject or object. The Theta-feature Criterion prohibits structures where the agent is subject and another agent is object or both the subject and object are themes. It is not clear whether Lexical Functional Grammar can rule out these instances.

9. In fact, this convention may be unnecessary if we assume, following Levin and Rappaport (1985), that a change of category can affect the argument structure of a lexical item. Thus, one might want to argue that the change from verb to nominal entails the inability of the constructions to realize theta-features syntactically.

10. We adopt Zubizarreta's use of the term *lexically realized* for a concept that equally well might be referred to as *semantically realized.* The agent role of a passive sentence is present semantically, as shown by its ability to control a purpose clause in (i), even when the agent is not expressed in a *by*-phrase (see Roeper 1987).

(i) The boat was sunk to collect the insurance.

11. We make no distinction between oblique phrases and derived oblique phrases (or chômeurs in terminology of Relational Grammarians).

12. Our reasons are that this distinction is not crucial to our analysis and that the question is quite controversial (cf. Marantz (1984) and Johns (1984a) for only a portion of this debate, and Johns (1987) for another view).

13. Woodbury rejects the characterization of antipassive as suppressing the direct object in favour of advancing ergative to absolutive.

14. Since first presenting this paper in the spring of 1985, other work on the topic of the morphosyntax of causatives (see Woodbury and Sadock (1986)) and antipassive (see Miyaoka (1984) and references cited therein) has come to our attention. With regard to the latter's claim, Miyaoka is correct in that the antipassive morpheme is associated with an adversative reading in certain constructions, e.g. the transitive clause *Jaaniup Miuri niqimik nirijijaa* 'John ate the meat on Mary.' It does not follow, as claimed by Miyaoka, that the intransitive forms must be derived from the transitive. Miyaoka assumes that transitivity alternations, if not mediated by morphology, involve reduction. An alternative approach is taken in Johns (1987), in which transitive morphology plays a major role. Nevertheless, as pointed out by Miyaoka, the transitive use of the 'antipassive' must be accounted for. In our opinion, the adversative meaning of these constructions derives not from the morpheme itself but from the context. This would explain the lack of adversative meaning in the intransitive forms. Clearly, further research is necessary.

15. While our proposal concerning *-jau-* holds little controversy, some might arise with respect to our analysis of *-si-*. Grammars of Eskimo treat the nominalizer *-ji-*/*-ti-* as separate from the antipassive *-si-*. A problem for our analysis pointed out by S. T. Mallon (personal communication) is the existence of nominals such as *ilinniaqtitsiji* 'teacher', which contains the sequence *-si-* plus *-ji-*.

16. These forms are less common in isolation than with possessive morphemes attached.

17. We have not discussed noun incorporation, which also is thought by many to involve a syntactic rule operating within the word boundary, cf. Sadock (1980) and Baker (1985). Di Sciullo and Williams (1986) argue for a lexical account of this phenomenon.

REFERENCES

Baker, M. 1985. *Incorporation: A Theory of Grammatical Function Changing*, Ph.D. Diss., Massachusetts Institute of Technology.

Bennis, H., and J. Koster. 1985. Call for Papers. *Glow Newsletter* 15:5.

Chomsky, N. 1970. Remarks on Nominalization. In *Readings in English Transformational Grammar*, R. Jacobs and P. Rosenbaum, eds., pp. 184–221. Waltham, Mass.: Ginn Publishing.

Chomsky, N. 1981. *Lectures on Government and Binding*. Dordrecht, Holland: Foris Publications.

Di Sciullo, A.-M., and E. S. Williams 1986. Noun Incorporation versus Cliticization. In *Proceedings of NELS 16*, pp. 126–35. Amherst, Mass.: Graduate Linguistic Student Association.

Fortescue, M. D. 1984. *West Greenlandic* (Croom Helm Descriptive Grammars). London: Croom Helm.

Grimshaw, J., and R.-A. Mester. 1985. Complex Verb Formation in Eskimo. *Natural Language and Linguistic Theory* 3:1–19.

Johns, A. 1984a. Case Assignment and Grammatical Relations in Eskimo. *Cahiers linguistiques d'Ottawa* 12:49–87.

Johns, A. 1984b. Dative 'Movement' in Eskimo. In *Proceedings of the Parasession on Lexical Semantics,* pp. 162–72. Chicago: The Chicago Linguistic Society.

Johns, A. 1987. *Transitivity and Grammatical Relations in Inuktitut.* Ph.D. Diss., University of Ottawa.

Johnson, M. 1980. *Ergativity in Inuktitut (Eskimo) in Montague Grammar and in Relational Grammar.* Bloomington: Indiana University Linguistics Club.

Kaplan, R., and J. Bresnan. 1982. Lexical-Functional Grammar: A Formal System for Grammatical Representation. In *The Mental Representation of Grammatical Relations,* J. Bresnan, ed., pp. 173–281. Cambridge: MIT Press.

Levin, B., and M. Rappaport. 1985. The Formation of Adjectival Passives. *Linguistic Inquiry* 17:623–61.

Lieber, R. 1983. Argument Linking and Compounds in English. *Linguistic Inquiry* 14:251–85.

Marantz, A. 1984. *On the Nature of Grammatical Relations.* Linguistic Inquiry Monograph 10. Cambridge: MIT Press.

Miyaoka, O. 1984. On the So-called Half-Transitive Verbs in Eskimo. *Etudes Inuit Studies* 8 (supplementary issue), 193–218.

Roeper, T. 1987. Implicit Arguments and the Projection Principle. *Linguistic Inquiry* 18:267–310.

Sadock, J. M. 1980. Noun Incorporation in Greenlandic: A Case of Syntactic Word Formation. *Language* 56, 300–19.

Schneider, L. 1972. *Inuktituorutit: Grammaire purement esquimaude: Cours d'initiation au dialecte de l'Ungava.* Québec: Direction générale du Nouveau-Québec.

Smith, L. R. 1982a. An analysis of Affixal Verb Derivation and Complementation in Labrador lnuttut. *Linguistic Analysis* 10:161–89.

Smith, L. R. 1982b. Labrador Inuttut (Eskimo) and the Theory of Morphology. *Studies in Language* 6:221–44.

Williams, E. 1981. Argument Structure and Morphology. *The Linguistic Review* 1:81–114.

Williams, E. 1984. Grammatical Relations. *Linguistic Inquiry* 15:639–73.

Woodbury, A. C. 1977a. Greenlandic Eskimo, Ergativity, and Relational Grammar. In *Syntax and Semantics 8: Grammatical Relations,* P. Cole and J. Sadock, eds., pp. 307–36. New York: Academic Press.

Woodbury, A. C. 1977b. The Greenlandic Verbal Suffix *-ut:-* Interaction of Linguistic Form and Grammatical Function. In *Proceedings of the*

Third Annual Meeting of the Berkeley Linguistic Society, pp. 251–69. Berkeley: University of California.

Woodbury, A. C., and J. M. Sadock. 1986. Affixial Verbs in Syntax: A reply to Grimshaw and Mester. *Natural Language and Linguistic Theory* 4:229–44.

Zubizarreta, M. L. 1985. The Relation Between Morpho-phonology and Morpho-syntax: The Case of Romance Causatives. *Linguistic Inquiry* 16:247–89.

THE NATURE OF POLYSYNTHESIS IN ALGONQUIAN AND ESKIMO

J. Peter Denny

INTRODUCTION

The Algonquian languages, like so many other Canadian native languages, present us with the problem of the complex polysynthetic verb that often conveys a whole sentence, e.g. Ojibwa *šōškw-ēk-inā=n* 'smooth-sheetlike-by hand=OBJ' = 'he smooths something sheetlike by hand' (- indicates polysynthetic boundaries within the stem, and = the stem-inflection boundary).[1] These words seem to involve some sort of word-internal syntax because they include combinations of: noun with verb, e.g. *cīšš-ākon-ēhikē* 'clear-snow-do by tool to things' = 'he clears snow away' (with incorporated noun *-ākon-* 'snow'); adverb with verb, e.g. *omp-ipitē* 'up-move' = 'it flys up'; and adjective with noun *kakāno-kāt-ē* 'long-leg-have' = 'he has long legs'. As the English glosses show, such combinations are made by syntactic connections of separate words in isolating languages. Yet, we are reluctant to understand these polysynthetic combinations in the same syntactic terms because that would deny the functional significance of the word, including the fact that speakers often handle these words as remembered lexical units. It is the search for a middle position, in which polysynthetic combination is similar to but significantly different from word-external syntax, that I will pursue in this paper. This problem involves the narrower, and probably older, sense of polysynthesis, for which Robins (1967, 177) summarizes Humboldt's definition: "the essential structure of the sentence is incorporated into a single word." It does not directly concern the newer and larger sense in which polysynthetic simply describes the word-morphology as involving many bound morphemes (Bloomfield (1933) uses the separate term *synthetic* for this newer sense). This paper offers the idea that the polysynthetic combination of verb, adverb, noun, and adjective morphemes within a complex verb arises from distinct rules of polysynthesis that are *not* syntactic and *not* derivational.

The greatest challenge for such a project arises when verbs contain elements that seem to be part of the noun phrase, as happens in noun incorporation and also when noun classifiers appear in the verb. Both of these phenomena occur in Algonquian languages—in fact both kinds of morphemes occur in the middle of the verb stem, with other elements before and after them, and therefore are known as *medials*. In the examples, we saw classificatory medial (i.e. noun classifier) *-ēk-* 'sheetlike' and incorporating medials (i.e. incorporated nouns) *-ākon-* 'snow' and *-kāt-* 'leg'. This paper emphasizes these polysynthetic combinations of noun elements with verbs; a detailed account is given for Algonquian cases, but attention also is given to the somewhat different phenomenon of Eskimo noun incorporation.

The problem will be pursued in the general framework of logical semantics, which has developed since 1970. This actually is a diverse set of approaches founded by scholars such as Cresswell, Montague, Dahl, Bartsch, and Keenan, to mention some pioneers, but mostly I follow the practices outlined in McCawley (1981). As we proceed, it will become apparent that logical semantics involves quite different emphases than those of generative grammar with its autonomous syntax. or structuralist linguistics with its separate study of syntax, morphology, semantics, etc. Logical semantics puts primary emphasis on meaning and discourse—the speaker uses word meanings to communicate information; since they cannot express it all at once it must be spread out in time in an intelligible discourse. Secondary emphasis is given to syntax and morphology—these are seen as structures for conveying semantics and discourse to the listener. Following this approach, the paper considers how semantic and discourse structures are conveyed by polysynthetic morphology.

In coping with polysynthesis, in the sense of incorporating non-verb morphemes into the verb, we have to make a crucial distinction that is advocated by Goddard (1987) in his analysis of Fox verbs: *categories* (manipulated by rules) must be separated from *processes*. Since English combines adverb and verb using separate words whereas Fox, like other Algonquian languages, often combines them within a word, the same categories, adverb and verb, are combined by different processes, a syntactic process of word combination in English and a morphological process of word formation in Algonquian. Dowty (1978) has advocated the same separation for logical semantics, saying that "rules" combining categories such as adverb and verb are separate from their realization by either syntactic or morphological processes.

So far we have emphasized different processes used for the same rules, i.e. those combining the major lexical categories: noun, verb, adverb, and adjective. However, in studying these rules, which may be conveyed by either word-external syntactic processes or by polysynthetic morphology, we will contrast them to other rules, derivational ones. These latter rules, such as the deriving of a noun from a verb, usually are conveyed only by morphology, although some have syntactically processed analogues. I will call rules combining the major lexical categories when conveyed by word-forming morphology *polysynthetic rules* to contrast them with derivational ones.

1. POLYSYNTHETIC WORD FORMATION WITHOUT GRAMMATICAL CASE

In accordance with the theoretical outlook in Jensen and Johns (this volume), I hypothesize that Algonquian verb stem formation cannot involve manipulations of grammatical case, e.g. subject and object. This places me in opposition to Goddard (1987), so I will argue the case from two of his Fox examples. He starts from an example in which a sentence and a complement are conveyed in separate words (morpheme boundary symbols are those used in this paper; the symbol – marks the boundary of preverb modifiers with verb):

[1] ni:h–kehk-e:nem=ekwa e:h–katawi–nepo:hiw=aki
me should–know-by thought=3sg→1sg that–about to–die on=1sg→3sg
ni:hka:na
my friend
'my friend should know about me that I am about to die on him'

Both verbs are inflected for both participants, *kehk-e:nem=ekwa* '*he* knows about *me*' and *nepo:hiw=aki* '*I* die on *him*'; therefore Goddard argues that the complex sentence is formed by *copying* the subject of the lower verb as object of the higher verb. This seems fine, but he also applies the same argument to another example in which there is no inflected verb but just an "initial" morpheme within the main verb:

[2] ke=ki:shi–meko yo:we nep-ow-e:nem=enepena
you=already–really in the past die-INITIAL FORMER-by thought=1pl→2
'we had thought you were already dead'

Here, the transitive verb of thinking, the "final" morpheme *-e:nem-*, is modified by an adverb of dying, the initial *nep-ow-*, which was derived by adding the initial former *-w-* (a grammatical morpheme; Bloomfield (1946, 104); Drapeau (1979)) to the verb stem *nep-* 'die'. The inflection, combining prefix *ke=* and suffix *=enepena* indicates 'we' acting on 'you', i.e. the participants in the action of thinking described by the main verb. The subject of the lower verb of dying in the previous example has no counterpart in this case, since the dying is only encoded by an adverbial initial. The complex verb of thinking with its adverb of dying signals *some* coreferentiality of the participants in the two actions. From this, the hearer can make the unavoidable inference that the 'you' being thought about is the same 'you' doing the dying—after all 'we' cannot be thinking about *'you'* that *'we'* are dying. Given this ease of inference and lack of any overt marker of the subject of a putative lower verb of dying, we should not claim that the notion of a subject is involved in this kind of word-internal combination.

This position, that grammatical case is not involved in word formation, is very important for understanding incorporated nouns, i.e. Algonquian incorporating medials. When there is an external noun instead, that external noun can be a grammatical direct object, e.g. Cree *maskisin=a kēciko-nam* 'he took off (his own) shoes' (see note 1). The verb here is 'transitive inanimate', i.e. it takes a grammatical object that is an inanimate noun such as *maskisin=a* 'shoes'. However, when the same situation is described with an incorporating medial *kēt-askisin-ē=w* 'he takes off (his own) shoes', we do *not* want to claim that *-askisin-* 'shoe' is an incorporated direct object. One reason is that the medial may be non-referential (e.g. *nōcih-iskwēw-ē=w* 'he chases women, is a woman-chaser'), whereas the external noun must have at least indefinite reference (*iskwēw=a nōcih=ēw* 'he pursues a woman'). In connection with these Cree examples from his paper, Wolfart (1971) points out that the incorporated noun version often has some specialization of meaning, such as 'he is a woman-chaser', not found for the external noun version. Such specialization points to the fact that instead of being a direct object, the incorporated noun in fact is a modifier of the verb. The complex verb stem *nōcih-iskwēw-ē=* 'to seek women' is narrowed to convey prototypical ways of seeking women.

The view that incorporated nouns are verb modifiers, not grammatical direct objects, is defended in detail in Mithun (1984). In support, she emphasizes that, in Iroquoian languages, the words formed with incorporated nouns are lexical items; speakers are very aware of whether a particular word is a part of their speech, and they notice idiolectal and dialectal differences for such words. These points apply to noun classifiers as well, since for Mithun classifiers are only a *sub*-type of one kind of incorporated noun, type IV, 'classificatory noun incorporation'. Similarly, in Algonquian languages such as Ojibwa and Cree, I have observed that speakers often remember verbs containing incorporated nouns or noun classifiers as single lexical units. To be able to defend this view in detail, for both incorporated nouns and noun classifiers, requires some analysis of the semantic differences between the two.

1.1. Incorporated Nouns and Noun Classifiers

Although noun classifiers are not distinguished grammatically from incorporated nouns in Iroquoian languages, the semantic differences between them still show up. Only noun classifiers can co-occur with full independent nouns, as in Mithun's (1984, 870) Mohawk example:

[3] . . . rabahbót wahu-tsy-ahní:nu . . .
bullhead he-fish-bought
'he bought a bullhead'

Here the classifier *-itsy-* 'fish' co-occurs with the noun *rabahbót* 'bullhead'. In contrast, incorporated nouns can only co-occur with *other* elements of the external noun phrase such as a determiner, number, or adjectival verb. An example from Mithun (1984: 870) of the last of these possibilities is:

[4] kanekwarúnyu wa'-k-akya'tawi'tsher-ú:ni
dotted PAST-I-dress-make
'I made a polka-dotted dress'

These facts are congruent with the basic semantic distinction between incorporated nouns and classifiers that will be argued for in this paper: incorporated nouns express noun *predicates* that, therefore, cannot be repeated or contradicted by an external noun, whereas noun classifiers express sorted *arguments* that can co-occur with a noun predicate expressed by an external noun. The difference can be illustrated by the following partial formalizations of these examples. In example [3], 'bullhead he-fish-bought' the classifier 'fish' gives a sorted argument: Bullhead (fish) & Buy (he, fish). But, in example [4], 'I-dress-make', the incorporated noun 'dress' gives a predicate: Dress (thing) & Make (I, thing). (Beyond illustrating the difference between classifiers as sorted arguments and incorporated nouns as predicates, these formalizations are inadequate and are replaced later in the paper.)

For Algonquian, the most important difference arising from this semantic distinction is that incorporated nouns are *never* coreferential with the subject of the verb, whereas noun classifiers often are. Since the incorporated noun expresses a predicate, there can be no external noun duplicating this role, which serves as subject. Furthermore, the incorporated noun cannot be the subject itself, since incorporated nouns do not provide the definite reference necessary for such typical subject properties as control of reflexivization. However, classifiers can express the sorted argument for the subject which is expressed by a noun or pronoun, e.g. Cree *wāsē-yāpisk-isō=w* 'he (grammatically animate) glows in heat as stone'.[2] In this sentence, the subject is conveyed by the inflectional pronoun *=w* 'it', and the classificatory medial (noun classifier) *-āpisk-* indicates that it is drawn from the sort 'mineral solid'. We will see later that this coreferentiality of classifiers with subjects is limited in Algonquian languages by other lexical and grammatical properties. A further difference between the two kinds of medials also accords with the theory: since incorporating medials express only noun *predicates,* which may refer to nothing at all, they can occur with intentional verb predicates like *nōt-* 'seek' (e.g. *nōt-atihkw-ē=w* 'he is hunting deer') for which no reference to actual things is being sought. However, since classificatory medials express sorted *arguments* for nouns, they must always be referential and, therefore, cannot occur with *nōt-* 'seek'. Consequently even trees, which are very frequently referred to by classificatory medials—e.g. *-āskw-* 'organic solid' in *nōtim-āsko-si=w* 'he (tree is a grammatically animate noun) is round'—have to be described by an incorporating medial with *nōt-*—e.g. *-āhtikw-* 'stick-like'[3] in *nōt-āhtikw-ē=w* 'he is logging'. We see, then, that our theory is congruent with two important differences between the two kinds of medials: incorporating medials cannot describe subjects, and classificatory medials cannot occur with intentional (non-referring) verbs.

The semantic analysis I have given claims that noun classifiers express sorted arguments. Other scholars have suggested instead that classifiers express some special sort of predicate (McCawley 1981, 172–175; Lappin 1981), as I did previously (Denny 1976). However, in Denny (1985a), I presented detailed evidence from Conklin's (1981, 70–88) study of Thai classifiers that shows my current position to be correct. In the syntax of Thai noun phrases, classifiers are omitted just when we would expect it if they express arguments, i.e. when reference to individuals is not wanted. On the other hand, nouns are omitted when reference to the *property* they express is not needed. This distinctive pattern of omissions supports my view that only nouns express predicates, whereas classifiers express arguments.

1.2. Algonquian Classifiers

Mithun discusses other important relationships between external nouns, which have grammatical case, on the one hand, and, on the other hand, incorporated nouns and noun classifiers, which do not. Of these two groups, only external nouns can introduce participants into discourse, i.e. participants remembered across clauses so that the nouns need not be repeated. The incorporated nouns and noun classifiers operate only at the level of the clause and therefore have to be repeated in each clause that involves the participant they describe. An example of this involving the Ojibwa noun classifier *-ākkw-* 'organic solid' comes from the texts of Andrew Medler (Bloomfield 1957). At this point the hero, Nenabush, already is a discourse-level participant. Just as he is about to eat, he is annoyed by two trees, one introduced into the story as a discourse participant by the noun *mettikw* 'tree' but the other only referred to at the clause level by the classifier.

[5] mettik etašš āsw-ākku-ssin(=Ø) emā pēššo
tree and then across-solid-lie=(he) there near
'there was a tree leaning against another tree close by there'

[6] mī tašš ēši–kesīpwēwēškā=t.
thus–scraping noise move=he
'it moved with a creaking noise' (as it rubbed the other tree)

[7] mī tašš kī–ēšā=t wī–ekkawē–nīss-ākku-pin=āt.
went thither=he to–beforehand–down-solid-pull= he him
'so then he went over there to pull it loose from the other tree beforehand' (i.e., before he ate)

Once the first tree is introduced to the discourse by the noun in sentence [5], it can be referred back to by the inflectional pronouns in sentence [6], in which it is the (grammatically animate) subject of the verb, and in sentence [7], in which it is the (grammatically animate) direct object of the second verb. Similarly, the already introduced hero is referred back to by the inflectional pronouns of both verbs in sentence [7]. However, the second tree is separately referred to in sentence [5] and in sentence [7] by two occurrences of the classifier *-ākkw-* 'organic solid'—it never reaches the level of a discourse participant. These references, of course, are inferences, as discussed in subsequent sections, since the classifiers are verb modifiers.

1.3. Eskimo Incorporated Nouns

So far, we have seen that the incorporated nouns and noun classifiers of Algonquian (and Iroquoian) languages do not have grammatical case and do not introduce discourse participants. It is important to show that the same is true of Eskimo incorporated nouns, since they do have some distinctive properties. Fortescue (1979) argues for their lexical, non-syntactic status within a generative framework, essentially paralleling the arguments I will give within logical semantics. Usually, Eskimo incorporated nouns cannot establish a discourse referent and the noun must be repeated in a subsequent clause, e.g. *killaaq* 'hole' in

[8] Piita killaa-liuraaningmat, qimmiq katalauqtuq killaar-mut
Peter hole-when he had made, dog he fell in hole-to
'after Peter had made a hole, the dog fell into the hole'

However, Sadock (1980, 1986), in presenting and extending the analysis of Rischel (1972), has claimed that Eskimo incorporated nouns sometimes can introduce discourse referents, based on evidence such as the following from Greenlandic dialect:

[9] Suulut biili-liorsimavoq
Soren car-he has made
'Soren has made a car'

[10] sikaat karsikkuannik sanasimavaa
cigars boxes with he has made it
'he made it with old cigar boxes'

The inflection for direct object of the verb in [10] refers back to the car introduced by the incorporated noun *biili-* in [9]. It is hard to know what to make of this exception. From its content, it appears to be from a modern children's book, possibly translated from Danish; perhaps, it represents a recent accommodation to Danish grammar. At any rate, examination of traditional Eskimo texts (Spalding 1979) shows that a discourse referent is introduced only when an incorporated noun is accompanied by an external noun phrase element, such as a nominalized adjectival verb. Here is an Aivilingmiut dialect example (Spalding 1979) from a tale told by Thomas Kusugaq:

[11] inuk-sigiblutik ajagaqtualungniguuq
person-they coming across great cup and ball players
'they came across people, great cup and ball players'

The incorporated noun *inuk-* 'person' appears in the intransitive verb, but it is accompanied by an external noun phrase element, a nominalized adjectival verb *ajagaqtualuk* 'great cup-and-ball player' inflected as a noun in the (plural) instrumental case, *ajagaqtualung=nik* (with clitic *-guuq* 'they say'), the particular oblique case that occurs with the patients of intransitive verbs. This noun serves as the *whole* external noun phrase and suffices to place the people it refers to into the discourse register. They are then the pronominal subject of the next clause:

[12] marruungniguuq ajagaqaqłutik
two they having cup and ball game
'who (each) had two cup and ball games'

When incorporated nouns occur by themselves, they fail to establish their referent in the discourse. The above method of establishing a discourse referent is by no means the usual one; normally a full external noun is used. Five things are referred to in the next passage [13], only one, *maniq* 'lamp-wick moss', by an external noun, and only it is referred back to (twice) in subsequent clauses. Three others, 'boots', 'porch', and 'stone-lamp' all are referred to within their clauses by incorporated nouns and never referred to by pronominal inflections in later clauses. As pointed out earlier, and discussed later, these references are inferred not expressed, since the incorporated nouns are nominal modifiers of the verb. The fifth thing, 'oil', appears only in a local case noun. When 'porch' is referred to a second time, the noun is repeated in a local case (the six clauses are lettered):

[13] **a.** kamik-kami
boot-when she put on
b. tursuung-muaqłuni
porch-she going to
'. . . when she put on (her) boots, going to the porch,'

c. manir=mik tigusibluni
lamp wick moss=INSTR she grabbing
'she grabbed (some) lamp-wick moss,'

d. tursuung-niguuq qulliq-tagarmat
porch-in lamp-since there is
'(and) since there was a stone-lamp in the porch,'

e. ursu-mullu misukłuniuk
oil-into and she plunging it
f. ikibluniukłu
and she lighting it
'she plunged it into the (lamp's) oil, and she lit it. . .'

The moss introduced in clause [13c] is referred to by pronominal inflections in [13e] and [13f]: the heroine plunges the moss into the lamp's oil, then removes the moss and lights it, and as the story continues, goes outside carrying the lighted moss. Since it is indefinite at first mention it is an oblique (instrumental) case patient of an intransitive verb; nonetheless, it is established as a discourse referent by the external noun. For the incorporated nouns, what we have seen confirms very clearly what Mithun claims: incorporation backgrounds the noun in the discourse, and since it does not establish its referent as a discourse participant, the noun has to be repeated if the referent is wanted in a subsequent clause.

Sadock appears to accept that Eskimo incorporated nouns are not subjects or direct objects, but he claims that they are in an oblique grammatical case, which contrasts with the theory supported here that they are verb modifiers. However, similar objections to those given earlier against the notion that Algonquian incorporated nouns have grammatical case apply to Eskimo as well. First, the main oblique grammatical case ending, the instrumental case used on external nouns for the patients of intransitive verbs (e.g. *anguti=mik takuvunga* 'I see a man') never appears on incorporated nouns. Second, specialized meanings arise when the modifying noun and the verb become fully lexicalized, e.g. Fortescue's (1984) example from Greenlandic (*anurlir-puq* 'it is windy' from *anuri* 'wind' and *-lir-* 'provide with'). Third, many combinations are remembered by speakers as lexical items.

We have seen that Eskimo incorporated nouns are just like Iroquoian and Algonquian ones in the two most crucial properties: they are not grammatical subjects or objects, and they normally do not establish discourse referents. In other ways, however, they are significantly different. Sadock suggests the differences arise because Eskimo noun incorporation is more a matter of derivation, whereas Sapir's (1911) "noun incorporation", which would be exemplified by Algonquian, is more a matter of compounding. However, these labels do not seem to capture the several distinctions that are found. The Algonquian (and Iroquoian) patterns are regarded as true cases of noun incorporation because the noun elements appear within regular, independent verbs. The Eskimo pattern seems to be only loosely labelled noun incorporation because, as Fortescue (1984) points out, the nouns are not 'incorporated' into regular verbs, but have affixed to them a limited set of dependent verb suffixes that occur only after nouns (or the empty root *pi-*). One consequence of this is that two of these dependent verb suffixes have the special role of permitting the noun to which they are suffixed to introduce discourse referents: *-taar-* 'get' and *-gar-* 'have'. An example from Sadock (1986) is

[14] erner-taar-put, atserlugulu Malamik
son-get-they, and they called him Mala
'they got a son, and they called him Mala'

The object inflection on the second, transitive verb refers back to the incorporated noun *erneq* 'son'. Although Sadock claims this shows a syntactic connection of the incorporated noun to the verb, it seems more likely that the incorporated noun, as usual, is a nominal modifier of the verb, and that the derived verb has the syntactic property of introducing the discourse referent. This is likely to be the case for verbs of having and getting, since their main function is to indicate things possessed by their subjects, many of which will be new to the discourse.

A second distinctive feature of Eskimo noun incorporation is that the actual noun stems are incorporated. In contrast, in Algonquian, a separate lexical class of morphemes, the incorporating medials, are incorporated; and in Iroquoian, the noun root is incorporated, which in an independent noun requires other derivational affixes. Because, in Eskimo, the actual nouns are being incorporated, they sometimes are inflected in part as nouns, although most often they are not. The inflections that appear are the local cases and the possessed endings; grammatical case and number inflections, which are the most important for syntax, do not occur. For example, certain verbs of motion take a local case on the incorporated noun, e.g. [13b.] *tursuung-mu-aq-łuni* 'she going to the porch' has noun *tursuuk* 'porch', inflected with allative case *-mut* 'to', incorporated into verb *-aq-* 'go'. However, Fortescue (1984) indicates that, in Greenlandic dialect, the original local case endings have fused with the verb suffix to form a new verb suffix, with distinctive 'singular' and 'plural' forms, *-mukar-* 'go to (a place)', *-nukar-* 'go to (places)'. Similarly, under lexically restricted conditions, possessed endings may appear; e.g. in Greenlandic dialect *angut-* 'man' with possessed endings means 'father', so when 'father' is incorporated the endings appear, e.g., *angu-si-sar-poq* 'he resembles his father' with possessed inflection *-si* before the verb *-sar-* 'resemble' (from Sadock 1980).

Most surprisingly, an external noun in genitive case can appear expressing the possessor of the referent of the incorporated noun, e.g. in Greenlandic,

[15] tuttu-p neqi-tor-punga
reindeer-GEN meat-eat-I
'I ate reindeer's meat'

Here, incorporated 'meat' has external possessor 'reindeer's.' Sadock treats genitive case for a possessor and ergative case for ergative subject of a transitive verb, e.g. *tuttu-p takuaa* 'the reindeer sees it', as one grammatical case which he calls *relative*. Although many ergative languages have a similar homonymy of forms, the complete separation of grammatical function suggests that these are two grammatical cases not one: the ergative case marker as well as the transitive inflections on the verb probably are derived historically from the genitive case and the possessed inflections. If genitive is a separate case, then neither the external possessor nor the incorporated possessed bear a grammatical case relation *to the verb*. Instead, we have a complex noun phrase, one segment of which is incorporated; the polysynthetic rule works on the output of the syntactic combination of the possessor and possessed nouns by incorporating only the possessed member of this noun phrase. This polysynthetic combination is prior to any grammatical linkage of the noun phrase to the verb and, of course, precludes such linkage, since the whole noun phrase becomes a nominal modifier of the verb.

Sadock (1986, 24) gives a further example of syntactic relations that appear to be confined within the noun phrase and not involve any grammatical link to the verb:

[16] puisi-kkaangamili, orsu-ata ila-a
seal-whenever he caught but fat-3sg POSS GEN part-3sg POSS
nerisarpaa
he would eat it
'but whenever he caught a seal, he would eat part of its fat'

In this example, an incorporated noun in the first clause is established as a discourse referent that serves anaphorically as the possessor of another explicit possessor of the direct object noun of the verb in the verb clause. The double possessive construction in question is 'seal's fat's part': the seal is introduced only by an incorporated noun in the first clause, *puisi-kkaangamili* 'but whenever he caught a seal', but it is indicated to be the possessor by the inflection on the possessed noun for 'fat' in the verb clause, *orsuata ilaa nerisarpaa* 'its fat's part he would eat it' = 'he would eat part of its fat'. This example demonstrates that, although incorporated nouns cannot have grammatical case relations with their verb (or establish discourse referents having grammatical case relations with subsequent verbs), in the case of Eskimo, since the incorporated elements are actual nouns, their syntactic relations to other nouns remain undisturbed, including the possibility of establishing a discourse referent for linkage to a subsequent noun phrase.

Some of the facts of Eskimo noun incorporation we have just reviewed require us to recognize that the nouns being incorporated may already belong to syntactically formed noun phrases: incorporation removes the noun from the noun phrase, converts it into a modifier of the verb, and leaves behind the remainder of the noun phrase. This conception helps us understand the most frequently occurring external noun phrase component, the nominalized adjectival verbs, with which we began this discussion. Here is another example abbreviated from Sadock (1986, 23):

[17] . . .qusanar-tu-mik qaan-nior-paa, unnermillu
beautiful-one-INST kayak-make-he him and with white sealskin
amer-tillugu
cover-simultaneously he it
'he made a beautiful kayak for him, and covered it with white sealskin'

The noun *qajaq* has been incorporated in the verb *-lior-* 'make' but the nominal modifier *qusanartumik* 'a beautiful one' remains as an external noun phrase that establishes the discourse referent referred back to as object of the verb in the verb clause, *amertillugu* 'he covering it'. A formation such as this proceeds as follows: [1] the noun phrase *qusanartuq qajaq* 'a beautiful kayak' is formed syntactically; [2] the noun *qajaq* is incorporated in the verb—in this case, we know that the speaker remembers the whole lexical item *qaannior-* 'to make a kayak', since Sadock reminds us that Rischel (1974) has shown that the phonology involved is now unproductive; in other cases, the speaker would join noun and verb suffix at the time of utterance; [3] the remainder of the noun phrase then is linked syntactically to the resulting incorporative verb, becoming the oblique object in the instrumental case, *qusanartu-mik*. By recognizing that this adjectival noun and the head noun have been related syntactically to each other prior to incorporation, we also recognize that the semantic relation of adjectival modifier to noun has been established prior to incorporation, as needed for examples such as that in [18] (Sadock 1986, 30) (the incorporative verb 'make-money' has been nominalized).

[18] peqquserluut-inik aningaas-iortoq
false ones-INST PL money-one who makes
'a counterfeiter'

This preexisting link of modifying noun to incorporated noun also explains why, as Sadock points out, such a modifying noun must be accompanied by an incorporated noun in order to introduce a discourse referent. The semantic link to the incorporated noun is needed to identify the kind of entity referred to by the external modifier, although as Mithun (1986, 35) points out sometimes this may be inferrable from context. The pre-incorporative link of modifier to noun also explains cases of lexically specified number agreement as in the example cited by Sadock (1980, 309) of the grammatically plural noun *qamutit* 'sled, carriage, car' whose external modifiers must be plural:

[19] ataatsi-nik qamute-qarpoq
one-INST PL car-has he
'he has one car'

In considering these cases, we also have recognized that the lexicalization of the noun-verb combination is variable; for frequent combinations there will be a remembered unit, whereas rarer ones may be constructed anew. This possibility of variable lexicalization is an important feature of polysynthesis, i.e. links between morphemes from major lexical classes, rather than derivation, i.e. other morpheme combinations. As will be described in section 2, only polysynthetic combinations may be either constructed at the time of utterance or remembered; derivations always are remembered, since they evolve slowly and unconsciously within the speech community.[4] A related aspect of this property of polysynthetic combinations is called *semi-lexicalization* by Fortescue (1979, 26); when the combination is remembered for production as a unit, the separate meanings of the incorporated noun and the verb are maintained. For example, although *qaannior-* must be remembered as a unit, its separate meaning components remain 'kayak' and 'make'.

1.4. Conclusion

Our consideration of the exceptional cases in Eskimo noun incorporation indicates that they all are concerned with syntactic and semantic relations within the noun phrase and that none of them alters the status of the incorporated noun as a nominal modifier of the verb; in no case does the incorporated noun have a grammatical case link to the verb.

The special features of Eskimo noun incorporation seem to be permitted because the actual nouns are incorporated not a special class of morphemes such as the Algonquian incorporating medials. These latter, in contrast, are always followed by one particular verb final *-ē-*, e.g. Cree *sāpopē-skisin-ē=w* 'he has wet shoes'; in addition, they usually are distinct morphologically from the nouns referring to the same thing, e.g. noun *maskisin* 'shoe' and medial *-askisin-* 'shoe'. Similarly, Iroquoian incorporated nouns are only noun roots, which have to be accompanied by other derivational morphemes in a full noun. Interestingly, Algonquian languages also have the Eskimo-style of noun incorporation, in which a regular noun can have suffixed to it a restricted set of dependent verb finals, e.g. Cree *-iwan* 'to be or be characterized by a thing' in *askī-wan* 'it is earth'. At least one of these finals requires that the noun have a possessed inflection; this final *-i-* forms verbs of possession, e.g. *o=mohkomān-i=w* 'his=knife-have=he' = 'he has a knife'.

Our survey of Algonquian, Iroquoian, and Eskimo examples has shown that incorporated nouns and noun classifiers occurring in verbs do not have grammatical case—subject, direct object, or oblique—and do not introduce discourse referents that serve as subjects or objects. In this sense, they do not participate in the word-external syntax relating nouns to verbs. To understand further the distinctive nature of polysynthetic joining, we will proceed to compare it to derivation.

2. POLYSYNTHESIS AND DERIVATION

To compare polysynthesis and derivation, it is essential to recall the pertinent definition of polysynthesis used in this paper: polysynthesis consists of sentence-building combinations within a word. These are the junctures of morphemes from the major lexical classes—verb, noun, adverb, and adjective—which in isolating languages are combined word-externally. This definition excludes many other combinations of morphemes; these are the derivations. As we proceed with a detailed account of the difference between polysynthesis and derivation, it is clear that we cannot use the other definition of polysynthesis—many morphemes in a word—since this would eradicate any difference before we start!

In comparing polysynthesis with word-external syntax in the earlier sections of the paper, we have emphasized that polysynthetic combinations often are memorized lexical units. As we now compare polysynthesis to derivation, we have to look at the other side of this feature of polysynthesis: although the combinations often are lexicalized, they need not be, an individual speaker at the time of utterance may construct new polysynthetic combinations or reconstruct old ones if he has forgotten them. Here are examples of polysynthetic words unlikely to be a part of anyone's lexicon:

[20] Ojibwa: miskw-āpikk-itē-naniw-ē
red-metal-heated-tongue-have
'he has a hot as red metal tongue'

[21] Eskimo: pik-annga-a-qatau-juq
right up there-from-come-with others-INDIC.
'he is coming with others from right up there'

This kind of individual creativity is an aspect of polysynthesis in which it is similar to word-external syntax, despite the differences described previously. As we will see, it is *not* true of derivations, since they are only arrived at by the unconscious drift of the whole speech community. For example, in [20] the morpheme *-itē-* 'heated' is formed derivationally by adding the derivational morpheme *-ē-* 'process' to the verb morpheme *-it-* 'heat'. Once the speech community has developed this juncture, no individual speaker can vary it. This difference in the role of the individual speaker in creating combinations has no connection with productivity: a derivational system may still be productive (as demonstrated later in this section), since the speech community is still producing new forms, but individual speakers cannot create new forms that will be accepted as normal speech, as can be done for polysynthesis.

This distinctive role of the speaker in creating new polysynthetic combinations arises out of a more fundamental difference between polysynthesis and derivation. Polysynthetic morphemes are members of the major lexical classes, each of which refers to separate aspects of the situation the speaker is describing, as illustrated in [20]. These are open classes of morphemes, new ones being created to describe new things, properties and occurrences. Since they refer to elements of the situation, the speaker must be free to combine them as communication requires and also to have a conscious awareness of what they mean, e.g. in [20] knowing that one is describing a 'tongue' as 'red' and 'hot'. None of this is true of a derivational morphene like *-ē-* 'process' in [20]: that heating is a 'process' is not a separate aspect of the situation but just a more abstract re-classification of heating. Because of this, it need never be consciously recognized nor manipulated creatively by the individual speaker.

In comparing polysynthesis and derivation, we are talking about rules not processes. Both polysynthetic rules and derivational rules are realized by morphological processes, since only such processes are available within the word. Let us examine a Cree verb to which both kinds of rules have applied (the boundaries marked / are the derivational boundaries): *āt-akām/ak-is/in* 'he is blocked by open (water)'. Polysynthetic rules combine the adjectival initial *-āt-* 'blocked', the classificatory medial *-akāmak-* 'open space' (from which water is inferred), and the verb final *-isin* 'become'. Since the adjective, the classifier, and the verb all refer to properties, things, or events the speaker is trying to describe, speakers report their awareness that this word contrasts with the non-incorporating verb *āt-isin* (~ *āc-isin*) 'he is blocked' and that various other medials such as *ākonak-* 'snow' could appear in the verb describing other things he was blocked by. Just as Mithun points out for Mohawk speakers, I have observed Cree speakers discussing such incorporating words and indicating which ones are in their dialect and which they have heard in neighboring dialects. Thus, there is a high degree of awareness of the polysynthetic boundaries and of the meanings of the individual components being joined.

In contrast, derivational morphemes do not describe elements of the situation being referred to. Instead, they derive one class of morpheme from another. When they contribute any meaning it is a supplement to the meaning of another morpheme, quite different from the independently varying meanings of polysynthetic combinations. Also, speakers do not report any awareness of the derivational boundaries. In our example, the classificatory medial *-akām/ak-* is derived, by "post-medial" *-ak,* from the incorporating medial *-akām-*, (e.g. *wās-akām-ē=w* 'he makes a circuit', i.e. he goes around an intervening space). The suggestion that there is some kind of boundary at the derivational juncture is regarded by speakers as a false way of looking at the language, pointing to the entirely unconscious nature of derivation. Similarly for the derivational boundary within the verb final *-is/in,* the first morpheme is the "bare final" *-is-* 'become' and the second is the "verb class marker" that provides the "aspect class" (called "aspectual character" by Lyons 1977, 706) of the verb, *-in-* 'event'.[5] Again, speakers are entirely unaware of this boundary. It may be objected that this is because these combinations were once transparent but have coalesced over time. However, this does not seem to be the case. These derivational rules are still being unconsciously manipulated. For example, the Plains Cree bare final *-pay-* has been changing its meaning from 'go' to 'become'. In the last fifty years, between Bloomfield's Plains Cree fieldwork and that of Ahenakew and Wolfart (Ahenakew 1986), speakers have begun to change the verb class marker to *-in* 'event' to fit the new meaning 'become' of the bare final, e.g. *piko-pay/in* 'it is broken' rather than older *piko-pay/i=w, pāst-ipay/in* 'it cracks, bursts' replacing *pāst-ipay/i=w.*[6] Furthermore, one cannot argue for historical accretion unless there is a known source in previously productive combinations, in this case combinations of the other kind, i.e. polysynthesis and not derivation. There is no such evidence that the bare finals and verb class markers once were manipulated consciously in this way as elements in polysynthesis. In contrast, a case where we *can* argue for historical accretion of previously productive polysynthesis is in the formation of new unitary initials from old stems, e.g. the now unitary initial *kiskinaw-* 'teach' in *kiskinō-hamaw=ēw* 'he teaches it to him' is an accretion of initial *kisk-* 'know' and final *-inaw-* 'see', arising from their frequent occurrence together as a stem used as an initial for secondary derivations.

The two cases of derivation, rather than polysynthesis, we have been discussing, postmedial *-ak* and the verb class markers, show the functioning of derivation, which is to derive one class of morpheme from another. The more usual case is postmedial *-ak,* since it contributes no meaning of its own but just marks the grammatical shift from incorporating medial to classificatory medial. (Mithun, 1984, argues that noun classifiers are derived from incorporated nouns in a variety of other language families). The verb class markers fundamentally are the same in that they derive finals from bare finals or from monomorphemic bare stems, but they are unusual in adding a component of meaning, the verb class of the verb. So far, we have illustrated verb classes of the aspect class type, i.e. either state, event, or process, but the verb class markers sometimes signal other verb class information such as the *semantic* case (of the subject or direct object). For example, marker *-aw* added to bare stem *nāt-* yields the transitive animate final *nāt/aw=* in *nāt/aw=ēw* 'he fetches (him) for him'. The marker *-aw-* signals that the direct object is the beneficiary not the patient, in contrast to *nāt=ēw* 'he fetches him' in which Ø marker indicates that the patient is the direct object (Denny 1985b).[7] This transitive animate bare stem *nāt-* is unusual in being able to take three different markers (also *-amaw-* signalling beneficiary as direct object and an oblique *inanimate* patient, *nāt/amaw=ēw* 'he fetches *it* for him'); most bare stems or bare finals take only the one marker that signals their appropriate verb class. Because of the very limited nature of the meaning combinations, compared to the enormous variety of nominal and verbal combinations available in polysynthesis, it is correct to regard the verb class markers as derivational morphemes that produce finals and stems from bare finals and bare stems.

To see the contrast between derivation and polysynthesis, it is helpful to compare the derivational verb class markers to their very close relatives, the polysynthetic abstract finals. The latter are themselves, in fact, derived from a few of the former. For example, marker *-i-* for aspect class 'process' is the likely source of abstract final *-ī-* that combines polysynthetically with classificatory medials, e.g. *-askamik-* 'ground' in *kotāw-askamik-ī=w* 'he sinks into the ground', and with adverbial initials, e.g. *kiyip-ī=w* 'he is quick'. In both cases the resulting complete stem still belongs to the aspect class 'process'. However, the abstract finals, unlike the verb class markers, combine freely with other morphemes in a way that depends upon the situation the speaker is describing. For example, the classificatory medial (noun classifier) *-askw-* 'cloud' appears with either abstract final *-ā-*, derived from the '*spatial* state' marker *-ā-*, or with abstract final *-an-*, derived from the unmarked (i.e. 'nonspatial') 'state' marker *-an-*. If a spatial pattern of cloud is involved the 'spatial state' final is used, e.g. *mamēn-askw-ā=w* 'it is partly cloudy', *osāwipē-skw-ā=w* 'it is a sky with yellow spots', but for uniform conditions of the sky the unmarked 'state' final appears, e.g. *wāsē-skw-an* 'the sky is clear', *yīkw-askw-an* 'it is overcast'. The verb class markers can not be manipulated in this way to refer to particular situations; they give a fixed supplementary meaning, i.e. verb class, to a bare final or bare stem to which they are linked derivationally, e.g. marker *-ā-* 'spatial state' accompanies bare final *-sk-* 'be abundant', *nisk-isk/ā=w* 'there are lots of geese'. As before, it is important to remember that this is not a difference in productivity, since it was shown earlier that these semantic verb class markers are still productive.

Other derivational morphemes include *-t,* which derives transitive inanimate (TI) bare finals (or bare stems) from certain transitive animate (TA) ones, e.g. TI *-ēyih/t-* 'think about it' from TA *-ēyim-* 'think about him'. Several other derivational processes are described for Fox in Goddard (1987); they can be exemplified in Cree. One of great interest is a morpheme *-w*, which converts (verbal) bare finals and bare stems into (adverbial) initials. For example, the bare stem *kiskis-* in *kiskis/i=w* 'he remembers' becomes the initial *kiskis/w-* for use with other finals, e.g. *kiskis/o-m=ēw* 'he reminds him' (literally: 'he tells him to remember') with final *-im-* 'by speech'. Another group of derivations are those that yield the incorporating medials from nouns, e.g. *-āpēw-* 'man' from noun *nāpēw* 'man'. Finally, there is the derivation of finals from monomorphemic stems, e.g. *-āpam-* 'see' in *atim-āpam=ēw* 'he sees him going your way' from *wāpam-* 'see' in *wāpam=ēw* 'he sees him'. The variability in these last two kinds of derivations is described in Wolfart (1973).

We now can summarize what we have learned about word formation. First, syntactic rules involving grammatical case and the discourse register lie beyond word formation. Second, polysynthesis is a distinct set of word formation rules in which morphemes with referential meanings from lexical categories, such as noun, verb, adjective, and adverb, are combined using morphological processes. Likewise, derivation is a distinct set of rules in which morphemes of one class are derived from those of another—the derivational morphemes either have no meaning or contribute a supplementary meaning.

3. SENTENCE SEMANTICS AND PROPOSITIONS

The view of incorporated nouns and of noun classifiers occurring in verbs that I have described claims that they are nominal modifiers that combine with the verb to produce a new verb. However, in many cases, for the hearer to grasp the speaker's message, the hearer must infer a proposition in which there is a semantic case relation between an entity indicated by the incorporated noun or classifier and the occurrence described by the verb. Clearly, there is a gap between the meaning of the sentence itself and the proposition the hearer infers from it. For example, in sentence [7] from Medler's Ojibwa story about the two trees, the classifier *-ākkw-* 'organic solid' (i.e. wood and bone) is a nominal modifier of the verb *nīss-ipin=* 'to pull down' when they are combined in the stem *nīss-akko-pin=:* this stem conveys only that the pulling down was of a kind that involves organic solids. But for the hearer to understand the situation he must infer a semantic case relation to the action for the second tree in the situation (which the classifier describes), in this case a locative relation, since the hero is pulling the first tree down *from* the second one so as to stop the creaking noise made by their rubbing together.

The notion that sentences do not specify propositions fully is widely accepted in logical semantics. It was first fully studied for deictic words, when it was recognized that, from a sentence such as *I am here now,* one must infer a proposition such as 'John Smith is in Room 7403 at 12:30 PM'. However, it is recognized now that anything in a sentence may require inferential completion. This fact arises naturally out of the costs associated with any act of communicating information. There always is a tendency to transmit less and let the recipient infer more. Incorporated nouns, and noun classifiers appearing in verbs, essentially are devices for abbreviating messages. When the entity in question does not play a major role in the discourse it can be backgrounded by these incorporations. However, the task of inferring the role played by the entity in the situation remains for the hearer.

Not only must semantic case be inferred but the degree of reference as well: as Mithun (1984, 859) points out, these incorporated nominals are "unmarked for definiteness, number, or case". From a given occurrence, a hearer may infer that a classifier is purely adverbial and does not refer at all, as in the Ojibwa example *miskw-āpikk-itē-naniw=ē* 'he has a hot as red metal tongue'. Here the classificatory medial *-āpikk-* 'mineral solid' is not inferred to have any reference—there is no metal in the situation—it simply is the case that the tongue is *like* metal in its red hotness. This example shows nicely that adverb is the default role of incorporated nominals. However, frequently, the situation does involve entities described by the incorporated morpheme, and then any appropriate degree of reference may be inferred (Mithun 1984, 856, describes a variety of possibilities); in this word the incorporating medial *-naniw-* 'tongue' is inferred to have specific reference. Once an inference is made that a medial refers to something in the situation, the basic semantic difference in reference between noun classifiers and incorporated nouns applies: the classificatory medials are inferred to convey sorted arguments that must have actual references; therefore, as we saw earlier, they cannot occur with non-referential verb predicates like 'seek'. However, the incorporating medials are inferred to convey noun predicates, and thus, may refer to a property of a potential referent linked to a verb like 'seek', e.g. Cree *nōt-atihkw-ē=w* 'he is hunting deer'.

Next, we will look at an example comparing in detail, on the one hand, the structure of the sentence conveyed by a polysynthetic word, and on the other hand, the separate structure of the proposition inferred from it. We will use the Ojibwa verb mentioned in sentence [7] from Medler's story about Nenabush and the trees, stripped of its preverb modifiers for simplicity: *nīss-ākko-pin=āt* 'he pulls him down from a solid'. In the sentence structure shown in [22] the classificatory medial *-ākkw-* 'organic solid' is adverbial as is the initial *nīss-* 'down', both modify the verb final *-pin* 'pull' (the inflection also signals conjunct mode for a clause that is coordinated with other clauses).

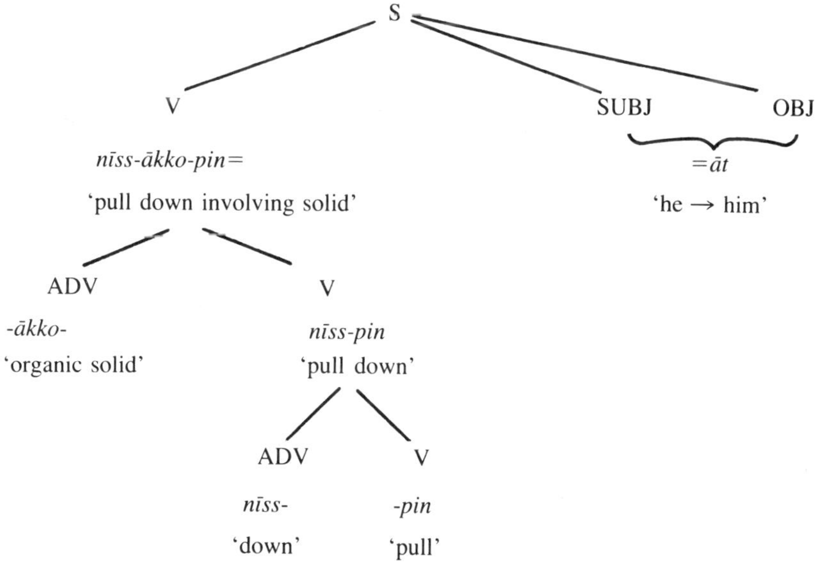

From this sentence the hearer infers the proposition that Nenabush is pulling down one tree from another tree. To capture the logical semantics of this proposition, we have to represent the noun sort 'organic solid' for the second tree, since it is conveyed explicitly by the classificatory medial *-ākkw-*. Noun sorts, as already argued, are the sorted arguments of noun predicates, so that for each noun predicate our logical representation will supply a sorted argument. We also have to represent the inferred semantic case relations of the participants to the action. A semantic case will take a noun sort as one of its arguments, and must have a verb sort to be its other argument if it is to relate the participant to the action. The verb sorts are the aspect classes conveyed by some of the verb class markers we saw previously, either 'process', 'event', or 'state'. Thus, the logical form of the example will be a conjunction of several sentences, most of them giving semantic case relations among various noun sorts and the verb sort 'process'. The logical form is

[23] (∃ inanimate: Tree inanimate) [(∃ organic-solid: Tree organic-solid)
(∃ process) Pull-down process ∧ Agent nenabush, process
∧ Patient inanimate, process ∧ Source organic-solid, process]

to be read 'there is an inanimate that is a tree, such that, for some organic solid that is a tree and for some process, the process is pulling down, Nenabush is the agent of the process, the inanimate is the patient of the process, and the organic solid is the source of the process' ('source' or 'ablative' case means the organic solid is the place from which the movement process begins). A tree diagram [24] in the manner of McCawley (1981), may help show the structure.

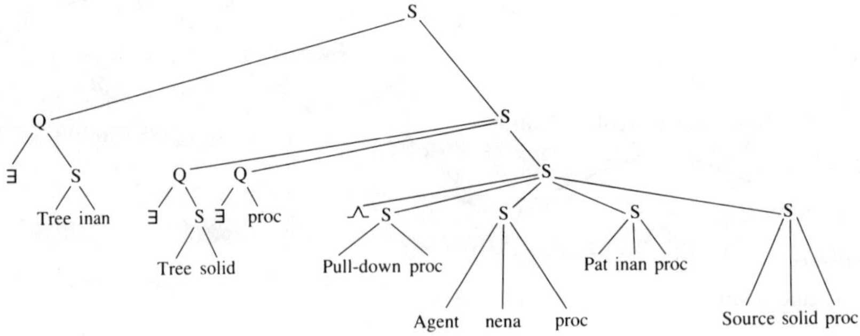

Some parts of this proposition are carried over from previous discourse, particularly the name *Nenabush* and the noun predicate 'tree' for the first tree that is the patient of the pulling down; also, the grammatical animate gender of the tree is replaced by its semantic sort 'inanimate'. This information is represented in the quantifier, which is outside the matrix of the proposition (the latter shown in square brackets in [23]), since it cannot be at issue for the truthfulness of *this* proposition. Within the matrix, the verb sort 'process', the 'agent' semantic case for the subject, and the 'patient' semantic case for the object all are provided by the hearer's lexical knowledge of the verb in the utterance, final *-pin-* 'pull'. However, it is the three inferences concerning the classifier *-ākkw-* 'organic solid' in which we are most interested. As we have seen, all that is signalled in the utterance is the adverbial notion that the action of pulling down is *of a kind* that involves organic solids. First, the hearer has to infer that there is reference to an actual organic solid. Then he has to infer that it is likely to be a tree. (These two inferences probably also were made from the previous occurrence of *-ākkw-* in the first sentence [5] quoted). Finally (and only for this sentence), he has to figure out what role a second tree could play when the first one is being pulled down—given the earlier parts of the story, that the hero is bothered by the noise of the two trees rubbing together, the semantic case 'source' is the obvious inference. It is worth noting, parenthetically, that several features of this logical representation have been recommended by other scholars. First, McCawley (1981, 118) advocates the use of restricted quantification in which noun predicates appear as parts of quantifiers. Second, Davidson (1967) has claimed that verb predicates have their own 'event' arguments, here realized as the sorted verb argument 'process'. I have defended this view with data from Eskimo 'only' (Denny 1984); another recent defence is Peterson (1985). Third, Sondheimer (1978) has argued that it is events that are located not their participants, in this case the process of pulling down is located by a source relation with respect to an organic solid (the second tree).

The most dramatic cases of semantic case inferences are those where only context guides the hearer's choice among as many as three cases, patient, instrument, or locative. For example, Cree *kip-āpisk-aham* 'he closes or locks it *with* or *as* metal' involves inferring either 'instrument' or 'patient' for the inferred referent of classificatory medial *-āpisk-* 'mineral solid'—typical contexts of closing or locking make the inference of 'locative' case improbable but do not rule it out. This latter possibility is prominent in the next example, involving classificatory medial *-āskw-* 'organic solid', *micim-āskw-aham* 'he fastens it *as* or *to* a solid by tool', where the choice is largely between 'patient' and 'locative' cases; however, fastening *by* an organic solid also might be inferred in some situations (both verbs have final *-aham* indicating the use of some instrument or other).

Besides the semantic cases relating participants to actions, there also is a semantic case relating participants to each other, i.e. possessor and possessed. This relation most often is inferred for body parts when they are conveyed by incorporating medials, e.g. (transitive) *kāsī-hkw-ē-n=ēw* 'she washes his face'. The incorporation allows the possessor to be direct object inflected on the verb but the hearer has to infer that the body part is possessed. Whether or not this inference will be made depends upon situational context; it is not directly signalled by the word, as illustrated in the following pair (of intransitives): *nanīc-ikan-ē=w* 'he has lumps on his joints', and *os-ikan-ē=w* 'he boils bones' (to collect fat). To infer that the bones in the second case are *not* possessed, the hearer has to know that one does not usually boil them while still attached to the owner! On the other hand, washing usually will be interpreted as affecting a possessed body part, e.g. (intransitive) *kāsī-hkw-ē=w* 'he washes his (own) face'. The inference that an object described by an incorporating medial is possessed is not limited to body parts but may apply to other objects, e.g. *mahk-astotin-ē=w* 'he has a big hat'. As before, depending on the situation, possession may not be inferred, e.g. *kimot-astotin-ē=w* 'he steals a hat', presumably not his own!

Voegelin and Voegelin (1973) have pointed out that the body part described within a transitive verb not only is inferred to be possessed by the participant who is direct object but also is the inferred location of the action; thus *kāsī-hkw-ē-n=ēw* is better glossed 'she washes him *on* his face'. They support this view by pointing out that the related sentence, in which there is an external noun for the body part and in which the verb still has the possessor as direct object, requires a locative suffix on the noun. This is seen in their Shawnee examples:

[25] ni=peʔš-ičāl-ē-n=a
I=touch-nose-ABSTRACT FINAL-by hand=1→3
'I tweaked him on his nose'

[26] ni=peˀš-en=a ho=čāl=eki
I=touch-by hand=1→3 his=nose=LOCATIVE
'I touched him on his nose'

In [25], the incorporating medial *-čāl-* 'nose' appears, but in [26] the external noun *čāši* 'nose' has the locative suffix *-eki,* giving explicit indication of the locative case relation, which is only inferred for the incorporated noun. (The meaning of this lexicalized incorporating verb usually is narrowed to include playful intention, hence the gloss 'tweaked'). The two semantic case relations into which the incorporated noun enters, possessed and locative, are easily represented in the kind of logical semantic representation advocated in this paper since they are relations of one argument to two other separate arguments: the possessed relation holds between the body part and the patient (inflected as direct object), whereas the locative relation holds between the body part and the sorted verb argument, i.e.

[27] ($\exists$ animate$_1$:Speaker animate$_1$) ($\exists$ animate$_2$:Third-person animate$_2$)
[($\exists$ process) ($\exists$ x) Tweak process $\wedge$ Agent anim$_1$,process
$\wedge$ Patient anim$_2$, process $\wedge$ Located process, x $\wedge$ Nose x
$\wedge$ Possess anim$_2$, x]

to be read 'there is an animate who is the speaker, and another animate who is a third-person, such that, for some process and some x, the process is tweaking, the first animate is the agent of the process, the second animate is the patient of the process, the process is located at x, x is a nose, and the second animate possesses x'. We can see in this example another reason for following Davidson's view that verb predicates have their own verb arguments (as well as Sondheimer's view that events, i.e. verb arguments, are located, not the participants in the event). In this discussion of incorporated body parts, I have stressed inferences that they are possessed. Other important facts about them are discussed in the Voegelins' paper and more briefly in Mithun and in her Algonquian source, Frantz (1971).

Although semantic case is inferred and not signalled explicitly by incorporated nominals, there are some linguistic constraints on the semantic cases which can be inferred. Since these differ for incorporated nouns and for noun classifiers, I will discuss incorporated nouns first. The Algonquian incorporating medials are never inferred to describe agents. In large part, this is due to the restriction discussed earlier in the paper that incorporated nouns cannot be subjects; usually agents are subjects. However, even in lexical passives such as Cree *it-ācim-iko/si=w* 'he is thus narrated of', no incorporating medial for the agent, e.g. the narrator, ever appears. I think this is because agents cannot be construed, even for purposes of compact linguistic communication, as mere verb modifiers, i.e. as just further characteristics of the action described by the verb. Certainly, in Algonquian languages, agents are given preferred status in a variety of grammatical ways, which is likely to block such radical semantic downgrading.

The same semantic restriction applies to Iroquoian incorporated nouns; Chafe (1970, 50) says that only patient nouns are incorporated, where 'patient' is a macro-semantic case including patients narrowly defined, beneficiaries, and the subjects of stative verbs.[7] A puzzle arises in these latter cases because the incorporated nouns are coreferential with the subjects of the verb, e.g. Chafe's Onondaga example:

[28] ˀo-nǫhs-aká:yoh 'the house is old'
it-house-is old

In section 1.1, it was shown that incorporated nouns never can be subjects. Certainly, in Algonquian languages, the incorporating medials never appear in such stative verbs, only *classificatory* medials can appear, e.g. Ojibwa *miškaw-akkamik-ā* 'it is hard ground'. However, for Iroquoian languages, there is no morphological distinction between incorporated nouns and noun classifiers, and Woodbury (1975, 13), writing of Onondaga, says that "all noun incorporation is classificatory" by which she means that they refer to objects as members of a class. Thus, Iroquoian incorporated nouns are neutral with respect to the morphologically required distinction in Algonquian between incorporated noun proper and noun classifier. Because of this, occurrences like that in [28] involve the incorporated noun taking on a classificatory function in some contexts; in this example, we have to regard *-nǫhs-* 'house' as a noun classifier that provides the sorted argument for the subject, as classifiers are free to do. There is another way these Iroquoian stative verbs might be interpreted: the incorporated noun can be a predicate nominal so that our Onondaga example could mean primarily 'it is an old house'. This solution, however, cannot apply to the non-stative cases, such as Onondaga *ˀo-nǫhs-okhas* 'the house is leaking', therefore the more general solution is to claim that these incorporated nouns have taken on a classificatory role. They are not full classifiers, because the restriction that incorporated nouns cannot be agents still applies; in the earlier examples, the pronoun indicates that the subject is a patient.

Restrictions on the semantic cases that can be inferred for Algonquian noun classifiers appearing in verbs arise from quite different sources. Classifiers, in general, are able to specify the sort for any participant in any semantic case relation to the action; this is especially clear in languages like Eskimo or Chinese, in which noun classifiers are associated with demonstratives, which may appear in any noun phrase. However, when the noun classifiers appear in verbs, as the Algonquian classificatory medials do, other grammatical properties of the verb system contribute to preventing them from ever giving the sort for an agent. As Piggott (1979) has described, all agents in Ojibwa have to be *semantically* (not just grammatically) animate: sentences in which an inanimate thing might be an agent in other languages, such as *the stone broke the window,* are paraphrased to avoid construing the inanimate thing as agent.[8] This grammatical restriction is coupled with the lexical restriction that there are no classificatory medials for animates: 'man', 'woman', 'dog', etc., are expressed only by incorporating medials. These animacy restrictions produce the atypical result, for noun classifier systems, that Algonquian classifiers cannot provide the sort for an agent.

4. SUMMARY

The main argument has been that syntax, polysynthesis, and derivation are separate kinds of rules of combination. Derivational rules produce morphemes of one class from those of another class; sometimes the derivational morpheme contributes supplementary meaning. In contrast, polysynthetic rules combine morphemes from the major lexical classes: verb, noun, adverb, and adjective. They do so without recourse to syntactic categories, such as subject and object, and without establishing discourse referents. Polysynthetically combined morphemes, unlike derivational ones, refer to independent aspects of the situation spoken about and, therefore, are sometimes manipulated creatively by speakers.

Emphasis was placed upon two classes of polysynthetic morphemes: incorporated nouns and noun classifiers, both of which are nominal elements appearing within verbs. Both are related adverbially to the verb in the utterance but often are inferred by hearers to refer to entities in the situation described, which entities are inferred to bear semantic case relations to the action.

These two types of nominal elements differ in their inferred reference properties since the incorporated nouns provide a noun predicate but the classifiers give a sorted noun argument. Because of this, the former cannot be coreferential with the subject, and the latter cannot appear with non-referential verbs. With respect to inferred semantic case, in Algonquian languages, neither can be agent for different reasons: incorporated nouns are semantically restricted from this role in most languages, whereas classifiers, which normally allow it, are prevented from it in Algonquian because agents are restricted to animates and there are no classifiers for animates.

To capture these phenomena, a logical semantic model was used in which there are separate sorted arguments for noun predicates and for verb predicates, the two kinds of arguments being linked by semantic case relations. Within this model, the information conveyed by a sentence was separated explicitly from that inferred so as to complete the proposition.

NOTES

1. Following Piggott (1979) I have analyzed this transitive inanimate verb as having a stem ending with verb class marker *-am*, *šōškw-ēk-in/am=*, followed by inflection *=n*, although Algonquianists usually include this morpheme in an inflection *=ān*. Semantic reasons for this change of view are given in Denny (1983).

2. Most Cree words cited are from Bloomfield's unpublished lexicon of Plains Cree. I am very grateful to Charles Hockett for providing a photocopy of Bloomfield's manuscript and to John Hewson for providing a computer printout of this lexicon.

3. This morpheme is an incorporating medial when followed by *-ē-* but is homophonous with a classificatory medial.

4. Sadock (1986) offers three other examples in support of a syntactic relation between incorporated noun and verb. In my opinion the first one involves only a link in inferred thought structure but no anaphoric link in the discourse: *kangerlu-liaqatigisimavaa, tikikkamillu* 'fjord-he accompanied him going to, and when they arrived'—it is inferred in thought that they arrived at the fjord but there is no anaphoric reference to it in the discourse and, consequently, the incorporated noun did not establish a discourse referent. The other two cases involve noun phrases in apposition to sentences with an incorporated noun: [1] *Joorut palasi-nngorpoq tusaamasoq* 'Jorgen became a famous priest'—I think this is really 'J. became a priest, a famous one', since the adjectival noun follows the verb and is in absolutive case; [2] *P. 276-inik ammassat-torpoq, nipasallu ilivitsut marluk* 'P. 276-ones sardine-ate, and lumpfish whole two' = 'that P. ate 276 sardines and two whole lumpfish'—the second clause containing three nouns in the absolutive seems to me to be conjoined to the first clause as a whole not conjoined to the incorporated noun 'sardine'.

5. The term *verb class marker* emphasizes their function, therefore, I have used it to revise the terms *abstract final* and *abstract subfinal* used in earlier papers, e.g. Denny (1985b).

6. This change occurs only for *intransitive* inanimate (II) verbs and apparently not for *animate* intransitive (AI) ones. The old marker *-i-* in final *-pay/i-* does not exist in the synchronic II system, so that these verbs were either AI verbs borrowed in the II system or archaic II verbs. If they are AI verbs, the marker *-i-* meaning 'process' fits the old meaning of the bare final 'go', since processes are subdividable occurrences, as are movements. The new meaning 'become' requires marker *-in-* 'event', since events are unitary occurrences of which the prototypical example is 'become'. The pressure for bare final *-pay-* to change from 'go' to 'become' presumably arises from the narrowing of the finals AI *-s/in-* and II *-ht/in-*, from 'become' to 'fall' and 'lie'. The change from II *-pay/i-* to *-pay/in-* is recorded in Faries (1938) Cree dictionary, e.g. *pikopayiw* or *pikopayin* 'it breaks' (forms transliterated into phonemic orthography), therefore, what we may be observing is the spread of this change into Plains Cree from some other dialect. Since Bloomfield and Ahenakew and Wolfart worked at different although neighboring communities in northern Saskatchewan, there is the possibility of subdialect differences. Two reasons why the marker may not have been changed for the AI verb are [1] marker *-i-* is a regular marker of the AI system, [2] marker *-i-* is semantically the most unmarked or neutral category of the AI system, as discussed in Denny (1985b). None of these complexities invalidates the main point that these derivational morphemes have been manipulated productively in recent decades.

7. Because there are many typographic errors in the printed article, readers interested in this paper are invited to write for a corrected reprint to the author,

Department of Psychology, University of Western Ontario, London, Ontario, N6A 5C2.

8. For example, in three Ojibwa tales about love medicine, Medler never encodes the medicine as an agent causing love in the recipient. A typical avoidance pattern is, in translation: "Then this young woman made use of this love medicine. Then this young man fell in love with her" (Bloomfield 1957, 210).

REFERENCES

Ahenakew, F. (ed.) 1986. *Stories of the House People*. Winnipeg: University of Manitoba Press.

Bloomfield, L. 1933. *Language*. New York: Holt, Rinehart & Winston.

Bloomfield, L. 1946. Algonquian. In *Linguistic Structures of Native America*, H. Hoijer et al., eds., pp. 85–129. New York: Viking Fund.

Bloomfield, L. 1957. *Eastern Ojibwa*. Ann Arbor: University of Michigan Press.

Chafe, W. 1970. A Semantically Based Sketch of Onondaga. *International Journal of American Linguistics* 36(2:Part II).

Conklin, N. F. 1981. *The Semantics and Syntax of Numeral Classification in Tai and Austronesian*. Ph.D. Diss., University of Michigan. (University Microfilms 8125090).

Davidson, D. 1967. The Logical Form of Action Sentences. In *The Logic of Decision and Action*, N. Rescher, ed., pp. 81–85. Pittsburgh: University of Pittsburgh Press.

Denny, J. P. 1976. What Are Noun Classifiers Good For? *Papers from the 12th Regional Meeting*, pp. 122–32. Chicago: Chicago Linguistic Society.

Denny, J. P. 1983. Semantics of Abstract Finals in Algonquian Transitive Inanimate Verbs. *Canadian Journal of Linguistics* 28:133–48.

Denny, J. P. 1984. Lexical Semantics and Logical Form: Locatives, Event Arguments and Conditionals. In *Papers from the Parasession on Lexical Semantics*, pp. 107–16. Chicago: Chicago Linguistic Society.

Denny, J. P. 1985a. The Semantic Role of Noun Classifiers. In *Noun Classes and Categorization*, C. Craig, ed., pp. 297–308. Amsterdam: Benjamins.

Denny, J. P. 1985b. Semantic Verb Classes and Abstract Finals. In *Papers of the 15th Algonquian Conference*, W. Cowan, ed., pp. 241–71. Ottawa: Linguistics, Carleton University.

Dowty, D. 1978. Applying Montague's Views on Linguistic Metatheory to the Structure of the Lexicon. In *Papers from the Parasession on the Lexicon*, pp. 97–137. Chicago: Chicago Linguistic Society.

Drapeau, L. 1979. Aspects de la Morphologie du Nom en Montagnais. Thèse de PhD, Université de Montréal.

Faries, R., ed. 1938. *A Dictionary of the Cree Language*. Toronto: Church of England in Canada.

Fortescue, M. 1979. The Relation of Derivation to External Syntax in West Greenlandic. In *Proceedings of the Fifth Scandinavian Conference of Linguistics,* T. Petterson, ed., pp. 23–38. Stockholm: Almqvist & Wiksell.

Fortescue, M. 1984. *West Greenlandic*. London: Croom Helm.

Frantz, D. G. 1971. *Toward a Generative Grammar of Blackfoot*. Norman, Okla.: Summer Institute of Linguistics.

Goddard, I. 1987. Post-Transformational Stem Derivation in Fox. *Papers and Studies in Contrastive Linguistics* (Poznan), 22.

Jensen, J. T., and Johns, A. This volume. The Morphosyntax of Eskimo Causatives.

Lappin, S. 1981. *Sorts, Ontology and Metaphor*. Berlin: de Gruyter.

Lyons, J. 1977. *Semantics*. Cambridge: Cambridge University Press.

McCawley, J. D. 1981. *Everything that Linguists Have Always Wanted to Know about Logic*. Chicago: University of Chicago Press.

Mithun, M. 1984. The Evolution of Noun Incorporation. *Language* 60:847–79.

Mithun, M. 1986. On the Nature of Noun Incorporation. *Language,* 62:32–37.

Peterson, P. 1985. Six Grammatical Hypotheses on Actions, Causes and "Causes." Mimeo distributed by Indiana University Linguistics Club.

Piggott, G. L. 1979. Verb Classification in Ojibwa. *Montreal Working Papers in Linguistics* 12:149–86.

Rischel, J. 1972. Derivation as a Syntactic Process in Greenlandic. In *Derivational Processes,* F. Kiefer, ed., pp. 60–73. Stockholm: Research Group for Quantitative Linguistics.

Rischel, J. 1974. *Topics in West Greenlandic Phonology*. Copenhagen: Akademisk Forlag.

Robins, R. H. 1967. *A Short History of Linguistics*. London: Longman.

Sadock, J. M. 1980. Noun Incorporation in Greenlandic. *Language* 56:300–19.

Sadock, J. M. 1986. Some Notes on Noun Incorporation. *Language* 62:19–31.

Sapir, E. 1911. The Problem of Noun Incorporation in American Languages. *American Anthropologist* 13:250–82.

Sondheimer, N. K. 1978. A Semantic Analysis of Reference to Spatial Properties. *Linguistics and Philosophy* 2:235–80.

Spalding, A. 1979. *Eight Inuit Myths*. National Museum of Man, Mercury Series, Canadian Ethology Service Paper No. 59. Ottawa: National Museums of Canada.

Voegelin, C. F., and F. M. Voegelin. 1973. The Syntax and Semantics of Possession in Shawnee. Paper read at the Algonquian Conference, Green Bay, Wisc.

Wolfart, H. C. 1971. Plains Cree Internal Syntax and the Problem of Noun Incorporation. *Proceedings, 38th International Congress of Americanists,* Vol. 3:511–18.

Wolfart, H. C. 1973. *Plains Cree: A Grammatical Study*. Philadelphia: American Philosophical Society.

Woodbury, H. 1975. Onondaga Noun Incorporation. *International Journal of American Linguistics* 41:10–20.

RELATIONAL PARAMETERS OF REFLEXIVES: THE HALKOMELEM EVIDENCE

Donna B. Gerdts

INTRODUCTION

Although reflexives have been given significant attention in all syntactic theories, studies generally have shared a common focus: the statement of appropriate constraints on possible antecedents. Various binding parameters intended as cross-linguistic generalizations have been posited; for example, Chomsky's Binding Conditions and Perlmutter and Postal's Reflexive Rank Law. However, these are uninsightful for languages like Halkomelem, a Salish language spoken in southwestern British Columbia, which have morphological reflexives with the antecedent limited to subject.

The line of research pursued in this paper takes as its focus an entirely different approach to the problem: the Relational Structure of reflexives, that is, the relations borne by the nominals at each level of structure. In order to control for the binding problem, I limit the class of constructions under consideration to cases of reflexives where, as in Halkomelem, the antecedent is the *subject* and the reflexive is the *direct object* at the appropriate level of structure. Within this limited class of data, it is easy to see that reflexives differ with respect to final transitivity and to the exhibition by the subject of properties customarily associated with nominals that head an object arc in an earlier stratum. Two concepts have been proposed within Relational Grammar to deal with these facts: *Cancellation* and *Multiattachment*. These concepts are defined and illustrated in section 1, where I also consider a proposal regarding their interaction.

Section 2 discusses two Halkomelem reflexive constructions, one of which provides evidence for a type of reflexive that has not been noted previously.[1] On the basis of the Halkomelem evidence, I propose that Cancellation and Multiattachment are independent parameters of Universal Grammar; taken together, they predict that *four* types of reflexive constructions occur in natural language, as discussed in section 3. That concepts available in Relational Grammar allow for the parametricization of reflexives, as empirically justified herein, provides support for this theory, especially since, as section 4 discusses, other theories, because they have dwelt on a two-way dichotomy of reflexives (e.g. lexical versus syntactic reflexives), do not provide the mechanisms for an adequate account of the various reflexives. In particular, I consider the analysis of reflexives posited by Marantz (1984), which comes closest to mirroring the relational account. On the basis of data from Halkomelem, I show that the relational grammar approach is superior to Marantz's approach.

1. BACKGROUND

1.1. Cancellation

It is a well-noted phenomenon that reflexives are finally transitive in some languages but finally intransitive in others. This is seen most clearly in ergative languages, where the case marking/verb agreement of the clause will differ depending upon whether the final subject is an *ergative* (subject in a transitive stratum) or an *absolutive* (subject in an intransitive stratum or object in a transitive stratum).[2]

For example, in Tzotzil (Aissen 1982) subjects of reflexives determine ergative agreement as seen in [1]:

[1] 7i-s-nak'	s-ba	'He hid himself.'
cp-E3-hide	his-self	

E(rgative)-agreement is used for final 1s in a transitive stratum, as seen in [2], while A(bsolutive) agreement is used for final 2s and final 1s in an intransitive stratum, as seen in [2] and [3].

[2] L-i-s-maj 'He hit me.'
cp-A1-E3-hit

[3] Ch-i-bat 'I'm going.'
inf-A1-go

That the reflexive clause in [1] exhibits E-agreement provides evidence for its final transitivity.

In contrast, in Halkomelem, the subject of a reflexive determines absolutive rather than ergative agreement, as seen in [4]:[3]

[4] ni kʷə́ləš-θ-ət kʷθə swə́yˀqeˀ
aux shoot-tr-self det man
'The man shot himself.'

In terms of agreement, Halkomelem is a split ergative language (Gerdts 1981a); ergative versus absolutive is distinguished only for 3rd persons in nonsubordinate clauses. A third person final 1 in a transitive stratum determines the agreement suffix *-əs* (cf. [5] while a third-person final 1 in an intransitive stratum has Ø agreement, (cf.[6]).

[5] ni kʷə́ləš-θ-ámˀš-əs kʷθə swə́yˀqeˀ
aux shoot-tr-1obj-3erg det man
'The man shot me.'

[6] ni ˀíməš kʷθə swə́yˀqeˀ
aux walk det man
'The man walked.'

That the ergative agreement suffix is *not* possible in a reflexive, as [7] shows, gives evidence for the final intransitivity of the clause; further evidence will be discussed in section 2.

[7] * ni kʷə́ləš-θ-ət-əs kʷθə swə́yˀqeˀ
aux shoot-tr-self-3erg det man
('The man shot himself.')

Given the assumption that reflexives in Tzotzil and Halkomelem have equivalent initial structures—the antecedent is an initial 1 and the reflexive is an initial 2—then the final transitivity of Tzotzil is expected, whereas the final intransitivity of Halkomelem requires some explanation.[4] Aissen (1982), citing data from several languages, argues that what is involved is Cancellation: a nominal, which bears a relation at one level, does not bear any relation at the subsequent level, as represented in the relational network in [8].[5]

[8]

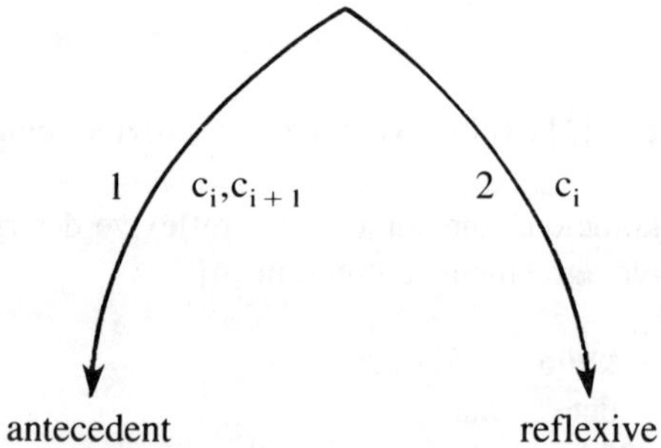

Although the reflexive heads a 2-arc in the c_i-stratum it heads no arc in the c_{i+1}-stratum, in contrast to the antecedent, which heads a 1-arc in both strata. Note that the arc itself is cancelled; therefore, the structure in [8], although it is initially transitive, is finally intransitive.

Taking the presence or absence of Cancellation as a parameter of variation, we see that there are two types of reflexives: those like the Halkomelem reflexives that involve Cancellation, and those like the Tzotzil reflexives that do not.

1.2. Multiattachment

Reflexive constructions in many languages exhibit some unexpected properties. Rather than patterning with constructions involving 'straight' subjects (that is, subjects at all levels of structure), reflexives sometimes pattern with passive or unaccusative constructions. As discussed in Perlmutter (forthcoming) and Rosen (1981), the Italian *si* reflexive, when occurring in the past tense, selects the auxiliary *essere* 'be' rather than *avere* 'have', as seen in [9].

[9] Ugo si è difeso. 'Ugo defended himself.'

Unaccusatives like [10a] as represented in [10b] and passives like [11a] as represented in [11b], also select *essere*.

[10] a. Ugo è caduto. 'Hugo fell.'

b.

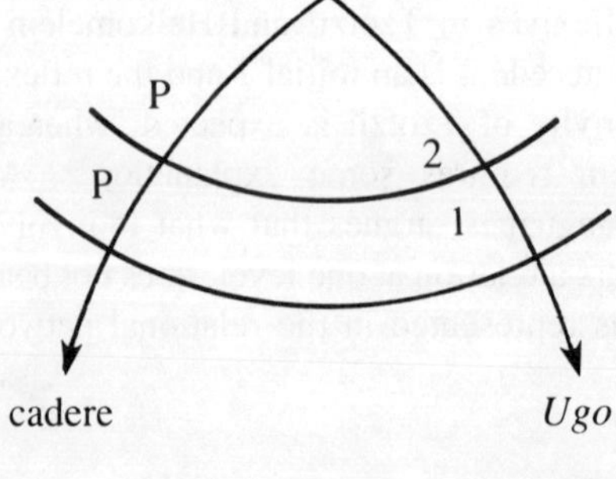

[11] **a.** Il gruppo sarà accompagnato da un interprete.
'The group will be accompanied by an interpreter.'

b.

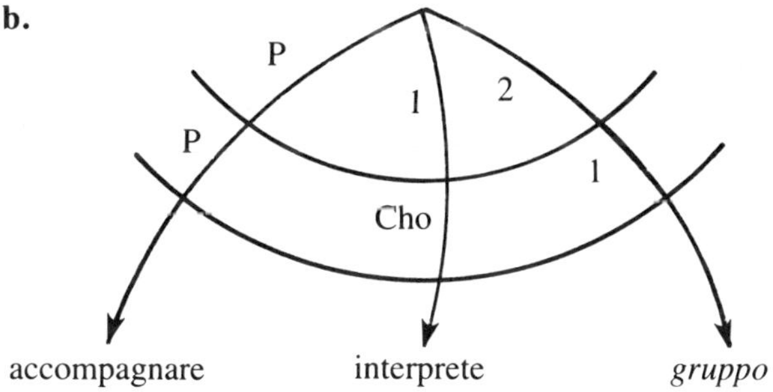

In contrast, unergatives like [12] and active transitive clauses like [13] select *avere*.

[12] **a.** Ugo ha reagito. 'Hugo reacted.'

b.

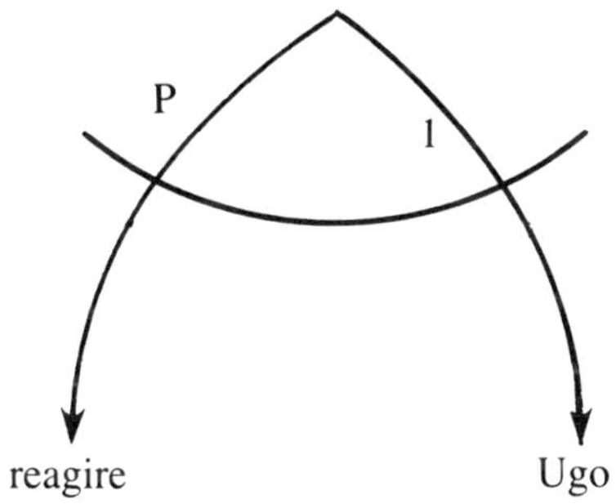

[13] **a.** Ugo ha difeso Anna. 'Hugo defended Anna.'

b.

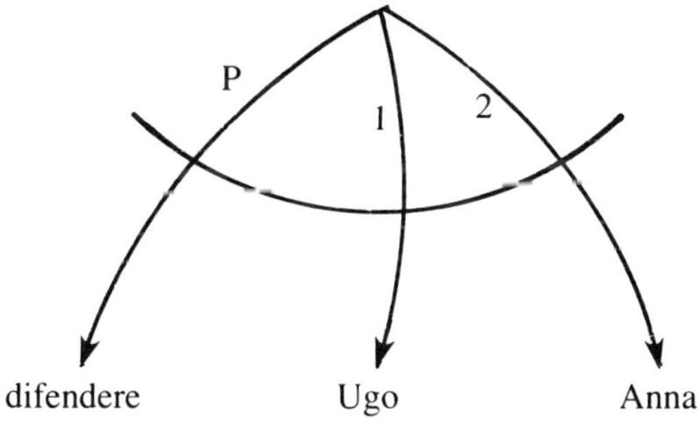

This distribution follows from the rule of Auxiliary Selection given in Rosen (1981):

[14] Select *essere* 'be' in any clause that contains a 1-arc and an object-arc with the same head, otherwise select *avere* 'have'.

In unaccusatives and passives, since a single nominal (italicized above) heads a 2-arc (in the initial stratum) and a 1-arc (in the final stratum), *essere* is selected. Returning to the reflexive in [9], *essere* is selected, indicating that a single nominal heads both an object-arc and a 1-arc. An analysis of reflexives involving Multiattachment, as discussed in Perlmutter (1980, forthcoming) and especially Rosen (1981), would meet this requirement: in Multiattachment, a single nominal heads more than one arc in a single stratum. Thus, the initial level of [9] could be represented as follows: since the 1-arc and the 2-arc have the same head, *essere* will be selected as stipulated in [14]:

[15]

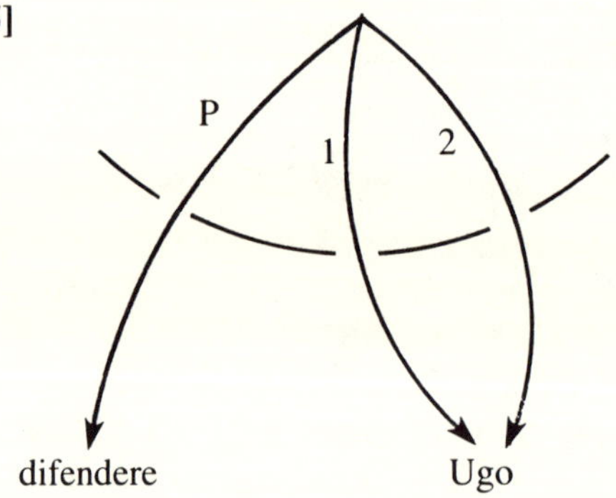

Rosen points out a second reflexive construction in Italian, formed with the anaphoric pronoun *sé stesso*. As seen in [16], such reflexives select *avere*, which would follow from an analysis without Multiattachment, as given in [17]:

[16] Ugo ha difeso sé stesso. 'Hugo defended *himself*.'

[17]

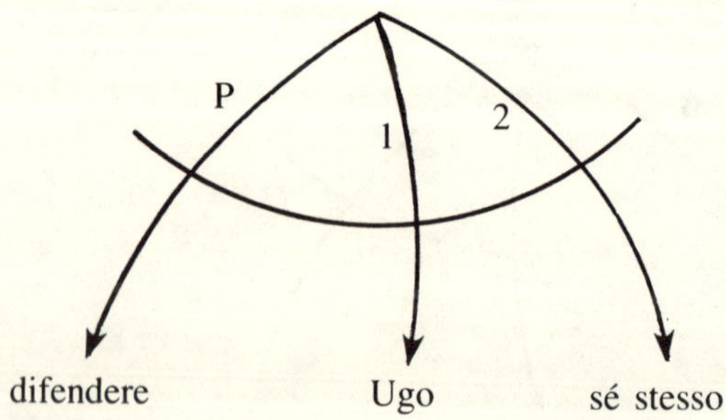

Thus, the two Italian Reflexives differ with respect to Multiattachment, which serves as a parameter of variation.

1.3. Parameter Linking

In the earlier sections, two parameters of reflexives, Cancellation and Multiattachment, have been discussed. The question arises, Are these parameters linked in some fashion? Earlier work on this topic, on Italian by Rosen (1981) and on Albanian by Hubbard (1980), leads to the suggestion that Cancellation and Multiattachment are correlated.

As we have seen, there are two reflexives in Italian, with and without Multiattachment. Rosen also points out that the two reflexives differ with respect to final transitivity.

The *si* reflexive is finally intransitive but the *sé stesso* reflexive is finally transitive, as evidenced by their behavior in causatives. As discussed by Rosen (1981, also see her references), Italian causatives are typical cases of Clause Union (Perlmutter & Postal 1974); each element in the downstairs clause is assigned a relation in the upstairs clause. In Italian, the downstairs final 1 is assigned its upstairs relation according to this schema:

[18] downstairs final relation		union relation
1 of an intransitive	=	2
1 of a transitive	=	3

Thus, in [19], the downstairs clause is finally intransitive and the downstairs final 1 is a union 2, hence the ACC clitic *lo*: whereas in [20] the downstairs clause is finally transitive and the downstairs final 1 is union 3, hence the DAT clitic *gli,* as these data from Rosen (1981) show:

[19] Bruno voleva farlo piangere.
'Bruno wanted to make him (ACC) cry.'

[20] Bruno voleva fargli raccogliere le monte.
'Bruno wanted to make him (DAT) pick up the coins.'

In a causative with an embedded *si* reflexive, as in [21], the final 1 is ACC not DAT giving evidence for final intransitivity.[6]

[21] Quell'episodio rischia di { ?farlo odiarsi. / *fargli }
'That incident is likely to make him (?ACC/*DAT) hate himself.'

In contrast, in a causative with an embedded *sé stesso* reflexive, as in [22], the final 1 is DAT not ACC giving evidence for final transitivity.

[22] Quell'episodio rischia di { fargli odiare sé stesso. / *farlo }
'That incident is likely to make him (DAT/*ACC) hate himself.'

In summary, *si* reflexives involve both Multiattachment and Cancellation, as represented in [23], while *sé stesso* reflexives involve neither, as represented in [24].

[23] *si* Reflexives:

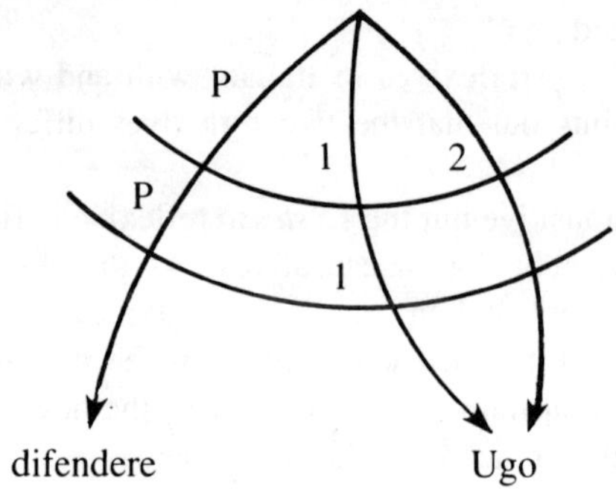

[24] *sé stesso* Reflexives:

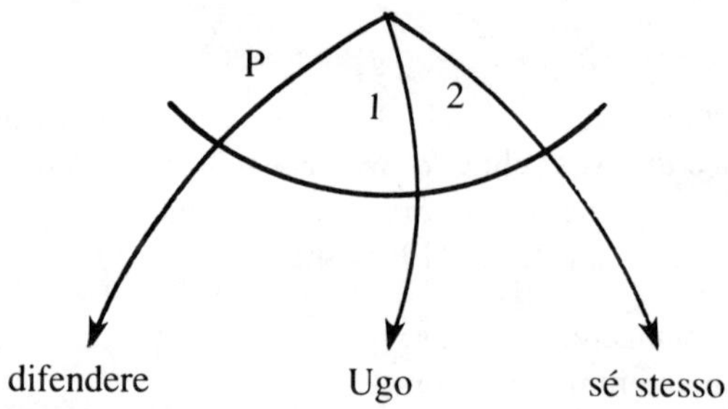

The same conclusion can be reached regarding Albanian reflexives (Hubbard 1980). One reflexive, e.g. [25], marked by "Neopolitan" morphology (which also occurs on passives and unaccusatives) involves both Multiattachment and Cancellation.

[25] Burrat lahen.
men-the wash
N 3pPRNACT
'The men wash themselves.' / 'The men are washed.'

A second reflexive, e.g. [26], which involves an anaphoric pronoun and "active" morphology, has neither Multiattachment nor Cancellation.

[26] Agimit lan veten.
N wash self-Ac
3sACT
'Agim washes himself.'

Thus, previous work on the topic leads to the suggestion that the parameters Multiattachment and Cancellation are linked. However, I argue on the basis of Halkomelem reflexives that these, in fact, are independent parameters.

2. HALKOMELEM REFLEXIVES

As in Italian and Albanian, there are two means of forming reflexives in Halkomelem. However, both are morphological in the sense that they involve verbal morphology rather than an anaphoric pronoun. The $-\theta$*ət* reflexive, the segmentation of which will be discussed presently, is illustrated in [27]–[28]:

[27] ni q'ʷáqʷ-əθ-ət ɬə sɬéniʔ ʔə kʷθə sqə́məlʔ
aux club-tr-self det woman obl det paddle
'The woman clubbed herself with the paddle.'

[28] ni cən lə́x̌ʷ-əθ-ət
aux lsub blanket-tr-self
'I covered myself with a blanket.' (literally: 'I blanketed self.')

Second, the -*əm* reflexive, is illustrated in [29]–[30]:[7]

[29] ni tší -qʷʔ-əm ɬə sɬéniʔ
aux comb-hair-intr det woman
'The woman combed her own hair.'

[30] csé-t cən ceʔ ɬə sɬéniʔ ʔu q'ʷə́l- əɬc-əm-əs
tell-tr lsub fut det woman lnk bake-adv-intr-3ssub
ʔə kʷθə scé.ɬtən
obl det salmon
'I'm telling the woman to bake the salmon for me.'

The two reflexive constructions have different distributions. The -*θət* reflexive is used only to reference initial objects: the reflexive refers to the patient nominal in [27]–[28].[8] In contrast, the -*əm* reflexive is used only when a non-initial object is involved. For example, I have argued in Gerdts (1981b; 1981c) that clauses like [29] involve possessor ascension and lexical suffixation (the Salish equivalent of noun incorporation), so that the reflexive is an initial possessor that ascends to object; thus, examples like [31a], represented in [31b], are taken to be the non-reflexive counterpart of [29].

[31] a. ni tší -qʷʔ-t-əs ɬə sɬéniʔ kʷθə sqʷəméyʔ
aux comb-hair-tr-3erg det woman det dog
'The woman combed the dog's hair.'

b.

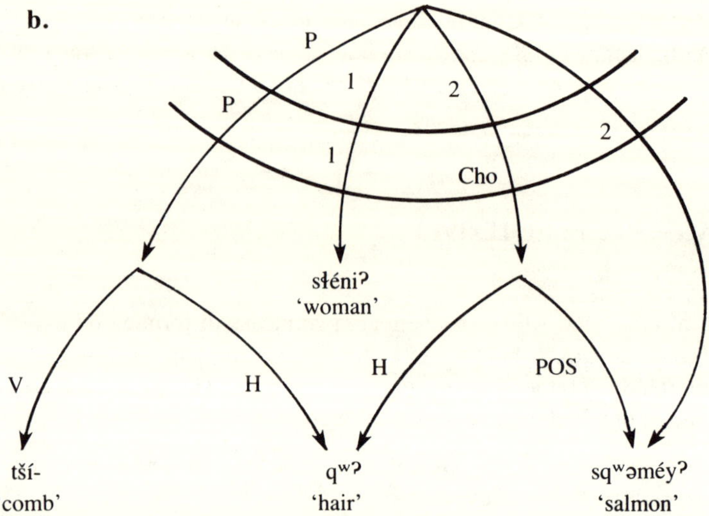

The *-əm* reflexive clause in [6] involves Ben-2 advancement (see Gerdts (1981a) for discussion). The reflexive references an initial Ben that is advanced to 2, as evidenced by the presence of the advancement suffix *-ɬc* and the oblique case (used to mark nonterms) of the initial object. The nonreflexive counterpart is given in [32]:

[32] a. csé-t cən ceˀ ɬə sɬéniˀ ˀu q'ʷəl-əɬc-θ-ámˀš-əs
tell-tr 1sub fut det woman lnk bake-adv-tr-1obj-3ssub
ˀə kʷθə scé.ɬtən
obl det salmon
'I'm telling the woman to bake the salmon for me.'

b.

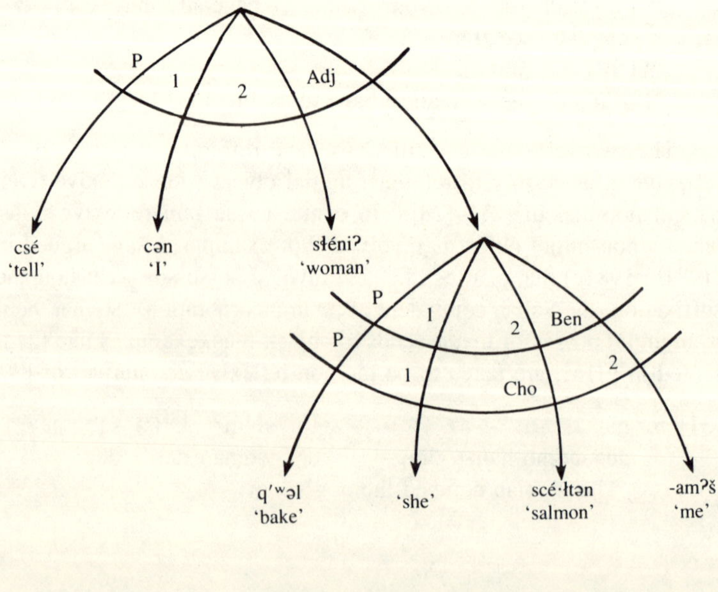

Thus, *-θət* reflexives reference initial 2s, while *-əm* reflexives reference non-initial 2s.

2.1. Cancellation

Turning now to the relational properties of the two Halkomelem reflexives, both reflexives involve Cancellation; that is, they are finally intransitive. Evidence for this comes from the lack of third person ergative agreement in reflexives like [27] and [29] (see section 1.1). Furthermore, Halkomelem, as discussed in Gerdts (1981a) bans clauses where the final ergative is a proper noun, hence* [33].

[33] *ni q'ʷə́l-ət-əs ɬə Mary kʷθə scé.ɬtən
aux bake-tr-intr det det salmon
('Mary baked the salmon.')

However, a proper noun can serve as a final absolutive, as in the intransitive clause in [34] and the antipassive clause in [35].

[34] ni ʔiməš ɬə Mary
aux walk det
'Mary walked.'

[35] ni q'ʷə́l-əm ɬə Mary ʔə kʷθə scé.ɬtən
aux bake-intr det obl det salmon
'Mary baked the salmon.'

As seen in [36] and [37], proper nouns can serve as final ls in reflexive clauses; thus, they are final absolutives and the clauses are finally intransitive.

[36] ni kʷə́ləš-θ-ət ɬə Mary
aux shoot-tr-self det
'Mary shot herself.'

[37] ni tší -qʷʔ-əm ɬə Mary
aux comb-hair-intr det
'Mary combed her own hair.'

Further evidence for the intransitivity of *-θət* reflexives comes from causatives, which will be discussed in section 4.

2.2. Multiattachment

Thus, both Halkomelem reflexives involve Cancellation of a 2-arc and therefore are finally intransitive. However, I claim that the two reflexives differ with respect to Multiattachment: *-θət* reflexives involve Multiattachment, whereas *-əm* reflexives do not. Evidence for this comes from the rule of transitive marking in Halkomelem. The reflexive suffix *-θət* actually is a complex form, composed of the transitive suffix *-t* and a reflexive object suffix *-sut.*[9] Evidence that the reflexive form *-θət* involves a transitive suffix comes from limited control marking. Transitive suffixes in Halkomelem appear in two forms: the general transitive suffix *-t* and the limited control suffix *-n.*[10] The latter is used in situations where the agent is not in full control of his actions as illustrated in [38b] and [39b].[11]

[38] a. ni kʷələš-θ-ám^ʔš-əs kʷθə swə́yʔqeʔ
aux shoot-tr-1obj-3erg det man
'The man shot me.' [on purpose]

b. ni kʷələš-n-ámʔš-əs kʷθə swə́yʔqeʔ
aux shoot–l.c.tr–1obj–3erg det man
'The man shot me accidentally.'

[39] a. ni kʷə́ləš-θ-ət kʷθə swə́yʔqeʔ
aux shoot-tr-ref det man
'The man shot himself.' [on purpose]

b. ni kʷələš-nám-ət kʷθə swə́yʔqeʔ
aux shoot-l.c.-ref det man
'The man managed to shoot himself.'
/ 'The man shot himself accidentally.'

Thus, the morphological evidence supports the claim that the *-θət* reflexive contains transitive marking, whereas it is clear that the *-əm* reflexive does not.

Gerdts (1981a) formulates a rule for transitive marking to account for the distribution of the transitive suffix *-t;* [40] is an updated version of this rule:[12]

[40] Transitive marking occurs in clauses where there is a nominal that heads both
(i) an Acc-arc (i.e. the 2-arc in a transitive stratum) *and*
(ii) a final nuclear term arc (i.e. final 1-arc or 2-arc).

This rule accounts for transitive marking on monoclausal transitives like [41a], as represented in [41b], and passives like [42a], as represented in [42b].

[41] a. ni kʷələš-θ-amʔš-əs kʷθə swəyʔqeʔ
aux shoot-tr-1obj-3erg det man
'The man shot me.'

b.

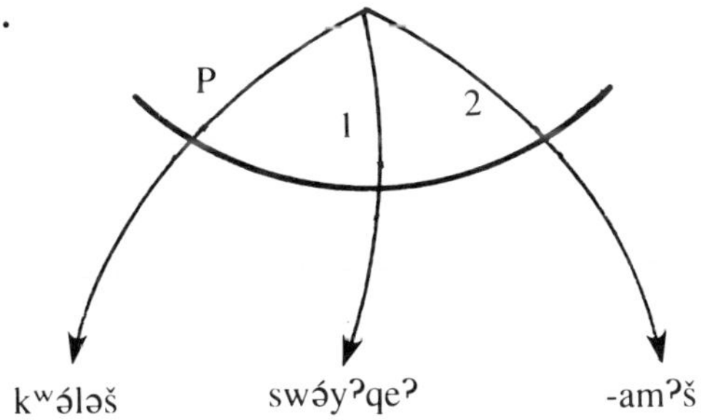

[42] a. ni q'ʷəl-ət-əm kʷθə sce.łtən ˀəƛ' Mary
aux bake-tr-intr det salmon obl-det
'The salmon was baked by Mary.'

b.

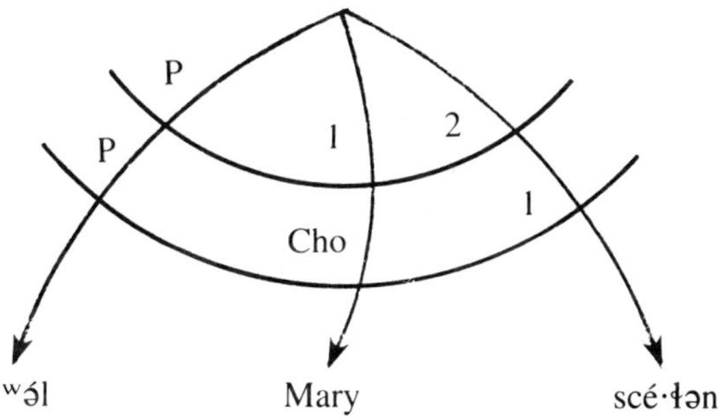

Furthermore, [40] accounts for the impossibility of transitive marking on monoclausal intransitives (cf. [43]) and antipassives (cf. [44]).[13]

[43] a. ni ˀíməš kʷθə swə́yˀqeˀ
aux walk the man
'The man walked.'

b.

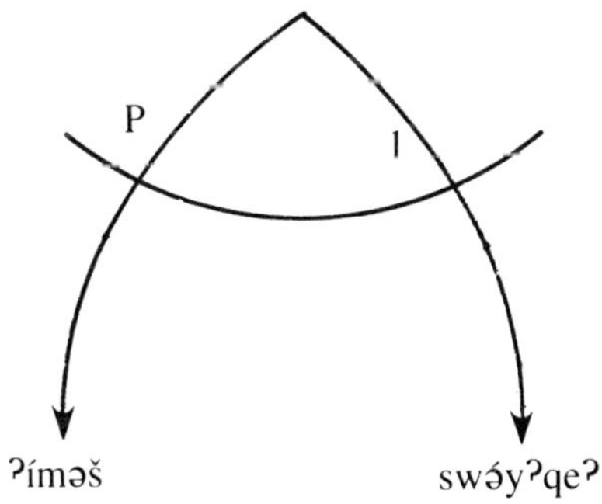

[44] a. ni q'ʷə́l-əm ɬə Mary ʔə kʷθə scé.ɬtən
aux bake-intr det obl det salmon
'Mary baked the salmon.'

b.

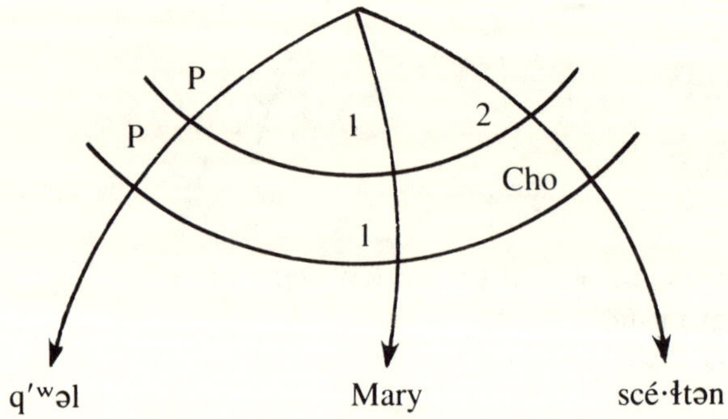

The contrast in transitive marking on passives and antipassives forms the basis for the statement given in [40]. While both [42] and [44] involve a nominal heading the 2-arc in a transitive stratum, in [42], where there is transitive marking, the nominal is a final nuclear term (the final 1), but in [44], where there is no transitive marking, the nominal is a final chomeur—not a final term.

Returning to reflexives, an analysis involving Multiattachment for reflexives like [27] together with the rule for transitive marking in [40] would predict the presence of transitive marking. Thus, [27], which would involve both Multiattachment and Cancellation, would be represented as in [45]: there is a single nominal that heads the 2-arc in a transitive stratum and a final nuclear term arc (the 1-arc).

[45]

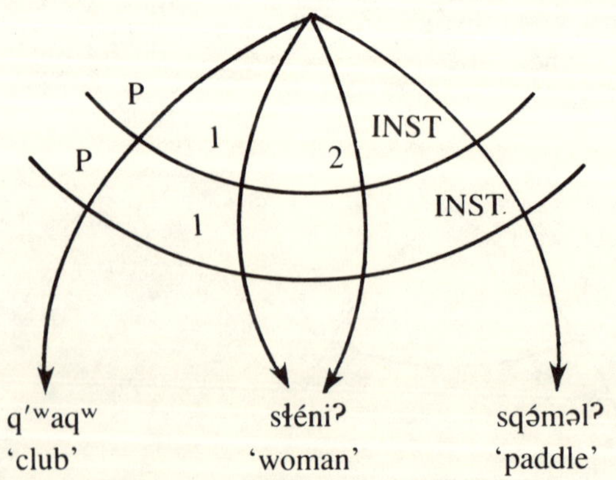

In contrast, since the *-əm* reflexive lacks transitive marking, Multiattachment is not involved. Thus, an -*əm* reflexive like [29] involves Cancellation but not Multiattachment, as represented in [46].

[46]

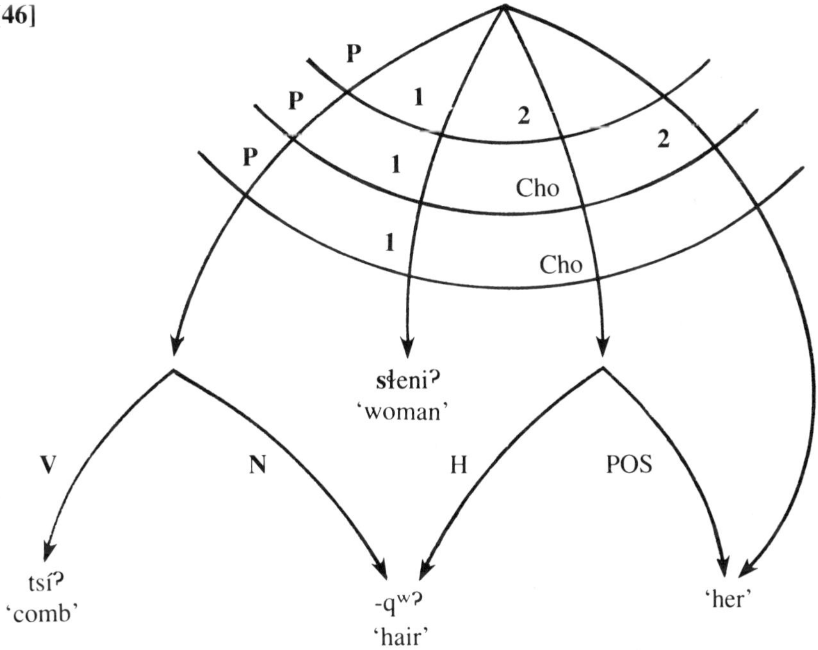

Therefore, the Halkomelem data show that Cancellation and Multiattachment operate as independent parameters, since the -*əm* reflexive involves Cancellation but not Multiattachment.

3. A CROSS-LINGUISTIC TYPOLOGY

So far in this discussion, three types of reflexives have been exemplified: reflexives with both Multiattachment and Cancellation, like the Italian *si*, the Albanian morphological reflexive, and the Halkomelem -*θət* reflexive; reflexives with neither Multiattachment nor Cancellation, like the Italian and Albanian anaphoric pronoun reflexives; and reflexives with Cancellation but without Multiattachment, like the Halkomelem -*əm* reflexive, as summarized in [47]. This raises the question: Is there a fourth type of reflexive, one that involves Multiattachment but not Cancellation? In work concurrent to my research, Berinstein (1984) argues for an analysis of the K'ekchi Mayan reflexive that would fill this last box.

[47]

	Cancellation	No Cancellation
No Multiattachment	Halkomelem (-*əm* reflexive)	Italian (*sé stesso*)
Multiattachment	Italian (*si*) Halkomelem (-*θət* reflexive)	K′ekchi (Mayan)

3.1 Multiattachment Without Cancellation: The Mayan Reflexive

In K′ekchi, as in Tzotzil (discussed in section 1.1), the reflexive clause is finally transitive as evidenced by the fact that the final 1 determines ergative agreement (=A3), as [48] exemplifies.

[48] Ani x-Ø -x-sac′ r-ib?
who tns–B3–A3–hit A3-self
'Who hit himself?'

However, as Berinstein shows, subjects in reflexive clauses exhibit one property—extraction—generally reserved for final absolutives. In non-reflexives, only the final 2 and not the final 1 can extract in a finally transitive clause, as seen in [49].[14]

[49] Ani x-Ø- x- sac′?
who tns–B3–A3–hit
'Who did he hit?' /*'Who hit him?'

In contrast, final 1s in reflexive clauses (even though they determine ergative agreement) can extract, for example, in [48]. This would follow under the analysis posited by Berinstein which involves Multiattachment (thus, the final 1 would head an Abs-arc in the initial stratum) but not Cancellation (the arc 'unattaches' through the *birth* of a nominal 2-arc, as originally suggested then rejected for Italian in Rosen 1981), as represented in [50]:

[50]

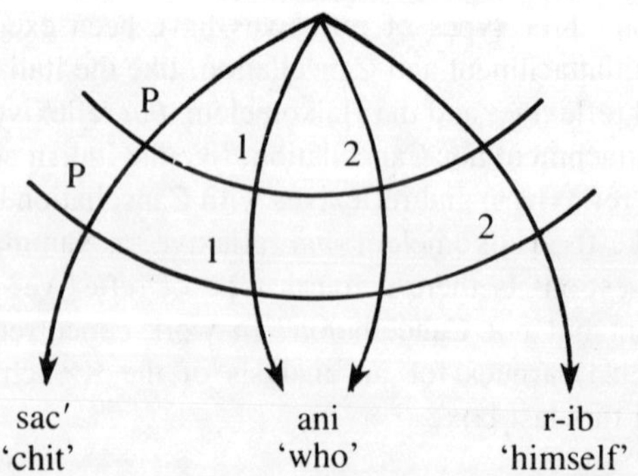

Under this analysis, K'ekchi provides the fourth type of reflexive and again, as Berinstein points out, gives evidence that Multiattachment and Cancellation are independent parameters.

3.2. The Morphology of Reflexives

This discussion has led to the conclusion that, as far as relational parameters are concerned, there are (at least) four types of reflexives in Universal Grammar. In contrast, when the form of the reflexive is considered, only two patterns exist cross-linguistically: either the reflexive is an independent pronoun or the reflexive is morphological, i.e. a verbal affix or clitic. This raises the question: Are the relational parameters in any way linked to the form of the reflexive?

Although this discussion of reflexives lacks a broad enough data base to answer this question conclusively, there nevertheless appears to be a correlation between Cancellation and the form of the reflexive. As evidenced by Italian, Albanian, and K'ekchi, the presence of an anaphoric pronoun seems to correlate with the absence of Cancellation. Furthermore, morphological reflexives seem to correlate with the presence of Cancellation, as evidenced by Italian, Albanian, and the two Halkomelem reflexives.

In contrast, Multiattachment is not correlated with the form of the reflexive, since the two Halkomelem reflexives are morphological but differ with respect to Multiattachment: conversely, both K'ekchi and Italian have constructions with anaphoric pronouns but the K'ekchi reflexive involves Multiattachment although the Italian *sé stesso* reflexive does not.

4. REFLEXIVES IN OTHER THEORIES

In the discussion, it was argued that the relational parameters Multiattachment and Cancellation accommodated four types of reflexives in Universal Grammar and it was posited that, although Multiattachment is independent of the form of the reflexive, Cancellation reflexives are morphological whereas no Cancellation reflexives involve anaphoric pronouns. This section briefly discusses analyses of reflexives in two other theories from the perspective of the relational analysis of the data.

Lexical Functional Grammar easily accommodates two types of reflexives: lexical (marked morphologically and exhibiting intransitive properties) and syntactic (with an anaphoric pronoun and exhibiting transitive properties). Furthermore, the LFG account offered by Grimshaw (1982) gives an insightful account accommodating the Multiattachment and the Cancellation properties of the Romance clitic reflexives. However, it is not clear how her account could be extended to the Halkomelem *-əm* reflexive, which is 'lexical' but lacks Multiattachment properties, or to the K'ekchi reflexive, which is 'syntactic', but nevertheless exhibits Multiattachment properties. The data thus present a challenge to an LFG account of reflexives.

Marantz (1984), in a theory designed to incorporate grammatical relations into a transformational analysis, also falls short of accommodating four types of reflexives. Again, he basically divides reflexives into lexical and syntactic. He posits that lexical passives actually are instances of passive (with the reflexive pronoun in a deleted *by* phrase); this analysis is cast in relational terms as follows:[15]

[51]

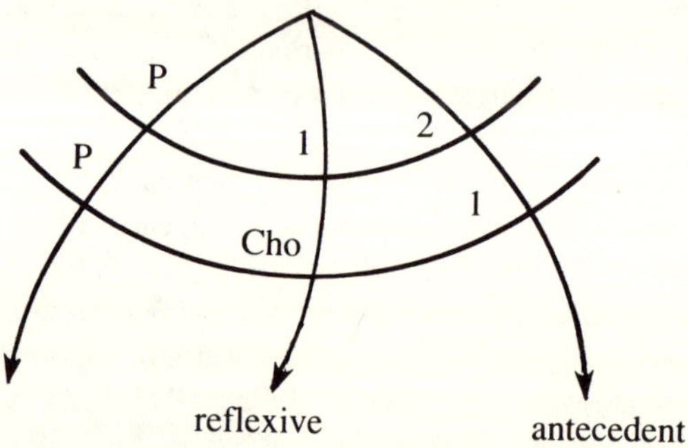

Under this analysis, it is no accident that reflexives pattern like passives in many languages; thus, Multiattachment 'effects'—such as Auxiliary Selection in Italian, Neopolitan morphology in Albanian, and transitive marking in Halkomelem *-θət* reflexives—are easily accounted for, since these phenomena also are exhibited by passives in these languages.

However, Marantz's analysis fails to account for the syntactic properties of reflexives in Halkomelem because in this language reflexives and passives are not parallel in several respects. For example, as mentioned in section 2, the *-θət* reflexive only references initial 2s, thus, possessor ascension constructions, like [52] are incompatible with *-θət* reflexives, since a non-initial 2 is referenced by the reflexive.

[52] *ni tší -qʷʔ-θ-ət ɬə sɬéniʔ
aux comb-hair-tr-self det woman
('The woman combed her own hair.')

However, 2s in possessor ascension constructions can advance to 1 in a passive clause, as exemplified in [53]:

[53] ni tší-qʷʔ-t-əm ʔə-ƛ' Mary kʷθə sqʷəméyʔ
aux comb-hair-tr-intr obl-det det dog
'The dog's hair was combed by Mary.' (literally: 'The dog was hair-combed by the woman.')

The data in *[52] versus [53] shows that reflexives and passives do not share the same domain.

Reflexives and passives also differ with respect to causatives. As discussed in Gerdts (1981a), Clause Union causatives in Halkomelem require the downstairs final 1 to be the initial 1; that is, only constructions with a 'straight' 1 (the same nominal is the 1 in every strata) allow causative clause union. Thus, causatives like [54], which involve a downstairs unergative clause, are possible although causatives like [55], which involve a downstairs unaccusative clause, are not.

[54] ni cən ʔíməš-stəxʷ kʷθə swə́yʔqeʔ
aux 1sub walk-cs det man
'I made the man walk.'

[55] *ni cən q'ʷə́l-stəxʷ ɬə scé.ɬtən
aux 1sub bake-cs det salmon
'I made the salmon bake.'

Downstairs passives, since they involve 2–1 advancement, also are banned in causatives, as *[56] shows.

[56] *ni cən q'ʷəl-ət-əm-stəxʷ kʷθə scé.ɬtən ʔə ɬə sɬéniʔ
aux 1sub bake-tr-intr-cs det salmon obl det woman
'I made the salmon be baked by the woman.'

Marantz's proposal concerning reflexives and the relational account make opposite predictions regarding causatives with downstairs reflexives. Under Marantz's analysis, since passive is involved, reflexives should be banned from causatives; under the relational account, since there is a nominal—the antecedent—which is a 1 in all strata, downstairs reflexives should be allowed in causatives. The data in [57] and [58] show that the relational account makes the correct prediction.

[57] ni cən ləx̌ʷ-əθ-ət-stəxʷ kʷθə John
aux 1sub blanket-tr-self-cs det
'I had John cover himself with a blanket.'

[58] ni cən lem-əθ-ət-stəxʷ kʷθə John
aux 1sub look-tr-self-cs det
'I had John look at himself.'

Thus, Marantz's suggestion that lexical reflexives are passives is compatible with some of the properties of Halkomelem reflexives but not with others.

5. CONCLUSION

This study has explored the relational structure of reflexives from a cross-linguistic viewpoint. I have argued that Cancellation and Multiattachment are not linked but rather independent parameters of universal grammar. Taken together, they accommodate four types of reflexives cross-linguistically. My evidence for this hypothesis was based on the two Halkomelem reflexives; since both involve Cancellation but only one involves Multiattachment, the independent status of these constructs was established.

Furthermore, I speculated on the linking of the form of a reflexive and the Cancellation parameter. Morphological reflexives—that is, reflexives that involve a verbal affix or clitic—appear to involve Cancellation (as do the two Halkomelem reflexives), although independent pronoun reflexives do not. Conversely, Multiattachment is not linked to the form of the reflexive; although both of the Halkomelem reflexives are morphological, only one involves Multiattachment.

That concepts available within Relational Grammar allow for the parametricization of reflexives provides support for this theory, especially since proposals regarding reflexives in other theories have been shown to be inadequate. Thus, the Halkomelem data, besides having significance to the Relational theory of reflexives, also provides a challenge to the analysis of reflexives in other frameworks.

NOTES

I would like to thank Guy Carden for his comments on the draft of this paper. Earlier versions were presented at the 1983 RG Festival, Cornell University, CLA 1983, NYSCOL 1983, and ESCOL '84; I appreciate the questions and comments I received from participants in those conferences.

1. For an introduction to the basic concepts of Relational Grammar, see Perlmutter (1980) and the papers in Perlmutter and Postal (1983).

2. A transitive stratum is one that contains both a 1-arc and a 2-arc; an intransitive stratum is one that is not transitive.

3. The Halkomelem data are from the late Arnold Guerin of the Musqueam Reserve, Vancouver, British Columbia. My work on Halkomelem has been supported by the Elizabeth and Melville Jacobs' Fund and the National Museum of Man, Ottawa.

The following abbreviations are used in the glosses of the Halkomelem data:

adv	advancement suffix
aux	auxiliary
cs	causative
det	determiner
erg	ergative
intr	intransitive
l.c.	limited control suffix
lnk	linker
obj	object
obl	oblique marker
ref	reflexive
sub	subject

ssub	subordinate clause subject
tr	transitive
1	first person
2	second person
3	third person

4. Postal (1977) suggested that final intransitivity in reflexives was due to antipassive; for arguments against this proposal, see Aissen (1982) and Gerdts (1981a).

5. Aissen concentrates on the cancellation of 3s, giving evidence from Tzotzil and Georgian, and discusses the cancellation of 2s, citing data from French, Turkish, and Dyirbal, only briefly.

6. See Rosen (1981) for a discussion of the acceptability of downstairs *si* reflexives in Causative Clause Union.

7. This intransitive suffix also is used in main clause passives, some antipassives, and some initially unergative clauses.

8. A second difference between the two reflexives is that *-θət* reflexives refer to clausemate antecedents but *-əm* reflexives may refer to the subject of the next higher clause, as seen in [30].

9. The transitive suffix *-t* regularly combines with an object suffix beginning with *-s* giving *-θ*; this is seen with the first person objective suffix in [5].

10. After the limited control suffix *-n-*, the initial *-s-* of the pronominal affixes is deleted.

11. I have no account to offer of the allomorphy of the limited control marker: *-nəx*^{w} ~ *-nam* ~ *-n*.

12. This rule resembles the rule of Auxiliary Selection in Italian, given in [14], in that it is stated conjunctively.

13. I am assuming a spontaneous demotion version of antipassive; see Postal (1977) for discussion.

14. Berinstein (1984) points out that a 2–3 retreat construction is used when the notional 'subject' of a transitive is extracted; since this construction is finally intransitive, the final 1 is a final absolutive.

15. In 'deep' ergative languages, reflexives would have the form of an antipassive. However, this analysis is not tenable for Halkomelem reflexives; see Gerdts (1981a) for evidence that Halkomelem reflexives do not involve antipassive.

REFERENCES

Aissen, J. 1982. Valence and Coreference. In *Syntax and Semantics 15: Studies in Transitivity,* P. Hopper and S. Thompson, eds. New York: Academic Press.

Berinstein, A. 1984. *Evidence for Multiattachment in K'ekchi Mayan.* Ph.D. Diss., University of California, Los Angeles.

Gerdts, D. 1981a. *Object and Absolutive in Halkomelem Salish.* Ph.D. Diss., University of California, San Diego.

Gerdts, D. 1981b. Possessor Ascension and Lexical Suffixation in Halkomelem. Paper presented at the Annual Meeting of the Canadian Linguistic Association, Halifax, Nova Scotia.

Gerdts, D. 1981c. A Syntactic Analysis of Lexical Suffixes in Halkomelem Salish. Paper presented at the Seventh Annual Meeting of the Berkeley Linguistics Society, Berkeley, California.

Grimshaw, J. 1982. On the Lexical Representation of Romance Reflexive Clitics. In *The Mental Representation of Grammatical Relations,* J. Bresnan, ed., pp. 87–148. Cambridge: MIT Press.

Hubbard, P. 1980. *The Syntax of the Albanian Verb Complex.* Ph.D. Diss., University of California, San Diego.

Marantz, A. 1984. *On the Nature of Grammatical Relations.* Cambridge: MIT Press, Cambridge, Mass.

Perlmutter, D. 1980. Relational Grammar. In *Syntax and Semantics 13: Current Approaches to Syntax,* E. Moravcsik and J. Wirth, eds., pp. 195–230. New York: Academic Press.

Perlmutter, D. Forthcoming. Multiattachment and the Unaccusative Hypothesis: The Perfect Auxiliary in Italian.

Perlmutter, D., and P. Postal. 1974. Lectures from the Linguistic Society of America Summer Institute, Amherst, Massachusetts.

Perlmutter, D., and P. Postal, eds. 1983. *Studies in Relational Grammar 1.* Chicago: University of Chicago Press.

Postal, P. 1977. Antipassive in French. *Lingvisticae Investigationes* 1, 333–74.

Rosen, C. 1981. *The Relational Structure of Reflexive Clauses: Evidence from Italian.* Ph.D. Diss., Harvard University.

INDEX

G

H

I

J

K

L

M

N

O

P

T

U

V

W

X

Y

Z